Strategic Debate

GLENCOE

Strategic **Debate**

Roy V. Wood
University of Denver

Lynn Goodnight
Northwestern University

New York, New York   Columbus, Ohio   Chicago, Illinois   Peoria, Illinois   Woodland Hills, California

To
Alan G. Price and Walter Ulrich
who were a testimony to the
best in our profession

Credits for photographs and illustrations are on page 422,
which represents a continuation of the copyright page.

Editorial Consultant
Kandi King
Tom C. Clark High School
San Antonio, Texas

Copyright © 2006 by The McGraw-Hill Companies, Inc. All rights reserved. Except as
permitted under the United States Copyright Act of 1976, no part of this publication may be
reproduced or distributed in any form or means, or stored in a database or retrieval system,
without the prior written permission of the publisher.

Printed in the United States of America

Send all inquiries to
Glencoe/McGraw-Hill
8787 Orion Place
Columbus, OH 43240-4027

ISBN: 0-07-872995-5

2 3 4 5 6 7 8 100/055 11 10 09 08 07

CONTENTS

PREFACE

Most students get involved in debate for the same reasons that they join other school clubs or organizations: the activity looks interesting, and other students seem to be enthusiastic about what they are doing. The new debater soon discovers that debate is a great deal of fun. There's a real joy in matching one's research and verbal skills against those of another person.

As the new debater struggles through the process of learning to debate, he or she discovers that good debating involves being able to perform well on many levels; intellectually, analytically, and verbally. He or she quickly discovers that learning to do all this well takes a year or more of hard work and practice. But somehow it is worth it.

As debaters begin to master the skills (usually, let's face it, in order to win more debates), they discover that how to win is not the only thing being learned. As they begin to think critically, their classwork in general improves. As they begin to listen critically, they become increasingly well informed about current events, contemporary issues, and the matter of ethics.

Strategic Debate is designed to help debaters at all levels. Though primarily intended for beginning debaters, even intermediate and advanced debaters will find useful advice. This new edition has a wide range of activities to provide the debater with opportunities to try out the strategies being presented. There are also six "Strategies in Action," features interspersed throughout the text, that focus on applying specific debate skills in real life.

Beginning debaters often find the vocabulary of debate confusing. Coaches may talk about preparing a "prima facie case" to meet the affirmative "burden of proof." Speeches are called "constructives" and "rebuttals" (each with a different purpose and set of rules). Debaters are sent out to get as many "quotes" as possible to support the "contentions." This text defines these basic terms (and others) and explains why such concepts are essential to strategic debate. By helping new debaters understand the rationale behind the concepts, *Strategic Debate* helps them become thinking debaters.

Strategic Debate also helps new debaters thoroughly understand the strategic and tactical obligations and possibilities of both the affirmative and the negative position. This text presents the practical aspects of strategic debate for beginners.

Finally, *Strategic Debate* helps new debaters understand the strategic implications of debate as a communicative activity. Thinking debaters realize that, no matter how well the fundamentals of debate are mastered, arguments and analysis must be communicated to the judge. Experienced coaches know that their beginning debaters "have arrived" when they stop explaining losses by blaming the judges and begin to study how they failed to communicate with that judge.

However, this text is also designed to aid advanced debaters. Analyzing the "path of most resistance" to championship debating, *Strategic Debate* provides insights into the strategic approaches used by championship debaters. Debaters at the advanced level often are surprised at the refinements that really good competitive debate involves. *Strategic Debate* helps advanced debaters take a fresh look at the fundamental concepts and techniques and to see new subtleties.

Acknowledgments

The authors and publisher would like to express their gratitude to the many people who helped formulate the material presented in this new edition of *Strategic Debate*. The members of the Northwestern University (Evanston, Illinois) debate team and the high school students enrolled in the Debate Divisions of Northwestern University's National High School Institute helped generate new insights into debating. Gail Bush provided valuable insights into library research and computer indexing and research, serving as an invaluable sounding board for how this technology can be used in debate. Steve Foral and his debate students at Lincoln High School provided insights and materials on Lincoln-Douglas debate. Grateful acknowledgment is given to Matt Whipple, head debate coach at Glenbrook South High School, Glenview, Illinois, for reviewing new material and providing suggestions for the affirmative and negative chapters of this new edition. Scott Deatherage, Director of Forensics at Northwestern University, and Jim Hunter, debate coach at Oak Park and River Forest High School, advised on the current as well as future trends in debate and graciously provided materials. Betty Martin, Barbara Pollard, Jennifer Rapp, and Sheryl Wasserman (staff at the National High School Institute, Northwestern University) and Tzu-Hsiang Yu (University of Denver) provided a great deal of assistance in the preparation of this fifth edition.

Finally, grateful acknowledgment is also extended to three special people. James M. Copeland, Executive Secretary of the National Forensic League, Ripon, Wisconsin, assisted with general advice and provided many of the illustrations. Tom Goodnight, Northwestern University, advised and helped prepare the new chapter on logical and critical thinking. Kandi King, Director of Forensics and Speech at Tom C. Clark High School, San Antonio, Texas, served as consulting editor and was invaluable in keeping this new edition a practical, contemporary tool for classroom use.

Fundamentals of Strategic Debate

Objectives

After studying Chapter 1, you should be able
1. To discuss the educational as well as competitive values of debate.
2. To explain the differences between propositions of fact, value, and policy.
3. To understand what constitutes a properly worded proposition.
4. To explain the requirements of a prima facie case.

Key Terms

After reading this chapter, you should understand the following debate terms:

critical listening
critical thinking
proposition
proposition of fact
proposition of value
proposition of policy
burden of proof
presumption
prima facie case
burden of rejoinder

Every year thousands of students participate in academic debate. With so many students, the range of approaches to the activity and the depth of experience in debating vary greatly. There are those who debate for only a short period of time, yet they gain valuable exposure to the skills required in academic debate. There are others who compete for seven or eight years during high school and college. Many of these debaters become experts on a variety of debate topics and authorities in their own right on debate theory.

The majority of debaters fall somewhere between these extremes. Their experience is not so short that they gain only a brief exposure, but neither do they make debate a career. Many are fortunate enough to be introduced to debate through their school's curriculum. For most, though, debate is an extracurricular activity that is learned for its educational value and enjoyed for its competitive thrills. This text is designed, first, as an introduction to the concepts and skills that form the basis of debate and, second, as an explanation of the basic and advanced aspects of debate as a competitive, strategic activity.

Debate as a Competitive-Educational Activity

Debate isn't just an educational activity or just a competitive activity. Debate is a competitive-educational endeavor. The skills and values that can be learned from it are as vital to the educated, democratic person in the twentieth century as they were to the Greeks, who developed debate as an aid to training orators. Debate teaches much within the context of a competitive situation. Former president John F. Kennedy identified many of the benefits of debate in an address he delivered on August 22, 1960: "I think debating in high school and college is most valuable training, whether for politics, the law, business, or for service on community committees such as the PTA and the League of Women Voters. A good debater must not only study material in support of his own case, but he must also, of course, thoroughly analyze the expected argument of his opponent. The give and take of debating, the testing of ideas, is essential to democracy. I wish we had a good deal more debating in our educational institutions than we do now."

One of the most valuable skills that debaters acquire is the ability to communicate orally in a situation that demands spontaneity and clarity. Few students, except debaters, get the opportunity to speak before trained listeners who provide feedback on the quality and effectiveness of their presentations.

Debaters also learn to design concise, compelling arguments that can stand up under almost immediate attack from a skilled opponent. When asked about his view of debating in 1964, Malcolm X noted "I'd put myself in my opponent's place and decide how I'd try to win if I had the other side; and then I'd figure a way to knock down those points." There are few other situations in which speakers can find such highly motivated critics of their own thinking. A debater can be sure that if the judge does not comment on arguments that are logically weak, the opposition will.

One of the most valuable skills learned through debate is **critical listening**.

Listening is too often a passive activity. Most people tune out the majority of what is said around them or directly to them. As passive listeners, they retain only approximately 25 percent of what they do hear. Often politicians, businesspeople, teachers, parents, and even students argue endlessly over issues because they are absorbed with what they will say next instead of listening to what others are saying.

It is not easy to listen effectively—it is hard work. But to debate effectively, you must be an active listener. This means you must work to grasp the facts being presented. You must establish eye contact and watch facial expressions, as well as take in information. In debate if you do not listen to what the opposition is saying, your response is likely to be ineffective or irrelevant.

Listening theorists have identified four specific actions one can perform to become an active listener:

1. Anticipate what the opposition is likely to say. What will the next point be?

2. Continually review or summarize what the opposition has been saying.

3. Pay attention to the evidence being used.

4. Watch for "hidden meanings." What are the nonverbal messages?

Effective debaters learn to employ all of these skills. They also take notes on what is being said in an effort to better refine these skills. Debaters can then tailor their responses to their opponents' points—many times using their opponents' words—and turn their opponents' arguments to their own advantage. (The role of notetaking to enhance critical listening will be explored further in Chapter 4.)

Debate also teaches students to employ critical thinking skills. Every day, people find themselves in situations that require them to think clearly and critically about things. In many of these situations, difficult choices must be made. Debate teaches students to evaluate both sides of an issue before making a decision. Debate encourages students to ask questions and challenge the current state of affairs. The debate works as a problem-solving forum, in which informed individuals are always analyzing the issues and then reasoning to a conclusion.

The ability to listen critically also is widely recognized as an important skill learned in debate. But debate also teaches students to speak extemporaneously, or on the spur of the moment. Malcolm X described the experience of speaking extemporaneously in debate as one of power: "Standing up there, the faces looking up at me, the things in my head coming out of my mouth, while my brain searched for the next best thing to follow what I was saying, and if I could sway them to my side by handling it right, then I had won the debate—once my feet got wet, I was gone on debating." You have probably had the experience of thinking of a brilliant rejoinder hours after an argument. Debaters must think of those snappy responses immediately and express them fluently to their opponents and judges.

Finally, debate teaches organization skills. These skills enable debaters to place arguments in a framework that makes the ideas easy to follow but difficult to forget.

During political campaigns, debating controversial issues becomes a media event.
Above, Democratic candidate for U.S. Senate from Illinois Barack Obama listens to his
Republican rival Alan Keyes during a debate October 21, 2004, in Chicago, Illinois.

In debate the critic and the opposition take nothing for granted. If the organization of
arguments is even slightly confusing, the debater's opponents will push for clarity.
This kind of pressure forces debaters to become highly skilled in presenting their
ideas.

In addition to teaching specific skills that can be developed, debate also teaches
values that are essential for individuals living in a democracy. The debater not only
learns to recognize a valid argument when it is presented but also develops an
appreciation for the case that is well developed, no matter which side it represents.
At the same time, the students of debate learn to identify the fallacious, or misleading,
arguments and to avoid them.

In debate, competition is never separate from education. "Winning at any cost"
is never condoned, because it is only the students who learn the primary skills and
values of debate—who are willing to commit themselves to the intellectual rigor
required by debate—who are able to compete successfully at the highest levels. Too

In his remarks to the National Forensic League in 1964, President Lyndon Johnson noted "As debaters, you must search for the truth and you must speak the truth; and you must surrender yourself to the truth, for the genius of our democracy is that it admits variety and it permits criticism. Knowing always that in the long run truth will prevail. . . ."

Photo courtesy of the National Forensic League.

often, debaters mutter that debate is an educational, not a competitive, activity only when they need a rationalization for not winning. This claim is often an excuse for not caring enough about the activity to learn the persuasive, research, analytical, and refuting skills that are so necessary to debate. However, successful debaters know that the techniques needed to win a debate embody the very skills and attitudes that provide the educational benefits of debating.

Debate as a Thinking Activity

Critical thinking is a prerequisite for truly successful debating. Successful competitive debaters develop reasons to back up their position. They critically analyze a position by exploring reasons against it. Finally, they understand the reasons behind the opposition's position and they explore the opposition's arguments to see if those arguments can refute their own position.

One of the worst approaches to debate is the nonthinking approach. Believe it or not, some debaters participate in debate for an entire year without employing the techniques of critical thinking.

How does this happen? The coach teaches the students standard methods of organization and procedure. Debate textbooks and handbooks provide basic content. Speaking style is learned by simply imitating other debaters. Therefore, nonthinking debaters never really understand the particular debate topic, the strategies behind methods of organization and refutation, or the persuasive tactics that make debate a form of communication. Such debaters never bother to think about what they are doing.

Debaters who are critical thinkers understand why particular types of organization and procedure are used. Because they understand the grounds of the debate, they seek out the best evidence—from the library, correspondence, debate handbooks, or many of the other resources discussed later in this text. They think about the evidence being used and know exactly what it does for their arguments. They think through the possible responses to their arguments. And they also continually reexamine their speaking style and use of language so that they do not simply imitate other successful debaters, but instead become powerful communicative speakers in their own right.

Debate as a Strategic Activity

Early in their studies, military cadets learn that there are two elements to winning a war. First, a commander must have a general plan of attack. Should the enemy be taken by land or by sea? Will the enemy be demolished or starved into surrender? After arriving at a general plan, the commander must then discover methods that will make the goal attainable. Will aircraft carriers or submarines be used? Will nuclear weapons or the infantry be employed?

When the commander has answered such questions and developed a battle plan, the commander will have arrived at the strategy and tactics to be used in the campaign. *Strategy* is the overall plan of attack; *tactics* are the specific techniques to be used to fulfill the plan.

A symphony conductor also must develop a strategy and tactics. What is the general plan? Will the performance demonstrate the composer's mathematical skill in creating the work? Or will the performance bring out the subtleties of emotion present in the piece? Whichever direction is taken, the conductor must employ specific techniques in order to produce the desired effects in performance.

Debate requires a similar kind of planning. When students are preparing to debate competitively, they must have an overall plan of attack and specific methods for carrying out that plan. The debate team must think critically in order to weigh many important considerations. What are the demands of the topic? What are the potential strengths and weaknesses of the research materials that have been gathered? Which approach to analysis seems most potent for the debate? What might the opponents be expected to do? How might the judge be expected to react to various plans of attack?

After the strategy has been developed, the team must decide on tactics. When and how will the arguments be presented? What will each speaker do? What evidence would be the best to use during the debate? What style of presentation would be the best to use?

In its best forms, debate involves carefully considering the best strategic approach that should be taken in light of the topic, team, opponents, and audience. That is why this text is titled *Strategic Debate*: it evolves out of a consideration of the strategic implications—the strategies and tactics—of competitive debate.

And this is the time to dismiss the idea that there are shortcuts to successful competitive debating. Although some debaters look for them, there are no tricks, deceits, or gimmicks that really help in debate. All shortcuts to winning have serious

Students discuss the strategies and tactics their debate team will use.

disadvantages, not the least of which is that they are unethical and therefore completely counter to the spirit of competitive debate. The debater who uses unethical tactics will never be successful in the long run, and he or she will sacrifice many real benefits along the way. The authors have learned, from watching debaters at all levels of competition and at all levels of competence, that there is only one path to successful competitive-educational debate—the path of *most* resistance.

The Basics of Debate

It is certainly possible for debaters to get by on their natural abilities, just as unpracticed athletes might get by on natural talent; but the really good debater knows that to get the most out of debate one must continually refresh one's fundamental understanding of the activity. For this reason, the rest of this chapter has been designed to fill two needs: to introduce the fundamentals to new debaters and to provide a review—and even new insights—to experienced debaters.

The first question debaters ask at the beginning of a new season is "What's the topic this year?" There are two things debaters can be sure of as they wait for the answer to their question: (1) the debate topic always involves a particular type of proposition; and (2) the topic is always worded in a particular way that determines the grounds of the debate and kinds of arguments debaters can (and cannot) develop. Therefore, the rest of this chapter presents basic information about propositions and the obligations of both sides in a debate.

Propositions

By definition, a **proposition** is no more than a judgment expressed in words. If one person says to another, "This summer has been cooler than normal," that person has offered a proposition for acceptance or rejection. To say "I think teenagers ought to be allowed to set their own curfews," is also to offer a proposition. To suggest, "Dress codes for high-school students should be abolished," is again to express one's feelings in the form of a proposition. Each of these examples, however, involves a different type of proposition, a different type of judgment.

The first example, "This summer has been cooler than normal," is an example of a **proposition of fact**. The person expresses a judgment about an actual event—a belief that the temperatures have been lower than normal. The validity of this judgment can be checked rather easily: all the individuals have to do is check the daily temperatures of the current summer against the normal temperatures listed in an almanac. A comparison of these two lists would then determine whether the proposition were accurate.

Types of Propositions

Proposition of Fact
"This summer has been cooler than normal."

Proposition of Value
"I think teenagers ought to be allowed to set their own curfews."

Proposition of Policy
"Dress codes for high-school students should be abolished."

"I think teenagers ought to be allowed to set their own curfews" is a different type of proposition. It is a **proposition of value**. The speaker expresses a judgment about the worth or value of a particular idea. It is not as easy to check the validity of this kind of judgment as it is to verify a proposition of fact. In fact, propositions of value often make the best topics for open discussions and TV talk shows because the participants can argue for hours and never arrive at a solution. Lincoln-Douglas debate—sometimes called value debate—uses a proposition of value rather than a proposition of policy. These value propositions involve beliefs, which cannot be proven true or false. They tend to fall into one of two categories: value conflict and value judgment. In Lincoln-Douglas debate you do not argue about changing a policy, but rather about whether a particular value statement is preferable.

The last example, "Dress codes for high-school students should be abolished," illustrates the third type of proposition, a **proposition of policy**. The speaker suggests that a specific action or policy should be adopted: the dress code should be eliminated. A proposition of policy, unlike propositions of fact and value, does not involve verification; instead, it involves deciding whether a policy should be adopted or abolished. Sometimes the decision is easy to reach, and sometimes it is not. In the example given, different individuals might argue about the advantages or disadvantages of the dress code, and such arguments could go on indefinitely. On the other hand, a proposition such as "We should all go to the party together" would require a simple *yes* or *no* from the individuals involved.

It is possible to debate any one of the three types of propositions. Lawyers debate propositions of fact when they argue whether a person is guilty of a crime as charged. Legal procedure provides a carefully worked-out system for deciding whether a charge is true. The jury is allowed to hear only certain types of evidence, and the judge makes sure that the rules are not violated and that the jury fully understands the implications of the law.

Many people enjoy debating propositions of value. Anyone who listens to radio or television talk shows is bound to hear debates about value judgments. Value questions create great audience interest because the listeners can get personally involved in such issues as when adoption is the best option for parents and children or whether violence on TV breeds violence in society. Even though it is difficult to arrive at answers to such questions, the purpose of such a debate generally is to create interest and to clarify points of view rather than to arrive at solutions.

Policy questions also frequently come up for cross-examination debate. When a legislature debates a bill, it is almost always trying to decide whether a policy should be adopted. When a student council argues about how funds should be spent, it too is concerned with policy matters. The decision, then, about whether to accept a policy usually comes in the form of a vote that expresses the feeling of the majority. The majority simply decides whether a proposed change represents the best policy for the organization to adopt at that time.

When a proposition is being considered as a national debate topic, the first demand placed on it is that it be debatable for an entire year. There should be enough evidence on both sides of the proposition to keep students interested throughout the season. Second, the debate propositions should deal with a subject area that interests and challenges serious students. Finally, the proposition for debate should deal with contemporary issues that will make debaters feel that they are engaging in more than just an academic exercise.

Policy propositions generally meet all of these requirements. There are almost always pressing policy problems, involving issues of national or international policy, that can be selected for the academic debate topic. Propositions that suggest a change in national or international policy often are interesting to students, and after a year of research, debaters generally have learned some worthwhile facts about the real world.

A further advantage of policy propositions is a very practical one. Over the years, debate coaches and judges have arrived at a set of criteria, i.e. topicality, harm, inherency, and solvency, for evaluating policy debates. Debaters, then, can be fairly sure—no matter which part of the country they might debate in—that the judges will expect about the same sorts of things from the affirmative and negative teams. More important, debaters from Vermont, for example, who meet a team from California, can be comfortable in the knowledge that their opponents will interpret the proposition within the framework of the basic criteria. Regional differences in debate style, of course, need to be taken into account.

Wording of the Proposition

Cross-examination debate is standardized not only by the type of proposition but also by the wording of the proposition. Debaters can always be certain that the topic will be phrased in such a way that the affirmative and negative teams' responsibilities will be clear. A look at the following propositions will clarify this point:

Resolved: That the federal government should implement a comprehensive program to guarantee retirement security in the United States.

Resolved: That the United States government should significantly increase space exploration beyond the earth's mesosphere.

Resolved: That the federal government should significantly increase social services to homeless individuals in the United States.

Resolved: That the United States government should reduce worldwide pollution through its trade and/or aid policies.

Resolved: That the federal government should guarantee comprehensive national health insurance to all United States citizens.

All of the propositions above, which were actual National Forensic League annual debate topic resolutions, have several common characteristics. First, the propositions are worded so that the affirmative team (the side advocating the proposition) is on the side suggesting a change in the present system. The negative team, which would answer *no* to the proposition, is always placed in the position of defending the present system, or the *status quo.*

Second, all of these propositions advocate only one change in the present system. Although it might be interesting to debate "*Resolved:* That law enforcement agencies should be given greater power and Congress should have the right to overrule decisions of the Supreme Court," such a topic would be subdivided into two separate propositions:

Resolved: That law enforcement agencies should be given greater power.

Resolved: That Congress should have the right to overrule decisions of the Supreme Court.

The rules that govern the wording of Lincoln-Douglas debate propositions are not as complex as those for cross-examination debate. Generally, the proposition to be used in Lincoln-Douglas debate is a value proposition—or topic statement that makes a subjective evaluation of an event, idea, person, place, or thing. The affirmative argues that the value implied in the resolution ought to be adopted, but does not actually propose a specific plan of action. Each value proposition will contain a value or ethical term such as the following: take priority over, justifiable, right to, more important than, or morally obligated. The proposition will usually involve a universal idea or a contemporary problem, for example, values relating to democratic ideals, the right of privacy, the right to die, or the rights of the innocent versus those of the guilty.

As with any debate topic, the Lincoln-Douglas debate proposition must be debatable. This means that both sides—the affirmative and the negative—must have an equal chance of winning each round. The wording of the topic must not bias the proposition to one side over the other. For example, the proposition "Resolved: Violence in the media is an unconscionable affront to the puritan ethic" would be difficult for any negative team to win because of the severity of the language. Another issue regarding debatability is the amount of evidence available for topic research. Materials need to be available as evidence on *both* sides of the proposition. In many academic debate leagues, four propositions are debated each season. (In some areas, up to seven propositions are debated annually.) This leaves little time for research. While Lincoln-Douglas debate does not place the same emphasis on evidence as does cross-examination debate, the debater will need to research the proposition and pull some evidence on the issues. Following are sample Lincoln-Douglas propositions:

Resolved: The principle of majority rule ought to be valued above the principle of minority rights.

Resolved: When in conflict, the spirit of the law ought to take priority over the letter of the law.

Resolved: That secondary education in the United States ought to be a privilege, not a right.

Resolved: When in conflict, protection of the innocent is of greater value than prosecution of the guilty.

Because the propositions deal with large enough issues, there is still plenty to debate even though the resolution is restricted to only change in the present system. The affirmative may decide that there are several harms within the resolution that need to be addressed. The affirmative could present two or more harms within the resolution and offer a solution to each. The negative could then argue that the harms aren't really a result of the present system or that the affirmative's plan to solve the harms won't work.

For example, under the national health insurance topic, the affirmative might decide to present two problems: (1) that a lack of health care leads to increased costs to treat illnesses and (2) that a lack of health care causes economic devastation for individuals and families when a catastrophic illness strikes. These problems would call for separate solutions—providing preventive care coverage in an effort to prevent some of the illnesses and providing comprehensive insurance so that no one is devastated economically by a catastrophic illness—but each would fall under the national health insurance topic.

The fact that the affirmative and negative have something to debate depends on one key word in the propositions. *Should* is perhaps the most important word in the resolutions. *Should* implies the policy change, and it characterizes the affirmative's position in the debate. The affirmative does not suggest that the policy change *will be* enacted, nor that it *can be* adopted, but that the change *ought to* be made. This concept is referred to as the *should-would argument*.

The affirmative team, therefore, usually does not have to prove that the change would be accepted by the government. The affirmative need only demonstrate that legislators *should* vote for the change. However, the negative may find it profitable in some cases to argue that lobby groups or attitudes of the administration would prevent the implementation of the affirmative plan.

Should is generally defined by the affirmative as meaning "*ought to* but not necessarily *will.*" More fundamentally, the word means that the affirmative's proposal would be *the most desirable policy at the present time*. The affirmative is bound to demonstrate that the proposition, as it develops and analyzes it, would be the best policy and that the status quo therefore should be changed.

Finally, the proposition is worded so that it does not reflect a bias and so that the terms will be relatively clear to both the audience and the debaters. The national health insurance topic on page 12 would have been worded improperly if its authors had written that the government should guarantee a "burdensome, heavily regulated, comprehensive national health insurance"; such a wording would have shown a clear bias. Also, if the proposition contains a specific formulation, such as "comprehensive national health insurance," the negative can be much more certain of how the affirmative will interpret the topic.

Returning to the imaginary debaters who asked "What's the topic this year?" it is easy to see that the answer will fall within certain limits:

1. The topic will be a resolution that is expressed in the form of a proposition policy (for cross-examination debate) or of value (for Lincoln-Douglas debate).

2. The topic will deal with a subject that is controversial and that will yield ample evidence for both sides of the question.

3. The topic will always place the affirmative team in the position of advocating a change in the present system, or status quo.

4. The topic will suggest only one change in the status quo.

5. The topic will always contain the word *should* so that the duties of the affirmative will be clearly spelled out and, at the same time, limited.

Propositions of Policy and Team Obligations

A properly worded proposition of policy implies obligations for the two teams engaged in the debate. The decision about which team won a debate may well depend on the critic's judgment about which team best met its obligations. The fundamental obligations of affirmative and negative debaters can best be understood by first looking at another situation, the law.

In the legal system, criminal action against a person involves a carefully developed set of rights and obligations that closely parallel those of the debate situation. The state, represented by the prosecution, brings charges against a citizen, who is represented by the defense attorney, and the trial begins with a basic **presumption:** that the defendant is innocent until proven guilty beyond a shadow of doubt. This presumption, a characteristic of most Western law, defines several elements in the criminal trial. The defendant does not have to prove that he or she is innocent; instead, the prosecution must establish the defendant's guilt. Lawyers say, then, that the **burden of proof** is on the prosecution. Because the presumption of innocence is with the defendant, the only way the prosecution can overcome the presumption is by meeting its burden of proof.

The burden of proof is so important in a court of law that the defendant does not have to go to trial until the prosecution has demonstrated to the court that it has at least the minimal case required for it to meet its burden of proof. Accordingly, the prosecution is usually asked to show its evidence to a grand jury or to a magistrate at the time of the arraignment so that the trial judge can be assured that the state has a minimal case. Such a case, which represents the minimum evidence required to meet the burden of proof, is called a **prima facie case.** If the prosecution does not have a prima facie case, it cannot meet the obligation implied in the fundamental presumption that the defendant is innocent until proven guilty beyond a shadow of a doubt.

If the prosecution has a prima facie case, the defendant is brought to trial. At the trial there is a new set of obligations. The defense is now faced with a case that was judged prima facie—that the minimum evidence exists to meet the burden of proof. The defense must show that the case does *not* prove, beyond a reasonable doubt, that the defendant is guilty. The defense's obligation to answer is called the **burden of rejoinder.** Only by meeting the burden of rejoinder can the presumption of innocence be regained.

So far, this analysis has focused on obligations that apply only to either the prosecution or the defense. A final obligation falls on both the prosecution and the defense: both sides must prove what they assert. Much of a lawyer's training involves learning the criteria for proof and the legal precedents for proof.

As you probably know, the order of presentation in a trial is standardized. The prosecution always begins and ends the trial. The prosecutor initiates the action against the defendant in a carefully developed case, one that is composed of arguments and evidence that satisfy the burden of proof of the charge. As the prosecution proceeds, the defense is allowed to cross-examine the witnesses and to question exhibits of evidence in an attempt to refute the prosecutor's case. After the prosecution has rested its case, the defense presents its side. After the defense has developed its arguments and the prosecution has cross-examined, both sides are given the opportunity to summarize their stands for the jury. The defense begins the summation period, and the prosecution ends it.

As you may have guessed, the obligations of debaters are very similar to the obligations of lawyers. At the outset, the affirmative team is in the position of advocating a change in the present situation. As in the case of the defendant, the status quo is held to be "innocent until proven guilty." It is the job of the affirmative to present an indictment of the status quo that will overcome the presumption held by the negative team. In debate this affirmative team obligation is called the burden of proof of the proposition.

Some debaters get confused about this point, but it is important to remember that the burden of proof is *always* with the affirmative team. Although the negative must prove what it asserts (burden of rejoinder), it is usually not in the position of trying to prove that the proposition should be adopted. Even if the negative agreed that the present system should be changed, it would argue that the need for change falls outside the area of debate described by the proposition. (If the negative supported a change within the area covered by the proposition, there would be no debate, since both teams would be arguing for the proposition.)

To understand this, think about what happens in the legal system when the defendant admits to being responsible for the death of someone but disagrees as to the specific charge being brought before the court—first-degree murder. A trial still takes place to determine the validity of the charge, and the prosecution still has the burden of proving that the defendant is guilty as charged (that is, that the act was one of first-degree murder). The same is true in the debate. Even if the negative agrees that there is a problem with the status quo, the affirmative still has the burden of proving that the present system must be changed according to the specific policy suggested by the debate resolution.

Also like in the legal system, debate operates under the assumption that the affirmative can overcome presumption and meet the burden of proof only by presenting a prima facie case. In debate, a prima facie case is the minimal argument required to support the resolution. Just as a trial judge can begin by assuming that the prosecution has at least a minimal case, the debate judge can assume that the affirmative would not advocate a change unless it had a case that would support the proposition. (The specific approaches that the affirmative can take to develop a prima facie case are considered in a later chapter.)

After the affirmative has met its burden of proof, overcoming negative presumption, the negative team is faced with the burden of rejoinder. Obviously, the negative cannot win its argument unless it presents a well-developed argument. Like the defense in a court of law, the negative in a debate will usually establish that the affirmative's case does *not* prove that the present system should be changed in the way the affirmative suggests. (Negative approaches are discussed in detail in a later chapter.)

Summary

Debate is an academic activity that provides a multitude of rewards as well as challenges. The skills and values you will acquire in cross-examination or Lincoln-Douglas debate can be applied in virtually every walk of life. Every day you will make decisions and value judgments. It may be as simple as whether to spend your time at work or at play, by yourself or with others—or as complex as planning for the future. The skills learned in debate will help you in your schoolwork (researching and writing papers), in developing and presenting an argument, and in examining other individuals' arguments from an objective viewpoint. Debate enables you to do this because it is modeled after decision-making situations in the "real world". Through debate, you gain the skills to effectively take sides on an issue because you learn to analyze a problem and its solutions. You have begun the process by looking at the three types of propositions. Analyzing the characteristics of the problem area and the nature of the debate propositions gives you specific directions in which to discover the basic issues in problem-solving. In the next chapter you will look at logic and how it serves as the beginning point for debate.

Questions

1. List three of the valuable skills a debater can acquire.

2. What are four actions you can perform to become an active listener?

3. In a court of law, what type of proposition do lawyers debate? What types of propositions do academic debaters debate?

4. What are the criteria necessary for a debatable proposition of policy?

5. What constitutes a prima facie case in a court of law? In a debate?

Discussion Opportunities

1. People who debated in high school or college often say that the debate experience was one of the most valuable things they ever did. Why do you suppose they say this?

2. Some people believe that honesty and fairness are even more important in debate than in other academic activities, because debate involves persuasion. Based on your reading and your knowledge of debate so far, do you agree or disagree with this statement? Why?

3. The term *should* is described as perhaps the most important word in the national debate topic. Why is this so?

4. Why does the burden of proof in a debate always rest with the affirmative team?

Writing Opportunities

1. Attend a meeting of the city council, school board, or student activity group. During the meeting take notes on the issues being discussed and proposals put forth. Write each of the proposals discussed in the form of a proposition. Are the propositions debatable? Why?

2. The following are examples of poorly worded propositions. Identify the problem with each and rewrite the propositions correctly.

Resolved: That efforts should be made to curtail our rising unemployment.

Resolved: That this winter has been worse than any other.

Resolved: That harmful unemployment should be stopped.

Resolved: That English study develops skills in grammar and punctuation.

Resolved: That the United States should adopt programs to fight inflation and guarantee a future supply of energy.

Resolved: That United States citizens should not be denied access to medical care.

Resolved: That modest changes should be made in the jury system in the United States.

Resolved: That the worldwide expansion of pollution and weapons should be controlled.

3. Formulate a proposition of fact, a proposition of value, and a proposition of policy on one of the following general topics: arms sales, education, disposal of toxic wastes, pollution, the federal deficit, health care, or discrimination. Outline the issues you think are important about the proposition.

Critical Thinking Opportunities

1. Discuss debate as a thinking and as a strategic activity. What role do strategies and tactics play in everyday life?

2. Identify which of the following propositions are propositions of fact, value, or policy.

   Resolved: That infant mortality is highest among the poor.

   Resolved: That high medical costs create needless death and suffering.

   Resolved: That reading skills in elementary and secondary schools are declining.

   Resolved: That three years of physical education are not necessary for a well-rounded education.

   Resolved: That the United States' balance of trade deficit is continuing to rise.

   Resolved: That the United States should significantly change its foreign trade policies.

   Resolved: That a judge is better qualified to render a verdict than a jury of one's peers.

   Resolved: That the jury system should be abolished.

   Resolved: That Americans drive more imported cars than American-made cars.

   Resolved: That the United States should provide a guaranteed annual income for all citizens.

   Resolved: That enlistments in the armed forces are decreasing.

   Resolved: That the federal government should take measures to guarantee the United States' military superiority.

3. Presumption is a jealously guarded feature in criminal law in the United States. Why? What are its implications in nonlegal areas, such as politics and debate?

4. Using one of the propositions and issues you developed in Writing Opportunity 3, prepare a two- to three-minute speech that analyzes why a debater would need to address the issue if debating the proposition. Be prepared to present the speech.

Logical Argument and Critical Thinking

Objectives

After studying Chapter 2, you should be able
1. To explain the Toulmin model of argumentation.
2. To explain and demonstrate the different kinds of argumentation.
3. To sort arguments into categories and weigh their strengths and relevance.

Key Terms

To analyze the role of logic in debate, you will need to understand the following terms:

Toulmin model
argument from authority
argument from expertise
argument by
   generalization
counterexample
causal argument
causal chain of reasoning
alternate causality
argument from sign
argument from analogy
argument from precedent
slippery-slope argument

validity	claim
data	warrant
rebuttal	reservation
qualifier	backing

Debate offers an opportunity to learn many things: to speak effectively, to listen critically, to undertake research, and to write in well-considered and logical terms. The most basic skill that debaters may learn, however, is argumentation. Argumentation involves everything from the development of individual arguments to complicated cases that advocate change or oppose alteration of the status quo. Before taking on the larger topics of case making, it is helpful to focus first on how to make and criticize a single argument.

At the most basic level, an argument always involves a movement from what is known to what is unknown; or to put it differently, from that which is secured or believed by everyone to that which an advocate wishes to establish as true. Now, everyone knows all about arguing: people engage in informal arguments about what is true with brothers and sisters, friends, spouses, and relatives.

However, there is a difference between knowing intuitively how to argue and making well-founded and considered arguments. This difference is especially important in debate. Not only are the topics relatively well balanced between affirmative and negative evidence, but you will meet opponents who are responsible for bringing maximum criticism to bear on your ideas. How can you be sure that you are making and defending good arguments?

Fortunately, logic and argument are topics that have interested thinkers for quite a while. The most common process of thinking about advocacy argument began over 2000 years ago, when the Greek philosopher Aristotle combined the logic of scientific reasoning with the requirements of presenting sound arguments for public deliberating bodies. Debaters today have a pretty good idea of what constitutes an effective argument and what the elements are that are required to secure a reasonable link between data (evidence) and a claim. The latest version of Aristotle's theory of argumentation is the model developed by the British philosopher, Stephen Toulmin. Toulmin's model is the basis for this chapter.

This chapter explores the theory of reasoning in debate and the basic strategies for building a complete argument. Next, it examines the tactics for effective argument in debate. Last, it looks at the kinds of arguments and how they work for debaters.

The Nature of Argument

Philosophers have long deliberated about whether certainty exists. Can we, in most areas of science and human life, really even talk about "facts" that we know exist and will forever be true? For all practical purposes, most people can agree that gravity exists and that the sun will come up tomorrow. But few people know for certain that tomorrow will be better than today or that there is one right way to do things.

However, there *are* relative degrees of certainty. People can count on some things being almost always true. Warmth and light are needed for life. Politicians once in office will raise taxes. You should look before crossing the street. Other propositions are true most of the time but not always. For example, it is true that most of the time planting the fields in the springs will bring a fall harvest, but not always because floods and draught sometimes intervene. Still other propositions are true only rarely; these kinds of claims are possibilities. For example, it is possible that the United States will suffer another economic depression like the one of the 1930s, but it isn't likely.

Argumentation involves dealing with uncertainty. Sometimes you may wish to convince others that a claim is absolutely true. In order to secure this position, you need very strong data (or evidence) that the claim is true. At other times, you may know that a claim is not true everywhere and all the time, but you can establish that it is probably true in most situations. To prove this kind of claim, your data does not have to be as strong, but it still must be very good and the exceptions to the claim must be small. At other times, you may wish to establish that a claim simply might be true in a few cases. Although much weaker evidence will work to establish the *possibility* of a proposition being true, you still need to show that there is at least some relevant proof for the claim. To make an effective argument, then, you need to determine how strong the evidence is for a claim. This chapter will deal both with special types of claims and the relative merits of different ways of linking proofs and claims.

The Toulmin Model

As we mentioned earlier, scholars have studied the nature of argument for thousands of years. There are, therefore, hundreds of approaches to argument that you could consider. However, there is one approach that many debate teachers and coaches use and that the authors feel is especially appropriate for those who want to learn to do the best possible job of debating: the **Toulmin Model.**

Stephen Toulmin's system of argumentation is based not just on a theory of how logic and argument should lead to truth, but on how practical argumentation takes place, with all its varying degrees of certainty and probability. Toulmin has studied how people develop arguments and, more importantly, how listeners process those arguments to determine their validity. **Validity** is simply a test for the logical coherence of an argument: to be coherent, an argument must follow the rules of reasonability, and an argument that is not reasonably constructed is not valid. It is important to remember that it is the audience—or, in debate, the judge—who determines what constitutes reasonable rules for making an argument. Toulmin's model is useful for debaters because it is more sensitive to the rules of audience judgment than some other systems of logic.

Claims, Data, and Warrants

You already know the basic ideas that lie behind the Toulmin model. In the Toulmin model, an argument moves from what you know to what you *claim* to be true. You start with *data* and try to persuade the judge that you are *warranted* in moving from the data to the claim.

A **claim** is a conclusion of reasoning: it is the proposition that the arguer desires to be accepted. The claim is the end or object of making an argument. You might think of the claim as a destination, an arrival point. How do you get to a well-secured and believable claim? The answer depends on what kind of claim is involved: fact, value, or policy. (As you may guess, these kinds of claims relate to the three kinds of propositions discussed in Chapter 1.)

A *factual claim* involves a statement that something either is or is not the case. Sometimes such claims are made through observation. For example, the sky is either blue or grey or mixed blue and grey on a given day. To make a claim about the color of the sky, you need merely observe the state of the sky and state your observation. Obviously, this particular claim is not really open to much argumentation, since another person could easily verify it by looking at the sky.

However, factual claims are argumentative when observation is not possible and conclusions have to be reached from making inferences. Factual claims must be supported by offering proof that evidence has been completely and reliably gathered, and that the evidence offered is the best, most relevant set of observations of the facts under consideration.

A *value claim* involves a statement about what an individual thinks is good or bad. Whereas factual claims typically apply to the identification of things or phenomena in nature, value claims apply to what people hold to be important, sacred, and dear. Value claims are established by showing that either most or the best people hold a certain set of preferences. If you wish to claim that certain values are more important than others, then you must bring evidence that elevating one value over another is somehow better or more appropriate for a given community.

A *policy claim* involves a statement about what should or should not be done. Policy claims involve questions of action. Ultimately, in proving a policy claim you must establish that the consequences of pursuing a policy are of immediate importance. Policy claims differ from factual claims insofar as you cannot know the results of a policy claim before enacting the law or program. Thus, the future is always to some extent uncertain and unpredictable. Policy claims differ from value claims because you must do more than simply confirm a set of values or choose among values. When confronted with a policy claim, people are being asked to act in a way that is either consistent with professed values or that challenges them to pursue new ones.

After the claim, the next part of the Toulmin model is data. The term **data** signifies the information that is offered in support of a claim. Sometimes the term data is called *proof* or *evidence*. What the three terms have in common is that *data*, *proof*, and *evidence* are offered as statements that everyone would agree with, even the opposition.

Although there are many kinds of data, the most common are testimony, examples, and statistics. *Testimony* is opinion that is offered on behalf of the truth of a claim. Good testimony is authoritative. There are many different kinds of authority, some based on experience and others on general reputation. *Examples*, or instances, are used to demonstrate a claim's validity. Such data should be relevant to the claim, clearly observed, and defined. Finally, *statistics* are gathered by mathematical sampling techniques and scientific methods. Statistics are used to demonstrate the widespread effects of a claim. It is useful to study social science methods for gathering statistics, because statistics can involve a number of highly specialized assumptions that may either strengthen or undercut the validity of the claim.

The **warrant** is a key part of the Toulmin model. It satisfies only one question, but a very important one: how do you get from data to claim? The warrant certifies the relevance and importance of the relationship between data and claim. Another word for the warrant is *inference*. In building an argument, the evidence *infers* that a claim is true; in other words, the evidence taken on its face is sufficient to establish the truth of a claim.

At this point, it may be useful to consider an example that puts data, warrant, and claim together. Suppose you wish to make the claim that if you study hard, you will make good grades. In this case, the claim would be one of policy: study hard and make good grades. You could probably come up with a number of examples in which work in classes resulted in high test scores. Your data would be a number of examples: hard study in music, history, and language arts. Your warrant would be an inference called a *generalization*; that is, if a series of examples all point in the same direction, then you can infer a general conclusion that builds from the examples. The argument is relatively clear because all examples point in the same direction and support the claim.

Data	Warrant	Claim
Hard study and A grades in music, history, and language arts →	Hard study in this representative sample of cases leads to a sound generalization →	Hard study leads to good grades.

But suppose there was a counterexample. Suppose you studied hard in chemistry and didn't make a good grade? Worse, suppose that there were a number of counterexamples, cases where there was hard study and still the grades did not turn out well. Is there any way to save your generalization? Yes. But to do so, you have to turn to the second part of the Toulmin model, which involves the components of *rebuttal, reservation,* and *qualifier.*

Rebuttals, Reservations, and Qualifiers

Toulmin knew that data were often mixed. He recognized that in most argumentative situations involving practical decisions there would be some evidence in favor of the claim and some evidence against it. So, he developed components to his model that would allow arguers to take into consideration exceptions to the rule and to define more precisely the kind of claim and the conditions for its acceptability.

A **rebuttal** is a possible condition under which the relationship between data and claim would not hold. Think of the rebuttal as the exception to the rule. In the example above, there are counterexamples where hard study was not sufficient to produce a good grade. In building a sound argument, you must think of all the potential rebuttals and decide if they are serious or not and how they should be treated in developing your argument.

A **reservation** is an announced exception to the rule, a point at which you account for why the warrant (linking data and claim) does not really hold. In the sample argument, the reservations may be that hard work produces good grades, *unless* either the subject matter is too hard or one has talents in some courses but not in others. Thus, the argument develops not as an absolute rule, but as a more considered generalization. It is acceptable to admit reservations as long as you can account for them, leaving the argument true on the whole. For instance, you might add that while you can't guarantee better grades with better study habits, in all cases study is likely to produce better grades than would result without such effort.

A **qualifier** is simply a term that expresses the degree of confidence that you have in the relationship between data and claim. If your degree of confidence is high, then you might say: It is *almost certainly* the case that studying will get you good grades. If your degree of confidence is low, then you might say: It is *simply possible that. . . .*

Most of the time, a good argument uses the term *probable* to identify the relationship between data and claim. An accurate qualifier protects an argument against quibbling. If there are many (or significant) exceptions to the rule you are trying to establish, you can admit those safely if you intend to establish only a possible relationship between data and claim. If there are a few exceptions to the rule, then you do not have to prove a contention as universally true.

The following chart illustrates how the sample argument now looks.

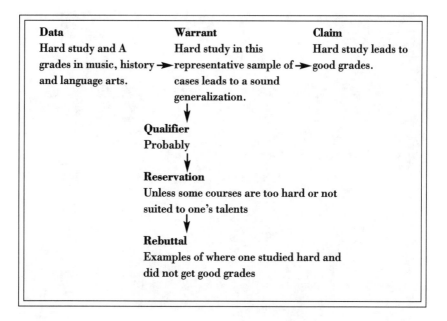

In thinking through an argument for debate, you need to look at it from both sides. On the one side, it is useful to find the best evidence and warrants that prove claims important to supporting the resolution. On the other side, it is just as useful to see exceptions to those arguments and to put them into proper perspective in building a case.

Backing

There is one final component in the Toulmin model: backing. **Backing** refers to the general area from which the warrant or data/evidence is drawn. For instance, you might look into the causal relationship between study and grades. Why is it that study produces performance?

While this question is beyond the scope of the particular argument being debated, it is still relevant. To develop the argument further, you might consult the fields of education and human development. Principles of learning and developmental psychology might help you develop more evidence and different warrants to refine your claim. Backing, then, involves all pertinent, general, and authoritative background that can be brought to bear in answering questions about the warrant or data.

Types of Argumentation

There are ways of establishing claims that typically bring together certain forms of data and warrants. Such recurrently linked data-warrant units can be considered as

A seasoned debater is prepared to back up her claim with sufficient proof.

separate kinds of arguments. Each of these different argument types has rather distinctive proof requirements. This section explains how these argument types are developed, some of their typical uses for making arguments in policy debates (the development and use of argument in Lincoln-Douglas debate are discussed in Chapters 12 and 13), and relevant tests of validity.

Remember that *validity* refers to whether or not an argument meets the rules of reasonability. If the validity of an argument is weak, then one of its parts is defective and it should not be accepted. If an argument is well designed, then its validity should be strong, and you should be relatively confident that your claim will be stated precisely and backed with relevant, sufficient, and authoritative proof.

Authority

A claim whose validity is based on authoritative testimony is called an **argument from authority**. In a complicated world, people cannot investigate everything individually—they have to take someone else's word for it. So how do people separate a person whose word is credible—or authoritative—from someone who does not state things that are believable? This is a quite complicated question.

Let's begin with a tough case. In a presidential election, politicians are contesting over who has the best vision of the future for America. Where does the vision come from? Why should it be believed? Can politicians be expected to be committed to their promises to think only of the American people and not of private gain? These are difficult questions to answer, especially when each politician faces an opponent who is doing his or her best to show that the other side does not have an authoritative claim.

One way to meet the test of authority is to ground arguments in a meaningful personal experience, one that creates both knowledge and commitment to a cause, ideal, or policy. This is what Al Gore, then a Vice Presidential candidate, did when he discussed finding purpose in his own life in the car accident that involved the near tragic death of his own son. At the 1992 Democratic National Convention, Gore said:

> But, ladies and gentlemen, I want to tell you this straight from my heart;
> that experience changed me forever. When you've seen your six-year-old son
> fighting for his life, you realize that some things matter a lot more than
> winning. You lose patience with the lazy assumptions of so many in politics
> that we can always just muddle through. When you've seen your reflection
> in the empty stare of a boy waiting for a second breath of life, you realize
> that we were not put here on Earth to look out for our needs alone, we are
> part of something much larger than ourselves. (Speech Accepting the Demo-
> cratic Vice Presidential Nomination. *Facts on File*, 16 July 1992: 521).

By dedicating himself to a higher purpose, Gore claimed the moral authority of a commitment to a set of values. For many, this helped show that he had a substantive commitment to politics. *Moral authority*—opinions backed with deeds, long-term commitments, and actions—is used to support arguments about values that society ought to pursue.

Often in debate, moral authorities are useful in setting out the importance of the goals that the affirmative case is pursuing. The more recognized the social leader or the more diverse the number of people from different religions, nationalities, and walks of life that are committed to such values, the greater the moral consensus over the desirability of common values.

Expertise

Another kind of authority comes not from the world of values, but from the world of factual observation and measurement. The validity of an *argument from expertise* is determined by the trustworthiness of a source. A trustworthy source is one who has been judged competent to make an evaluation by a consensus of experts.

No expert is entirely neutral. Humans inevitably come to problems with predispositions, presumptions, and interests. Expertise, however, has to do with reliability—

the notion that reasonable people can make the same observation under the same conditions and come up with similar conclusions. To the extent that the opinion of an individual is accepted as credible among a body of experts, that person might be said to be an expert.

Expertise needs to be considered carefully. It may be the case that a person who is qualified to be an expert in one area may not be credentialed in another. Advertisers have long used the halo effect to borrow the authority of figures who are very well-versed in one area to speak about something they can make little claim to in others. For example, is there anyone else that you would consult about a jump shot if you could talk to Michael Jordan? Of course not. But just because Jordan was a whiz on the hardwood court does not mean that he can make any better determination about whether to buy a Chevy Blazer or new Bronco than anyone else. The basic question has to be asked: is the expert an expert in the claimed field of knowledge that requires judgment and experience?

In debate, expertise is difficult to establish. The qualifications of an authority are usually read so quickly that you may have no idea who the person is who has reached a conclusion or why that conclusion has been reached. Yet, authority is an important part of debate. Much of the time the credibility of the claims that are made depends upon the believability of the source. Moreover, when there are differing opinions, how do strategic debaters win?

Here are four suggestions. First, build a case that is supported by strong authorities. When you have a choice, for example, between citing a prestigious Supreme Court Justice and *The Daily Worker* on the centrality of privacy in American life, quote the Supreme Court Justice. If you are careful in picking out the sources, the case you argue in a round will develop an aura of credibility. Moreover, if you become noted for picking out and using evidence from the best sources, your own reputation as a debater will grow. There is strength in credibility by association.

Second, determine the strength of authorities by tracking critical reviews of sources that are used extensively. *Book Review Digest* or *Cumulative Book Review Digest* will give you access to scholarly reviews of books. Many times authors will write texts that seem to identify important problems and support novel programs. For example, in debating NASA policy, many debaters used testimony from science fiction writers as if it had the same credibility as scientists. Examining book reviews on such testimony will help put claims into perspective.

Third, when examining the comparative merits of sources, you can look for a number of people who are saying the same thing. Especially where there are key points of evidence in contention, it is important to have different authorities saying relatively the same thing. This can help you establish a consensus view.

Fourth, in many cases where there is a direct clash of opinion, you will need to discredit the opposing point of view. Discrediting opposing authorities can be done in a number of ways. First, show that the sources have contradicted themselves elsewhere, or that they have made some other points or "reservations" that support your position. Second, if no contradiction can be found, see if the sources have been discredited. Sources may be regarded as beyond the mainstream consensus or as having forwarded their opinions for self-gain. Finally, challenge the source's ability to make a conclusion—to know what is purported to be known. For instance, in debating a crime topic, it is popular to use think-tank estimates that suggest a high percentage of guilty criminals get off on legal technicalities. While this may be true, how could anyone know the precise number? In the United States, the court system is the only method available for authoritatively determining guilt or innocence.

Generalization

A generalization is a claim supported by a number of examples. **Argument by generalization** is a kind of inductive reasoning. Sometimes argument by generalization is referred to as *reasoning from example*.

Consider the following commitment to deficit cutting made by President Bill Clinton in his 1993 "State of the Union" address:

> We are not cutting the deficit because the experts tell us to do so. We are cutting the deficit so that your family can afford a college education for your children. We are cutting the deficit so that your children will someday be able to buy a home of their own. We are cutting the deficit so that your company can invest in retraining its workers and retooling its factories. We are cutting the deficit so that government can make the investments that help us become stronger and smarter and safer. ("State of the Union 1993." *Vital Speeches of the Day*, 15 March 1993: 324.)

Clearly, this is not an argument from authority. Clinton doesn't rely on expertise, which he might have done. Instead, he uses a different kind of logic.

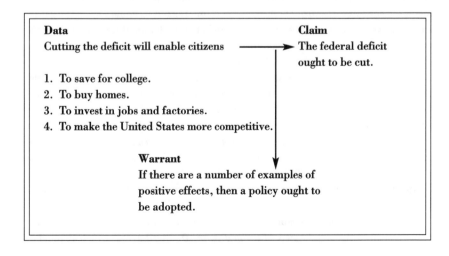

Data

Cutting the deficit will enable citizens

1. To save for college.
2. To buy homes.
3. To invest in jobs and factories.
4. To make the United States more competitive.

Claim

The federal deficit ought to be cut.

Warrant

If there are a number of examples of positive effects, then a policy ought to be adopted.

Note that the argument here works by generalization. There are a number of examples in which a policy has a positive outcome; therefore, the conclusion can be reached that a policy will work.

The argument can also work to establish a negative conclusion, of course. For example, in debating the question of homelessness, you might cite examples of how homelessness affects different classes of citizens. For children, homelessness may mean insufficient schooling or nutrition. For women, homelessness may mean decreased safety and vulnerability as well. For men, homelessness may mean being subjected to crime on the streets and reduced security. Thus, since homelessness creates problems for every class of citizens, you could generalize that homelessness is undesirable.

Generalizations work well when you can show that the preponderance of examples clearly points in a single direction: either establishing the existence of a social harm or pointing up the workability or desirability of a solution. Generalizations, however, always involve some exceptions to the rule, requiring that you anticipate potential rebuttals and have ready appropriate reservations or reasons that account for exceptions to the rule.

Consider the example of school vouchers. It may be the case that voucher systems, which allow parents to get a tax break when choosing a private school for their sons and daughters, have worked well where they have been tried. Students have gone to schools of their own choosing and test scores have increased. The generalization that is drawn is that voucher systems work well. If this generalization is then applied at a national level, a debater might argue that voucher systems would be a great success in all school districts. How could you deal with this kind of reasoning?

Note first that it may be possible to find examples where the voucher system did *not* work well. A *counterexample* is an instance that would bar the generalization. If it can be shown that in a number of instances the voucher system did not work and that the net result of choosing a private school was decreased rather than increased educational satisfaction, then the counterexample would negate the generalization. Note, however, that the strategic debaters understand this potential problem to begin with. Since generalizations are by definition simply general rules, smart debaters anticipate exceptions to the rules.

It is important to be aware of counterexamples that don't really affect the rule. For example, it may be the case that in some cases the voucher system did not work for peculiar reasons. Perhaps the system was not tried seriously, or ran into some administrative obstacles, or was implemented in school districts where little has ever worked. To the extent that you can show that counterexamples are (1) small in number, and (2) limited to a particular place, then the counterexample does not impair the generalization. To launch a good objection to a generalization you must be able to show that the counterexamples are large, relevant, and go to the heart of the matter.

Generalization is an important type of argument. In putting together a generalization, remember the simple tests of an argument: Do you have a sufficient number of examples? Are the examples pertinent to the generalization? Are there a large number of counterexamples? Can the counterexamples be discounted as peculiar or idiosyncratic?

Causal

Causal argumentation is usually deployed in debate for one of two purposes. First, debaters wish to find out the cause of a problem to isolate conditions in the status quo that give rise to socially threatening or undesirable situations. The assumption is that if you know what causes a problem, steps can be taken to eliminate those causes and bring about a satisfactory resolution. Second, debaters wish to find the causes of a successful policy so that they can be preserved or protected and the policy process can be strengthened.

For an example of causal argument, turn again to the 1992 presidential election. In his speech accepting the Republican nomination, then President George Bush stated:

> Make no mistake, the demise of communism wasn't a sure thing. It took the
> strong leadership of presidents from both parties, including Republicans
> like Richard Nixon and Gerald Ford and Ronald Reagan. And without
> their vision and the support of the American people, the Soviet Union
> would be a strong superpower today, and we'd be facing a nuclear threat
> tonight.

In this speech, Bush claims that wise American presidential foreign policy was necessary for bringing down the Soviet Union, that the fall of communism was neither a historical accident nor an event that occurred purely because of internal factors. Further, he seemed to be making the implied causal argument that Republican presidents made further progress in rolling back communism than Democratic presidents. The causal argument is deployed here to support the ultimate claim that since Bush is the standard-bearer of a Republican foreign policy process that has brought about good results in the past, it would be wise to insure the causal relationship in the future by reelecting Bush as President.

If this example seems a little convoluted, that is not surprising. Causal argument is like this much of the time. Cause is linked to effect, which itself becomes a cause of a further effect, and so on. This linking of cause and effect is known as a **causal chain of reasoning.** Such a chain simply means that an effect has multiple, independent causes that together become sufficient to bring about an effect.

Again, consider former President Bush's nomination address, which provides a more forceful example of causal argument:

> The world is in transition, and we are feeling that transition in our homes.
> The defining challenge of the '90s is to win the economic competition—to

win the peace. We must be a military superpower, an economic superpower, and an export superpower.

Here President Bush says that a desirable condition, peace, requires that three conditions be fulfilled: military strength, internal economic well-being, and trade prowess. Put in the language of formal validity, the President is saying: a single effect, X, has three independent causes. What strategies of attack and defense are suggested by this argumentation?

Note first that the claim of three and only three causes is one that should be tested. Does peace have other conditions? For instance, are issues of human rights, racial relationships, and religious conflicts important to peace? If these issues might also cause war and cannot be solved either militarily or economically, then an alternate causality has been established.

An **alternate causality** is one in which a condition may be brought about by a force not considered in the original argument. To the extent that you could establish that the alternative cause is important—indeed, *more* important than the causes established to support the original argument—then the claim is in jeopardy. For example, President Bush's argument might be challenged by the claim that future wars are going to center on questions of ethnicity, race, and religion, and that therefore a new foreign policy is needed—one different from the Cold War.

The discovery of alternate causality does not necessarily diminish the credibility of a claim. Sometimes what are claimed to be alternative causes are really not significantly different from the main causes, or merely lead to incidental reservations. In this example, it might be conceded that questions of ethnicity, race, and religion do jeopardize the peace in some areas of the world, but that these are smaller, regional conflicts. While of great importance in the areas that undergo such sufferings, such conflicts are not the key components of overall national policy.

At other times, what is claimed to be an alternate causality might turn out to support the main argument rather than jeopardize it. For instance, it may be the case that economic and military power are necessary to reduce the *impact* of future wars, even if they cannot prevent such conflicts from occurring. You should pay careful attention to the introduction of alternative causality in debate. Look at the strategic implications of whether the objection hurts or helps the ultimate claim.

Causal argument is very important to the process of debate because it provides a comparative basis for evaluating the outcome of policy. At a minimum, evidence is required to show that a single cause can produce an effect. If you claim that a policy will bring about a state of affairs, be it bad or good, then you must meet the test of showing that the cause has sufficient weight or potency to produce the effect. If you can find a similar case in which the cause produced the effect, then you might argue a similar result would occur in the present situation. If you can find a similar case in which the cause did *not* produce the effect, either now or at some time in the past, then the cause-effect relationship is put in doubt. These arguments usually become key contentions in policy debate.

When arguing in a debate that the adoption of a policy will bring about a set of unique consequences, the following causal tests should be applied. First, if policies similar to the current one have been adopted without either good or bad effects, then it is not likely that the policy will have a substantial effect. Even if similar policies have been adopted with substantial consequences, debaters still assume the burden of proving that the current conditions are similar in basic respects.

Second, if a policy has multiple effects, then it may be the case that what appear to be undesirable consequences could be offset by the policy's secondary effects. For instance, it might be the case that increasing government taxation hurts the economy and generally results in depressing economic growth. However, if a program increases taxes in order to retrain people in jobs, the resulting increases in productivity (the ability of workers to perform well) could stimulate the economy. Thus, strategic debaters must map out and consider the interaction of causes and effects.

Sign

Argument from sign is based upon a correlation of characteristics and objects. Sign arguments give a sense of measurement, features, or characteristics of things or situations. For example, in his 1993 "State of the Union" address, President Bill Clinton said the following:

> I well remember, twelve years ago Ronald Reagan stood at this podium and told the American people that if our debt were stacked in dollar bills, the stack would reach 67 miles into space. Today, that stack would reach 267 miles.

This example contains a number of uses of sign reasoning. First, former President Reagan begins the sign argument: the dollar bills stacked "67 miles into space" is a sign that the U.S. deficit is really substantial. President Clinton tops Reagan by saying that if you thought the deficit was big then, now the stack stands at 267 miles—a sign that things are really going the wrong way!

Note that these sign arguments are not at all like causal arguments. The fact that dollar bills could be stacked so high does not tell us anything about the harms of the deficit. (Indeed, Clinton's comparison was a little dubious, since in real purchasing power the dollar was really "smaller" in 1993 than when Reagan drew his conclusion.) Rather, signs merely guide expectations; signs act as signals that something is going well or badly, that you can anticipate or not anticipate something coming about.

Consider the most simple and common sign argument. In the days before satellites, televisions, radios, and weather observatories, when people wondered about the weather all they had to go on was an almanac and their own experience with nature. Was it going to be a cold winter or a dry spring? People searched nature for clues. If the trees turned color early, the squirrels appeared to be unusually busy in foraging, the birds took flight south quickly, and an individual's rheumatism started acting up, then these were all taken as signs that winter was soon on the way. Reading the signs of nature could allow people to take prudent action quickly. If the signs were read incorrectly, then a condition would be mistakenly anticipated.

Like other forms of argument, sign argument is based upon a number of factors coming together and pointing in the same direction. The more people see signs of winter about us, the more they can confidently predict that winter is on its way. Signs are sometimes ambiguous, however. Signs can conflict: some pointing to an early winter, others to an Indian summer. When signs conflict in a debate, debaters must apply criteria to separate more important from less important signs, and to weigh the risks of various actions.

In policy debate, sign argument is used in several ways. Most frequently, sign argument is used to identify symptoms of a problem. For example, if you wanted to argue that environmental protection standards are not enforced adequately, then you might collect a variety of symptomatic evidence: a decreasing number of prosecutions for toxic waste dumping, delay in implementing Superfund site cleanup moneys, court cases that indict EPA administrators for submitting to illegal lobbying. All of these characteristics plagued the first Reagan administration and were taken by many as signs of a lax environmental commitment. Note that such activities are not said to *cause* an anti-environmental attitude but are said to be *symptoms* of an underlying problem. Sometimes you may wish merely to treat symptoms rather than solve a problem.

Analogy

Argument from analogy involves comparing two dissimilar ideas, situations, things, persons, or policies. A *literal analogy* is a comparison in which the objects under comparison seem to have more in common than not. A *figurative analogy* is a comparison in which the objects have a striking similarity, but as a whole have more difference than commonness.

Policy debate involves both kinds of analogies. For example, consider former President Bush's comparison of the 1992 Democratic bid for the presidency to past bids. In his 1992 speech accepting the Republican nomination, President Bush stated:

> Look, look this is serious business. Think about the impact on our foreign policy failures the last time the Democrats controlled both ends of Pennsylvania Avenue. Gas lines. Grain embargoes. American hostages blindfolded.

The argument that President Bush was making is one by analogy, a historical analogy. President Bush argued that a Democratic federal government is not good for the country; therefore, even if you were Democratic, it was wise to split the ticket and vote for a Republican for President.

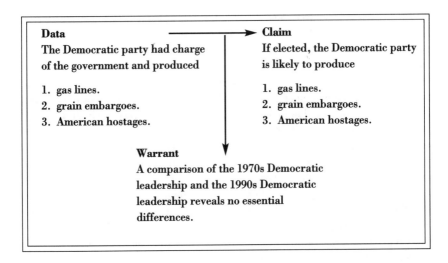

How do you rebut an argument from analogy? The answer to this question is very tricky. Consider the difficulty of dealing with President Bush's analogy. To begin with, you might effectively point out that the conditions that made the analogy pertinent had changed: that the early 1970s could not be compared to the 1990s. OPEC, the oil cartel that caused the embargo leading to gas lines, is much weaker now than then, and measures have been taken to reduce dependency on foreign oil. The grain embargo, a measure taken to punish the Soviet Union for human rights violations, is no longer a threat—since there is no more Soviet Union. By showing that the conditions of the past are no longer relevant in the present, the analogy should be refuted.

However, the point of President Bush's argument was not literal but figurative. He was not merely saying that the Democrats will bring back the same problems, but that the problems of the past show the Democratic party's weakness, one that will find its way into new problems. Sometimes, the only way to refute such a figurative analogy is with a counter-analogy, a response that makes another comparison outside the original frame of reference.

Precedent

An important argument that is often used by debaters is an argument from precedent. An **argument from precedent** simply says that one should follow an established way of doing things until and unless there is good reason for doing something differently. Argument from precedent is connected with a defense of presumption that the status quo should remain as is until there is a reasonable case for change.

The argument from precedent involves debaters in value debate. Imagine a case that identifies crime as being rampant in the United States. The affirmative team shows that a whole host of measures has been taken to solve crime within the existing state of laws and procedures, and that none of these measures has worked. They also show that if the rights of the defendants were reduced radically, perhaps by reversing the traditional presumption of innocence, then there would be more convictions and less crime on the streets. The lack of precedent for such a measure within American jurisprudence shows that this plan is a unique measure; and the analogy to lower crime rates of nations with no presumption of innocence may establish the crime-fighting desirability of such a program. But argument from precedent now becomes an important part of a policy debate.

One of the ways to justify setting aside precedent is to show that the current situation has unique problems that are so extraordinary that the current precedents are no longer workable, and that new approaches are needed. To the extent that current problems are large and unique to the present, precedent is transformed from a traditional value to an obstacle to action.

On the other hand, a radical departure from precedent creates opportunities for counterarguments. If one precedent can be overturned, then why not others? This is the logic of the **slippery-slope argument**. In the example given, the negative team might argue that if the precedent of innocent until proven guilty were reversed, then other individual protections might be struck down in the name of effective crime fighting. By magnifying the consequences of overturning precedent, it is possible to turn what seems to be even a minor or relatively innocuous action into something that may have very serious consequences. For example, advocates of gun ownership oppose a federal five-day waiting period for gun purchases not so much because they believe hotheads should have handguns, but because they believe the precedent of federal regulation could eventually curtail what they perceive to be a fundamental freedom: the right to bear arms.

Argument from precedent is subject to the following objections. First, if similar actions contrary to precedent were undertaken at other times and did not start the ball rolling down the slippery slope, then an objection to the current proposal may have less weight. In the case of gun control, a debater might note that although there have been many regulations on gun use and ownership, the right to bear arms has been sustained.

Second, if you can demonstrate that there are checkpoints to the slippery-slope argument, then you can argue that it is not inevitable that violating precedent will automatically result in a catastrophic state of affairs. The slippery-slope argument assumes an automatic slide to a bad end.

By now, you should have a good idea of the different kinds of arguments available to you: argument from authority, argument by generalization, cause, sign, analogy, and precedent. All of these are important kinds of argument for strategic debaters, and all have strengths and weaknesses. In the following section, you will learn how to put these different kinds of arguments together through the process of analysis.

Analyzing Arguments

Any topic chosen for policy debate will have a large number of issues attached to its discussion. The process of analysis begins with sorting these arguments into different categories and then weighing their strength and relevance to different possible positions.

As a strategic debater, you must engage in critical thinking. The process of analysis requires that you always ask the questions: what is the strongest possible evidence that this argument is true, and what is the strongest possible evidence that it is false? After you determine the relative truth of the argument, then you must ask the next two questions: does the truth of the argument make a big difference to the acceptability of the resolution, or does the truth of the argument make little or no difference to the acceptability of the resolution?

It is important that you ask both sets of questions. Sometimes there are issues that are hotly contested, and it is difficult to determine who is right and wrong on a position, but the determination of truth or falsity makes no difference to the outcome of the debate. For example, it is not clear if the Democrats or the Republicans contributed more to winning the Cold War, but the relative merits of *past* foreign policy are not necessarily germane to the issue of what policy is best at *present*. On the other hand, some issues will appear to be of great strategic significance but cannot be settled conclusively. If it could be established that a significant number of Americans were absolutely without health care, then perhaps a radical revision of American health care policy would clearly be warranted; but given the variety of alternative sources of care, this conclusion is not clear cut.

The essence of strategic debate is being able to undertake analysis so that you can know the relative merit of arguments. The best kind of argument is one that is important to the acceptability of the resolution and is relatively easy to prove in a conclusive fashion. The least useful argument is one that has little intrinsic importance to the resolution or that is relatively difficult to prove in a conclusive fashion. Because of the nature of debate topics, you should expect that the more important an argument becomes, the more contested it will be, and the more extended and focused should be the development.

The following analytical techniques should help you develop and test argumentation. Later chapters on case development and refutation will take you through the process of developing reasoning into cases, presentation, and refutation. But this is where the process begins.

Sorting

A lot of analysis is similar to the children's game of sorting shapes. Like things go together. The challenge is to find a set of clear categories that will permit you to effectively develop your argumentation. How do you find categories for developing analytical argument? Usually, your research will suggest the main issues under discussion, but you have to figure out how those issues shape the debate.

Consider the following statement from President Clinton's 1993 "State of the Union" address:

> The rising costs and the lack of care are endangering both our economy and our lives. Reducing health care costs will liberate hundreds of billions of dollars for investment and growth and new jobs. Over the long run, reforming health care is essential to reducing our deficit and expanding investment.

This statement is helpful for beginning the process of analysis, because it includes headings for a number of issues. Clinton noted no fewer than six major categories of the health care debate:*

1. Rising health care costs are harmful to the economy.

2. Rising health care costs are harmful to our lives.

3. Reducing health care costs will increase money for investment in the economy.

4. Reducing health care costs will increase money available for new jobs.

5. Reducing health care costs will reduce the deficit.

6. Reducing health care costs will increase opportunities for public investment for other government programs.

Now, it is clear from these categories that the economic effects of current health care on individual health, economic competitiveness, the government deficit, and social services are important issues in the debate. As such, they provide categories for the development of arguments.

Note that an important part of sorting is dividing up arguments into affirmative and negative territory. Most issues are clearly one or the other, and stay that way. Evidence that suggests health care costs are unnecessarily high indicates reasons for change; evidence that suggests that the current level of health care expenses are not unnecessarily high indicate support for the status quo. Conversely, evidence that suggests health care reform will not reduce costs, reduce the deficit, or increase job training counts for the negative side; and the reverse for the affirmative. This is an elementary step in reasoning.

Not all issues are so simple, and there are a number of issues that could go both ways, depending on the type of case that is argued or the slant of the opposition's arguments. It is wise to think of affirmative and negative ground not as statically defendable territory, but as territory that requires strategic assessment. For example, reduced economic growth caused by high health care costs might be a negative argument—if economic investment is a cause of greater pollution, and pollution is a more problematic threat than loss of jobs. This "turning" of what might apparently

---

*The health care question is an excellent historical example of a debatable issue. It will be referred to throughout the text.

be one side of the debate or the other requires careful analysis of strategy—a topic developed extensively in upcoming chapters.

Assessing Viability

For every debate topic, you will reach a point where you must decide to regard some arguments as true and unassailable, some arguments as strong but subject to harassment, some arguments as weak and subject to strong opposition, and some as intellectually interesting and perhaps strategically enticing (if true), but not supportable by reasonable evidence.

Arguments that seem to be true are those that are supported by strong data and a consensus of experts. Generally, a debate topic will include a good number of arguments that carry strong presumptive validity. *Presumptive validity* simply means that almost everyone believes that the argument is true. For example, in debating the crime topic, there is a strong presumption that crime levels are too high and that crime is not valuable, especially crime against property. There is strong evidence both that crime harms a large number of Americans and that people find the problem threatening. If this is indeed the case, you will recognize that it will do little good either to spend a great deal of time finding more evidence to establish the obvious or to try to develop arguments that will conclusively deny what seems to be a presumptively true position. This may seem like stating the obvious, but many debaters wish to argue everything, and they thus miss the most valuable part of analysis: figuring out what cannot be argued successfully!

More interesting are those arguments that are strongly defended but contestable. In the crime topic, for example, it seems to be commonly believed that crime is worse now than it was twenty years ago. The feeling that crime is getting worse creates a strong impetus for passing legislation, especially when politicians lose seats for appearing soft on crime, as in the 1993 interim elections. In reality, however, statistics show that crime is no worse now than it was twenty years ago. When there is a gap between what appears or is generally accepted to be the case, and hard evidence, then analysis yields the beginnings of a good argument. Note that you would develop such an argument by explaining *why* the contention appears to be true and *why* in reality it is false. For example, you might argue that people think crime is greater now because media reporting is more widespread, but in reality the crime problem is less urgent than what it appears to be.

Arguments that are generally strong but can be offset or mitigated are an important category for debate. Note these are not *the* most important types of argument, strategically speaking. You could debate relative crime rates for a long time without coming to any secure conclusions. Where evidence is relatively equal or offsetting, often the best that can be accomplished is a standoff. But even this is an important task, because it helps to mitigate what the opponent might present as overly significant and important claims.

A third kind of strategic argument comes from evidence that conclusively settles an issue. For example, there are many different opinions about the effectiveness of handgun legislation on reducing violence. This could and has been debated for a long time, but the key question is what really happens when laws are passed. You should be sure to spend a significant amount of time searching for precedents, studies, surveys, pilot programs, or other such authoritative evidence. Because general opinion is usually vulnerable to considerations of time and place, the more specific and detailed the evidence you find, the more convincing your argument will be. For example, it may be the case that gun control fails generally. There are simply too many handguns in the United States to ever be retrieved. But by gathering detailed, specific evidence, you may be able to argue that controlling the production and distribution of ammunition may have a different effect.

The final move in analysis is to find holes in the available evidence, a strategy that is described fully in the chapters on affirmative and negative positions. At this point, the most important thing to remember is that analysis is a constant process of weeding out the weakest (least provable and strategically less useful) arguments and finding stronger arguments to take their place. Analysis is a practice that occurs at the beginning of the year, when you are first becoming acquainted with the topic; and it is a process that continues throughout the year as you encounter stronger arguments and come to think about revision.

Summary

This chapter has investigated the uses of informal logic in the process of debate. We began by identifying the component parts of a single argument. The most basic parts are claim, warrant, and data. The claim of an argument is a statement that identifies what it is you wish to prove. In an argument, the data are comprised of evidence or proof that you believe is relevant to the truth of the claim. The warrant is the reasoning that links data and claim, an explanation of why the evidence is both relevant and sufficient to prove what it is that you are claiming.

We also identified useful secondary components of a single argument. In particular, we looked at rebuttal statements that located some reason why the data were not conclusive or completely relevant. We also examined expressed reservations. These are statements that identify exceptions to the rule. Reservations stem from an assessment of the strength of rebuttals and are strategically useful in establishing the candor and honesty of an argument. We also looked at qualifiers, which are terms such as *some, all, many, none* or *probably, possibly, certainly*. These terms regulate the amount of confidence one has in the relationship between data and claim. The term *backing* defines all the extra data and reasoning that could be used in support of an argument.

There are regular ways of constructing arguments that form a kind of topical logic. Each topic has a number of strategic considerations that are attached to building or criticizing reasoning of this kind. In particular, we examined arguments from authority, expertise, generalization, cause, sign, analogy, and precedent. In each case, strategic strengths and weaknesses of the different kinds of argument differ. Hence, the advocate must be able to use informal reasoning with careful analysis in complicated advocacy situations.

Analysis works best when two-sided thinking is emphasized, leading an advocate to look for the components that support and those that oppose the arguments relevant to a topic. Strategic analysis requires assessing how relevant and important arguments are to the acceptability or truth of a resolution under debate. Analysis requires both an assessment of all relevant arguments and picking and choosing among those that develop affirmative and negative ground for particular cases.

Questions

1. What are data, warrant, and claim? How are they related?
2. What are the differences between rebuttals, reservations, and qualifiers?
3. Define backing.
4. Define argument from authority.
5. Define causal argument from sign.
6. Define analogical argument.
7. Define causal argument.
8. Define argument from precedent.

Discussion Opportunities

1. To what extent would you announce reservations and rebuttals to the arguments you wish to develop? If you admit that there are exceptions to the rule, do you weaken your own case? Why?
2. The argument from precedent says that a great deal of weight should be given to the question of whether we are acting within tradition or violating it. Should argument from precedent be important?
3. Discuss the process of analysis of arguments and the ways to sort out important areas for research and thinking from minor or unimportant ones.
4. Discuss what is the best way of analyzing issues pertaining to a topic of major national discussion, such as crime, health care, or free trade.

Writing Opportunities

1. Take a public issue, like the controversy over wearing fur garments, and isolate the major arguments for and against the issue. Write a short paper analyzing the arguments. You should try to be comprehensive, yet frame the paper so that you systematically cover only the major issues.

2. Form a slippery-slope argument and explain why it raises needless fears.

3. Create an argument that differentiates the causes of good government from those of bad government. Distinguish between what you think are the major causes of good government from those that are only accidental or relatively minor.

Critical Thinking Opportunities

1. Suppose you overhear an individual arguing that money causes happiness. This person has known several very wealthy people in his life, and they are all happy. How could this argument be countered and developed?

2. Develop an argument from example. Show how your examples support a major claim, and demonstrate how a counterexample does not hurt the overall thrust of your argument.

3. Develop an argument from sign. Show how the signs work together to prove that the claim is true.

STRATEGIES IN ACTION

In her world history class, Maria is required to write a term paper. Her history teacher has posed a very broad question for this assignment: Geography Today—Redrawing the World's Maps: What Does It Mean? Each student in Maria's class is required to identify an area of the question about which to research and write a term paper. Many students in the class seem at a loss about how to complete this assignment. Rather than panic or worry, Maria—a debater—puts her analytical and research skills to work. Take a look at the course of action Maria put together for herself:

- Outline what you already know about one area—the break-up and reshaping of various countries in Russia and Eastern Europe.
- Compile a list of readings—background information on what has been happening in Russia and in Europe, in general. Determine three or four sources that discuss the most recent changes, such as *Time* and *Newsweek*.
- Go back to the outline and add any issues that have come up in your background reading.
- From your research, develop a one- to two-sentence answer to the question "Redrawing the world's maps: what does it mean?" This answer will become the thesis for your research paper (your affirmative case, sort of speak).
- Go back to the issues that you outlined. Select those that support your answer to the question.
- Using those issues, list key terms that can be used for looking up resources in indexes. Do a computer search. Begin with the *Readers' Guide Abstracts*. Next, search the *Social Issues Research Series* (SIRS). To include newspapers in your search, consult ProQuest. (The now more than 4000 newspapers and periodicals covered in this index will provide ample information.) To include books, use the computerized card catalog.
- Develop a bibliography of resources for your term paper. Gather together the relevant materials from your search. Remember, some of the materials will need to be printed straight from the computer indexes you researched. The abstracts from the other indexes will help you identify those articles likely to be of value.
- Read and mark evidence or data that can be used as quotations to support statements in your term paper. Then, put the quotations on index cards. Organize them by subject area.
- Using your evidence and your outline, begin writing your term paper.

The strategies Maria uses in debate are the same ones she used to set up the course of action for her project in World History—research skills and evidence-gathering techniques.

Research Strategies and Tactics

Objectives

After studying Chapter 3, you should be able

1. To explain how to make the best use of research time.
2. To conduct a useful library survey on the current debate resolution, using indexes, books, periodicals, legal publications, and government documents.
3. To develop a list of places and sources to write to for material on a particular debate resolution.
4. To explain and test the guidelines for ethics in research.
5. To process a primary source and properly record and file evidence cards from that source.
6. To explain the criteria for high-quality evidence.
7. To create a list of key terms to use when researching a debate resolution.

Key Terms

To research effectively, you will need to know the following terms:

competent
form
fact
value judgment
empirical evidence
opinion evidence
validity
reliability

To the casual observer, debate doesn't seem to be a very difficult activity. If a person is sufficiently glib and has a better-than-average knowledge of a subject, it might be assumed that he or she would be a fairly decent debater. Moreover, the typical debate takes only about an hour and a half to run its course, and each speaker spends only about fifteen minutes speaking. An observer might think, then, that all a debater has to do is be prepared to give the equivalent of a fifteen-minute speech—hardly an overwhelming task.

Like many other things, however, the true nature of debate is hidden beneath the surface. For every minute that he or she spends before the audience or judge, a good debater spends several hours in preparation. The bulk of this time is devoted to research, to getting the evidence to support the arguments that will be used in debate. Championship debaters are quite willing to work for many days to obtain the evidence necessary to develop a single argument in thirty seconds.

Why is research so important? The main reason is that debate, by its very nature, requires a tremendous amount of evidence. Debate is formalized argument, and argument is the process of reasoning from the known to the unknown—from *evidence* to a *conclusion*. Any argument, then, requires evidence if the audience or judge is going to accept it as valid.

As a debater, you must be prepared for more than just one argument. A typical debate might contain as many as a hundred different arguments, and you will participate in more than just one debate. You need to be ready to deal with many different cases and analyses. Thus, you will need tremendous amounts of evidence just to deal intelligently with the arguments that will be advanced in the course of a debate season. In addition, you will need to have a thorough understanding of the issues and elements in the topic area, so that your analyses will be as strong as the evidence.

To participate in championship-level debating demands even more research, because you will want the best and most recent material available on the topic. One national collegiate champion asserted that although all the other elements of debate are important, the most successful debaters are those who have the most thorough knowledge of the topic and the best evidence to support what they assert.

This chapter deals with the strategy and tactics of debate research. The first matter for concern is the overall strategy of research—what to do first, what to look for, and how to make the best use of your research time. Then this chapter presents tactics for research: where to find evidence, how to file it, how to retrieve it, and how to maintain it.

The Research Strategy

One theme of this text is that debaters should have the highest standards for their own work. It is never profitable to look for the easy way out; instead, you should seek the path of most resistance. This attitude is essential if you are going to get the maximum educational advantage from debating—and if you hope to be a successful competitor. Your research strategy, therefore, should grow out of this philosophy.

The research strategy for debate can be stated in one sentence: debaters should strive to obtain a thorough knowledge of the topic and the highest-quality evidence to support their arguments. If you succeed in carrying out this strategy, not only will you learn a great deal, but you will win more debates than other less informed debaters.

Quality research is more than gathering "quote cards." A debate topic involves much more than isolated statistics and assorted quotations that relate to its major issues. Debaters who operate on this superficial level are making a serious tactical mistake.

Some debaters spend hundreds of hours looking for quotations and statistics and end up, when the season is completed, knowing very little about the topic and its issues! How can you spend countless hours researching and still not understand the topic? Ironically, the answer is a simple one. These debaters get caught up researching specific issues without understanding how those issues relate to the general topic.

Superficial research has its disadvantages on the competitive level. The authors have seen several debates lost—even at the end of the season—simply because the debaters didn't understand the topic. They had plenty of evidence cards, but they didn't know or understand the important background facts that any informed person would know about the topic. Evidence may not always be the key to defeating an opponent's argument. If you have a good understanding of the topic, you may be able to develop or defeat an argument through reasoning even when there is no evidence in your files to support your argument.

How do you gain a thorough knowledge of the topic? How do you obtain the highest-quality evidence? The first step is to decide to carry out the research strategy. Every debater wants to be good—but not all are willing to do the work needed to be good. The second step is to develop specific criteria for judging the quality of your research. After all, it does little good to set a strategy for obtaining high-quality evidence unless you know what high-quality evidence is. Finally, you should develop specific tactics for carrying out your research strategy.

Obtaining the Highest-Quality Evidence

Deciding upon the kind of evidence that is best is not easy. Because evidence is used to try to obtain agreement from an audience or judge, the basic question you need to ask is what it will take to get the judge to decide that your argument is valid. Some people require very little in the way of evidence to support what they already feel to be true. Even the best evidence might not cause other people, whose opinions have already been formed, to change their minds. And some audiences require extremely sound evidence, while others seem to believe anything that has appeared in print.

Fortunately, although it is true that debate judges are people first and judges second, you can be more certain of what the debate judge will require in the way of evidence than can, say, a public speaker who addresses lay listeners. Debate judges have arrived at some fairly standard criteria for judging the quality of evidence. They are inclined to award the debate to the team that has done the best job of meeting the evidence criteria in supporting their arguments.

In examining the criteria for debate evidence, you must first consider two general questions. The first question is what can be said about the *external* qualities of the evidence—how can the *source* of the evidence be evaluated? The second question is what can be said about the *internal* qualities of the evidence—how *truthful* is it?

External Criticism

Questions of external criticism (how good is the source?) can be divided into two areas: the quality of the publication from which the material is drawn and the competence of the author of the material. Debaters use several criteria in judging the quality of the publication and the qualifications of the author.

First, debaters ask if the publication is **competent** to testify on behalf of a given argument. To find competent publications you should seek sources that are known to be objective and responsible in reporting factual and opinion material. For instance, if a magazine claims to report current events, does it report these events reliably and responsibly, or does it slant and interpret events to fit a particular editorial bias? Many debaters have fallen into the trap of believing a publication that sounds good but really is biased. Although in most speaking situations an advocate can get by with biased material, as a debater you can be very sure that your opponents will have done enough research to show that the evidence is faulty.

Along with the competence of the source, debaters also need to be concerned about the **form** of the evidence. This issue can become quite complex. For example, two debate teams may differ as to what was or was not said in a presidential address, only to find that one team has been quoting from a source that used an advance copy of the speech, while the other team has been quoting from a source that used the speech as it was actually given. Authorities speaking on television in an interview format or on a discussion panel have been known to make inconsistent statements (compared to their written works).

Which form carries the greatest validity? The general rule is that the more permanent the form, the more reliable the information. Authorities are likely to be more careful in a scholarly book that will be available for many years than in a television encounter. An expert is likely to weigh every word carefully in the prepared text of a speech, because every word will be carefully read, but that same person may feel freer to exaggerate and dramatize in off-the-cuff remarks. As a debater, therefore, you will want to seek the most permanent forms of evidence because they typically represent the best material.

In addition to questioning the quality of the publication, debaters also question the competence of the author of the material. The first question to ask here is: who is the author? Most debaters insist that an author be considered an expert, not a layperson, in the area being debated. The author should be professionally qualified and competent to state facts or opinions, should be respected by other authorities in the field, and should have a reputation for responsible reporting. An author should not be biased.

Generally, this means that you should avoid authorities who have a vested interest in their subject. For instance, you would expect a spokesperson for a drug company to argue that the prices charged for drugs are not out of line, that drug companies do not have high profit margins. You might also expect certain doctors to support the increased use of medical tests under the guise that such testing improves medical diagnosis. And you probably wouldn't be surprised to discover that heads of government agencies are usually eager to point out the effectiveness and necessity of their agencies.

At the same time, however, when you are researching a given authority, you should also look out for evidence that supports opinions other than that authority's own biases. Take the example of the doctor. A doctor's arguments that many of the tests ordered by doctors are unnecessary and are ordered only when covered by insurance or government programs would be very valuable evidence.

The second question about the competence of the author is whether the author is an expert in the particular field. Authorities in one field commonly state opinions about other fields in which they are not qualified. An expert in military strategy might be heard advancing opinions about foreign policy. A physicist might offer medical advice to a friend. While being a layperson does not make one's opinion false, any more than being an expert necessarily makes it true, as a debater you want to be careful to gauge accurately the qualifications of the author of the evidence.

Third, you should ask *when* the author got the information. Generally, the closer the author was to the event, the more likely it is that the information will be right. When debating current events, this usually means that the most recent evidence is the best.

It should be noted that only newspapers carry the most recent evidence, because only newspapers print information within hours of availability. Magazines give the impression of being as up-to-date when they are not: for example, a *Time* magazine issue dated the first of the month actually came off the press at least one week before.

On many issues or arguments, the date of the evidence could determine who wins the issue. For example, the issues debated in the 1993–94 national health insurance topic are prime examples of the need for the most recent evidence. Since the Clinton administration was developing a health care policy at the same time high-school debaters were debating the topic, the dates of evidence became very important. A newspaper article on the woes of individuals without health insurance (with no chance of getting coverage) became outdated with the next press release discussing White House proposals for covering those individuals. In such instances, public opinion polls might be out of date as soon as a new poll is published. On the other hand, when considering historical events it may well be that the oldest source is the most accurate. An ancient Greek's comments about life in ancient Greece may be more accurate than comments in a modern, idealized history of that country.

As a debater you should be cautious about the copyright date on books. Books generally are not printed with the same speed as magazines or newspapers; thus a book with a copyright date of 1994 may have been written in 1992 or 1993. A good way to judge the timeliness of a book is to check the footnotes. The dates on footnotes and in the bibliography will give you a good idea of when the book was actually written and how current the research materials are.

Internal Criticism

Internal criticism, the truth of the evidence, frequently is overlooked by inexperienced debaters. They feel that if the source is sound and the authority reputable, the evidence must be true. But this is not always the case. In early 1990, former President George Bush argued that the United States was in an economic downturn but not a recession. President Bush repeated this line many times at press conferences and on the campaign trail. Late in 1991, he was forced by events to admit that the economic downturn was much worse than he had thought and that the United States was in fact in a recession.

You should always read materials with a sense of caution. Make sure that you evaluate both what the evidence says and how consistent it is.

When evaluating the validity of evidence, the first and most obvious consideration is: what does the evidence say? What does it report, and does this report make sense? Does the evidence report actual events—facts—or does it make inferences about what is probably true, based upon what is already known? Perhaps the statement is a **value judgment** about the nature of events, based on inferences drawn from facts.

Most logicians and debate judges feel that the further the statement is from the fact level, the more likely it is to contain error. The following is an example of an irresponsible leap from fact to inference to conclusion:

> *Fact*: Some American tourists are obnoxious.
>
> *Inference*: All American tourists are obnoxious.
>
> *Value*: Yankee, go home!

Many inexperienced debaters depend on opinion evidence in which bias and error are likely to exist. It is best to present evidence that is factual in nature and let the judge follow your logic in arriving at your conclusions.

You can also judge the truth of evidence by checking to see if it's consistent within itself. It is not unusual to discover inconsistencies in evidence, and a careful researcher often can disprove an opponent's arguments by showing that the opposing team didn't read enough of the quotation to indicate the true opinion of the authority. By reading further from the same article or from other articles by the same person or source, you may be able to show that the so-called authority seems unable to make up his or her mind. Inconsistency, then, may be one of the first indications that a piece of supporting material is not valid.

Finally, you can gauge the validity of evidence by determining whether it is consistent with other information. Do other authorities or sources agree? Is the same fact consistently observed by others? You should beware of arguments for which only one supporting source can be found. You also should be careful of a quotation that runs counter to the bulk of other information.

Criteria for Selecting the Highest-Quality Evidence

A. External criticism (How good is the source?)
  1. How competent is the source of the evidence?
    a. Is it objective?
    b. Is it responsible?
    c. Is it relatively free from bias?
  2. What is the form of the evidence?
    a. How permanent is it?
    b. Did the source intend permanence and strict interpretation?
  3. Who is the author of the evidence?
    a. Is the author an expert in the field?
    b. Is the author relatively free from bias?
    c. How was the information obtained?
      1) Firsthand observation (primary source)?
      2) Obtained from someone else (secondary source)?
    d. When did the author get the information?
  4. How recent is the evidence?
    a. Does it represent the latest material available?
    b. Have important events occurred since the evidence was written?
B. Internal criticism (How truthful is the evidence?)
  1. What does the evidence say?
  2. On what level of abstraction is it?
    a. Is it a factual report?
    b. Is it an inferential report?
    c. Is it a judgmental report?
  3. Is the evidence consistent within itself?
  4. Is the evidence consistent with other information?

Research Tactics

The tactics of research are simply the procedures that debaters use to acquire background knowledge of the topic and the highest-quality evidence to support their arguments. This section suggests some tactics you can use to make the best use of your research time.

Acquiring Background Knowledge

Although all research obviously contributes to your knowledge of the topic, debaters usually have something more specific in mind when referring to "acquiring background knowledge." A pool of evidence—"quote cards"—and background information are two different things. Evidence represents specific, relatively independent information that pertains to the arguments debaters expect to use or encounter. Knowledge of the topic—background information—refers to a more general understanding of the issues, ideas, and relevant facts that pertain to the topic area. Good debaters put almost as much emphasis on understanding the topic as they do on gathering evidence.

The process of acquiring background information begins the day the proposition for the debate year is announced. At this point, usually in the spring, debaters begin background reading. However, they do not proceed without first organizing their time and energy.

The first step in organizing the background reading phase of research is to find out what is already known about the topic. At this point, many debaters simply make a rough outline of what they already know about the debate topic. Then, often working with their partners or other squad members, they list the major areas that are likely to be important, along with subissues that will probably come into play.

It's not unusual for debaters to find they know very little about a new debate topic. Beginning debaters especially may have only very superficial knowledge about such topics as the global environment, space exploration, or even health insurance. Therefore, many debaters find they need to begin with a general discussion of the topic area and issues that might be explored. Sources such as debate handbooks or the *Forensic Quarterly* (published by the National Federation of State High School Associations) can be useful at the early stages of research. Such sources provide overviews of the topic and introduce areas for possible research. They may also include preliminary bibliographies and affirmative and negative cases. All such sources provide a good general background on the topic and can help to get you thinking. Once you are familiar with the topic, you will be ready to move on to the next phase of background research.

The next phase of acquiring background knowledge involves carefully reading three or four key books about the topic and its major issues. As mentioned, you can usually find several good books to read in the bibliographies of handbooks and other topic books. At this point, you should attempt to cover one or two major books that reflect relatively objective approaches to the topic. If possible, you should also try to read one book that represents the bias of those who tend to support the topic, and one book that represents those who tend to oppose it.

In familiarizing yourself with the extreme biases on any topic, you will likely encounter the standard and emotional arguments that will turn up in debates during the year. Also, the authors of work that show a bias will likely refer to other works that share that bias, and you can keep such sources in mind for later reference. A good way to locate sources on either side of the topic is to write to the pressure groups that usually are active in any major policy question.

Although standard, objective sources usually are more difficult to find than biased ones, there are ways to locate them. Your school librarians may offer suggestions, or a teacher may be available to recommend the text on which most experts depend. Objective texts should acquaint you with the major arguments and issues, as well as provide other authorities who can be investigated later.

Since researching a topic is time-consuming, you need to be as efficient as possible. Efficiency begins by reading only relevant material. In selecting materials you should check the title, table of contents, index, and chapter heads to focus your search for evidence. When researching, skim rapidly, skipping all material that is clearly irrelevant and reading slowly any materials of possible importance. Don't worry about missing something by skimming; it will be more than compensated for by the increased amount of material you will read. Also, don't limit yourself to reading books. You should also consult magazines, newspaper reports, government documents, and pamphlets.

It isn't easy to decide when and how to terminate the general knowledge part of your research. However, there will come a time when you will feel ready to move on to gathering specific evidence for actual debating. At this juncture many debaters simply stop their background reading and let their knowledge lie fallow in their minds. Others feel it is important to synthesize their background reading more formally.

To gain a formal synthesis, some debate squads divide into small groups to discuss the major issues or points of controversy. After the groups have reached some consensus as to what seems important, they frequently assign specific issues to various students. These issues, which may be broken down further into negative and affirmative aspects, are researched individually or in groups.

While the analysis of these issues will not be extensive, since all the debaters are still learning about the topic, group discussion and analyses can speed up the process of gathering background material. Group research can also help a squad spot potential affirmative cases. It is generally a good idea to have each group or individual write up statements to be duplicated for distribution to the entire squad. Those statements should provide background material, highlights of areas that need additional research, sources for background reading, and any viable arguments that were discovered while researching.

Regardless of which tactics you use to gather background information, eventually you will be ready to gather evidence—a development that most debaters eagerly await. Now is the time to compile quote cards.

Researching Specific Evidence

It was mentioned earlier that argument is the process of reasoning from evidence to a conclusion. Most debaters have little trouble arriving at conclusions, but they have to work hard to find evidence that will support those conclusions. That is the purpose of this phase of research. You should approach each piece of evidence with four questions in mind:

1. What does the evidence say?
2. How does the evidence say it?
3. What will the evidence do?
4. How good is the evidence?

This first question, "What does the evidence say?" is rather obvious. As you read quickly through masses of materials, you will become "tuned in" to the material that seems most applicable to the debate topic. At this point, you should be looking for factual, inferential, or judgmental material that will support affirmative or negative arguments.

The second question, "How does the evidence say it?" addresses an issue of quality. It is always sad when a researcher finally finds just the information he or she has been looking for, only to discover that the material is so poorly written or so lengthy that no judge would respond to it. There is little you can do in such a situation, because no one has the right to rewrite the evidence to make it more palatable. Although some debaters would paraphrase the material, it's best simply to keep looking for usable evidence.

The third question, "What will the evidence do?" has many elements. You need to consider what the evidence will do in a debate. Will it support the argument in the mind of the judge? How will the other team react to it? How easy will it be for the opposition to cast doubt on it? How does it fit with or contradict the other evidence you plan to use?

You can answer these questions at least tentatively before actual competition begins. However, the best way to find the answers is to use the material to see what it will do. Sometimes debaters are pleasantly surprised to find that a piece of evidence they thought was weak appears to have won a debate for them. At other times debaters may find that favorite quotations had disastrous effects or caused more trouble than they were worth.

The basic consideration is: does the evidence have the power to convince? If you carefully consider how a piece of evidence will support your arguments, there is every likelihood that it will be convincing. Then it can be tried in debates, against good opposition, to see how it stands up. Having given careful thought to these matters, you can be well on the way to meeting the strategic objective: to have the best evidence possible.

The last question, "How good is it?" is one that is conditioned by the many standards that are used to judge evidence. The general standards of external and internal criticism have already been discussed. In addition to these, many debaters rank evidence according to its quality for debate.

Evidence can be divided into two general categories. **Empirical evidence** is based on controlled observations and factual and inferential data. **Opinion evidence** usually is judgmental in nature. Empirical and opinion evidence can be ranked from the best—experimental data—to the most doubtful—layperson opinion.

Empirical Evidence

Empirical evidence includes experimental data and observational data. Experimental data are the results of scientific experiments conducted to explore some causal relationship. Experimenters begin with a *hypothesis*, or prediction about the nature of things. It supposes a relationship between two or more things or concepts.

For example, an experimenter might hypothesize that "A causes B to happen to C." If it is suspected, for example, that a particular virus causes a particular disease, the experimenter might set up a test to see if the virus causes the disease in laboratory animals. If it does, the experimenter can be more sure that the virus is the cause. Or a supposed cause might be removed. If, for instance, a police chief thinks the crime rate is high because there aren't enough police officers, the force might be doubled in an experimental area to see if the crime rate drops. If it does, the cause of the high crime rate may have been found.

Of course, there are many more types of experiments. The point is that such data often are considered the very best debate evidence because they represent the best way to establish causation. However, experimental evidence is superior only when it is based on sound research. In any case, evidence that can be verified is always preferable to evidence that cannot.

The current trend in debate, in both high school and college, is to rely more heavily on statistics and quantitative studies. In recent years there has been increased experimentation in social, economic, and political areas, as well as more valid data. While this may improve the quality of available evidence, it can create problems for the debater if not approached with caution.

In evaluating experimental data, you should ask three questions: (1) How well were the variables controlled? (2) Has the experiment been replicated with the same results? and (3) Can the results of the experiment be generalized to more than just the cases that were used in the experiment?

Always be sure to examine the methodology used to arrive at empirical data. You should have some idea of how the data were collected. When studies are used to support an argument in a debate round, check to see if the debate's proposal contains the same conditions and mechanisms as the studies being cited for support. Most abuses of experimental data occur in this area.

In addition to experimental data, empirical evidence also includes observational data. Observational data include statistics and carefully developed examples. The main criteria for judging the quality of observational data are **validity** and **reliability**. To judge validity, you need to ask whether the observer actually observed what he or she claimed to be measuring. To judge reliability, you need to ask if the same results would be obtained if the observations were repeated or if they had been gathered at the same time by a different observer.

Political polls are good examples of types of observations that have had to overcome major validity and reliability problems. Early pollsters picked Alfred Landon to defeat Franklin D. Roosevelt in 1936 because their measures weren't valid. They thought they were gathering data about the feelings of all the voters when they conducted telephone interviews, but they overlooked the fact that millions of Democratic voters couldn't afford telephones during the Depression.

Reliability, on the other hand, was the problem for the pollsters who picked Thomas Dewey to defeat Harry S. Truman by a landslide. Polls that were taken two weeks before the election simply weren't accurate two weeks later. As the campaigns began for the 1992 presidential election, then-President Bush was identified in the polls as a shoo-in for a second term. The polls virtually declared President Bush the winner prior to the first presidential primary. The result was that many Democratic front-runner candidates stepped back to wait until 1996 to run when there would not be an incumbent president (Bush would not be eligible to run in 1996). As the campaign progressed, the President's standings in the polls dropped. How could anyone have known that a third-party candidate would pose a real threat to the election of a candidate from either party? On the eve of the election, the polls and the media speculated on what would happen if neither President Bush nor Democratic Party candidate Bill Clinton received the required electoral votes for election. The election became too close to call. The nation waited with bated breath. The result: By the time the polls had closed in the Midwest, the media had declared Clinton the winner.

Experienced debaters like to use observational data. If the data are reliable and valid, such evidence is difficult to overcome in a debate and is frequently very persuasive.

Opinion Evidence

The second major category of evidence is opinion evidence. Like empirical evidence, opinion evidence also is divisible into two categories: *expert testimony* and *testimony from a layperson*. A person who fulfills the standards mentioned earlier in this chapter is probably an expert. Otherwise that person should be considered a layperson, no matter how prestigious the person's qualifications.

Even though most debate coaches would like to see less use of opinion evidence, they know that debaters will always make great use of it. Opinion evidence usually is easier to find and easier to use than other evidence. It is easier to find because almost everybody is eager to state an opinion or conclusion in print. Some students feel that it's easier to use because an authority does their thinking for them. Thus, the biggest danger in using opinion evidence is that it contributes to the nonthinking style of debating.

However, despite the prejudices of a large number of coaches (including the authors), opinion evidence can be very useful to debates. It can be useful, however, only if the debaters take the time to understand *why* the authority arrived at a particular conclusion. If they can explain this to the judge, the opinion card can save a great deal of time in a debate. Expert testimony, however, is the only type that can be used for proof. Testimony from laypeople should be reserved for the persuasive effect of illustration.

Debaters must assess their opinion cards in terms of
why the authorities came to their conclusions.

Hierarchy of Evidence

Best: experimental data
Second best: observational data
Third best: expert opinion
Weakest: layperson opinion

Sources of Evidence

Most debaters use a two-pronged attack in looking for evidence. Early in the season,
they search for material that looks as though it will be useful for background reading.
Later they look for evidence to support specific arguments and cases.

The most productive time begins when your team has tentatively arrived at the affirmative case that it will use. You can then sit down and work out the major topics and subtopics that fit under your particular analysis. Then you can exhaustively research each element of the case to get the evidence you need and to see what the weaknesses of the case may be.

Usually, team members divide their efforts to avoid duplication. They not only research the arguments that support their case but explore the arguments they would use if they were on the negative team. In this way they can anticipate negative attacks, or they may even throw out a case because of the weakness of such arguments if the opposition should use them.

It is important to note that many good debaters double-check one another on the most important evidence. They know that debates have been lost by teams that copied quotations inaccurately. By making sure the evidence is correctly cited and recorded, they avoid the embarrassment of having a judge think they cheated.

To prepare for the negative side of the question, most teams detail probable affirmative arguments for thorough research. Because many arguments often are involved, some debate squads divide the labor among all the members.

The values of thorough research have been extolled. Now it is time to consider some tactics for doing such work. These tactics vary considerably from person to person, because most researchers develop systems that work best for them. You will have to decide which system will work best for you.

Very few debaters begin their research by reading the first book or article they encounter; such a system is simply too inefficient and you have no guarantee that the first find will be the best. In fact, if you follow this system you are likely to become tired of reading or to run out of time before finding the best data. Instead, it is better to begin by building a bibliography of the material that is available; then you can get an overview of what lies ahead.

A bibliography can be built by first making a list of words that might relate to a topic. It does not hurt to use your imagination when compiling the list. Once you have completed a list of key words, the next step is to go to the periodical indexes and the card catalog. Looking up each word will provide a tremendous supply of possible sources. Start with the source that looks best and then work down through the list. Do not hesitate to add to the list of possible sources while you read through material. Footnotes and bibliographies can prove invaluable in locating good source material.

At first you should read quickly, skimming the material and marking the parts that look good enough to commit to evidence cards. By skimming, even slow readers can at least superficially exhaust the available evidence. Then you can return to the most valuable sources and authors for in-depth reading.

The main tactic, at this point, is to *have* a tactic! So much evidence is available on most topics that debaters rarely can cover all of it. By carefully following the best plan of attack, many debaters end the season with as many as seven to ten thousand quality evidence cards. Their equally energetic, but disorganized, colleagues may end up with just a few hundred or, at best, a thousand cards. Quantity, however, should never be confused with quality in debate; it is possible—and necessary—to have both.

Developing Key Terms

Resolved: That the federal government should guarantee comprehensive national health insurance for all United States citizens.

insurance	health care
Medicare	Medicaid
preventive care	malpractice
HMO	homelessness
AIDS	immunizations
unemployment	doctor choice
nursing homes	deductibles
drugs	coverage
experimental procedures	orphan drugs
socialized medicine	fixed-income
fraud	quality of life
medical care	nursing homes

The following sections detail twelve major areas in which the best debate evidence can be found. The list includes sources of evidence that debaters have found to be profitable over the years. The areas to be covered include: (1) bibliographies, (2) indexes, (3) computer searches, (4) reference books, (5) topic-related books, (6) magazines and journals, (7) newspapers, (8) pamphlets, (9) legal periodicals, (10) government documents, (11) debate handbooks, and (12) debate institutes. By exploring a combination of these sources, you can be confident that you have done your basic research.

Bibliographies

Many debaters are surprised to discover that some reference books are entirely bibliographical. There are even bibliographies to bibliographies. Formal bibliographies are normally found in the reference section of the library. Here is a sample of available bibliographies that you may wish to consult:

Bibliographic Index. A bibliography of bibliographies.

Books in Print. An annual listing of published works by subject, author, and title.

Forthcoming Books. A bimonthly listing of all books scheduled for publication within the next five months.

Book Review Digest. An excellent place to find critical reviews of major sources.

Public Affairs Information Service (PAIS) Bulletin. Contains an assortment of books, documents, reports, and journal articles.

Specialized bibliographies can be found on any of the debate topics. These bibliographies are often annotated with brief descriptions. These descriptions allow the debater to evaluate the value of a particular source without having to actually look at it. Such annotated bibliographies can save valuable time when researching. Listed below is a sample of specialized bibliographies that were available on some of the past annual debate topics.

Space Exploration

Lawrence, Robert M. *Strategic Defense Initiative: Bibliography and Research Guide.* Boulder, CO: Westview, 1987.

Magill, Frank N., ed. *Magill's Survey of Science: Space Exploration Series,* Vols. I-IV. Englewood Cliffs, NJ: Salem, 1989.

Prison Reform

Logan, Charles H. *Privatization and Corrections: A Bibliography.*

Storr, CT: University of Connecticut Press, 1986.

Whittingham, M. D. "Crowding and Corrections A Bibliography." *Criminal Justice Abstracts 17* (September 1985): 392-404.

Indexes

Indexes are another source for exploring the availability of sources. Many indexes contain useful references to source materials. Books, periodicals, journal articles, research reports, editorials, and collections of factual materials are a sampling of the types of materials that can be found in various indexes. Listed below are some of the available indexes that you may find helpful. This list is by no means exhaustive.

Current Index to Journals in Education

Education Index

Economic Index

Catholic Periodicals Index

Book Review Index. An excellent source of references to critical reviews.

Cumulative Book Index. Good source for current books.

Biography Index

Vertical File Index

Social Sciences and Humanities Index

International Index to Periodicals. Good source for finding materials on international topics.

Readers' Guide to Periodical Literature. Probably the most widely used source among debaters (at least at the beginning levels), this is the most comprehensive guide to popular materials. For more specialized materials, consult the more specialized indexes discussed in the section on Periodicals.

New York Times Index

Official Index of the Times (London)

Index to Legal Periodicals

External Research. This State Department list is of scholarly interest.

U.S. Government Printing Office: Monthly Publications Catalog. A reference catalog all debaters should know; it lists all government publications by subject headings.

U.S. Government Printing Office: Congressional Information Service Index. Contains annotated listings of all publications from the legislative branch since 1970 (also available on computer searches).

United National Document Index. Very useful but frequently overlooked.

Congressional Record Index

The indexes listed here are but the tip of the iceberg of those available. In any given field of research, you will find an index listing the materials in the journals of that field. In some fields you may find more than one index. Many of the indexes listed here (as well as some of the more specialized ones) will be discussed in greater detail in the appropriate sections that follow.

Computer Searches

One important change in libraries across the country is the availability of technology for computerized searches. More and more libraries are installing computerized data systems as replacements for the traditional card catalogs and bound indexes. For the library users who take the time to understand them, these systems can offer tremendous advantages for research.

To be sure, some researchers still view computerized searches with some hesitation. Some critics see the advent of computerized library indexes as another annexation of everyday life by computer technology. In addition, this group might automatically assume that the opportunity to use computerized data systems for research is only available to the expert programmer. But this is not so. Most computerized systems are designed to be "user friendly." That is, they are designed so that anyone can use them. It usually takes only a few minutes to master a particular system.

Many libraries have installed computerized catalogs so that researchers can search for books by author, title, or subject. Instead of flipping through cards one by one, researchers find the sources on a computer monitor. Suppose you were looking for books on the debate topic, "*Resolved:* That the federal government should guarantee comprehensive national health insurance to all United States citizens." One of the key terms to be explored would be *health care*, and the computer menu would allow you to do a subject search on that term. While all computer systems differ, generally you would begin your search by typing the term *health care* and entering it. The computer would then indicate how many entries were found relating to health care, and you could begin to look at each entry individually.

Most computer catalogs and databases offer a variety of information about each listing. The information includes everything you are used to finding in traditional card catalogs (such as the call number, publication information, and a summary of contents), as well as much more. Computer catalogs can tell you the present status of the book—whether it has been checked out, other libraries where the book might be found, and so forth—so that you don't have to waste a trip to the shelf to discover that the book has been checked out. In addition, most computer catalogs allow you to continue to narrow your search by adding additional key words. For example, you could add the term *unemployed* to your original term *health care*. Then you could add *insurance*. Each additional term would help you focus your search. (A specific example of a search on the national health insurance topic is provided in the section on books.)

Many periodical indexes are now available on computer databases. (Check with your librarian to see which systems your library subscribes to.) These bibliographic databases will give you a bibliographic citation, or reference. The most common computerized periodical index is the *Readers' Guide Abstracts*. This system may be available on-line, which means it can be accessed via a modem from home, or the library may subscribe through CD-ROM. This system is similar to that of the computerized catalog. You begin a subject search by entering a particular key word, such as *health*. Then you can narrow the search by moving to what is called a multiple subject search and adding a second term, such as *unemployment*. The abstracts provided for each entry are very useful: you can look at them quickly to determine if the articles are likely to hold pertinent information.

The example provided here shows entry two of ten, using a multiple search with the terms *health* and *unemployment*.

Two of the more widely available research databases are the *Social Issues Research Series* (SIRS) and *Lexis-Nexis*. SIRS is becoming available in many high schools around the country and is available on CD-ROM in many public and university libraries. Because it is only available on CD, SIRS is only as current as the CD program, which is generally updated only a few times a year. SIRS carries the full

Readers' Guide Abstracts

```
2 RGA
      AUTHOR:   Perlmutter, Cathy
       TITLE:   Cushion your health in hard times
      SOURCE:   Prevention (Emmaus, Pa.) (ISSN 0032-8006) v44
                p44-50+ May '92
    CONTAINS:   illustration(s)

SUBJECTS COVERED:
Business recession/Psychological aspects
Unemployment/Psychological aspects

ABSTRACT: Financial insecurity or job loss can lead to recession
stress.  University of Michigan researchers studied unemployed
workers during the mid-1980s recession and found that the
unemployed had far more health problems than a stably employed
comparison group.  Stanislav V. Kasl, a professor of epidemiology
at the Yale School of Medicine, says that even the fear of
unemployment may cause physical and psychological harm.  Herbert
Benson, a leading stress expert and author of The Relaxation
Response, says that job panic can lead to increases in blood
pressure and can trigger headaches, disrupt heart rhythms,
exacerbate pain, and lower the body's immunity to disease.  The
article discusses ways to cope with job loss and presents
information on contacting support groups for the unemployed.
```

text of magazine and newspaper articles about current issues, and it works much the same as the *Readers' Guide Abstracts.* The primary difference between the two systems is that while the *Readers' Guide Abstracts* provides only abstracts, with SIRS you can pull up an entire document. This means you can review the document immediately, as opposed to having to go and find it in the library. You can even print out the document to take home with you. The drawback, however, is that you can only print the text of the document, not any pictures, charts, or graphs. Also, if there are any boxed articles within the pages designated in the magazine for the article (perhaps pertaining to the subject area), they will not appear on the screen or printout.

The second common system is Lexis-Nexis (services of Mead Data Central, Inc.). This system is found predominantly in university libraries and is available on-line. The advantage of Lexis-Nexis is that it is as up-to-date as any printed material in the library. To save time when researching with this system, you may want to check with the librarian about transferring the material being researched to disks and then printing it at home or back at school.

The partial example on page 66 was on a research project looking at rap music. The terms that had been entered were *rap, issue, black, image,* and *comparison.* This example is the beginning of the 193rd entry.

Computerized indexes are also available for newspapers. One index that is becoming available in many libraries is *ProQuest.* This system indexes eight newspapers

Example of Lexis-Nexis

PAGE   90

193RD ITEM of Level 1 printed in FULL format.

Copyright 1992 Southam Inc.
Calgary Herald

March 1, 1992, Sunday, FINAL EDITION

SECTION: ENTERTAINMENT; Pg. C4

LENGTH: 705 words

HEADLINE: Two views of Rap

BYLINE: GREG KOT, CHICAGO TRIBUNE

BODY:
   Rap is the most vital and volatile form of music to emerge in the last decade, and also the most misunderstood and despised.

To its detractors, it is a monolith of big beats and macho threats that are offensive and dehumanizing.

To its creators and fans, it is a rainbow of voices and rhythms, the truest and richest expression of the black cultural experience of the last decade, from the melodicism of P.M. Dawn to the aggression of Public Enemy.

The best of the message-oriented rappers - KRS-One of Boogie Down Productions, Ice- T, Ice Cube, the Jungle Brothers, Public Enemy - are hardly an aberration. Rather, they're inheritors of a heritage that dates back to the drumming and chanting of African tribes and on through gospel, blues, jazz, soul and funk.

---

with abstracts, including the *New York Times, Wall Street Journal, Washington Post, Christian Science Monitor, Los Angeles Times, Chicago Tribune, Boston Globe,* and the *Atlanta Constitution.* Unless your library has ProQuest on-line, this index is only as current as the CD program. You can search ProQuest by subject, and the index provides citations and abstracts.

In addition to computerized newspaper indexes, the *Chicago Tribune* also offers a computerized newspaper service called *NewsBank.* This service provides full text for articles in the *Chicago Tribune,* and it is an efficient way to move through a large amount of data. For example, using the national health insurance debate topic, a search of *health care* yielded 1,920 entries for 1992 and 1993. To narrow the search, the terms *insurance* and *unemployment* were added; with the addition of the third term the number of entries was narrowed to eight.

The example below shows the listing of the eight articles located by using the terms *health care, insurance,* and *unemployment* as it would appear on the computer screen. Next is a sample listing of the first article on the list. The last step would have been to print out the actual text of the article.

Research in government documents also has moved into the computer age. Using a program called *GPO on Silver Platter,* you can research the majority of government

Example of NewsBank Article Directory and Sample

```
ZDDDDDDD NewsBank CD News Newspapers on CDROM - Chicago Tribune 1993 DDDDDDD?
3                                                                       311
3 Below is a list of articles you have found. Use the Up and Down arrows   311
3 and Page Up and Page Down to move through the list.                    311
3 *To display the full article, highlight the article to view.           311
3 Press ENTER.                                                            311
3 *To print, see instructions at the bottom of the screen.               311
3                                                                        311
3                                                                        311
3IMMMMMMMMMMMMMMMMMMMMMMMMMMMMMMMMMMMMMMMMMMMMMMMMMMMMMMMMMM5LIST SCREEN: 1 of 18FM;311
3:Date            Page    Headline                                         :311
3:DDDDDDDDDDDDDDDDDDDDDDDDDDDDDDDDDDDDDDDDDDDDDDDDDDDDDDDDDDDDDDDDDDDDDDDDDDD:311
3:July 14, 1993     1       Rural health care at crossroads               :311
3:July 2, 1993      1       Missouri acts to broaden health care          :311
3:July 1, 1993      1       Six months into the year, this bull market's :311
3:June 17, 1993    23       Make plans public, but keep health care in pr:311
3:June 15, 1993     1       The nurse will see you now                    :311
3:June 5, 1993      1       In N.J. town, outlook is a bit sunnier  MAP: :311
3:May 9, 1993       7       A wolf in Social Security clothing? Commentar:311
3:May 5, 1993       5       Dow can't keep the pace                        311
3HMMMMMMMMMMMMMMMMMMMMMMMMMMMMMMMMMMMMMMMMMMMMMMMMMMMMMMMMMMMMMMMMMMMMMMMMMMM(311
3 F1-New Search   F2-Help            F3-Print Article     F4- Printing... 311
-Scroll         311
@DDDDDDDDDDDDDDDDDDDDDDDDDDDDDDDDDDDDDDDDDDDDDDDDDDDDDDDDDDDDDDDDDDDDDDDDDDDY11
   11111111111111111111111111111111111111111111111111111111111111111111111
```

```
                                                              Page: 1

NewsBank CD News Newspapers on CDROM - Chicago Tribune 1993  -- List of
Headlines

---------------------------------------------------------------------------

COPYRIGHT 1993, CHICAGO TRIBUNE

Headline:  Rural health care at crossroads
           Clinton reforms may pit clinics against single doctors

Date:      July 14, 1993          Section:     NEWS
Page:      1                      Edition:     NORTH SPORTS FINAL
                                  Word Count:  1275

Author:
William Neikirk, Tribune Staff Writer.

---------------------------------------------------------------------------
```

documents (with the exception of the *Congressional Record*). *GPO on Silver Platter* contains more than 250,000 citations to government documents listed in the *Monthly Catalog* and covers government documents from July 1976 to the present date. Included are periodicals, books, pamphlets, reports, hearings, maps, and other serials.

As with the other computerized searches, you use subject areas for *GPO on Silver Platter*. Beginning with a single term such as *health* would yield 23,441 entries—far too many to deal with! However, by combining two terms, such as *health* and *insurance*, your search would yield a smaller number; the search would be looking for documents having both terms in the same document. To narrow still further, you could add a third term, *administration*. The three terms together would narrow the field to 892 entries.

The two examples on page 68 could have been narrowed even further with

Example of *GPO on Silver Platter*

```
                                                          3 of 892
AN: 93083447
SU: HE 22.2:IN 3/2/992
SU: HE222IN32992
CA: United States. Health Care Financing Administration.
TI: Financing health care for persons with AIDS and HIV infection : the role of
the Health Care Financing Administration.
SO: [Washington, D.C.?] : U.S. Dept. of Health and Human Services, Health Care
Financing Administration, 1992.
SE: HCFA pub. ; no. 02194.
IT: 0512-A-01


 — — — — — — — — — — — — — — — — — — — — — — — — — — — —
                                                         22 of 892
AN: 93077686
SU: HE 22.2:M 46/34
SU: HE222M4634
CA: United States. Medicaid Bureau.
TI: National summary of state Medicaid coordinated care programs.
SO: [Washington, D.C.?] : Medicaid Bureau, Health Care Financing
Administration, U.S. Dept. of Health and Human Services, 1992 [i.e. 1993].
SilverPlatter 3.11     GPO on SilverPlatter (1976 - 8/93)
```

additional terms. In the first sample, the term *AIDS* could have been added; in the second, the search could have been narrowed again with the term *Medicaid*.

Additional Resources

Reference Books

Reference books are very useful for gathering background material and gaining a general understanding of the debate topic. Sometimes a reference book can be an excellent place to find specific pieces of information. Which reference books you consult will be determined by the specific topic being debated.

The following are reference books you may want to consider using. Some of them are fairly heavy reading, but they can help you become familiar with general terms and topics. This list is not intended to be all-inclusive—rather it is intended to be a starting point.

Statistical Abstracts of the United States. An exhaustive summary of current statistics.

Economics by Paul Samuelson. An excellent and very readable text in beginning economics.

The United States in World Affairs. Published by the Council on Foreign Relations, it provides a good history and analysis of world affairs for each year.

Editorial Research Reports. An outstanding reference series. Available only to newspapers and libraries, it presents in-depth analyses of currently important topics.

Political Handbook of the World. A good reference for specific information about foreign countries.

New York Times Economic Review and Forecast. A very good review of economic development in different areas of the world.

Relations of Nations by Frederick H. Hartmann. A good examination of foreign policy and foreign relations.

Treaties in Force. The State Department's annual list of all the treaties to which the United States is bound.

Legislation on Foreign Relations. Published by the Committee on Foreign Relations, U.S. Senate.

Annual Report of the Council of Economic Advisors. An outstanding source for an analysis of the economic problems facing the United States.

Black's Law Dictionary. The unquestioned standard work for legal terms and court precedents for concepts of law.

Who's Who in America. A standard source for obtaining the qualification of authors. In addition, there are several specialized Who's Who-type journals.

Brookings Institution Publications. A series of in-depth analyses of important issues.

Documents of American History

Constitutional Criminal Procedure. American Casebook Series.

American Constitution. Published by Lockhart, Kamisar, and Choper.

Constitutional Law. Gilbert Law Summaries.

Encyclopaedia Britannica. A thorough discussion of various topics at an adult level; thought by many to be the best encyclopedia.

Book of the States

Topic-Related Books

For any topic, you will be concerned with more than just reference books and textbooks. The starting point for finding topic-related books is the card catalog. The card catalog lists all the books in the library by author, title, and subject. Depending on the technology available in your library, the card catalog will be available in one of two forms.

The first form is the card catalog files. These files contain cards that list books by author, title, and subject. The subject cards can be very helpful. For example, if you were researching the 1993–94 debate topic, "*Resolved:* That the federal government should guarantee comprehensive national health insurance to all United States citizens," one of the subject areas you might look up would be *health care.* Under this heading you might find the following cards:

Health care

Bricker, P.W., L.K. Scharar, B. Conanan, A. Elvy, and M. Savarese, eds.

Health Care of Homeless People.

New York: Spring, 1985.

Health care

Institute of Medicine.

Homelessness, Health, and Human Needs.

Washington, D.C.: National Academy Press, 1988.

Health care

Wright, J.D., and E. Weber.

Homelessness and Health.

Washington, D.C.: McGraw Hill's Health Care Information
   Center, 1987.

The second type of card catalog is the computerized system. Many high-school libraries have begun to acquire computerized catalogs. Although the actual systems may vary from school to school, the basic concepts of how to use them are the same. Most of these systems are indexed by author, title, and subject (just like the cards found in the files). All you need to do to find a listing under a particular heading is to enter the heading into the system. The catalog would give you a list of entries in the catalog pertaining to the subject area. You could quickly browse through the entries or narrow your search. Then you could print out a list that would provide the subject searched, number of entries found, specific number of the entry being printed, title, author, publisher, description, location in the library, and call number.

The following examples show two entries that resulted from a search of the subject area *public health administration.*

```
Search request: S=PUBLIC HEALTH ADMINISTRATION                    NUcat
Book - Record 7 of 157 entries found                          Brief view
--------------------------- Screen 1 of 1  ----------------------------L604
        Title:  Administering health systems; issues and perspectives. Mary F.
                Arnold, L. Vaughn Blankenship <and> John M. Hess, editors.
    Published:  Chicago, Aldine-Atherton <1971>
  Description:  xvii, 444 p. 25 cm.
------------------------------------------------------------------------
    LOCATION:              CALL NUMBER                 STATUS:
1. MAIN                    350.841 A238
2. SCHAFFNER               350.841 A238



------------------------------------------------------------------------
COMMANDS:          LO  Long view        I   Index
                   N   Next record      G   Guide
O Other options    P   Previous record  H   Help

NEXT COMMAND:
```

```
Search request: S=PUBLIC HEALTH ADMINISTRATION                      NUcat
Book - Record 9 of 157 entries found                             Brief view
-------------------------------  Screen 1 of 1  ------------------------L604
         Title:  Administration for the effective control of heart disease: two
                 complementary studies.
      Published:  <Iowa City, University of Iowa, Graduate Program in Hospital
                 and Health Administration, 1973>
    Description:  xiii, 151 p. illus. 23 cm.
--------------------------------------------------------------------------
      LOCATION:            CALL NUMBER               STATUS:
   1. MAIN                 362.1961 A238




--------------------------------------------------------------------------
   COMMANDS:       LO  Long view        I   Index
                   N   Next record      G   Guide
   O Other options P   Previous record  H   Help

   NEXT COMMAND:
```

After you have located books through the catalog, you should pay special attention to footnotes, bibliographies, and indexes. These specific sections of a book will often direct you to other sources worth researching. In addition, they may save you time in finding subjects that may prove to be of special interest. In most cases, a quick look at the title page, table of contents, author's qualifications, and the date of publication will produce a reliable indicator of a book's merits.

However, you need to be able to distinguish between different types of books. For example, if you locate a survey of a subject intended for the general audience and an intensive, scholarly study of a subject, the latter is more likely to contain useful evidence. When reading anthologies of individual articles, you should keep in mind that the credibility of the evidence will depend on the qualifications of the authors and the dates of publication of the individual articles, not the dates of the edited collection.

To keep abreast of newly published books, you should consult *Books in Print*, which is an annual listing of published books by subject, author, and title. It is supplemented by *Forthcoming Books*, a bimonthly listing of all books scheduled for publication within the next five months.

Magazines and Journals

Periodicals are a good source of recent evidence. The best way to find relevant articles is to use an index. Every library will have at least one index to periodicals. The size of the library will determine the number of indexes carried as well as the number of periodicals. For example, every high school will have the *Readers' Guide to Periodical Literature*, but many (if not most) will not have the *Index to Legal Periodicals*.

The most comprehensive index to periodicals is *Ulrich's International Periodicals Directory*. This directory contains the name of almost every periodical published in the world, as well as what index it is listed in. Two other useful periodicals indexes are the *Chicorel Index to Abstracting and Indexing Services* and *Magazines for Libraries*. The *Chicorel Index* alphabetizes approximately 50,000 popular and scholarly magazines. It also indicates in what index they are listed. *Magazines for Libraries* describes approximately 6,500 magazines recommended for small to medium-sized libraries.

You will need to keep in mind that libraries do not subscribe to all the periodicals listed in a particular index. However, in most cases you can track down a copy of a periodical that your library doesn't carry through interlibrary loan.

The *Readers' Guide to Periodical Literature* lists titles of articles in such general-circulation periodicals as *U.S. News and World Report, Business Week, Time,* and *Fortune.* This is the index used most often by high-school students. The sources found in this index will usually contain evidence that is more general in nature. Of the more than 3,000 periodicals published each year, the *Readers' Guide* indexes only 200.

For many debate topics, your most productive reading will come from more limited-circulation periodicals, which are intended for a more specialized reading audience. Titles of articles in these kinds of periodicals can be found in special indexes such as the following:

Air University Library Index to Military Periodicals. Covers military training, air accidents, foreign air forces, unconventional warfare, national security, etc., in approximately 75 international periodicals.

Applied Science and Technology Index. Covers space science, computers, energy, fire technology, food industry, geology, transportation, etc., in approximately 180 periodicals.

Biological and Agricultural Index. Covers animal husbandry, botany, conservation, food science, pesticides, etc., in approximately 200 periodicals.

Business Periodicals Index. Covers accounting, advertising, banking, communications, international business, occupational health and safety, etc., in approximately 280 periodicals.

Criminal Justice Abstracts. Covers crime prevention, juvenile offenders, attitudes on firearms, etc., in approximately 160 international periodicals.

Current Law Index. A comprehensive index to over 700 law journals from the United States, Canada, the United Kingdom, Ireland, Australia, and New Zealand. This index does not overlap with the *Index to Legal Periodicals.*

Education Index. Covers preschool to adult education, school administration, audiovisuals, teacher education, etc., in approximately 200 periodicals.

Engineering Index. Covers structural, mechanical, industrial, chemical, and other kinds of engineering in technical reports, conference proceedings, books, etc., in approximately 1,400 journals.

General Science Index. Indexes approximately 90 periodicals representing all the sciences.

Humanities Index. Indexes journals and periodicals in fields such as history, philosophy, and literature.

Index to Legal Periodicals. Covers U.S. and international law in approximately 350 legal journals.

Index Medicus. Oriented toward specialized medical journals.

International Political Science Abstracts. Covers public opinion, foreign policy, military institutions, etc., in approximately 700 international periodicals.

Magazine Index. Microform index of over 350 magazines beginning with 1978.

Sage Family Studies Abstracts. Covers family life, child abuse, foster care, child development, etc., in approximately 260 periodicals.

Social Sciences Citation Index. Most comprehensive but also the most difficult of indexes to use. This bibliography subsumes all of the literature from the social, behavioral, and related sciences.

Social Science Index. Covers economics, law, criminology, political science, sociology, etc., in approximately 260 periodicals.

The following are a few examples of periodicals in a specialized index.

National Health Insurance

Medical World News
American Family Physician
Drug Topics
New England Journal of Medicine
Nursing Homes

When beginning your research, you should keep in mind that each index will include many broad subject headings. Use your imagination to develop a comprehensive list of key words to be used for research. Remember it is the key words list that will open the door to more articles and books.

For example, consider two debate resolutions from recent years. The first, "*Resolved:* That the federal government should guarantee comprehensive national health insurance for all United States citizens," suggests some obvious key terms:

insurance   preventive care

health care   catastrophic illness

Medicare	HMO
Medicaid	malpractice

However, if you look at the topic again, you may think of other areas or ideas that might be helpful for research, such as:

diseases	orphan drugs
AIDS	coverage
homeless	medical care
nursing homes	nurse practitioner
mental illness	experimental procedures
deductibles	retirement
fraud	unemployment
immunizations	nutrition
infant mortality	fixed-income
pharmaceutical	pensions
doctor choice	quality of life

Each of these terms relates to the subject of health care or health insurance. It may involve whether someone is currently covered, what sorts of items are covered by insurance, what services might be affected by national health insurance, and so forth. The key is to use your imagination to expand your options.

Now consider the second debate topic: "*Resolved:* That the United States government should reduce worldwide pollution through its trade and/or aid policies." At first glance, what are the obvious terms?

import	environment
export	clean air
pollution	acid rain

These are just the really obvious terms. If you think hard about pollution and the world economy, you may come up with other subject areas, such as:

energy	global warming
oil	disaster relief
nuclear power	children
greenhouse effect	housing
municipal waste	poverty

toxic waste	drugs
ozone depletion	weapons
rain forests	water
trade agreements	food chain
hunger	various countries
technology	

Each of these terms can be connected to pollution and trade. On an international topic, the list would also extend to any of the individual countries you could think of. The key is to keep thinking and to keep adding words to your list.

Periodicals are a good source of recent evidence. However, evidence from periodical literature should be carefully judged against the criteria of evidence. Some periodicals may represent one political bias or another. The best periodicals clearly separate editorial comment from reporting.

Newspapers

It is wise to stay abreast of current developments by reading a daily newspaper regularly. One of the best U.S. papers for debaters is the *New York Times*. The *Times* contains reports of congressional committee hearings as well as reprints of important testimony. Finally, the Sunday edition of the *Times* includes a special section, "The Week in Review," which summarizes and analyzes developments of the past week.

Carried by most major libraries, the *New York Times* publishes its own semimonthly index, which is cumulated annually. Each entry in the index includes a reference to the date, page, and column of an article (Nov. 8, 16:6). For Sunday editions, section numbers are also included (Dec 16, IV, 9:1). The index is valuable not only for finding articles in the *Times*, but also for locating accounts of similar events contained in other newspapers of the same day.

Other newspapers debaters tend to rely on are the *Christian Science Monitor*, the *Wall Street Journal*, the *Washington Post*, the *National Observer*, and the *Los Angeles Times*, just to mention a few. Indexes for individual newspapers include:

Christian Science Monitor Index

Los Angeles Times Index

Wall Street Journal Index

Washington Index

Pamphlets

Another, although less recognized, source of evidence is the large number of pamphlets published each year. Pressure groups, foundations, and academic departments are among the many issuers of pamphlets. A sampling of pamphlets from all issuers is listed in the *Vertical File Index*, established by most libraries. Most libraries maintain a vertical file of pamphlets and will order materials upon request.

The *Vertical File Index* also lists organizations from which you or your team might want to order pamphlets directly (many of these are at no charge). The best way to discover the identity of such organizations is to ask three questions:

1. Who might be interested in this problem area?
2. Who stands to gain from the adoption of the resolution?
3. Who would lose from the adoption of the resolution?

By answering these questions you will be able to identify a number of special interest groups, most of which will be more than happy to supply materials. A word of caution, however: you must remember that information received from such organizations must be analyzed very carefully. Many of these groups are not objective. The problem is not that their facts and statistics are necessarily false, it's that their interpretations of facts might be biased.

A small sampling of organizations that have crossed many of the debate topics include:

Institute of Research on Poverty

Bureau of Social Science Research

Center for Coastal and Environmental Studies

Council on Environmental Quality

American Association for the Advancement of Science

Department of Commerce

The Rand Corporation

Institute for Policy Studies

International Monetary Fund

Brookings Institution

Names of organizations can also be found in bibliographies and footnotes. Another source for finding relevant groups would be the *World Almanac*. The *World Almanac* lists more than 25,000 organizations. If read with caution, some of the materials from these organizations can be very good sources of evidence.

Legal Publications

With a few exceptions legal periodicals are not available in general libraries, but only in law and bar association libraries. Within a law library, you will find three especially valuable types of publications.

First, law libraries usually keep a large collection of books and pamphlets that are referred to as *treatises*. These are indexed in a card catalog similar to the catalog in a general library. Second, texts of court decisions in cases you may wish to investigate are also found in law libraries. You may not have a great need to investigate these materials if the debate topic involves international law, but they may be quite important in the case of domestic issues.

The decisions of our federal and state courts are printed in volumes referred to as *court reports*. Some of these reports, especially those of the Supreme Court, also may be available in general libraries that are classified as government depositories. If you are familiar with the system of citation employed in these reports, you will be able to find the cases you want without difficulty. A Supreme Court decision will be cited as 391 U.S. 1015 (1968). Translated, this citation means that the case in question was printed in Volume 391 of *United States Reports*, at page 1015, and that the case was decided in 1968. Similarly, a state citation such as 5 Cal. 3d 584 (1971) would mean that the case may be found in Volume 5 of the third *Series of California Reports*, at page 584, and that the case was decided in 1971. Citations for cases tried in courts of other nations or tried before international tribunals will be difficult to trace in American libraries, although the process would be roughly analogous to this procedure.

Even after reading the actual decision, however, you may be uncertain about the implications of the ruling or about the current state of the law. Clarification of these matters for American law would require consulting *Corpus Juris Secundum*, a reference work that is available not only at law libraries but also at major courthouses and in many general libraries. The Lawyer's Annotated Edition of *United States Reports* also includes annotations and commentary that may be helpful.

The third type of legal publication is the legal periodical. There are two principal kinds of legal journals. First, professional societies or groups publish journals containing material pertinent to their special interests. Examples of such journals are the *Journal of World Trade Law* and the *Journal of International Law and Economics*. Second, most of the nation's law schools publish law reviews. Law reviews usually are divided into two parts. The front section contains articles by judges, law professors, and practicing attorneys. These articles provide broad treatment of legal problems and should be read with great care. The back section, often titled "Notes" or "Comments," should be approached with some caution. These sections are written by student editors of the journal. They focus on new court rulings and discuss current problems in the law. Frequently, several law reviews will include comments pertinent to the case. These reviews may be sufficiently repetitive that it is unnecessary to read them all. Finally, you should recognize that unsigned citations to law reviews usually refer to the student-written "Notes" section.

Government Documents

You will probably find that government documents can provide valuable information. On most topics they can be a direct source of information as well as a major summary source for materials that are difficult to obtain directly. Special reports, for example, typically contain the results of commissioned studies, which may not be available elsewhere.

Another type of government document is the annual report of many of the executive agencies of the federal government. For previous high-school debate topics, such sources as the *Economic Report of the President, Federal Bureau of Investigation Uniform Crime Reports,* and the *Task Force on Medicaid and Related Programs* were found to be particularly useful.

In addition, congressional hearings and reports are especially good sources of evidence. Listed below are committees whose reports you might want to examine:

Poverty
Senate Committee on Government Operations
Senate Committee on Finance
Joint Economic Committee
Joint Committee on Education and Labor

Pollution
House and Senate Committees on Environment and Public Works
Committee on Science and Technology
House Committee on Agriculture
Senate Subcommittee on Toxic Substances and Environmental Oversight
House Subcommittee on Water Resources

Health Care
House Appropriations Committee
House Interstate and Foreign Commerce Committee
House Ways and Means Committee
Senate Labor and Public Welfare Committee
House Committee on Government Operations

To remain knowledgeable about current developments in congressional committees, you should frequently consult the *Congressional Quarterly*—a weekly résumé of activities in Congress. The calendars of these committees, which list the most recent committee publications and scheduled hearings, may be obtained free of charge, along with single copies of the transcripts of hearings. Write to either the chairperson of the committee or to your senator or representative.

A few hints may be helpful in reading the transcripts of congressional hearings. You will quickly discover that the transcripts of hearings are especially worthy of attention. Concentrate primarily on the statements of professors and professionals from such fields as sociology, pathology, toxicology, medicine, political science, economics, chemistry, and the law; representatives of academic research bureaus or technical organizations and pertinent government agencies; and directors of reputable foundations or groups.

You can also save a tremendous amount of time if you realize that hearings contain repetition. The same witnesses may give almost identical statements at different hearings concerning the same problem. There may even be repetition within the same hearing. Frequently, a witness will read a prepared statement orally and then will have the written version of the same statement also included in the record.

The dialogue between witnesses and committee members following the witnesses' formal statements should not be overlooked. This interchange often is a source of excellent information, particularly of qualifications or limitations that witnesses may have forgotten to place on their overly generalized preliminary remarks.

Finally, the reports of the committees, printed after the conclusion of the hearings, are also worthy of attention. Although frequently there is duplication between the hearings and the report, it also is true that the reports contain many ideas and opinions not presented in the original hearings.

Individual publications of executive agencies represent still another type of government document. While some agencies, such as the Department of Agriculture, publish valuable pamphlets and reports, you should be wary of propagandistic publicity pieces that are used by some agencies primarily as promotional items— leaflets, brochures, or handouts. Single copies of specific government agency publications generally can be obtained by writing directly to the issuing agency. It is a good idea to request, at the same time, a bibliography of related materials published by the same agency. The bibliography may contain publications not listed elsewhere.

The *American Statistics Index* is a monthly abstract and index publication with annual cumulations. It covers all statistical publications of the U.S. government, including congressional publications with substantial statistical data. Detailed information on how to use the index is included at the beginning of each publication.

It is always possible that unexpected evidence may turn up in the *Congressional Record*, the final type of government document. Unless you have virtually unlimited research time, however, reading the *Record* should be given a low priority. Many of the reprints in the *Record* are letters or editorials from obscure local newspapers. Should someone cite evidence from such a newspaper or periodical, however, your best chance of locating it is to peruse the *Record* for ten or fifteen days following the date cited. It usually can be found.

Federal government publications, of all the types that have been discussed, are indexed in the *Monthly Catalog of United States Government Publications*. Numbers in the subject index in the back of the volume refer to listings in the front section. These listings contain the complete citations to the pertinent publications. The February issue of each year consists of references to periodicals issued by government agencies. The *Monthly Catalog* is cumulated each year. Normally, however, its listings run about three months behind actual publication dates. Therefore, the *Congressional Quarterly of the Bulletin of the Public Affairs Information Service* should be consulted for notices of very recent releases. The *Monthly Catalog*, by the way, is not complete in its listings—some publications are not listed there.

In addition to the *Monthly Catalog*, the *Congressional Information Service Index* contains annotated listings of all publications from the legislative branch since 1970.

Your best bet for locating government publications, however, is to consult directly with the government documents supervisor or librarian at the nearest depository library. Government depository libraries regularly receive copies of most government publications. If you don't have a depository library nearby, most federal publications may be ordered at minimal cost from the Superintendent of Documents, U.S. Government Printing Office, Washington, DC 20402.

Debate Handbooks

Despite the protests of some debate coaches, nearly all debaters make some use of debate handbooks during the early stages of their research. These special references are compiled to aid debaters in identifying the major issues, basic evidence, and important authorities pertaining to the year's topic. Many debaters find such help very useful at the beginning of the debating season. Even those who debate at the championship level will admit to ordering handbooks, if only to see what they can expect from their weaker opponents.

Because handbooks are limited to a certain number of pages, there will always be evidence that was not included in the handbook. This usually does not mean the evidence was of no value. It often means that there was simply not enough room for the researchers to provide the information from as many sources as possible in the limited space available. The sources cited in the handbooks may produce valuable leads to additional primary sources.

Handbooks are designed merely to introduce students to a topic. They are not to be considered definitive sources. Because they must be prepared quickly and then condensed into a few hundred pages, it should be obvious that even the best handbook is likely to have its shortcomings. As long as you know that such shortcomings exist, there is no reason why you should not use a handbook as a beginning source. However, it is not appropriate to quote directly from a handbook during a debate round. Evidence should be quoted from the original source—and then only after it has been checked for accuracy and context. Checking handbook evidence is important; an error might have been made in the production of the handbook. This simple precaution of double-checking sources will insure that the evidence is accurate.

Many coaches protest the use of handbooks because some lazy debaters feel that they need go no further in their research for evidence. (Such students would be more properly called "oral interpreters.") One of the principal values and strategies of debate is learning the technique of independent research. Debaters who begin the season by buying as many debate handbooks as possible and spend the season cutting and pasting will find little long-term success in competition. As new ideas are developed by opponents, handbook researchers will find themselves lacking evidence unless they take the initiative to begin some original research.

If you do decide to buy a handbook, take care when deciding which one(s) to buy. Each year new handbooks enter the market, while others drop out. Choose only those with complete citations and a reputation for being thorough and accurate. Many handbooks advertise in the *Rostrum* (published by the National Forensic League) and other debate journals. Remember that an advertisement for a handbook in a debate publication does not automatically mean a debate organization has evaluated the product.

Each year the National Federation of State High School Associations publishes a journal covering the current high school debate topic. This publication, *The Forensic Quarterly*, is not a handbook of evidence cards, but rather four issues analyzing the debate topic for the upcoming year. These issues can provide an excellent starting point for background information as well as an extensive bibliography for beginning a library. *The Forensic Quarterly* can be ordered from the National Federation of State High School Associations, 11724 Plaza Circle, P.O. Box 20626, Kansas City, MO 64195.

Debate Institutes

Each summer dozens of universities and independent groups around the country offer institutes for high-school debaters. The structure varies from one institute to another, but to some degree each offers instruction in debate theory, topic lecturers, access to a university library, practice rounds on the new topic, and an opportunity to work with debaters from other high schools. Institutes vary in length, as well, with the shortest being two weeks and the longest five weeks. Costs vary as greatly as content, but many institutes offer scholarships.

An institute is like a handbook; it can be very beneficial when chosen with care, but it is not a guarantee of a successful season. Work cannot stop with the institute; it must continue throughout the entire season. When choosing an institute, compare and shop around. Look at staff, university facilities, reputation, and program offerings.

Each year the National Federation of State High School Associations publishes a *Directory of Summer Workshops*. You can request a copy by writing the National Federation of State High School Associations, 11724 Plaza Circle, P.O. Box 20626, Kansas City, MO 64195. Many summer institutes also advertise in the *Rostrum*, published by the National Forensic League. The National Federation and the NFL make no attempt to evaluate the institutes advertised.

Summary

This chapter has outlined some of the major strategies and tactics of debate research. Because argument in debate depends so much on evidence, debaters often are only as good as the evidence they present. Research should be approached with a planned strategy. The strategy has to be to collect better evidence than any of your opponents will have. Your research tactics should involve carefully gathering background material and specific evidence.

The thinking approach to debate applies as much to this area as to any other.

Debaters who research in a particular way because "that's the way everybody else does it," or who merely collect cards instead of convincing evidence, will join the many victims of nonthinking debating. These students won't learn much from the debate experience and won't win many debates.

Questions

1. What source of research is likely to produce the most recent piece of evidence?

2. Why is the copyright date on a book important?

3. Evidence can be divided into two categories: empirical evidence and opinion evidence. Explain the difference between the two.

4. If you are researching the newspapers for recent material, which indexes should you consult? Be sure to include computerized as well as print indexes.

5. In what catalog would you find a list of all government publications by subject headings?

6. Under what conditions should you spend your time going through the *Congressional Record*?

Discussion Opportunities

1. If you were asked to support the debate resolution, "*Resolved*: That alcohol commercials should be banned from television," would you look for empirical or opinion evidence to support your claims? What type of information would you be looking for in your evidence? Provide reasons for the type of evidence you would use.

2. How might you apply your knowledge of research techniques in other classes on other subjects?

3. Why is it important for evidence used in a debate to be of the highest quality? What are the consequences of using evidence that does not meet the test of highest quality?

4. Debaters will often use empirical data to prove a point. Why is it important for the debater to know the methodology (how the researcher arrived at the conclusions) of the study? If you research conclusions only, without understanding the limitations of the study, what can be the possible consequences?

5. Some debaters can't wait to get to the library and start gathering evidence on the debate topic. These debaters choose an affirmative case area and hit the library. What have these debaters sacrificed by not taking at least a little time to do some background reading?

6. Using the current debate topic or one provided by your coach or teacher, which reference books do you think will be of value? Why? Would these sources be used for background research or to find evidence?

7. What are the advantages and/or disadvantages of information found in pamphlets or received by sending inquiries through the mail?

Writing Opportunities

1. Using the current debate resolution or one provided by your coach or teacher, outline a strategy for research. Indicate the boundaries of your search and the sources you plan to explore. Choose one of the sources listed and put your strategy for research into action. The result could be the beginnings of a topic bibliography.

2. Compile a list of organizations that might have useful information on the current debate resolution (or one provided by your coach or teacher). Compose and mail letters to these organizations, requesting information concerning this resolution. When the information arrives, be prepared to explain why it is or is not useful for your research.

3. Using the current debate resolution or one provided by your coach or teacher, make a list of congressional committees that might have information about the topic. Write to each of these committees for information. Be sure to ask for any bibliographical information.

Critical Thinking Opportunities

1. What are the differences between research based on the nonthinking approach and research based on the thinking approach to debate?

2. Choose an issue of importance and follow it in the weekly newspaper and on the nightly TV news for one week. Evaluate the evidence being used to support various claims. Provide an example of evidence that meets the criteria for high-quality evidence. Also provide an example(s) of evidence that fall short of the criteria.

3. Using the current debate resolution or one provided by your coach or teacher, make a list of key terms that could be used for beginning your research. Follow up by exchanging lists with a teammate or classmate and looking for additional key terms to be added.

4. To test internal evidence, look for examples of individuals (public figures or experts) who appear to have argued on both sides of an issue. (Hint: This may be a politician who has seen the light or perhaps a researcher whose findings are proving different than once believed.)

5. What computer searches are available in your high-school library? In your

public library? Which of these would be of use for researching the current debate topic or one provided by your teacher? Outline briefly how you would use each of the computer resources (or pick up printed instructions from the librarian).

6. Why is it important for debaters to look at specialized indexes when researching the debate topic? On the topic "*Resolved*: That the federal government should guarantee comprehensive health insurance for all United States citizens," what is the difference in the type of evidence found in *Time, Fortune, Forbes, Newsweek,* the *New York Times,* or the *Washington Post,* and evidence found in *Medical World News, New England Journal of Medicine, Nursing Homes, Public Health Reports,* or *Health Affairs?*

Evidence, Briefs, and Flowing

Objectives

After studying Chapter 4, you should be able
1. To process a primary source and properly record it.
2. To develop and maintain a filing system.
3. To formulate an affirmative or negative brief.
4. To develop a system of abbreviations for flowing a debate.
5. To flow a debate.

Key Terms

In order to fulfill the objectives in this chapter, you will need to understand the following terms:

affirmative brief
negative brief
flowing
evidence card
simple alphabetical filing
    system
elaborate alphabetical
    filing system
notebook index filing
    system

The topic for the season has been announced. You have put your research strategy into action and pulled materials for view. You have identified which issues and arguments need supporting documentation. Now the reading begins: you must decide what portion of an article or book should be used to support a given argument.

When reading for supporting evidence, debaters generally mark the materials liberally. Most debaters find it is better to mark more evidence than might be needed, rather than narrow too much too soon. At the beginning of the season, especially, it is a good idea to mark a lot of potential evidence. At this point you are still learning about the topic. What may seem unnecessary early in the season could become important later on, because as the season progresses, the issues will evolve and change. It is always easier to weed out evidence later should it prove to be useless than to have to backtrack to find evidence that has become crucial.

As debaters learn to cut evidence, write debate briefs, and flow a debate, they develop three important skills: listening, thinking, and writing. It is through listening, thinking, and writing that debaters learn to identify and structure arguments, develop responses to arguments, and determine what kinds of support documentation to look for.

One of the key steps in preparing arguments for debate is marking (or cutting) evidence. Evidence should always be marked on copies of the materials and never on the originals. (The only exception to this rule would be if you own the materials being marked.) To begin, first determine which argument you want to research. Make a list from your bibliography of sources that appear to have evidence on the argument to be researched. Then pull those sources and start reading with an open mind. Copy out useful information, or photocopy relevant pages or complete articles. (Many debaters prefer to make photocopies. There are advantages to this approach that will be discussed in the next section on recording evidence.) Remember that the information in an article or book may take you in a different direction than originally planned. Also keep your eyes open for any evidence that may prove relevant to arguments other than the one you are concentrating on. These pieces of evidence can be cut and used later.

Recording Evidence

After you have read a number of articles or books on the topic, marking relevant supporting quotations, your task next becomes one of transferring the material into a form that is usable in a debate round. To do this requires recording the quotations onto an easily portable and accessible form and recording enough information to enable you to answer questions about the quotes' accuracy. The form used by most is called an **evidence card.**

The first step in developing an evidence card is taking the marked information and placing it on a file card in such a way that it will be easy for you to use in the debate round. Most debaters who use card file systems prefer to use three-by-five index cards. While these cards are small, they are preferred because when accumulated in large quantities (often as many as 10,000), they weigh significantly less than larger cards. Remember that whatever you research you will need to transport to each debate round!

A few debaters still record evidence on cards in longhand. This is usually done when recording evidence directly from the primary source while researching in the library. Others type the evidence on to the card. Typing evidence makes it easier for both colleagues to read the evidence in a debate round.

However, many debaters now write or type only the source citation on the top of the card and then cut and paste the actual quotation from a photocopy of the original. There are two advantages to this way of cutting evidence. First, it's faster to cut and paste the evidence than to write it out in longhand or to type it. Second, the evidence will be more accurate. When cutting the quotation from a copy of the original, you can be sure of the quote's accuracy. There is less likelihood that a word will have been inadvertently left out or numbers transposed.

When recording evidence you must be sure to record all relevant information on the card. This includes a full bibliographical citation at the top of each card. The citation should include: the author's name; qualifications; title of the article; title of the periodical, newspaper, book, or government document; date; and page number.

Citation Information

1. Topic heading for filing
2. Subtopic heading for filing where warranted
3. Author's name
4. Author's qualifications
5. Article title
6. Periodical, newspaper, book or government document title
7. Date
8. Page number

The author's qualifications are important in case the credibility of the source is challenged in a debate. A great piece of evidence can lose much of its impact if you have no idea of who the person being quoted is.

Nukes—Good

Harold B. Finger (Pres., U.S. Council for Energy Awareness), "Nuclear Energy is in Our National Interest." _The Environmental Forum_, May/June 1991, p. 38.

"Nuclear power plants are among our cleanest sources of energy. They emit no sulfur oxides, no nitrogen oxides, and no carbon dioxide."

Rationing: Oregon Bad

Joseph A. Califano (Former Sec., HEW), "Rationing Health Care: The Unnecessary Solution." U. OF PENNSYLVANIA LAW REVIEW, May 1992, p. 1528.

"The cost to doctors and hospitals to document the eligibility of patients, obtain approval of hospital admissions and other procedures, and bill patients, climbed to $62 billion in 1983. With the proliferation of pre-admission screens and other review mechanisms in the second half of the 1980s, this year will top $100 billion."

4C12

George Rimler (Prof. Management, Virginia Comm. U.) COMPENSATION AND BENEFITS REVIEW, May-June 1992, p. 48.

⟨ Patients who know that the details of their injuries and illnesses (particularly mental health issues) will be discussed with third parties may not confide completely in their physicians or other providers. ⟩

It is imperative that the source, date, and page number be accurate. A good quotation can lose its importance—maybe even the debate round—if the opposing team points out that they cannot find the quotation on the page that you have cited. This is where the earlier discussion about always checking out evidence researched by someone else comes into effect. Mistakes are easy to make when recording evidence, and the team presenting the evidence in the debate round is responsible for its accuracy. There is also the question of ethics to consider.

When creating your evidence cards, be sure to allow space at the top of the cards for filing headings. Many debaters like to box this area off so that the filing label or code does not get lost in the rest of the evidence. These filing headings or codes are the key to efficient retrieval during a debate. (Filing of evidence will be covered later in this chapter.)

Another key point to remember is that each card should include only one piece of evidence. While you may save a little money by placing two quotations on one card, this will cause a great deal of confusion when you are trying to retrieve evidence in the debate round. Similarly, if a quote is relevant to two separate arguments, you may want to copy it and file it in both areas.

When recording evidence you must take care to include all of the words from the original source. It can be quite frustrating trying to cut a piece of evidence that can be read quickly in a debate round. Some authors tend to be longwinded, and some seem to use a great deal of unnecessary verbiage to make a point. It is often tempting to omit words that appear to be unnecessary. This is not recommended. What one researcher considers unnecessary another (perhaps even the author) would consider important.

However, if you do choose to delete words from a quotation, this must be indicated with ellipses (. . .). Remember that adjectives, qualifiers, and such words as "not" are not considered unnecessary; to delete such words would distort and change the meaning of the evidence. The potential problem with cutting quotations are so great that one debate organization, the National Forensic League (NFL), requires that internal ellipses *not* be used unless the debaters are carrying the original, or a copy of the original, with them. In some cases a piece of evidence may contain ellipses in the original. This should be indicated in brackets on your evidence card, as follows: [ellipses in original].

How then do you deal with the quotation that is good but just too long? Instead of using ellipses and leaving out part of the quotation, it is recommended that you begin by putting the full quotation on the evidence card. Then you can use brackets [ ] to indicate which portion of the quotation will actually be read in a debate round. This enables you to delete material that makes the quotation unnecessarily long or confusing, but still leaves the entire quotation available for anyone who wants to check it. This also helps to cut down on the number of original or copies of articles you must carry with you to a debate. However, keep in mind that when you come across a source that is critical to the development of your affirmative case or of a really significant disadvantage, you will probably want to carry a copy of that source with you for reference. This way if your key source is challenged, you can offer the complete text to the opposing team.

A last item of importance when recording evidence is internal references. When marking evidence you must remember that the evidence will be placed on an evidence card and filed away separately from the source. Therefore, you must be certain that you understand what any piece of evidence says without having to refer back to the original source. Any references to *it, he, she, the act, the program,* and so on should have a notation as to what is being referred to. For example, note the qualification in the following piece of evidence:

> "Paradoxically, it [managed competition] would also antagonize many doctors and hospitals, but can promise neither relief from bureaucracy nor a durable solution to the health care crisis."

Without the words *managed competition,* the quotation would be useless. There would be no way to remember in a debate halfway through the season what the *it* was.

Filing Evidence

Once you have done all the work necessary to research and mark the many sources available on the topic, you will have invested a great deal of time and energy into accumulating a significant number of evidence cards. It isn't unusual for a debate team to research as many as 2,000 evidence cards by the first tournament. (This is particularly true for debaters who have been to a summer debate institute.) However, having a large number of evidence cards is valuable only if you can find and use the cards in debate rounds. Some debaters carry massive amounts of evidence around from tournament to tournament but use only a hundred or so cards on a regular basis. The usual reason for this is that the debaters simply don't know what evidence they have in their file boxes. There are also those who remember researching certain areas of the topic but can't seem to find where they filed the evidence. Information retrieval, as any professional will affirm, is as important as any other phase of scholarship.

To a certain extent, each debate team must develop a filing system that is best for its own use. Any system is adequate if you know at all times what you have and if you can quickly retrieve the evidence during a debate round. Thus, the important thing is not so much which system you use as that you have a system. However, there are several commonly used filing systems that have proved helpful to debaters. These vary in complexity, depending on how much evidence the debaters have gathered.

The common feature of all filing systems is that they divide evidence into categories. Then each category of evidence is stored in a file box behind index card dividers that indicate the categories. No matter what system you use, it is important that the number of cards in each category be kept small. If there are more than ten cards under a single heading, the chances increase that you won't know what the file contains and will use the first card that comes to hand. While the amount of preparation time allowed at each tournament will vary, such limitations mean that you can't make a leisurely search for evidence to read in the round. Even if you know what evidence is in your file, a category that contains twenty or thirty cards will require too much time to sort through in the actual debate round.

A filing system should make it as easy as possible to find evidence during a round. Three commonly used filing systems are the **simple alphabetical system,** the elaborate alphabetical system, and the **notebook index system.** Using the resolution "*Resolved*: That the federal government should guarantee comprehensive national health insurance to all United States citizens," the systems would work as follows.

Simple Alphabetical System

The most basic filing system involves dividing the cards into subject areas and filing them accordingly. If you have several cards on the single payer system, they are filed behind an index card divider labeled *single payer,* with *single payer* written in the upper right-hand corner of each card to facilitate refiling. This system is used most often by new debaters, and it works fairly well as long as you have only a small number of evidence cards. More evidence, however, requires a more elaborate system.

Elaborate Alphabetical System

As you accumulate more evidence, it becomes necessary to find a way to divide the cards into more usable categories. As your research continues, you will soon have thirty or more cards on an area such as the single payer system. Since prep rules do not allow enough time to sort through that many cards in a debate round, you need to develop ways to break down large categories of evidence.

The first step to dividing cards into a more usable system is to use two file boxes, one for affirmative and one for negative evidence. Then you take the cards that had been filed under one "single payer" category, divide them between affirmative and negative cards, and file them in the separate affirmative and negative boxes.

However, if you keep gathering evidence, it will soon become necessary to have additional dividers behind your main headings. For example, under the category *single payer* you may need to divide your affirmative evidence into smaller categories such as *less costly* and *benefits millions.* Your negative breakdown might include categories such as *not desirable* and *hurts patients.* Some debaters take this system a step further and use different colors of index cards when recording evidence to indicate the two sides of the question. This can help facilitate refiling at the end of a round. However, using two colors of index cards requires good insight and care in the early stages of recording evidence. To avoid having to recopy a tremendous amount of evidence, you must decide at the time a source is being researched whether a piece of evidence will be used to support affirmative or negative arguments. In many cases this may be difficult to determine. In addition, it frequently happens that debaters find that evidence originally researched to support one side of the proposition ends up supporting a position on the other side.

This expansion of the alphabetical system to accommodate more evidence has its problems. To begin with, it takes a great deal of time during a debate round to find the appropriate divider heading and then the best card in the section. Another drawback is that on some topics a sizable amount of evidence cannot be categorized as only affirmative or negative. For example, on the national health insurance topic, evidence that would be used by the affirmative to show how the single payer system has worked where used could also be used by the negative to show that individual states can develop their own systems. For these reasons, more experienced debaters usually use a notebook index system for filing their evidence cards. (Many debaters also use affirmative and negative briefs, which are discussed later in this chapter.)

Notebook Index System

In a notebook index system, evidence cards are still divided into categories, subcategories, and even sub-subcategories. The difference is that the divider cards are lettered and numbered instead of being labeled by subject. A listing or index of the categories is kept in a notebook for easy use. Some debaters also tape a copy of the particular section of the index inside each file box. The notebook index system allows debaters a better opportunity to organize their evidence when they have a large number of evidence cards and several file boxes.

The initial sorting of evidence is the same as with the alphabetical system. Cards are divided into general categories. From this point, you would work to subdivide the cards into smaller and smaller categories until the size of each category is manageable. Then you would assign labels to the general category and to each of the subcategories. Labeling can be done in a number of ways; the important thing is that the index system works for you.

One possible index labeling system would be to identify the major categories by initials. For example, *single payer system* would be labeled *SP*. Next, subcategories would be assigned letters. For example, *less costly* would be labeled *A* and *benefits millions* would be labeled *B*. Under *A* and *B* there would be an additional breakdown into sub-subcategories, such as *Canadian system controls health care costs* or *Canadian system more efficient*. These two sub-subcategories would be given numbers under the *A* subcategory (*A-1, A-2*, etc.).

A second possible way to label is by file box. If you have five file boxes, you could assign a code number to each box. Then you could assign a letter to the major heading(s) and numbers to the subcategories. As a team's research continues, it is not unusual for a major heading to fill an entire file box. When this happens this second labeling system is quite efficient.

This index system is easy to use. It allows debaters to file both affirmative and negative evidence in the same files divided by subject, rather than having to assign evidence to affirmative or negative files. You can quickly find evidence by simply looking through your index sheets, rather than looking through your actual files and reading the divider cards. Because evidence cards are divided into categories and labeled with the proper letter and number codes, during the debate you can turn immediately to the appropriate card. After the debate, you can also refile the cards quickly and easily.

As with any system, one key to using the index system is to keep the number of cards in each category small. You can do this by expanding your number of categories and subcategories as the number of evidence cards increases. For example, under the subcategory *Canadian system more efficient*, you can later subdivide by the reasons the system is more efficient. When dividing a category into smaller categories, be sure to reevaluate each card's value. If a card is no longer relevant or has become too general to be of value, it should be discarded.

The example provided on the following pages shows an index for evidence on the national health insurance topic. Blank spaces have been left in the index sheet to allow room for adding new categories. It is better to leave too many blank spaces than too few. When possible, type your index on a computer. This way when you need to add categories or subdivide further, you can generate a new copy without having to start from scratch.

Debaters who have used the following notebook index system report that it is a very effective way to handle large amounts of evidence. They say that the cards can be found easily and refiled quickly. This is probably true because many index headings are possible under a code designation and because the entire subject subcategory does not have to be written on each divider and evidence card. Yet enough detail can be provided in the notebook index to give debaters a clear idea as to what is filed in the category. Also, it is considerably easier to read the code than to read a lengthy heading when searching through a file box.

A word of warning, however: if you lose the notebook that contains your index, there is no way of knowing where the evidence is filed. It would be wise to carry a duplicate or two at all times, and to keep an extra copy of the relevant part of the index in each individual file box.

Maintaining Evidence Files

The final step in managing debate evidence is carefully maintaining the evidence file. Periodically, you should go through all of your material to see what you have. Cards that are never used should be discarded if they are not as useful as they once appeared. More often, however, when you go through your file you will find material

Sample Notebook Index System

File Box 3—Single Payer System

3A. Single Payer System is less costly

    1. Canadian system

        a. Less costly

        b. Health share of GNP lower in Canada

        c. Saves on billing costs

        d. Better able to monitor fraud

        e. Avoids expensive specialization

        f. More efficient

        g.

        h.

        i.

        j.

    2.

    3.

    4.

    5.

    6. U.S. system

        a. Bureaucracy is wasteful

        b. Employs twice as many staff

        c. Entrenches rich-poor gap

        d.

        e.

        f.

        g.

    7. Global budget constrains costs

    8. Single payer could save $100 billion

    9. Single payer superior to free market

   10.

   11.

   12.

   13.

   14. Studies

        a. Health Insurance Association of America cost study flawed

        b. Other studies confirm billions saved

        c.

        d.

        e.

Sample Notebook Index System *Continued*

    15. Single payer administrative savings enormous

    16. Single payer stops medical inflation

    17. Single payer saves hospitals money

    18.

    19.

    20.

3B. Single payer system benefits millions

    1. Canadian system

        a. Access to advanced care

        b. Choose their own doctor

        c. Waiting lines not serious

        d. Get long-term care

        e.

        f.

        g.

        h. Doctor fees reasonable

        i. Bed closings justified

        k.

        l.

        m.

        n. Canadians support their system

    2. U.S. system

        a. Denies coverage to millions

        b. Has multiple flaws

        c.

        d.

        e.

        f.

        g. On brink of financial ruin

        h. Costs constrain liberty, choice in U.S.

        i.

        j.

        k.

        l. Can be applied in U.S.

        m. Americans willing to sacrifice

3C. Single Payer System is not desirable

    1. Canadian system

        a. Costs rising

Sample Notebook Index System *Concluded*

1. b. Hidden costs mask expense
   c. No incentive for efficiency
   d. Overhead costs high
   e. Inflationary
   f.
   g.
   h.
2. U.S. system
   a. Costs similar to Canada
   b. Get more value per dollar
   c.
   d.
   e.
   f. Costs billions to implement in U.S.
   g. Would require massive taxation
3.
4.
5.
6.
7.
8.

3D. Single Payer System hurts patients
1. Treatment delays
   a. Financial loss
   b. Cause death
   c.
   d.
2. Rationing of care
   a. Elderly hurt
   b. Shortage of beds
   c.
   d.
   e.
3. Hurts freedom
4. Difficult to implement
5. Studies flawed

File Box 4—Managed Care

File Box 5—Play or Pay

File Box 6—Free Market

Well-organized, thinking debaters can retrieve evidence quickly, even from evidence files as large as those shown here.

you have overlooked because it was not used early on. That material might prove to be the best evidence in your file.

The important thing is to extend the thinking approach to debate to your evidence file. Because it has become a kind of status symbol among debaters to carry large amounts of evidence, useless material often hides valuable information—there are so many cards that going through them to see what is good and what is bad becomes an overwhelming task. Also, the size of the file can lull debaters into thinking the research job is done. Such nonthinking debaters can typically be identified by the large number of late-season losses they accrue. Remember that a large file is useful only if you know what is in it and can retrieve the information quickly. If that is not the case, you will develop only a good set of muscles by carrying around so much evidence.

Writing Briefs

To be successful, debaters must research many important issues and arguments. Only with current, expert evidence can debaters hope to prove points critical to their positions in a debate round. However, researching evidence is not enough to insure a win in a debate round.

Debate requires that advocates arrange evidence in a useful, organized manner so that the arguments can be effectively presented in the debate round. The most common way for organizing these debate arguments is called the *debate brief*. A debate brief is generally a page (or set of pages) of arguments, with evidence that can be read as the need arises in a given round. Each individual argument on the brief is preceded by a line (____). During a round, debaters will often check off or paperclip each argument they plan to read in the debate round. For an example of a brief, see page 102.

The debate brief is different from the prepared first affirmative speech in several ways. First, arguments are not entirely written out. While a first affirmative speech is presented as a polished oration, a debate brief simply uses labels to identify the arguments (and some explanation where necessary), along with the evidence to be used to support the argument. Because all speeches after the first affirmative respond to what has been presented thus far in the debate, polished speeches are not feasible. The debate brief provides the opportunity to prepare arguments prior to the debate yet still have the flexibility to adapt to the actual debate in progress. Therefore, the debater should arrange arguments so that relevant objections can be entered into the debate round.

Second, a brief differs from a first affirmative speech in that it speaks to only one major issue. Each brief concerns only one major issue pertinent to the defense of an affirmative argument or a negative attack. For example, the negative team may have developed a variety of disadvantages to an affirmative case. Each one should be briefed out separately, so that the arguments that best pertain can be selected for delivery and the others held in reserve. The reasoning for this is the same as the reasoning behind recording evidence cards. You want to be able to get to each brief quickly and efficiently, and having only one argument to a brief makes it possible to order your arguments for each debate without having to keep shuffling pieces of paper.

Finally, unlike a first affirmative speech, a brief contains several pieces of evidence, not all of which are read in every round of debate. If you expect that a particular argument is crucial for your affirmative case or negative position, you may wish to have two, three, or four quotations on the brief. It is not necessary to read all the evidence to prove the argument, at least initially. But if the argument becomes the focus of contention later on, the backup evidence will be useful in further establishing your point.

Developing Affirmative Briefs

There are three types of **affirmative briefs.** The first is the *case brief*, used to support the affirmative case. Briefs developed to support the affirmative case may include arguments that extend the harms or advantages of the affirmative case, or they may be responses to anticipated negative arguments (for example, inherency or topicality).

The second type of brief is the *plan brief*, designed to defend the affirmative plan. These are anticipated responses to solvency and workability arguments, as well as to negative disadvantages.

The third type of affirmative brief is the *extension brief*. These are briefs that set up a second or third line of argument. Basically, this involves the affirmative anticipating the following scenario: the negative will argue inherency argument "A"; the affirmative will respond with the inherency brief; the negative is likely to extend the inherency argument in the next speech with argument "B"; the affirmative prepares a response—an extension brief. Before developing any affirmative briefs, you must first take a serious look at your affirmative case and outline the possible arguments that might be raised against it. Using your list of arguments, begin your research; your briefs should be constructed to anticipate the arguments.

Plan briefs are developed to defend (or answer) the solvency and workability arguments, as well as disadvantages. The construction of plan briefs is much the same as for case briefs. The affirmative tries to anticipate what arguments might be run against the affirmative plan.

Plan briefs need to be written with two possible uses in mind. First, the answers to negative plan arguments need to be thorough. If the arguments are presented in the first negative constructive, the response will come in the second affirmative constructive speech, and this would allow time for the affirmative to develop a detailed response.

Second, however, plan briefs also need to be constructed in such a way that they can be shortened to respond to plan arguments that are presented in the *second* negative constructive and thus answered in the first affirmative rebuttal. Since the first affirmative rebuttal is short (five minutes) and responds to thirteen minutes of negative argumentation, answers must be to the point and evidence, short and precise. It is of little value to present a detailed long brief against a single disadvantage and then not be able to cover other important negative arguments.

Some affirmative teams make their plan briefs a bit longer and include extension arguments and evidence on them. This is material intended for use in later rebuttals. Others choose instead to develop extension briefs. For example, in the sample briefs on the following pages, the affirmative brief answers the negative disadvantage "AIDS research will be destroyed." The initial plan brief argues why there is little hope of solving AIDS now and that research will not be stopped (among several other responses). The extension brief is intended to extend the argument that researchers have little confidence of a cure, by providing reasons why there is little confidence. Many debaters like to develop their extension briefs separately because it is easier to decide which arguments to extend and makes for less paper shuffling at a point in the debate when time is at a premium. The affirmative topicality brief on managed competition, which immediately follows, is a sample of how a brief would appear. The page breaks for the remaining briefs in this chapter are indicated by a solid line.

Affirmative Topicality   MANAGED COMPETITION
(T) – F.C.: Managed Care = National Health Insurance to all U.S.
Citizens

_____. (MC) = Nat'l Health Ins. Covering all citizens.
Paul Starr (Prof. Sociology, Princeton U.) THE LOGIC OF
HEALTH CARE REFORM, 1992, p. 15.

> ⟨ In recent years the phrase *national health insurance* has increasingly be-
> come identified with a federally financed and regulated insurance system—
> a more narrow conception than was current only a decade ago. When I use
> the words national health insurance, I mean a system that provides access
> to a mainstream standard of coverage on the basis of citizenship rather than
> employment. All Americans would be included, and residents who are not
> citizens could qualify for coverage through their own or a family member's
> legal employment or study. ⟩

*Starr as we all know is one of the major proponents of (MC.)

_____. Rules of (MC) = Universal Coverage.
Alain Enthoven (Prof., Stanford) and Richard Kronick (Prof.
UCSD), NEW YORK TIMES, January 25, 1992, p. A23.

> ⟨ Many employers do not offer man-
> aged care programs; others offer
> employees a choice of fee-for-
> service and managed-care pro-
> grams. But employers frequently
> pay all or most of the premiums, no
> matter what plan an employee
> chooses. As a result, the employee
> gets little or no reward for choosing
> the less costly managed care. Fur-
> ther, the incentive for managed-
> care organizations to reduce costs
> is destroyed, because cutting pre-
> miums will not make their plans
> more attractive to employees. ⟩

> ⟨ Such organizations would find it
> easy to seek profit by covering only
> healthy people, who aren't likely to
> have large medical bills, and not en-
> rolling people who are likely to be
> sick. Rules are needed to make sure
> everybody gets covered—including
> the unemployed and the 37 million
> uninsured—and that the organiza-
> tions aren't disadvantaged by en-
> rolling too many sick people. ⟩

**Enthoven is also a major proponent of (MC.)

Affirmative   HIPC Topicality   1/3
Pseudo —(T)
MComp ≠ Risk Discrimination

_____. No plan can reject consumers based on past/present
health conditions.

Senator John Breaux (La), CONGRESSIONAL RECORD, March
11, 1993, p. S2698.

> "No plan can reject any consumer for coverage based on current health
> status or past illnesses. In the current health insurance system, insurers
> often reject coverage for individuals or small businesses if those consumers
> have some pre-existing medical problems."

_____. Sponsors ensure equity in coverage.

Alain Enthoven (Prof. Stanford), HEALTH AFFAIRS
SUPPLEMENT, 1993, p. 31.

> ⟨ **Sponsors establish rules of equity.** The sponsor has several important
> functions in managed competition. First, through contracts with the partici-
> pating health plans, it establishes and enforces principles of equity such as
> the following: (1) Every eligible person is covered or at least is offered
> coverage on terms that make it attractive, even for persons with low ex-
> pected medical costs, and at a moderate financial cost. Health plans accept
> all eligible persons who choose them. ⟩

_____. Non-discrimination benefits private & public
sectors.

Sen. John Breaux (La), CONGRESSIONAL RECORD, March 11,
1993, p. S698.

> "Under the CALPERS program, none of its participating health care plans
> may deny a consumer coverage or charge higher prices based on past or
> current health problems. CALPERS administrators attributed the program's
> success to aggressive negotiations as a 'health insurance purchasing coop-
> erative' and believe this approach may offer significant benefit to both the
> public and private sectors around the country."

Affirmative   HIPC Topicality   2/3
_____. HIPCs would be required to accept patients with
pre-existing conditions.

Richard Kronick (Prof. UCSD), HEALTH AFFAIRS,
SUPPLEMENT, 1993, P. 89.

⟨ All health plans under contract to HIPCs would be required to accept, during an annual open enrollment, any person choosing to enroll, without preexisting condition exclusions or waiting periods. All plans would be required to report standardized information on enrollee satisfaction and outcome measures. Premiums would be determined in negotiation with the HIPC and would be the same for all persons purchasing coverage (although, as discussed by James Robinson elsewhere in this volume, the HIPC would pay health plans based on risk-adjusted rates). It is important to allow firms with more than 1,000 employees to decide voluntarily to purchase coverage through the HIPC.⟩ To avoid adverse selection, large firms that choose to purchase through the HIPC should make payments based on the demo

_____. HIPCs would be required to offer universal coverage.

Alain Enthoven (Prof. Stanford), Hrgs of Comm on Labor and Human Resources, Senate, ACHIEVING EFFECTIVE COST CONTROL IN COMPREHENSIVE HEALTH CARE REFORM, December 16-17, 1992, p.54.

"The HIPC would also contract with participating employers. It would accept all appropriate employment groups located within its area. It would not be allowed to exclude groups or individuals based on health status. It would assure continuity of coverage and not allow exclusions for pre-existing conditions. The HIPC would manage competition, applying business judgment in determining the numbers and identities of competitors. At the outset, the availability of managed care varies so widely from one geographic area to another that HIPCs would be allowed wide latitude in their initial choice plans until registered AHPs are generally available.

Affirmative   HIPC Topicality   3/3

_____. HIPCs Ø exclude on basis of health status.

Alain Enthoven (Prof. Stanford), HEALTH AFFAIRS SUPPLEMENT, 1993, p. 36.

⟨ HIPCs would be nonprofit membership corporations whose boards would be elected by participating employers. HIPCs would contract with participating employers and would accept all qualifying employment groups in their area. They would not be allowed to exclude groups or individuals because of health status. HIPCs would manage competition, applying business judgment in determining the numbers and identities of competitors, and would carry out all of the sponsor functions described above. ⟩

_____. HPPCs Ø exclude.

Alain Enthoven (Prof. Stanford), Hrgs of Comm on Labor and Human Resources, Senate, ACHIEVING EFFECTIVE COST CONTROL IN COMPREHENSIVE HEALTH CARE REFORM, December 16-17, 1992, p. 41.

> ⟨ Such employment groups—and individuals—should be pooled through the creation of a national system of Health Plan Purchasing Cooperatives (HPPCs) that would function as sponsors on behalf of all small employers and individuals in a geographic area. Each HPPC would accept all qualifying employment groups in its area. They would not be allowed to exclude employment groups or individuals because of health status. ⟩

Affirmative   Inherency
                          SQ Markets Flawed

_____. People who get sick have higher premiums.

Alain Enthoven (Prof. Stanford), HEALTH AFFAIRS SUPPLEMENT, 1993, p. 30.

> ⟨ First, insurers have strong incentives to group their customers by expected medical costs and to charge people in each group a premium that reflects their expected costs. This practice is known as experience rating or underwriting. The consequence is that those people having high predicted medical costs face high premiums. Many sick people find such premiums unaffordable and may go without insurance, taking their chances that they will receive free care. ⟩

_____. SQ = Inequity

Paul Ellwood (Pres and Co-Founder of the Jackson Hole Group) and Lynn Esteredge (Health Policy Analyst) HEALTH CARE STRATEGIC MANAGEMENT, January 1993, p. 1.

> ⟨ The effectiveness of the current system has been further eroded by segmentation of markets, biased risk selection and inequitable underwriting practices in the private sector, and uneven or incomplete coverage of the elderly, poor, and disabled in the public sector. ⟩

_____. Market segmentation = ↓ price competition

Alain Enthoven (Prof Stanford) Hrgs Comm on Labor and Human Resources, Senate, ACHIEVING EFFECTIVE COST CONTROL IN COMPREHENSIVE HEALTH CARE REFORM, December 16-17, 1992, p. 51.

> "Market segmentation minimizes price competition. Because of the huge number of complex services covered in health insurance contracts, carriers

and managed care organizations can segment markets and minimize the number of persons who would actually change health plan because of price."

_____. Only the healthy get health insurance.

Sen. Jeff Bingaman, CONGRESSIONAL RECORD, May 7, 1992, p. S551.

⟨I believe we should begin our journey by taking steps to reform the small group insurance market. The insurance marketplace is replete with failings, but none is as egregious as the failure of the small group insurance market. Insurance for employees of small business has become a luxury few can afford. Insurers have found creative ways to cover healthy individuals, while increasing premiums for individuals who actually need or use their health insurance.⟩

Affirmative   DA Answers   1/2

Answers to AIDS DA

Impax

_____. Researchers have little confidence of a cure.

Mark Harrington, CONGRESSIONAL RECORD, Feb 18, 1993, p. S1838.

Since 1987, the activist critique of AIDS research has worked its way back: from drug approval at the regulatory level of the US Food and Drug Administration (FDA), to expanded access for drugs still under study (Parallel Track), to the design and conduct of the controlled clinical trials themselves by the National Institutes of Health (NIH), pharmaceutical companies and, community-based clinical trial centers. While this work has generated some useful reforms in an inefficient system (and expanded access and expedited approval for several useful therapies), it often seems that all these accomplishments go for naught. HIV keeps spreading, AIDS keeps striking people down, and researchers appear to have little confidence in the rapid development of a therapeutic cure or an effective vaccine.

_____. n/u—AIDS work halted.

Rep. Stark, CONGRESSIONAL RECORD, Aug 4, 1992, p. H8131.

⟨Right now, there are reports from the National Institute of Allergy and Infectious Diseases (NIAID) of one AIDS vaccine trial that will not be initiated and a second that is being stopped because of liability concerns. These two impeded clinical trials are likely to be representative of others that have been stopped at an earlier stage or not even initiated because of similar concerns. If these claims are accurate and research will be halted on even a small number of potential vaccines, the overall prevention effort will suffer. If clinical trials are halted on the most promising and advanced of vaccines, which may be the case at present, and even if these vaccines are not ultimately the chosen candidates, significant ramifications result. 〉 H 8/3/

_____. AIDS impax exaggerated by AIDS activists, government, and media.

Fumento (author), NATIONAL REVIEW, Oct 18, 1992, p. 50.

〈 To counter this, <u>the NCA and the AIDS establishment—which includes Federal Government health agencies, AIDS activist groups, and the media—have worked tirelessly to spread the perception of an epidemic growing by leaps and bounds and increasingly spilling over from the original risk groups to the population at large.</u> In the AIDS alarmist lexicon, some persons might be more at risk but nobody is less at risk. Thus, it's PC to say that blacks and Hispanics are at greater risk, and the NCA has done so, but it is not at all PC to say that whites are at less risk. 〉

Affirmative   DA Answers   2/2

_____. National Health Insurance helps AIDS patients.

Leonard Robins, (Professor of Public Administration), Roosevelt University, and Charles Backstrom, (Prof. Political Science) University of Minnesota, 1991, *Health Politics and Policy*, p. 384.

〈 A third major issue is whether AIDS will trigger fundamental revisions in the system for paying for health care in the United States. One of the major improvements that could occur would be if the health care system were reformed through enactment of national health insurance. Regrettably, the health care system has up to now successfully resisted this direction, and in and of itself AIDS seems insufficient to produce such a major change. 〉 384

_____. HIV doesn't cause AIDS.

Tom Bethell (editor of American Spectator and Media Fellow at Hoover Institution), NATIONAL REVIEW, Aug 17, 1992, p. 22.

HIV ∅ HURT CELLS OF ANYTHING

〈 Down the hall from Duesberg at Berkeley's Stanley Hall is the lab of Professor Harry Rubin, another skeptic. <u>He also believes that HIV has not been shown to be the cause of AIDS.</u> I spoke to Bryan Ellison, a doctoral candidate with Rubin. Retroviruses have never been observed to kill cells, he told me. "If you microscopically vaccine healthy cells in a dish, and a virus such as polio is added to them, the virus multiplies inside the cells and bursts them open in a matter of hours. Soon you can see nothing but debris and garbage and dead cells," he said. But if you put HIV, or any other retrovirus, into the same dish with healthy cells—an environment when the body's immune system cannot interfere—the cells just sit there and continue healthy growth. >

NOTE: This brief contains extensions which would be used on the answers provided in the Affirmative Answers to AIDS Impax DA. It should be noted that each extension begins a new brief. This enables the debater to pull only the extensions which will be used.

Affirmative Extensions Off 1   DAs

Extensions for Answers to
AIDS Impax

EXTENSION OFF RESPONSE 1

_____. The fact is, the vaccine is a long way off.
June Osborn (Michigan School of Public Health), JOURNAL OF HEALTH ADMINISTRATION, Winter 1992, pp. 26–27.

> Myth Number Four: "I heard they've made some progress with a vaccine." This one makes me a bit tired, for I am a veteran of old vaccine wars; a perfect vaccine ready at hand would not do much for us at our present juncture. It would be a great help in countries where the nearly complete lack of health care infrastructure makes AIDS a cataclysmic "last straw" but in the United States we would not even be tempted to temporize or wait. The fact is that a vaccine for widespread use against AIDS is a long way off, despite intermittent excitements in the press. It is relatively little the fault of the scientists involved in the important search for a future vaccine strategy that every technological tidbit or twitch commands such brassy media attention; we should know from past experience that vaccines are not panaceas. > 26-27

_____. Testing would be more effective than a vaccine.
FUTURIST, March/April 1991, p. 47.

> Johnston and Hopkins propose a universal routine voluntary testing program, which would enable people to sexually segregate themselves on the basis of whether or not they are HIV-positive. They believe that such testing will be far more effective in limiting new HIV infections than any medical advances—even an AIDS vaccine—that could be developed during the 1990s. > 47

Affirmative Extensions   DAs 1/2

Extensions for Answers to
AIDS Impax

Extension Off Response 3

_____. Who exaggerates the impax—so they get more
money.
MacLEANS, April 27, 1992, p. 58

⟨Every three months, the Geneva-based World Health Organization publishes a report on the estimated number of people worldwide who are infected with human immunodeficiency virus (HIV) and the number who have,
as a result, developed the debilitating and ultimately fatal acquired immune
deficiency syndrome (AIDS). The WHO's latest report, published in mid-
February, portrayed a rapidly spreading disease, with one million new HIV
infections during the previous eight months, bringing the total worldwide to
about 12 million. It predicted an even grimmer future, with as many as 40
million people HIV-infected by the year 2000. But a growing number of
critics, in both Canada and the United States, contend that the WHO estimates are unrealistic and misleading. In fact, they say that the spread of
the deadly virus in North America peaked during the mid-1980s, and that
a two-year-old decline in the number of new AIDS cases diagnosed annually
is a trend that will continue through the 1990s. Said Joel Hay, a health
economist at the University of Southern California in Los Angeles: "I don't *58*
trust the WHO reports on the number of people infected with HIV, in Africa
or anywhere else. Their estimates have been widely exaggerated." ⟩

MacLEANS, April 27, 1992, p. 58.

⟨ And the University of Southern California's Hay contends that the study deliberately overestimates the number of HIV infections, largely for political reasons.
Said Hay: "They and other AIDS bureaucracies have a vested interest in paint-
ing the bleakest picture possible, because that's how they get their money." ⟩ *58*

Affirmative Extensions Off 3   DAs 2/2

_____. AIDS activists exaggerated impax on AIDS
MacLEANS, April 27, 1992, p. 58.

HETEROSEXUAL RISK

⟨But Canadian and U.S. government statistics show that, despite warnings
that AIDS could spread rapidly among heterosexuals, in North America
AIDS remains overwhelmingly a disease that affects homosexual and bisex-
ual men and intravenous drug users. Some experts now contend that AIDS
activists in both countries have made misleading claims about the disease's
potential for spreading among heterosexuals in order to encourage funding
for AIDS research and prevention. Said Alexander Langmuir, a former chief

epidemiologist with the Atlanta-based Centers for Disease Control: "There are no signs of a rampant new wave of AIDS. It's clearly a disease that is largely restricted to gays and drug addicts." 〉 *58*

_____. CDC proves HIV has not increased in prevalence. Fumento (author), NATIONAL REVIEW, Oct 18, 1992, p. 50.

〈 Looking at the epidemic as a whole the June 1992 CDC report concluded "Thus, serosurveillance overall has indicated relative stability rather than clear increase or decrease in HIV prevalence." Actually, the two largest populations being tested, military applicants and first-time blood donors, have shown a steady drop in infection since 1985, and although the CDC correctly claims that there has been certain skewing of the figures, since persons suspecting they are infected usually don't get tested, this doesn't explain why after, say, 1987, the numbers continued to drop. 〉
〈 The better things get, however, the louder the NCA screams, with the result that rhetoric and reality move further and further apart. Most recently, the NCA claimed that nothing short of a Cabinet-level position is necessary to wage its idea of a war on AIDS. 〉

Affirmative Extensions   DAs

Extensions for Answers to
AIDS Impax

Extension Off Response 5

_____. HIV is harmless and it does not cause AIDS.
Tom Bethell (editor of the American Spectator and Media Fellow at the Hoover Institution), NATIONAL REVIEW, August 17, 1992, p. 23.

〈 Another possibility is that HIV doesn't have anything to do with AIDS. This is what Peter Duesberg of UC Berkeley has been saying for five years: that HIV doesn't attack the immune system, doesn't cause AIDS, and is in fact harmless. A professor of molecular biology, Duesberg is one of the world's leading experts on retroviruses. I called him at his Berkeley lab and asked what he thought of the news from Amsterdam, and the possibility that we may now have one more lethal virus to worry about. 〉

_____. Drugs are the real cause of AIDS.
Tom Bethell (editor of the American Spectator and Media Fellow at the Hoover Institution), NATIONAL REVIEW, August 17, 1992, p. 23.

〈 Duesberg goes further and claims that drugs are the real cause of AIDS. If he's right, the emaciated patient in the AIDS ward corresponds to the emaciated junkie in the opium den. One-third of AIDS patients are admittedly intravenous drug users—covering about 75 per cent of heterosexual AIDS cases. The real figure is probably higher: drug use is illegal, and no doubt underreported. Duesberg adds that homosexuals from the "bathhouse culture" are (or were) heavy drug users (including non-injection drugs such as "poppers"). In the course of their encounters they tend to pick up whatever is going around, including HIV and other germs. But he says that HIV itself is a harmless "hitchhiker"—a marker for risk behavior, as the scientists say.

Developing Negative Briefs

Negative briefs are also divided into case, plan, and extension briefs. The starting point for preparing negative briefs is the same as that for affirmative briefs. First sit down with your teammate or squad and brainstorm what cases might be run on the current debate topic. Once a list has been generated, your work can begin.

For example, on the debate "*Resolved*: That the federal government should guarantee comprehensive national health insurance to all United States citizens," possible affirmative case areas might include single payer proposals (including Canadian plan, Universal Health Care Act, Medicare Universal Coverage Expansion Act of 1991), pay or play proposals (including AmeriCare, U.S. Health Care Program Act of 1991, Pepper Commission Health Care Access & Reform Act), socialized medicine (including the British Model, U.S. Health Service Act), or fill-in-the-gap proposals (including Managed Competition, Managed Care, Medical IRA's). As your research continues through the season, new case ideas will surface.

Negative *case briefs* involve the negative arguments that are being made against affirmative contentions or advantages. Basically, these case briefs are organized around the stock issues: topicality, inherency, and significance. The arguments developed in the negative briefs are designed to undermine the credibility of affirmative studies or the rationale behind the affirmative's arguments. A negative topicality brief should be well prepared so that any steps a plan might take beyond the scope of the resolution can be countered; otherwise, the affirmative might be able to preemptively anticipate disadvantages. Negative case briefs dealing with inherency arguments generally work to defend the status quo or present system. Negative inherency briefs should demonstrate the successes of the present system or show why there have been failures and how the present system can repair their failures.

For example, for an affirmative case claiming death and needless suffering to the unemployed, a negative team might develop negative case briefs showing that Medicare and Medicaid are available to take care of these people. Since the affirmative is likely to argue that while these programs do exist they have shortcomings, the negative would want to plan ahead and develop extension briefs on Medicare and Medicaid showing how the problems in the system can be repaired without adopting the resolution or to show how these programs can be expanded to cover the needs outlined by the affirmative.

Since the idea of the *extension brief* is the same for the negative as the affirmative, it will be discussed before negative plan briefs. Generally, to develop a negative extension brief, debaters follow a basic four-step process. First, the negative identifies the possible affirmative case; next, the negative develops case briefs; third, the negative analyzes the briefs, brainstorming possible affirmative responses to the arguments; and finally, the negative develops extension briefs to answer the affirmative responses.

Negative plan briefs are constructed a bit differently. Most of the negative plan arguments are directed at the specific solvency/workability of the affirmative plan or at the disadvantages that will result if the plan is adopted. The negative plan brief on solvency or workability is usually fairly straightforward. For example, it might involve a position on the national health insurance topic that the affirmative cannot guarantee insurance to all U.S. citizens. This position would be developed in a general form, addressing one of the affirmative case areas listed above. The negative would have to adapt the position in the specific round to show how it applies to the actual affirmative plan being presented.

Constructing the Negative Disadvantage Brief

1. The thesis of the disadvantage must be understandable.
2. The disadvantage needs a specific link to the affirmative case.
3. The negative must identify a specific impact to the disadvantage.
4. The disadvantage must show how the links and impacts are connected.
5. The disadvantage must be unique to the affirmative plan.

A disadvantage brief is structured differently from the other affirmative or negative briefs. A disadvantage must be carefully written so that it cannot be dismissed as irrelevant, trivial, or contradictory when viewed alongside the negative position on case. There are five steps to developing a good negative disadvantage. First, it is important that the thesis of the disadvantage be understandable. Many refer to this as the "label" for the disadvantage. The first sentence of the disadvantage needs to be clear, and it should be easy for everyone in the round—judge included—to understand what the central focus of the disadvantage will be. To label a disadvantage with just one or two words, such as "kill medical research," is not enough. Such a label is far too broad and can lead to confusion.

Second, the disadvantage needs to have a specific link to the affirmative case. The negative will be anticipating the sorts of disadvantages that can be run against the various affirmative cases. It is not enough to argue that any new spending on the affirmative proposal will eliminate research on AIDS; instead, the negative must show how the affirmative plan becomes the link to the elimination of research.

Third, the negative must identify a specific impact to the disadvantage. A good example of this is provided by Rich Edwards in the 1993 *Forensic Quarterly* (Vol. 67, No. 1). Edwards describes the case of a first negative speaker who presents the links to a "growth bad" disadvantage:

> The second affirmative speaker turns the links by arguing that the affirmative plan will actually result in less economic growth since the plan would increase the deficit. The second negative speaker then "reverses" the disadvantage by arguing that growth is actually good rather than bad, arguing that the economy is just coming out of a recession and needs the stimulus of additional federal spending.

In this example, the negative has actually reversed its position during the debate, leaving the affirmative in an impossible position of not knowing whether the negative is for or against economic growth. When presenting a disadvantage the negative is obligated to clearly indicate what the bottom-line impact is so the affirmative can respond. Remember, there is no reason for the judge to vote on a disadvantage unless it has some level of impact.

Fourth, the disadvantage must show how the links and impacts are connected—how one leads to the other. Consider the AIDS research disadvantage. When the negative claims that decreasing the profit margins of health providers will result in no more AIDS research, the negative is obliged to show (1) how reducing the profit margins will lead to the cuts, (2) that without increased research there will be an unchecked AIDS epidemic, and (3) what the ramifications of an unchecked epidemic will be.

Finally, the disadvantage must be unique to the affirmative plan. It must be pretty clear that it is the affirmative plan (and it alone) that causes the harms of the disadvantage. For example, the negative must be able to prove that health providers aren't looking to cut AIDS research anyway, and that the affirmative plan is only a handy excuse. If the negative argues that any increased spending will cause a deficit disaster, then it will be rather difficult to prove that whatever federal program is adopted next will have the same result. Unless a disadvantage brief contains all of these steps, the negative position is likely to be defeated by the affirmative or given little weight by the judge. The briefs on the following pages illustrate these points.

Negative   Topicality   1/2

Managed Competition
                    Comprehensive

_____. Managed Competition won't cover a single
              uninsured American.

Thomas Bodenheimer (Physicians for a National Health
Program), THE NATION, March 22, 1993, p. 22.

⟨ Managed competition is *not* universal health insurance; it will not cover a
single uninsured American. And as the Congressional Budget Office (Clinton's favorite source of economic analysis) recently reported, scant evidence exists that managed competition can control soaring health care
costs. ⟩

_____. Managed Competition won't include every
              community.

James Block (Chief Exec officer Johns Hopkins Hosp), Hrgs
Committee on Labor and Human Resources, Senate,
ACHIEVING EFFECTIVE COST CONTROL IN COMPREHENSIVE
HEALTH CARE REFORM, December 16-17, 1992, p. 144.

⟨ The problem that I see with the HIPC as it has been described this morning,
and the problems that I see with managed competition, are that they do not
encompass the entire community. It is not sufficient to say that we rely on
managed care plans to determine what providers they will purchase from.
There are critical institutions in every community which must survive for the
benefits of all kinds of people, and those institutions can be stabilized and
can also participate in cost containment if it is done in the context of a
regulated environment that also allows for competition. ⟩

_____. All Americans won't benefit from Managed
              Competition. ABC News, April 21, 1993.

⟨ GEORGE STRAIT: (ER SCENE) Some doctors don't like it, because competing to keep costs down could interfere with medical decisions. And some
advocates for the uninsured don't like it, because managed competition
does not extend benefits to all Americans.
DREW ALTMAN / KAISER FOUNDATION: Setting up a purchasing cooperative to bargain on behalf of people with insurance does precisely nothing
to make sure that people who don't have insurance get it. ⟩

Negative   Topicality   2/2
Managed Competition

_____. Managed competition doesn't offer much to
             Americans with health coverage.
Cockburn, NEW STATESMAN AND SOCIETY, May 21, 1993, p.
15.

> It is now becoming clear that Bill gave his wife an impossible task. "Managed
> competition" won't work for the same larger reason that managerial liberal-
> ism won't work. The system is too screwed up to be fixed this way. If all
> Americans were to be asked to pay, by way of new taxes, for a new health-
> care system that offered them all good care at reasonable rates and an
> underlying cost curve that pointed down, then they would no doubt support
> it. But "managed competition" doesn't offer Americans currently ensconed
> in company or union health plans much beyond the certainty of having to
> pay for those 37 million or so Americans who have no health coverage at
> all. And, politically, this will never fly. Clinton has already seen his minuscule
> economic stimulus package, pared down to $6 billion or so, filibustered out
> of existence by Senate Republicans. > *15*

_____. Employees from large firms won't receive coverage.

Paul Starr (Prof Sociology, Princeton), HEALTH AFFAIRS
SUPPLEMENT, 1993, p. 9.

> Under federal law, all American citizens would be guaranteed the right to
> a comprehensive set of benefits, defined in general terms by legislation and
> interpreted and adjusted over time by a National Health Board. The federal
> government would require all individuals and all employers, except perhaps
> the very smallest, to share the cost of health insurance. All—except, most
> likely, employees of large firms—would obtain coverage through new re-
> gional health insurance purchasing cooperatives (HIPCs). >

Negative   Case   1/3

Managed Competition
            Clinton Will Do Managed Competition
                      In Status Quo

_____. Managed Competition is crux of Clinton's Health
             Care Plan.

SACRAMENTO BEE, July 11, 1993 (Lexis), p. 17.

> Under GMC, Medi-Cal beneficiaries in the county will be able to choose
> from several providers based on the services they offer. "Managed competi-

tion," as it is known, encourages providers to offer a wider range of benefits and services in order to encourage Medi-Cal beneficiaries to enroll. Managed competition has been used for several years by the state Public Employees' Retirement System, which allows state employees to choose from several health plans and providers, and is expected to be a keystone of the Clinton administration's health care reforms.

_____. Clinton leaning to Managed Competition.
BUSINESS & HEALTH, March 1992, p. 51.

⟨ The immediate concern is whether managed competition can contain costs as dramatically as needed over the next five to 10 years. Serious doubts on that score have given rise to proposals to marry managed competition with firm price regulation and budgets—caps on annual premium increases, for example. The Clinton Administration is thought to be leaning heavily in this direction. ⟩   *51*

_____. Managed Competition is at the heart of health care.
Edwin Chen, LOS ANGELES TIMES, January 7, 1992, p. A18.

" 'We can begin seeing savings as a result of managed competition prior to any passage legislation' Ellwood said. 'What needs to happen is for the President-elect to simply signal his intention to lead the health system in this direction and . . . the system will quickly move toward accountable health plans all over the country.' " (ellipses in original)

___

Negative   Case 2/2
Managed Competition

_____. Consensus in Washington on Managed Competition emerging.
Tom Hamburger, THE OTTAWA CITIZEN, June 28, 1992, p.A6.

⟨ Despite disputes over fee schedules and coverage, release of the Senate Republican plan is a sign that consensus is developing among centrists in Washington around the concept of managed competition. ⟩   *A6*

_____. Managed Competition will pass in status quo.

Terese Hudson, (Sr Ed-HOSPITALS), HOSPITALS, February 5, 1992, p. 28.

"The various options for what reforms could be eventually passed narrowed after Bill Clinton's election, says one consultant to insurers. 'There is no question that some kind of managed competition will pass,' says Robert Laszewski, an insurance executive turned consultant."

_____. Clinton plan will include price controls.

Richard Dreyfuss, MOTHER JONES, May/June 1993, p. 19.

⟨ While the Clinton task force is toying with some form of a global budget, their managed competition plan will not in itself reduce spending. So, in an effort to restrain costs, the Clinton plan will probably involve direct price controls on an interim basis, likely including caps on insurance premium increases. But the Congressional Budget Office says that such price controls will be "painful" and will "require consumers to accept some real limits on the quality or quantity of health care." ⟩

_____. Clinton plan will be flexible for states.

Sen Dorgan (ND), CONGRESSIONAL RECORD, May 17, 1993, p. H324.

⟨ It is my understanding that the Clinton administration will encourage managed competition in those areas where it is appropriate and give States the flexibility to opt out of this kind of system when it just will not work. For rural areas where managed competition may not work, the Clinton administration envisions a system of managed cooperation instead of managed competition. The administration will look to HHS to develop models for rural network development that States may want to try.⟩ For example, a public

---

Negative   Case 3/3
Managed Competition

_____. States determine health care under Clinton plan.

BNA DAILY REPORT FOR EXECUTIVES (Lexis), July 13, 1993.

⟨ Robert Grossman, who coordinates legislative planning and environmental program review for the Hawaii Board of Health, said he thinks states will have to pay for care for uninsured people under federal reform.
    "People are being brought in with guarantees of coverage," Grossman said. "It will be the state that will be the responsible fiduciary party for the standardized benefits under the Clinton plan," he said, adding that Hawaii and other states are concerned about how much responsibility they can take given a flat economy. ⟩

_____. Clinton's proposal includes state managed competition.

Sen Dorgan (ND), CONGRESSIONAL RECORD, May 27, 1993, p.H324.

⟨ I am very supportive of all these ideas. Furthermore, I believe that the Clinton administration is planning to allow States to opt entirely out of a managed competition delivery system and put in a single payor system if they prefer. It is particularly important that rural States like Vermont have this flexibility. 〉

Negative   Solvency 1/2
Managed Competition
Utilization Review Bad

_____. Utilization Review ↑ health care costs.
NAATP REVIEW, Fall 1992, p. 12.

〈 And now doubt is growing about the new industry's most basic promise—lower medical costs. While utilization review often does cut such costs for employers, the administrative burden it imposes on doctors and hospitals may actually be increasing rather than lowering the nation's total medical bill. For every form a utilization firm sends out and every phone call one of its employees makes, someone in the medical community must respond, usually with equal or greater effort.
   "It's a cost that ends up getting passed on," says Sandra Harden Austin, executive vice president of the University of Chicago hospital. J. Ian Morrison, president of the Institute for the Future, a private research group in Menlo Park, Calif., that has researched medical economics, contends: "There's no evidence (utilization review) saves money." 〉

_____. Utilization review wastes millions.
NAATP REVIEW, Fall 1992, p. 12.

〈 In 1990, the inspector general of the U.S. Health and Human Services Department looked at review companies' scrutiny of 500,000 cataract operations paid for by Medicare. The Conclusion: THe U.S. paid $13.3 million to utilization reviewers to save $1.4 million in possibly unnecessary surgery. 〉

_____. Utilization review ↑ administrative costs.
NAATP REVIEW, Fall 1992, p. 12.

〈 Employers who hire utilization review firms don't always see past the initial savings. Their expenses appear to go down by more than the fee charged by the utilization review company as it cuts services. But the costs eventually come back in the form of higher service fees charged by hospitals and doctors required to offset their own increased expenses in dealing with the increased paper work, health economists say. 〉

Negative   Solvency 2/3
Managed Competition

_____. Utilization review ↓ access to treatment.
BUSINESS WEEK, February 18, 1991, p. 64.

> ⟨These days, such dramas are being played out in real life. Physicians are reeling under a new assault as employers and health insurers embark on another wave of health care cost containment. In the past, controls aimed to cut prices for procedures. Now, the idea is to stop doctors before they wield the knife. Such scrutiny, called utilization review, relies on computerized data banks to spot inappropriate or unnecessary care. Reviewers try to discourage doctors from providing such treatment. Later, they may flag physicians who order too many tests, or operate too often—and steer patients away from them.⟩

_____. Utilization review = doctor backlash.

George Rimler (Prof of Management, Virginia Comm U),
COMPENSATION AND BENEFITS REVIEW, May-June 1992,
p. 48.

> ⟨Some providers feel insulted and irritated by challenges to their autonomy and by the monitoring of their clinical decision making. They believe that the influence of utilization reviewers, most of whom have less clinical training, inappropriately challenges the legitimacy of the decisions they reach. In a similar vein, second guessing of provider decisions reduces the confidence patients have in the abilities of their providers. ⟩

Negative   Disadvantage 1/2
                    Medical Industrial Complex

A. U.S. Pharmaceutical Industry Strong.

Sen. Hatch, CONGRESSIONAL RECORD, February 27, 1992,
p.S3205.

> ⟨ Some will see the drug industry's relative strength and take it as fair game for increased taxation to help finance the problems of our ailing health care system. Others will take a different view and conclude that this is an area where America is the recognized world leader. ⟩
> We do not say that as often as we once did, or should say again in the future. And we should make no policies detrimental to this sector's health. Instead we should find ways to promote and build upon our leadership in the pharmaceutical industry as we enter the biological revolution of the 21st century.

B. Price Controls Reduce Medical Research.

Sen. Bradley, CONGRESSIONAL RECORD, March 11, 1992, p.S3191.

⟨ And although it is not easy to predict the reactions in the marketplace to Government intervention, this one is simple: Price controls, as envisioned in this amendment, will significantly reduce incentives for investment; a reduction in investment reduces funds for research; reduction in research will lead to fewer innovations, fewer cures, and fewer hopes for many Americans who are counting on medical breakthroughs to lengthen their lives. ⟩

C. Impact . . . AIDS Disaster!!!

_____. A cure is coming if we don't squash medical innovation.

Roy Vagelos (Chrmn, Merck & Co), VITAL SPEECHES, December 15, 1992, p. 145.

⟨ My point is that we will conquer AIDS and other diseases, saving millions of lives, and hundreds of billions of dollars. And our victories will be won through biomedical research with weapons forged through cooperation of industry, government and our nation's research universities.

This is why—in all healthcare reform—nothing is more critical than preserving our leadership in medical research and innovation. We must never trade away the future contributions of research in order to solve the financial problems of today. ⟩

Negative   Disadvantage   2/2

MIC

_____. Each delay results in thousands of deaths
John Platt (biophysicist), FUTURIST, Nov/Dec 1987, p.17.

⟨ Let us hope and push for this last possibility. Thousands of deaths could be prevented by every single day of advance in finding a vaccine or cure. ⟩

_____. Today's rates of increase produce one billion cases by 2025

Christopher B. Daily, CONGRESSIONAL RECORD, February 18, 1993, p. S1585.

"On a global scale, Hasaltine said, HIV is spreading rapidly in the Third World and has reached more than 20 percent of the general adult population in many areas, including Central Africa, India, Thailan_, ..., _nd parts of South America. At that rate and assuming no vaccine is forthcoming, by the year 2025 there could be one billion cases worldwide, Hasaltine said."

_____. All other concerns are secondary

John Platt (biophysicist), FUTURIST, Nov/Dec 1987, p.16.

⟨The continued spread of AIDS into the 1990s would transform the whole state of the world. It could make overpopulation, famine, environmental destruction, or the extinction of species seem like minor complaints—especially in the developing nations likely to be hit hardest.

AIDS may even transform the purposes of international politics. If the barriers do not become too high to communicate, the major powers will find a life-and-death interest in responding together to a mutual danger that laughs at the nation-state. Many of our nongovernmental organizations and networks, such as those interested in environmental protection, women's rights, and nuclear disarmament, could also shift their focus toward concern with AIDS and providing help across national boundaries.

Eventually, if it continues, AIDS will change the balance of power. Some countries will be destroyed by it, some badly hurt, and some almost unharmed. Those that suffer least will tend to dominate afterwards, as in previous epidemics.⟩

NOTE: This is an extension brief that would be used by the negative to extend the uniqueness of the MIC disadvantage.

Negative   Disadvantage 1/3
MIC
Extension on Uniqueness

Extension—U.S. Top of Medical Technology
_____. US has best medical technology in the world.

John Lee Clouse (Pres of the AMA), VITAL SPEECHES, December 15, 1992, p. 135.

⟨Good afternoon. Kon-Ichi-Wah. Thank you, Dr. Murase, for your kind introduction. This afternoon it is my task to discuss with you one of the great and tragic ironies facing world medicine today.

Let me begin with what's happening in the United States. At its best, medical care in America is the finest the world's ever known. Our great centers of medical education draw people from every land. Our scientific research produces incredible breakthroughs. Our ability to provide high quality, high impact, high technology care sets a standard that the rest of the world can only dream about.⟩ */35*

_____. US leads in biotech and genetic engineering.

Sen. Hatch, CONGRESSIONAL RECORD, Feb 27, 1992, p.S3578.

"The United States leads the world in biotechnology and genetic engineering patents. We lead the world and the reason we do is because we have the incentives in this country."

Negative   Disadvantage   2/3
MIC
Extension on Uniqueness
_____. U.S. leads in medical science advances.

Roger Butler (MD), TECHNOLOGY, BUREAUCRACY, AND HEALING IN AMERICA, 1988, p. 23.

⟨ If ours is the best health care in the world, then we should be proud of it— and we can be proud of our medical science and of the enormous advances our investment in health has brought to us and the world. We are preeminent still in this field in all the world and we shall undoubtedly lose some of that if we construct an environment in which the brightest young people increasingly elect other fields. We should remember too that our large investment in health, even if in ineffective practices, provides jobs in a service industry and a market for production industries, the income from which flows primarily into the American economy. ⟩

_____. Public perceives US has best medical care.

Roger Butler (MD), TECHNOLOGY, BUREAUCRACY, AND HEALING IN AMERICA, 1988, p. 23.

⟨ It is equally true, however, that most Americans who have experienced both systems would opt for ours. American reactions to our problems are in general that we must improve, that we have lost ground on cost control and access and equity issues, but that we still have the best medical care available in the world. ⟩

_____. US leads in use and development of medical technology.

Joseph Bast (Pres, Heartland Inst), WHY WE SPEND TOO MUCH ON HEALTH CARE, 1993, p. 146.

⟨ The U.S. leads the rest of the world in the development and use of medical technology. The US discovers new technologies, brings them to market, puts them to use across the country, and exports them to the rest of the world. Backed by government, private industry, and charitable gifts, the U.S. budget for health research and development dwarfs that of other nations. ⟩ /45

Negative   Disadvantage   3/3

MIC

Extensions on Uniqueness

_____. US has world technical superiority.
Sen Daschle, CONGRESSIONAL RECORD, Oct 5, 1992,
p.S17098.

> If the question about "the best" is posed in terms of "where is the cutting
> edge?" the answer is usually the United States. As Professor Fuchs point
> out, this is the country in which the most advanced technologies are found
> in the greatest abundance. It is here that ambitious young physicians most
> frequently come for advanced training and where the super-rich from Third
> world countries come when they want high-tech medical care. If technologi-
> cal superiority is the yardstick to be applied, then the assertion "we're
> number one" has some validity. > *S / 7098*

Sen. Daschle, CONGRESSIONAL RECORD, Oct 5, 1992,
p. S17098.

"Mr. President, in a recent article in the Journal of the American Medical
Association, Victor Fuchs, a Professor of Economics at Stanford University,
analyzed the assertion that 'Americans enjoy the best health care system
in the world.' Professor Fuchs uses an economist's point of view to evaluate
health care from the standpoints of its output—technology, public health,
and service—and considers each of these in terms of efficiency and distribu-
tional equity."

Victor Fuchs (Prof Eco, Stanford), quoted in CONGRESSIONAL
RECORD, October 5, 1992, p. S17099.

"One way to evaluate health care systems is to ask which country is in the
forefront of pushing out the technologic frontier. In which country do we find
the most advanced medical technologies in the greatest abundance? Where
do the world's most ambitious young physicians go for advanced training?
And where do the superrich from Third World countries go when they want
high-tech medical care? The answer to all these questions is usually the
United States. In this sense, we can accurately say that the United States
has the best health care system in the world. This country is the source of
many of the most notable technologic advances in medicine, and even
those developed abroad are usually more rapidly diffused in the United
States. New drugs are an exception; the Food and Drug Administration's
lengthy review may result in prior introduction abroad, even if drugs were
developed by US companies."

NOTE: This negative brief assumes that one of the affirmative's answers to the Medical Industrial Complex Disadvantage is "Clinton plan will decrease tech." The brief below outlines possible negative responses.

Negative   Disadvantage   1/2
MIC

Responses to Aff DA Answers
        Answers to: "Clinton Plan will Decrease Tech"
1. Plan avoids caps.

MINNEAPOLIS-ST. PAUL CITY BUSINESS, May 21, 1993
(Lexis).

⟨ The focus on physicians is high on the agenda of Hillary Rodham Clinton's health care reform efforts, now scheduled for release in mid-June. Despite fears from medical technology firms, reform is not likely to bring such things as price caps on devices or dictates about which hospitals can purchase which pieces of equipment. Instead, reformers are discussing ways to change how health care providers use medical technology. ⟩

2. Only plan is managed competition.

BUSINESS & HEALTH, May 1993, p. 44.

⟨ Spokespersons at the White House and HHS were not commenting on the disagreement. But sources close to the administration say they would be very surprised if Clinton announced a plan that was not anchored in a managed competition framework. "The president campaigned on that idea and he won on that idea. I don't think a government single payer system is a politically viable notion at this time," says Sen. Jay Rockefeller (D-W.Va). ⟩

Negative   Disadvantage   2/2
MIC

Responses to Aff DA Answers

3. Managed competition increases medical technology.

HEALTH AFFAIRS, Fall 1990, p. 63.

⟨ The point of these examples is that pharmaceutical manufacturers are being called on to reexamine their positions on a number of business practices, and many companies are moving quickly to change long-standing practices, to meet the demands of purchasers. This is a healthy sign. Over the long term, the techniques used by managed care will expand to all segments of the health care industry, placing new demands on providers and suppliers alike. The pharmaceutical firms that will survive in this environment will be large enough to sustain expensive research, diversified enough to rebound from the competition of new entrants into their product markets, flexible enough to adopt new marketing techniques in response to bottom-line decisionmakers and restrictions on product selection, and savvy enough to find opportunities in government-sponsored drug benefit programs instead of simply opposing anything that originates in Washington, D.C., or the state capitals. $>$ 63

4. Managed competition increases innovation.

Roy Vagelos (Chrmn of Merck & Co) VITAL SPEECHES, December 15, 1992, p. 146.

In terms of cost-sharing and risk-bearing: We believe that everyone should have more responsibility for the cost of their own healthcare, for making better choices in the care they receive, and for how they live their lives to prevent avoidable disease.

This seems obvious, but it's absolutely critical. The days of no-deductibles and no co-payments are gone forever, and with good reason.

They're not only unaffordable, they result in wasteful consumption of healthcare. If insurance pays the whole freight, healthcare is perceived as a free service, and there is simply no incentive to shop for value. It's like having a credit card with no requirement to ever pay the bills.

On the other hand if patients share in the cost of their healthcare, they do shop for value, and the market responds with innovation and competition. This is happening already as Managed Care is growing and competition is emerging across the country. $>$ 146

MAN. COMP = ↑ COMP q TECH

Checklist for Briefs

When developed with care, affirmative and negative briefs can be very useful tools. However, there are certain dangers to using them. The following checklist can help you avoid these dangers when writing and using debate briefs.

Debate Brief Checklist

1. Are statements precise and clear?

2. Does the evidence match the argument?

3. Is the brief flexible?

4. Is the brief current?

5. What briefs are compatible in the same debate round?

First, as with any writing, it is imperative that the statements used on debate briefs be *precise and clear*. Remember, there is not time in the debate round to rewrite the brief or to turn single word labels into clear, precise statements of an argument.

In the heat of the moment, you are most likely to read exactly what is on the printed page. If arguments in your brief are written out as a speech, they will be too difficult to adapt in the round. On the other hand, if arguments are indicated only by key words or phrases along with evidence, you might not explain the importance of an argument clearly enough or indicate why your source is more valuable than those presented by the other team. An argument in a debate brief must be short and concise, but it must also explain the argument clearly.

Second, it is important that briefs contain the best evidence. When pulling evidence for an argument in a brief, you need to be sure it matches the argument you are making. For example, on the disadvantage that AIDS research will be cut due to the decrease in profit margins for health providers, evidence that merely says health care providers will cut their research efforts does little to support the argument that AIDS research will be targeted specifically. Evidence that indicated that AIDS research would be the first to be cut would be of greater value.

Evidence that is slightly off-point, not credible, or out of date does little good in a brief. One weak piece of evidence weakens the credibility of your entire argument. Because the opposition will always focus on the weakest evidence in a brief, this can cause stronger pieces of evidence, which *are* right on point, to be lost in the shuffle. Generally, it is better not to make an argument at all than to spend the time developing an argument with weak evidence. And when structuring your briefs, it is always best to put your strongest quotations first. Supporting evidence should follow.

Third, one of the purposes of a debate brief is to enable you to plan your arguments ahead of time. To make this preparation work in the actual round, your briefs must be *flexible*. If a brief is long and complicated (with many sub- and sub-subpoints), you are likely to allocate your time poorly. On the other hand, a debate brief should not be so short as to leave the argument underdeveloped. In either situation the argument will end up being a loser.

When preparing a brief you should analyze the argument carefully. Exactly what steps are necessary to prove the argument? In what places should evidence be used? How much backup evidence is necessary? You should think about how the opposition will respond and try to anticipate those responses in your initial brief development. Such an analysis will also help you determine when and where extension briefs are needed.

Remember that you will not read everything on your brief in every debate round. The brief is designed to look at as many possibilities as possible. The key is planning. Unless a brief can accommodate a variety of uses, it might hinder good debating.

Next, debate briefs should always be *timely*. Revise and update your arguments

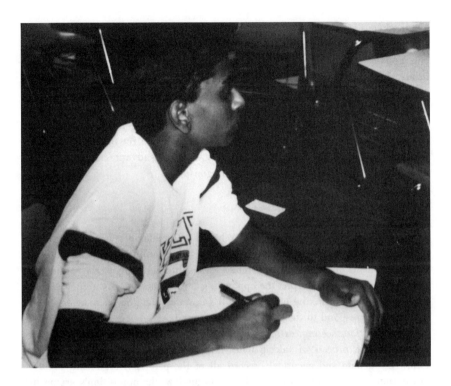

Flowing a debate quickly and accurately is an important skill for debaters.

throughout the debate season. It is a big mistake to think that once a brief has been written it can be filed and forgotten. Each debate does not happen in vacuum. You should continually look back at earlier debate rounds to see why you won or lost and to see what worked, what didn't, and why. This process should keep you revising cases and arguments.

Debaters who do not include reviewing debate briefs in their self-evaluation process are foolish. Some disadvantages presented early in the season will be turned, and they will continue to be turned if they are not reworked to try to eliminate the links that caused the turn. For many current topics, legislation will be enacted or pilot programs tried, and these will change the impact of some arguments.

Debaters should try to identify the weak links in a brief, then fix them or get rid of them. In the process, they might find a better link to that round-winning disadvantage. At the same time debaters will probably discover other arguments that need to be briefed. At the very least, though, debaters should always be looking to update the evidence being used in the debate brief.

Finally, as a team, debaters need to decide which briefs are *compatible*. It is always important that a team present a consistent position in the debate round.

You and your colleagues need to think through the implications of using various combinations of arguments, because those implications may not always be obvious. You need to be sure that briefs defending the present system do not contradict briefs that argue there are disadvantages to any measures that move toward resolving present system problems.

For example, if the first negative argues that the guarantee of comprehensive health care should be left at the state level, and uses the Oregon plan as an example of a state plan that works, it is probably not a good idea for the second negative to argue that government-run programs carry serious disadvantages and then read evidence about the shortcomings of the Oregon plan.

Flowing the Debate

The most basic tactic in refutation and rebuttal is to remember what has been said during the debate round. Surprisingly, many debaters simply don't listen carefully to the arguments of their opponents and, as a result, miss many of the subtleties of the case and often misinterpret the opponent's arguments. The first step, then, is to develop a system for taking notes that will guarantee that you hear the arguments and later can respond to them in the debate round.

Flowing, *flowsheeting,* or *taking a flow* are the terms that many debaters use to describe the process of taking notes during a debate round. The goal is to follow the debate and accurately record all of the principal arguments involved in the round. A flow also allows debaters to analyze the opposition's arguments, extend their partners' arguments, and prevent contradictions with their partners in the round.

The Large Case Flow						
1st Aff. Construc- tive	*1st Neg. Construc- tive*	*2nd Aff. Construc- tive*	*1st Neg. Rebuttal*	*1st Aff. Rebuttal*	*2nd Neg. Rebuttal*	*2nd Aff. Rebuttal*

Flowing can be done on a single sheet of paper so that you can easily see the flow of the arguments for any particular debate. When using a single sheet, the debate's plan and plan arguments flow onto the back of the sheet. Although using a single sheet of paper per debate may be economical, most debaters and judges find it is not practical and prefer to use multiple sheets of paper. The key in flowing a debate round is being able to follow what has been said and outlining where you want to go. Trying to do all of this on one page may defeat the purpose.

Typically, notes are taken on at least two large pads. Many debaters use legal-size pads, and others prefer large, spiral-bound sketch pads. The sketch pad probably is best because it provides the most space and because old flowsheets can be kept in the pad for later reference. Debaters usually choose a pad that stores easily inside the cases being used to carry their evidence. When using a legal pad or art pad, many debaters partition the pad ahead of time and allow one section for each speech in the debate.

The flow serves as a road map to show debaters and judges alike where particular arguments are going. Most speakers develop abbreviation systems that allow them to record information very quickly. Some championship debaters are so proficient at flowing that they can record the source, date, and page of each quotation used during a round. These debaters did not develop this skill by chance, however. They carefully practiced accurate flowing during many practice rounds.

The Large Plan Flow				
Aff. Plan	*2nd Neg. Constructive*	*1st Aff. Rebuttal*	*2nd Neg. Rebuttal*	*2nd Aff. Rebuttal*

The Art of Flowing

Most experienced debaters prefer to set up their own flowsheets. To do this, begin with an ample supply of paper. A good rule of thumb is that more is never too much! If you are making your own flowsheets, the process is pretty simple. The first sheet is devoted to affirmative case arguments, and divided into seven vertical columns. The first column begins with the first affirmative constructive speech, and each additional column is labeled according to speaker position. The only exception is the second negative constructive speech. These arguments are generally handled on one of two separate sheets of paper. (Some debaters prefer to divide their flowsheets into eight vertical columns to include the second negative constructive speech. When this is done, the arguments from the second affirmative constructive speech, which are then answered by the first negative rebuttalist, are indicated with an arrow drawn across the second negative constructive column.)

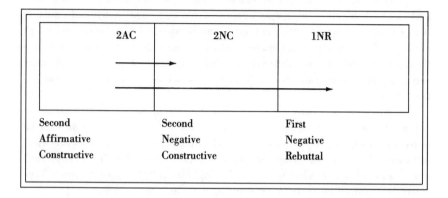

2AC	2NC	1NR
Second Affirmative Constructive	Second Negative Constructive	First Negative Rebuttal

With this exception in mind the flowsheet for all affirmative case arguments would look like the following.

Affirmative Case

1AC	1NC	2AC	1NR	1AR	2NR	2AR
First Affirmative Constructive	First Negative Constructive	Second Affirmative Constructive	First Negative Rebuttal	First Affirmative Rebuttal	Second Negative Rebuttal	Second Affirmative Rebuttal

The second sheet is for plan arguments first introduced into the debate by the negative. For beginning debaters, this is usually done in the second negative constructive speech. However, it is not uncommon for more experienced debaters to introduce plan arguments in the first negative constructive. When plan arguments are introduced in the second negative constructive speech, the flowsheet is divided into five vertical columns. In the first column is the affirmative plan. This is the reference point for the negative plan attacks, and it is not unusual for the negative to refer to planks of the plan when making the negative plan arguments.

Arguments Introduced by Second Negative

Affirmative Plan	2NC	1AR	2NR	2AR
	Second Negative Constructive	First Affirmative Rebuttal	Second Negative Rebuttal	Second Affirmative Rebuttal

The third sheet is used to handle arguments presented in the first negative speech that are *not* related to the affirmative case structure specifically. These might include topicality arguments, general observations, plan attacks, or counterplans. If the first negative presents disadvantages and a counterplan, you would want to flow these two sets of arguments on two separate flowsheets. This third sheet is divided into six columns beginning with the first negative constructive (1NC). It does not begin with the first affirmative constructive (1AC) because these arguments do not directly relate to the affirmative contentions or advantages as presented in the first speech.

Arguments Introduced by First Negative (But Not Related to Affirmative Case Structure)

1NC	2AC	1NR or 2NC	1AR	2NR	2AR
First Negative Constructive	Second Affirmative Constructive	First Negative Rebuttal or Second Negative Constructive	First Affirmative Rebuttal	Second Negative Rebuttal	Second Affirmative Rebuttal

Some debaters like to prepare their flowsheets prior to the debate. While this can be done to some extent, not all situations can be planned. However, if you use three pads with each divided as discussed above, you can prepare ahead of time. When preparing flows ahead of time, it's a good idea to prepare plenty of sheets, because you never know how many sheets will be needed in a given debate round.

Some debaters find it helpful to divide their flowsheets horizontally as well as vertically. The vertical lines are used to delineate the different speeches. The horizontal lines would be used to separate the individual arguments. Beginning debaters, in particular, may find this useful. This division makes it easier to follow an argument all the way across the flow. However, for this to work, you must remember to allow enough space on the flow between arguments. You can never leave too much space: there is nothing worse than trying to squeeze three more arguments into a space that was only meant to hold two. If you don't allow enough space, the result is arguments are not flowed next to each other, and the debater then has to use an elaborate system of lines and arrows to indicate the responses to the original argument. This makes it very difficult to decipher the road map and make extensions while speaking.

When in doubt, always allow more space. It is better to end the debate with a flowsheet that has lots of white space than with one in which the writing gets smaller and smaller and the responses more and more abbreviated in an attempt to make them fit into a small space.

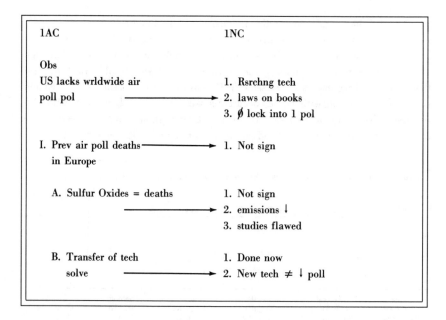

Symbols and Abbreviations

It is not possible for you to write down information word for word as quickly as another individual speaks. You need to develop a system to take down as much information as possible in a simplified way. One way of accomplishing this is to use an abbreviation system. Abbreviating words or concepts helps you record more information. Words that are used frequently can be abbreviated or indicated with the use of a symbol. For example, instead of writing out the word *dollars* or *money* each time it is used, the debater can simply use a dollar sign ($). There is no right or wrong list of abbreviations. Everyone's abbreviation system will be a little different. Systems will be modified as each season progresses. The important thing is that each you use some kind of system to flow the argument and record information quickly and accurately. Utility of the system is key. Below is a sample list of some of the more commonly used symbols and abbreviations.

Adv	advantage	>	greater than	NYT	*New York Times*
Circ	circumvention	<	less than	WSJ	*The Wall Street*
CP	counterplan	↑	increase		*Journal*
I	impact	↓	decrease	CR	*Congressional Record*
Inh	inherency	→	causes	SHrgs	Senate Hearings
PS	present system	↛	does not cause	HHrgs	House Hearings
T	topicality	=	equals	WP	*Washington Post*
EXT	extratopicality	≠	does not equal	NW	*Newsweek*
MR	minor repair	w	with	NR	*New Republic*
$	dollars, money,	w/o	without	USNW	*U.S. News & World*
	funding	bec	because		*Report*
Sig	significance	avg	average	BW	*Business Week*
XX	dropped argument			BL	*Black's Law*
???	used to indicate				*Dictionary*
	you may have				
	misflowed or do				
	not understand the				
	argument or				
	evidence				

In addition to general abbreviations and symbols that will be used year after year, you should develop a list of abbreviations specific to the topic being debated in a given season. On each topic there will be a significant number of terms that will be used quite often. Developing an abbreviation system for these specific terms will improve your ability at flowing more of the debate. For example, on the 1993–94 topic ("*Resolved*: That the federal government should guarantee comprehensive national health insurance for all United States citizens"), you might develop an abbreviation system that looks something like the following:

MIC	medical industrial complex
hc	health care
NHms	nursing homes
Mcare	medicare
Mcaid	Medicaid
pc	preventive care
sp	single player

hmlss	homeless
nhi	national health insurance
pp	play or pay
hmo	health maintenance organization
imm	immunizations
hsp	hospital

The list of specific abbreviations developed for the debate topic will grow as the season progresses and you note terms that are being used repeatedly. You should not begin each season by trying to develop a long list of abbreviations and then memorizing it. Such an approach usually does not work. An abbreviation is of little value if, in the middle of a speech, you look down at the flow and do not have the foggiest idea what the abbreviation means. If abbreviations are added slowly to the list and their forms are developed naturally, the system should work. If an abbreviation or symbol does not work for you, discard it, even if it made sense at one time or if other debaters are using it.

A final way of quickly taking notes during a debate is to write words without vowels. For example, "homeless" as "hmlss" or "Medicare" as "Mdcr". This system works for many debaters and with practice it becomes easy to do. Such a system can save you time in the debate round. Its value can also carry over to notetaking in the classroom. Again, the most important thing is not which system you use, but that it makes sense to *you* as the debater and helps you flow the argument quickly.

Deciding What to Flow

Each speech in the debate is structured. An outline format is used so everyone will know what is going on. You will want to flow at least this outline structure. For example, the first affirmative constructive speaker might say the following: "The first contention is the U.S. health care system is in trouble. Subpoint A. Costs for health care are skyrocketing . . . . Subpoint B. Millions of Americans have no access to health care. . . . Subpoint C. Many health care resources are misused. . . . Subpoint D. Many Americans die because of our health care policy. . . ." (*The Forensic Quarterly*, Vol. 67, No. 3, 1993, pp. 28–31). The flow of that contention would look something like this:

I. hc syst trble
    A. Csts hc ↑
    B. no access
    C. hc rsrcs misused
    D. many die

As a debater, you have to flow an argument whether or not you completely understand it. Even if its significance is not clear, the structure should be flowed. In the cross-examination period, you can go back and ask questions to clarify that which is unclear.

It is desirable to flow as much of the evidence being read as possible. This means flowing the name of the person being quoted, the publication, and the date. (For example, Smith, WSJ, 4/93.) As the debate progresses, the source may become important in terms of supporting the claim. Knowing that an argument is supported by evidence cited (such as *Time*, 93) can be of value when reading counter-evidence by a reputable individual. The date of the evidence can be very important on some topics. On the 1993–94 national health insurance debate topic, the date of the evidence could win or lose an argument. Since President Clinton's administration was proposing health care legislation at the time of the debate, knowing the date of the evidence was imperative for the debater. Reading evidence that indicated little forward movement on health care legislation could be easily taken out when more recent evidence indicated progress had been made. As you get better at flowing, you will learn to flow key phrases from the evidence. These key phrases will help you review the evidence to determine if what was read really does support the argument being claimed. It also helps to keep in perspective the impact of evidence as the debate progresses. The evidence that only claimed "adequate care for its patients" may otherwise be stretched to claim "comprehensive care" by the rebuttals.

As a debater you will want to flow as much detail as possible. For the negative team to make plan attacks and develop disadvantages specifically linked to the affirmative case, they will need to look at the specific wording of the case, plan, and supporting evidence. Using the same reasoning, the disadvantages (the harmful effects) should be flowed in detail. The negative will be claiming that the links or impacts of the disadvantage are independent, and that such impacts indicate that the affirmative case should be rejected. The links in the disadvantage are the triggers or causes of the disadvantage. When the negative argues that the links are independent, it is claiming that each link by itself could cause the disadvantage. If the links truly are independent, then the affirmative must beat all the links to beat the disadvantage. To be sure of doing this (and not missing one by accident), each link or impact needs to be flowed. If you have missed a link or impact, the negative (who is flowing each affirmative response and matching it to the appropriate link) is likely to claim that particular link is the winning argument in the debate. While flowing, you need to *listen*. Does the evidence say what the opposition says it does? Does it truly support the argument? If not, note this on the flow so it can be argued in the debate. If that point is not noted on the flow, it will not be remembered in the heat of your speech.

Should you flow your colleague's speeches? Ideally, yes. However, many debaters view their colleagues' speech times as opportunities to work on their own arguments. It should be noted that to use one's colleague's speech time as preparation time may be short-sighted. While using that period of time provides an opportunity to work on arguments, it can cause some real problems. Each debater spends time in the round extending arguments. These arguments do not evolve in isolation. It is difficult to extend your colleague's arguments when you have not flowed them (and really listened to how the arguments were developed and answered). Contradictions in philosophy and arguments usually result between team-members when one has not listened to what a colleague was saying. Being handed a colleague's flow to use for extensions can be disastrous. Abbreviations may not make sense to you, importance of individual arguments may be lost, notations on evidence may not make sense, and so on. You also run the risk of looking at someone else's flow halfway through the speech and not having the slightest idea what point was actually being argued. The result is usually a speech of repeated and non-extended arguments.

Another problem that is seen frequently is the use of contradictory position by either the affirmative or negative team. For example, the first negative might decide to argue inherency (the affirmative reason for change). The first negative position is that there is no reason to adopt the affirmative plan because the present system is already solving the problem. (On the national health insurance topic, the inherency argument against an affirmative arguing for immunizations would be that the system requires immunizations upon entering the school system, either preschool or at the kindergarten level.) Next, the second negative (who has not flowed the first negative constructive speech) runs a disadvantage on the harms that will result from solving the problem. (The negative disadvantage would be death or suffering from side effects from immunizations.) Arguing both positions in the same round is a contradiction (or inconsistency) in the negative position.

There can also be problems on the affirmative. If the first affirmative does not flow the second affirmative constructive speech, that team-member will not know what priority was given to the negative attacks. The result might be a changing of the priority of arguments by the first affirmative rebuttalist. At this point, no one would know what arguments the affirmative considers important. The result is that the judge becomes totally confused. Now it is not clear what is important and what is not. The second affirmative has outlined one set of arguments as significant and the first affirmative rebuttalist, another. This gives the second negative rebuttalist the opportunity to define the voting issues in the round. Many judges will find the second affirmative rebuttal a little late for the affirmative to sort out this confusion, however.

These problems can be avoided with planning, cooperation, and clear communication between debate partners. However, not flowing each other's speeches will leave room for error. You will always have a better idea of what is going on in the debate if you listen and flow all speeches.

To master flowing in such detail is not easy. It takes a great deal of practice. The key is to begin with the basic outline offered for each argument and add details as you gain experience. See Appendix A for an example of a flow from an actual debate.

Flowing the Cross-Examination

Far too often debaters view the cross-examination (cross-x) periods as a time to get information but not really as part of the debate. The cross-examination periods allow the debaters to ask direct questions of an opponent during specified periods between the constructive speeches. The cross-examination periods are part of the debate. They should also be flowed. Some debaters will flow important cross-x answers right on the flow where the argument will be developed and applied. Others choose to use a separate flow pad and then enter the answers on the flow where used. Which approach you use is a personal choice. Why should one flow the cross-examination? Too often, what is said in cross-examination is forgotten as soon as the next speech begins. Many judges won't vote on an issue raised in a cross-examination period unless it is then presented in a constructive or rebuttal speech. While most debates are not won or lost in the cross-examination periods, there can be some concessions or gains. For example, the affirmative can use the cross-examination period to pin the negative down to specifics on the disadvantages. The affirmative can ask about specific links to the affirmative. Evidence that does not appear to really support the impact of the disadvantage can be challenged specifically, or the negative can use the cross-examination period to show that the affirmative's actually applies to one state. You should note these answers to cross-examination questions on the flow and then use them in the upcoming speeches.

Follow-up

A flow of a debate has many uses after the actual debate round. Once a debate tournament is over, many debate squads will meet to discuss the tournament, the cases, and the arguments. From the flow sheets, squads can prepare a list of cases, arguments, and even extensions that should be worked on before the next tournament. From this list, research assignments can be made and preparation for the next tournament can begin. From the flows, each team can discuss the cases that were run at the tournament. Debaters can outline why the opposition seemed to have trouble. Teams can look at what negative attacks worked and what did not. Often, through discussion, they can determine why particular arguments did not work and how they can be improved. Teams can look back at the flows of their affirmative rounds to see where they had trouble. What points of the case seemed weak? What disadvantages were difficult to answer? If this information is determined, affirmative and negative briefs can be reworked and updated.

Each team or squad should keep a file of debate flowsheets. Each flowsheet should be labeled with the names of the teams debating, the tournament, and the winner of the round. When the squad receives an invitation for another tournament, they should use the file to find out if anyone on the squad had debated the schools that will be attending the tournament. Those flows should be pulled. This enables the teams to focus on specific cases and arguments when preparing for the next tournament.

While such an approach is quite useful in preparing for the next tournament, debaters should remember that other squads are likely to be doing the same thing. Other teams are likely to be changing their cases or arguments in response to their review of the flows. Reexamining the flows when preparing for the next tournament is a starting point and not an ending point.

As you become more efficient at flowing, you will be able to flow evidence citations. These citations can be very useful in aiding one in research. If you lose to a particular argument, the evidence as well as the answers to the argument should be evaluated. Using the evidence source from the flow, you can go and look up the evidence. Does the evidence in context support the argument that was made? It is possible that the source qualifications are not as valuable as they first appeared. The footnotes and the bibliography from the evidence may lead to other useful sources of evidence.

The Importance of Flowing

Unfortunately, many debaters do not pay enough attention to learning how to take a flow effectively. It is easy to spot the debaters who are not good at flowing a debate. Debaters who don't practice flowing arguments all the way through the debate repeatedly drop important issues in the constructive and rebuttal speeches. What is their problem? Often, in the heat of the moment, they forget anything that is not written down, no matter how important it is. At the other extreme are debaters who try to write down virtually every word said in the debate. The result is that they are so busy writing, they cannot critically listen to what is being said.

Teams that lose to the same arguments—or even to the same team, tournament after tournament—may have no idea which arguments they lost in a particular debate round, because they didn't keep a file of their flows. Reviewing flows from previous debates is probably the best way to determine where more work is needed. Poor flowing sometimes results in a losing team contending that "the judge didn't vote on the important issues" or "the judge didn't understand the argument" syndrome. The judge cannot be expected to understand or tell which arguments are important if the debaters don't organize and present the arguments in a proper fashion.

Summary

Debate is an activity that involves the performance of a great number of tasks. Debaters must listen to the operation, think about their own responses, pull evidence and briefs, and prepare speeches. In this chapter you have looked at how to use the evidence which has been researched to structure specific arguments for use in the debate. You have learned how essential it is to be a good listener and, at the same time, take notes in a debate round. Finally, you have considered how you can learn from previous debates, individually and as a debate squad.

Questions

1. What are the key pieces of information that need to be included on each evidence card?

2. What is the difference between an affirmative brief and the first affirmative constructive speech?

3. What are the three categories of affirmative briefs? What is the purpose of each?

4. What are the dangers you might encounter when developing and using briefs? Describe how briefs can be used effectively.

Discussion Opportunities

1. The pieces of evidence that follow are flawed. For each, identify the flaw.

"Health Care in the United States: The Overview." AMERICAN FAMILY, May/June 1991, p. 30.

> "Rep. Bill Archer (R-Texas) commented, 'We should not be lulled into simplistic alternatives for cost containment such as price controls. We know from experience that such approaches are inherently flawed and always make conditions worse.' "

Susan Hershberg Adelman (Past Pres, Michigan State Medical Society), AMERICAN MEDICAL NEWS, 1993, p. 24.

> "The most politically popular way to cut health care costs would be by cutting doctors' fees. Physicians received approximately 18% to 19% of the national health care dollar. But doctors who are self-employed have generally faced an overhead of 40%, most of it to pay salaries to ancillary personnel. It's now even higher due to new OSHA rules, the Americans with Disabilities Act, and CLIA. Under this formula, less than half of a private practice's gross receipts reaches the doctor as income. This income is further cut by taxes. Obviously doctors will not continue to work days, nights and weekends without some financial gain."

Congressional Budget Office. ECONOMIC IMPLICATIONS OF RISING HEALTH CARE COSTS, October 1992, p. 16.

> "First, the high salaries earned by physicians reflect the long hours they work and the rapid rise in the earnings of other highly skilled professionals during the last decade, . . . suggesting that at least some of the increase for physicians may be part of a general trend."

SAN DIEGO DAILY Transcript, June 4, 1993 (Lexis).

> "Also of concern to small biotech firms, Thomas said, is uncertainty in the marketplace, including waiting for new health planning from the government and waiting for the overall economy to improve."

Fumento, NATIONAL REVIEW, October 18, 1992, p. 49.

> "No matter. He did tell USA Today that, 'They came up with all the data he wanted. And he cut them down, left and right, in funding.' If that's true, it does matter. And it does matter that the man who may be our next President has concurred, saying, 'He knows that this Administration has not done anything on AIDS. We've got a good AIDS commission, a good AIDS report, good recommendations—no action.' "

Roy Schwarz, HEALTH SYSTEMS REVIEW, Jan/Feb 1992, p. 23.

⟨ It is the uniform opinion of the people who study technology that it will be a major player in the future economic growth of this country, and as economic growth goes, so will go the money we have for health care. ⟩

2. In this chapter the procedure for recording evidence has been outlined. Why is it important to record evidence that has been cited by the opposing team?

3. Why is it important to record all of a quotation on an evidence card, rather than deleting part of it with ellipses? If the evidence card is too long to read, having unecessary material in the middle of the quotation, how can you shorten it so it can be read in the debate?

4. What is the value of taking a flow in a debate round?

5. What can be gained by saving your flows and reviewing them before each tournament?

Writing Opportunities

1. Select or create a proposition that can be used for a debate. Find ten articles in the library that pertain to that proposition. Read, copy, then cut out the evidence. Record the evidence onto index cards.

2. Choose a controversial issue in your school or community. Outline the position being taken by a school or community leader or group. Prepare a brief (with evidence) for a counter position.

3. Draft a letter to the editor of a school or community newspaper in response to an editorial or opinion column published in a recent issue. Your letter should outline your position and supply supporting documentation.

4. Using an issue currently in national news, outline a position in brief form and include supporting evidence.

Critical Thinking Opportunities

1. List five types of business or professional activities in which flowsheeting would be an important skill to have. Explain why.

2. Find the answers to each of the following questions and indicate the source of your information:

   a. What percentage of students graduate from high school? Does the percentage differ between rural and urban areas?

   b. What percentage of high school graduates go on to college?

   c. What is the current rate of unemployment? the rate of inflation? the level of deficit spending?

3. Using the evidence that you have researched, divide them into categories and begin a filing system. Once this exercise is completed, it should become an ongoing exercise to prepare for future debates.

4. For the next week, use the list of symbols and abbreviations provided in the chapter (adding your own symbols and abbreviations) as you listen to class lectures, the nightly news, or a news radio broadcast.

5. What is the value of flowing the cross-examination periods in a debate? How should you use the information obtained from the cross-examination?

Debate Formats and Speaker Responsibilities

Objectives

After studying Chapter 5, you should be able
1. To explain the debate formats.
2. To outline the obligations of each speaker in a debate round.
3. To understand the use of preparation time and how the rules vary.

Key Terms

To debate effectively, you will need to know the following terms:

standard debate
constructive speech
rebuttal speech
cross-examination debate
preparation time
contentions
negative philosophy
negative block
voting issues
Lincoln-Douglas debate

Debate Types and Formats

At the high school level of debate there are two types—policy debate and Lincoln-Douglas debate. In policy debate there are two formats. The first format is standard or traditional debate and the second, cross-examination debate. Standard policy debate is used most often by beginning debaters (usually at the beginning of the season). Cross-examination debate is used for most tournaments at the high school and college levels. Lincoln-Douglas debate, often referred to as value debate, uses a two-person format centered around a value proposition. This value debate format is named after the historical debates between Abraham Lincoln and Stephen A. Douglas during the 1850s. It is far different from policy debate not only in its format, but in its style as well.

Standard Debate

The **standard debate** format was used almost exclusively until the mid-1970s. Many tournaments still offer standard debate for novice teams at the beginning of the season. This enables beginners to work on the fundamentals of debate before adding in the cross-examination periods. The standard debate format consists of two types of speeches: the constructive speech and the rebuttal speech. The **constructive speeches** are used to present each team's major points. They are usually eight minutes in length. The **rebuttal speeches** are used to refute or extend major arguments that were raised in the constructive speeches. The rebuttals are five minutes in length.

Standard debate usually involves two-person teams, although some novice tournaments involve four-person teams. When using a four-person team, two people debate on the affirmative side and the other two debate on the negative side. This allows the debaters to get used to debating one side of the topic before having to debate both affirmative and negative. In most areas where this format is used, after the first few tournaments or the first semester of competition, the four-person team is broken into two two-person teams. Each two-person team then has a chance to debate the affirmative and negative side of the topic using the standard debate format. Once novice debaters have mastered the basic skills of the constructive and rebuttal speeches, they then move on to cross-examination debate.

Cross-Examination Debate

The **cross-examination debate** format was first used in the 1930s. During the 1970s, cross-examination debate began to grow in popularity because debaters found it innovative and creative. It very quickly became the preferred academic debate format. Cross-examination debate is similar to standard debate, but with the addition of question-and-answer periods (the "cross-x") after each constructive speech. The question periods provide an opportunity for the debate teams to confront each other with regard to the issues.

Standard Debate Format

First Affirmative Constructive	8 minutes
First Negative Constructive	8 minutes
Second Affirmative Constructive	8 minutes
Second Negative Constructive	8 minutes
First Negative Rebuttal	5 minutes
First Affirmative Rebuttal	5 minutes
Second Negative Rebuttal	5 minutes
Second Affirmative Rebuttal	5 minutes

Cross-Examination Debate Format

First Affirmative Constructive	8 minutes
Negative Cross-Examination of First Affirmative Speaker	3 minutes
First Negative Constructive	8 minutes
Affirmative Cross-Examination of First Negative Speaker	3 minutes
Second Affirmative Constructive	8 minutes
Negative Cross-Examination of Second Affirmative Speaker	3 minutes
Second Negative Constructive	8 Minutes
Affirmative Cross-Examination of Second Negative Speaker	3 minutes
First Negative Rebuttal	5 minutes
First Affirmative Rebuttal	5 minutes
Second Negative Rebuttal	5 minutes
Second Affirmative Rebuttal	5 minutes

Lincoln-Douglas Debate

Lincoln-Douglas debate was first recognized by the National Forensic League as a competitive academic debate event in 1980. One of the reasons for offering Lincoln-Douglas debate was to offer an alternative to policy debate. Since 1980, over 100,000 students have competed at local, state, and national levels. Lincoln-Douglas debates today do not resemble the historical debates between Stephen A. Douglas and Abraham Lincoln. The original political debates between those two candidates entailed lengthy speeches; a match would last for hours. In Lincoln-Douglas debate format today, speeches are placed in a tight time format, as follows:

Affirmative Constructive	6 minutes
Negative Cross-Examination	3 minutes
Negative Constructive	7 minutes
Affirmative Cross-Examination	3 minutes
Affirmative Rebuttal	4 minutes
Negative Rebuttal	6 minutes
Affirmative Rebuttal	3 minutes

Preparation Time

The time that elapses between speeches is used by the debaters to prepare. It is called **preparation time** or *prep time*. There are various rules and practices for dealing with prep time. Three of the most common prep rules will be discussed here. However, you should never assume a particular rule is being used. When attending a tournament you or your coach should always check to see what policy will be followed with regard to preparation time.

With the exception of the first affirmative constructive speech, debate is an extemporaneous activity. While debaters can plan ahead (anticipating what arguments a particular team will run), it is not possible to plan exactly what arguments will be used in a particular round. To prepare for individual speeches, debaters flow the round. In the time between speeches, they jot down final notes, gather evidence and briefs, consult with their colleagues, and proceed to the front of the room to speak. Since it is unreasonable to allow unlimited time for preparation (many novice debaters would never be ready to speak), time limits have been set. The following are three examples of standard preparation rules. The first two are for policy debate and the last is for Lincoln-Douglas debate.

One- or Two-Minute Rule

The one- or two-minute prep rule applies to the individual speakers. Each speaker is allowed one or two minutes to prepare for each speech. If the speaker takes longer than the one or two minutes, the additional time is subtracted from his or her speaking time.

A coach and one of his debaters check over the tournament invitation for rules on preparation time.

Eight-Minute Rule

The most common prep rules are those that place limitations on the use of prep time by a team. Each team is given a total of eight minutes' preparation time to use as they wish. Preparation time is calculated from the time one speaker sits down until the next speaker begins speaking. The elapsed time is recorded by the timekeeper, and each team is informed as each minute of prep time elapses.

Each team is free to use the prep time as they see fit. For example, the affirmative might use two minutes before the second affirmative constructive speech, five minutes before the first affirmative rebuttal, and one minute before the second affirmative rebuttal. The negative will also determine how it wants to allocate its time. When a team has used the full eight minutes, any additional prep time is subtracted from subsequent speaking time for that team. Any unused preparation time is lost; it may not be saved for use in another round.

There are a number of variations on this rule. The five-minute and the ten-minute rules are the most common. The procedure is the same, but the total prep time for each team is shorter or longer. Which preparation rules are used are up to the tournament director.

Three-Minute Rule

In Lincoln-Douglas debate, each speaker (affirmative and negative) is allowed a total of three minutes preparation time. As with the eight-minute rule, the time is calculated from the time one speaker sits down until the next speaker begins speaking. The specific use of the three minutes is determined at the discretion of the affirmative or negative speaker. For example, the affirmative might use two minutes before the first rebuttal and then one minute before the last rebuttal. The negative, on the other hand, might find it more advantageous to use just one minute before the constructive speech and two minutes before the first negative rebuttal. When speakers have used their full three minutes, any additional prep time is subtracted from their speaking times. Since the amount of preparation time is only three minutes, it is unusual if a speaker does not use all of that time. However, should there be unused prep time, it cannot be used for another purpose.

Speaker Duties and Strategies

This section provides an overview of speakers' responsibilities to help you understand the rules of the game. Debate is a complex activity, and the strategies discussed later for the affirmative and negative will be easier to understand if you understand the basic role of each speaker.

The constructive speeches provide an opportunity for the affirmative and negative speakers to develop and critique contending positions. The rebuttal speeches are considerably shorter than the constructives and are for extending and summarizing arguments.

The affirmative always begins the debate. This is necessary so that the case to be debated can be outlined. Once the affirmative case has been presented, the negative refutes the affirmative contentions or presents plan-related arguments. The rebuttal speeches begin with the first negative and then alternate between sides. This gives the affirmative the last chance to convince the judge that a justification for change has been provided.

Apart from the first affirmative obligation to present a prima facie case and the disallowance of any new arguments in rebuttals, the speaker duties as presented here do not always occur in this precise sequence. For example, sometimes the first negative constructive might have an objection to the affirmative plan. In addition, to some extent the order of speaker responsibilities will vary by region of the country, depending on what judges prefer.

It should be noted that the duties of the negative speakers are flexible. In many parts of the country, the first negative spends a considerable amount of time attacking the plan, while the second negative presents additional plan arguments and works with the first negative to extend some of the plan arguments presented in the first constructive. Sometimes the second negative will decide to run an argument against the case. As long as the strategy is clearly defined and the judge does not object, such positioning is acceptable.

First Affirmative Constructive

The first affirmative constructive speech is all-inclusive. It includes **contentions**, or key points of the affirmative's arguments; the affirmative plan; solvency arguments; and advantages of the plan. The first affirmative constructive sets the stage for the development of arguments, a clear definition of the issues to be debated, and a greater opportunity for both teams to analyze and extend arguments.

The affirmative strategy in this speech is to present the strongest possible case for the resolution, and thus leave the affirmative in a strong offensive position. To do this, the first affirmative should:

1. State the resolution.

2. Define key terms when necessary.

3. Present the affirmative's justification for change.

4. Present the affirmative plan.

5. Show how the affirmative plan solves the need or harm.

6. Present any advantages.

7. Briefly summarize the affirmative's case.

The best order for steps 3, 4, 5, and 6 depends on the type of affirmative case being used.

Needs Case—First Affirmative Constructive

(Statement of the resolution)
I.   Harms that exist in the present system
II.   Inherency (justification for change)
III. Presentation of the plan
IV.   Solvency of the plan
V.   Summary

Comparative Advantages—First Affirmative Constructive

(Statement of the resolution)
I.   Attitudinal inherency
II.   Harm and its significance
III. Presentation of the plan
IV.   Advantages of the plan
V.   Summary

Outline For First Affirmative Constructive
Goals Case

I.   Statement of the goals of the present system
II.   Presentation of the plan
III. Present system fails to meet the goals
IV.   Affirmative plan better meets the goals
V.   Summary

Outline For First Affirmative Constructive
Net Benefits Case

I.   Statement of the resolution
II.   Presentation of the plan
III. Net benefits of present system
IV.   Net benefits of affirmative plan
V.   Net benefits of affirmative over present system
VI.   Summary

Outline For First Affirmative Constructive Alternative Justifications Case

I.   Statement of the resolution
II.   Presentation of plan 1
III. Presentation of plan 2
IV.   Presentation of plan 3
III. Net benefits of present system
V.   Presentation of advantage 1 (with inherency)
VI.   Presentation of advantage 2 (with inherency)
VII. Presentation of advantage 3 (with inherency)
VIII. Summary

First Negative Constructive

The first negative constructive speech usually focuses on responding to the affirmative case (harm, inherency, and advantages). However, the negative team also needs to decide if it agrees with the affirmative definition of terms and choice of topic area. If it does not, then the first negative provides the negative's alternative definitions and outlines the negative position on topicality. The negative must decide now what the **negative philosophy** will be—what position the negative will take against the affirmative case.

The negative strategy in the first constructive speech is to maintain the validity of the present system, to take the offensive away from the affirmative, and to expand the debate beyond the arguments presented in the first affirmative constructive speech. To this end the first negative speaker should:

1. Explain the negative philosophy or point of view in the debate.

2. Show how the negative will organize its analysis of the affirmative's arguments. (This is particularly important if the first negative is not following the affirmative case structure.)

3. Challenge the affirmative definition of terms and present an alternative (when appropriate).

4. Challenge the affirmative's topicality (when appropriate).

The affirmative takes a strong offensive position during a debate round.

5. Defend the present system by showing how the system is meeting the harms
    set out in the affirmative.

6. Summarize the arguments presented.

It is not necessary for the first negative to cover all six steps in every debate round.
For example, if the negative does not disagree with the affirmative definition of
terms, then no challenge would be made. However, if the negative does plan to
challenge the definition of terms or to make a topicality argument, it should be done
in this speech. (The only exception would be if the second affirmative speaker makes
an argument that causes the negative to decide that the definition of terms is no
longer valid or to question the affirmative's topicality.) The negative may also choose
to develop a negative disadvantage in this speech.

It is important that the negative team structure and label its arguments. If the
arguments presented are not easy to identify, they will be lost in later speeches.

First Negative Constructive

I.   Statement of negative philosophy
II. Challenge of definition of terms (if appropriate)
III. Topicality arguments (if appropriate)
IV. Refutation of affirmative points
    A. Statement of the affirmative point
    B. Statement of negative position
    C. Evidence supporting negative position
    D. Explanation of impact
V.   Summary

Second Affirmative Constructive

There are three things that need to be accomplished in the second affirmative constructive speech:

1. Reestablish the affirmative position and analysis in the debate.

2. Refute the major arguments presented by the first negative speaker.

3. Extend affirmative arguments and present any additional advantages to the affirmative case.

The second affirmative constructive speaker must be ready to extend and answer typical arguments against the affirmative case. In many cases the second affirmative speaker will have prepared for many of the negative's arguments prior to the debate. Any challenges to the affirmative's definition of terms or topicality should be taken seriously and should be answered carefully.

The key strategy for the second affirmative speaker is to uphold the affirmative's burden of proof; to remain on the offensive; and to narrow the range of arguments where possible. To accomplish this the second affirmative should:

1. Give a brief introduction reestablishing the affirmative position.

2. Defend the definition of terms (if necessary).

3. Defend topicality (if necessary).

4. Rebuild the affirmative justification for change.

5. Further establish with evidence the affirmative harm and its significance.

6. Demonstrate that the harm is caused by the present system or that the advantages are unique to the affirmative plan.

7. Present any additional advantages, time permitting.

8. Reestablish those affirmative arguments that have not been attached up to this point.

9. Summarize the arguments presented.

Should the first negative constructive speaker raise arguments against the affirmative plan, these too should be refuted. Where possible, the second affirmative should draw negative arguments back into the affirmative structure. This will help to reinforce the affirmative's offensive stance. The second affirmative may also present additional advantages stemming from the affirmative plan.

A word of caution, however: additional advantages should not be presented at the expense of rebuilding the affirmative case as presented. Winning an additional advantage doesn't do the affirmative much good if they lose inherency or give up more significant advantages because of an inadequate response in the second affirmative constructive speech.

Second Affirmative Constructive

I.   Introduction that shows the relationship between the affirmative case and the negative philosophy

II.   Defense of the definition of terms or topicality (if necessary)

III. Reestablishment of the affirmative inherency, showing how the negative arguments defending the present system are inadequate

IV.   Reinforcement of the affirmative harm and its significance

V.   Presentation of additional advantages (time permitting)

VI.   Emphasis of those affirmative positions dropped by the negative

VII. Summary

Second Negative Constructive

The second negative constructive speech usually deals with the affirmative plan. But this is not to say that the second negative cannot present a new argument on case should the need arise. It is possible that the second affirmative speaker will make an argument that will trigger a new line of argument for the negative. Since no new arguments can be presented in the rebuttals, the second negative constructive speaker would have to present any new case arguments. In addition, the second negative may need to present new arguments on the definition of terms or on topicality; in this case, care should be taken to explain why these issues have just now become relevant to the negative. However, the primary focus on the second negative constructive speech is to deal with three issues concerning the affirmative plan: 1) plan workability; 2) plan solvency; and 3) plan disadvantages.

The negative strategy for this speech is to outline arguments against the plan workability and solvency and to establish the disadvantages to adopting the affirmative plan. The negative wants to develop disadvantages that would outweigh any advantages gained by the affirmative. To accomplish this, the second negative should:

1. Outline what the speaker intends to do in this speech. This is important, since the structure of plan arguments departs from the affirmative case structure. It is also important for everyone to know if the second negative plans to present any new case arguments.

2. Show why the affirmative's plan is unworkable.

3. Show why the affirmative's plan will not solve the harms as outlined in the affirmative case.

4. Develop the disadvantages of the affirmative's plan.

5. Summarize the arguments presented.

The second negative constructive speech is the first speech of what is called the **negative block**. The first negative rebuttal, which follows immediately after the second negative constructive speech, is the other half of the negative block. This long block of speaking time provides the negative with a chance to drive home negative arguments, and team members should work together to decide how this time will be used. For example, the first negative may need for the second negative to extend some of the first negative arguments, thus enabling the first negative to cover the remaining first negative arguments. Or the first negative may want a new case argument introduced in the second negative constructive speech so that it can be extended further in the first negative rebuttal (or perhaps linked to another negative argument).

Solvency and workability arguments that arise in the second negative constructive may or may not be supported with evidence. Where possible, it is preferable to support all arguments with evidence; however, sometimes solvency and workability arguments are arguments of logic.

Disadvantages, though, must be proven with evidence. They should be developed with as much care as goes into developing the affirmative case. Successful disadvantages always demonstrate the link between the affirmative plan and the disadvantage, pointing out how the plan actually causes the disadvantage.

Second Negative Constructive

I.   Outline of structure of the speech
II.   New case arguments (if any)
III. Workability and solvency arguments
IV.   Disadvantages
V.   Summary

First Negative Rebuttal

The first negative rebuttal is the first of the rebuttal speeches. The rebuttal follows the second negative constructive speech (after the cross-examination of the second negative speaker in the cross-examination debate format). The second negative constructive speech and the first negative rebuttal comprise what is known as the negative block. The negative block is thirteen minutes of uninterrupted negative argumentation. When planned carefully, this block of time can have a significant impact on the affirmative case.

The primary duty of the first negative rebuttalist is to refute, extend, and develop the case arguments. If the first negative introduced any plan arguments, those would also be developed and extended. It is not possible for the first negative rebuttalist to cover every argument that was presented in the first constructive and to deal with any new advantages that were presented by the second affirmative constructive. Thus, it will be necessary for the first negative to make choices, by objectively identifying the winning arguments for the negative and the new arguments presented by the second affirmative constructive speaker. It is especially important to cover the new arguments now, since many judges will consider the second negative rebuttal too late for a first response to second affirmative constructive arguments.

The strategy for this rebuttal is to extend the negative case attacks (and plan attacks where appropriate) and to reinforce the negative position in the debate. To accomplish this, the first negative should:

1. Extend the position on the definition of terms, if necessary, and explain why the affirmative definitions still are not acceptable. (If the affirmative has adequately defended its definition of terms, this argument should be dropped.)

2. Extend the negative position on topicality, if necessary, and refute any second affirmative constructive arguments relating to topicality. (If the second affirmative constructive speaker answered the topicality challenges to the negative's satisfaction, the topicality argument should be dropped.)

3. Return to the arguments on case in the first negative constructive, refuting the affirmative's objections. Only the most important points should be developed and extended. Explain why these are the most important arguments in the debate.

4. Summarize the arguments presented.

For a strong finish, the first negative rebuttalist needs to relate the negative's position on case to the plan objections that were just presented by the second negative constructive speaker. The negative position at this junction is to say that there is no justification for change—but if there *were*, the disadvantages developed by the negative outweigh any advantages of the affirmative proposal. To end with the negative position on the debate shows the negative as a complete unit and in a very strong position.

First Affirmative Rebuttal

The first affirmative rebuttal is viewed by many as the most difficult speech in the debate. It is the only speech in which the speaker must respond to the arguments just presented by two speakers. The thirteen-minute block of negative argumentation must be answered by the first affirmative in just five minutes. Even for the best of debaters this is a significant task.

There are ways to make this task easier. First, the affirmative team must make good use of the affirmative cross-examination of the second negative constructive speaker. The affirmative should use this time to go through the negative disadvantages that were presented and ask questions regarding the link and impact of each. This will help to identify the weak points, and the responses can be used in the first affirmative rebuttal.

The first affirmative rebuttalist will also need good organization and a concise use of language. The first affirmative rebuttalist will need to know exactly which arguments on case need to be covered, the order in which they will be covered, and will need to provide concise labels for arguments on case and plan. The first affirmative rebuttalist must answer all new arguments that were presented by the second negative constructive speaker. Leaving any of these to the second affirmative rebuttal is not likely to go over well with the judge, since this would not give the negative an opportunity to respond.

The place to begin the rebuttal is with the arguments presented by the second negative; most often these will be plan arguments. The largest portion of the rebuttal (approximately three minutes) will be spent on these arguments, since they are new arguments presented by the negative and have never been responded to by the affirmative. The next one-and-a-half minutes or so should be spent responding to the arguments extended by the first negative rebuttalist. The last thirty seconds should be devoted to drawing through any arguments that the affirmative feels are crucial but were not covered by the negative in the negative block.

It is not possible for the first affirmative rebuttalist to cover every argument that has been presented in the debate thus far. As with the first negative rebuttal, choices will need to be made. The first affirmative should make those choices and make it clear to the judge that the arguments being extended are the most important arguments in the round.

The strategy for the first affirmative rebuttal is to ensure the affirmative has met the burden of proof; reinforced the workability of the affirmative plan; and narrowed the debate, both on case and plan. To accomplish this, the first affirmative rebuttalist should take the following three steps:

1. Refute the negative plan objections. Arguments should be labeled clearly and answers to the cross-examination questions should be pulled through where appropriate. On disadvantages, the focus should be on the links and impacts, and any weaknesses pointed out in the cross-examination period should be applied. Where possible, the negative disadvantages should be turned and claimed as additional affirmative advantages.

2. Return to the affirmative case and rebuild it. Narrow the debate by focusing on the key issues of the case: explain why these are the key issues and how the affirmative carries them.

3. Summarize the arguments presented.

The first affirmative must accomplish a great deal in this short speech. A great many issues must be covered but with enough thoroughness to have an impact on the debate. Just repeating labels and saying there has been no impact will do nothing for the affirmative. Instead, the affirmative must show why the argument goes to the affirmative.

The first affirmative rebuttalist will need to decide in each round how the time should be allocated. This decision should be made consciously before the start of the rebuttal and then the speaker should pace him- or herself during the speech. All too often first affirmatives get wrapped up in the plan attacks and finally return to case with only thirty seconds left. Although the disadvantages will have been beaten, there will be no justification for change in place. And without an affirmative justification for change, presumption rests with the negative—and the judge will vote negative.

Second Negative Rebuttal

The second negative rebuttal is the negative's last chance to speak in the debate. The second negative rebuttalist faces the same challenge as the other rebuttalists: not every argument can be extended in the time allowed. For this reason, the second negative rebuttalist should work with the first negative to choose carefully which arguments to extend.

This involves deciding what the **voting issues** are. Voting issues are not necessarily the winning negative issues, but the issues in debate that are crucial to determining whether the affirmative or negative wins. Because the affirmative and negative may not agree on what the voting issues are, the second negative will need to explain why the chosen issues should be identified as the voting issues. At the end of the second negative rebuttal, the negative wants the judge to view the arguments presented in this speech as the most important arguments in the round. They want the judge to view the other arguments as unnecessary.

As with the first affirmative rebuttal, the second negative rebuttalist needs to be careful in allocating the speaking time. It is recommended that the second negative spend the first two minutes on case arguments and the remaining three minutes on plan arguments. Because plan arguments are still the newest arguments in the debate, they will take the most time to cover and extend.

The key strategy for the second negative rebuttalist is to identify the case arguments the negative views as voting issues and to demonstrate that the winning disadvantages outweigh the affirmative advantages or the solvency of the affirmative harm. To accomplish this, the second negative rebuttalist should:

1. Outline which arguments the speech will be covering.

2. Deal with any topicality and definition of terms challenges (if still applicable).

3. Identify the voting issues on case and extend them.

4. Identify the voting issues on plan. It is not necessary to extend every workability, solvency, and disadvantage argument. The negative should choose the ones that they are winning (and that hopefully do the most damage to the affirmative case) and extend those; the rest can be dropped. The exception to this is that the negative does not want to drop a disadvantage that has been turned by the affirmative (claimed as an affirmative advantage instead of a negative disadvantage). These advantages must be responded to so that the affirmative cannot claim another advantage.

5. Summarize the negative position.

The second negative rebuttal is the last time the negative will speak in the debate. To make the best possible presentation in this speech, the first and second negative need to communicate with each other. Each speaker should identify which of his or her arguments are winners and should be extended. The first negative should also make sure the second negative knows why the argument is a voting issue and how it should be extended. To merely repeat the first negative arguments in the last rebuttal will do little good—they must be extended.

It is up to the second negative rebuttalist as to what order the arguments are presented. However, experience has shown that each debater will tend to always have enough time to cover his or her own arguments. With this in mind, it is recommended that the first negative arguments be presented first (about one-and-a-half minutes) and then the second negative arguments.

Some debaters like to organize the rebuttal by importance of arguments. This is fine as long as the grouping is by case arguments and plan arguments—everyone will get lost if the speaker jumps back and forth between case and plan. When there are a significant number of arguments in a round, this may be a good strategy. By beginning with the most important arguments, there is less danger of dropping the key argument in the debate should the time run out. Negatives can win the debate round by winning any one of the important voting issues.

Second Affirmative Rebuttal

The second affirmative rebuttal is the last speech in the debate. It is the final word on all arguments in the round. The second affirmative rebuttalist will need to decide how to present the affirmative's last word on the justification for change. As in any other rebuttal, the second affirmative cannot present new arguments or lines of reasoning in the rebuttal. The rebuttal must be a development and extension of those arguments that were presented in the constructive speeches.

The key strategy for the second affirmative rebuttal is to put the debate in perspective and to continue to advance the affirmative's basic strategies. To accomplish this, the second affirmative rebuttalist should:

1. Explain the order of arguments that will be covered.

2. Extend the answers to plan objections that were extended by the second negative rebuttalist. Point out any disadvantages that were dropped or that were turned (advantages for the affirmative).

3. Identify the central case arguments and show how they justify a reason for change. If these arguments are different from those identified by the negative, explain why these are the key voting issues.

4. Summarize the affirmative position.

The second affirmative rebuttal is unique. It is the only opportunity for someone to crystallize the entire debate for the judge. It is an opportunity to clarify arguments that have become muddled or confused. The second affirmative rebuttalist needs to explain what the central arguments mean in terms of the entire debate, for example, why the affirmative advantages or solvency of the affirmative harm outweigh the disadvantages the negative is winning. If some of the disadvantages have been turned, the second affirmative should explain why these disadvantages are really advantages for the affirmative (additional reasons to vote affirmative). Most importantly, the second affirmative rebuttalist should not misrepresent what has or has not been said in the round.

Summary

You should now be able to identify the elements of an academic debate, the duties of the speakers, and the obligations and opportunities of the affirmative and negative. You also should be able to identify ways to prepare for a debate and understand what must be done during a debate. With the basic rules of the game explained, you should now be able to see how the strategies discussed in later chapters are used by each of the speakers.

Questions

1. What is the basic difference between policy and Lincoln-Douglas debate?

2. Considering policy debate, what are the differences between the formats of standard and cross-examination debate?

3. Why is it necessary to have preparation rules in debate?

4. In cross-examination debate, under what circumstances would the second constructive speaker introduce a challenge to the definition of terms or to a topicality argument?

5. In the last two speeches of the debate, how should each speaker divide the time between case and plan issues?

6. What does the term *voting issues* mean?

Discussion Opportunities

1. What do you think are the advantages of cross-examination debate over standard debate?

2. How does the focus of the constructive speeches differ from that of the rebuttal speeches? Why do you think constructive speeches are longer than rebuttal speeches?

3. Is it desirable for the second affirmative constructive speaker to introduce additional advantages into the debate? Why or why not? If additional advantages are presented, where in the speech should they be placed?

4. What are the advantages of the negative block? How can the negative team structure its arguments to use the block effectively?

5. In the rebuttals, why is it important for each team to identify the voting issues in the debate? What should be done if the two teams are identifying different issues as voting issues?

Writing Opportunities

1. Attend (or watch on cable) a city council, school board, or student council meeting. Flow issues or arguments presented in one or two individual speeches. Write out a list of questions you would like to ask in a cross-examination period.

2. Using your flow from Chapter 4, write out a set of cross-examination questions you would ask the second negative constructive speaker in an effort to find the weak points in the attacks. Pay careful attention to how you label the arguments within the questions.

3. Listen to an academic debate that has been taped, or attend a debate in person—at a tournament or at your school. Outline the strategies being used by the negative team. Did they seem to work? What adjustments would you have made?

Critical Thinking Opportunities

1. Why do you think the speakers are not allowed to present new arguments or lines of reasoning in the rebuttals?

2. Using your flow from Chapter 4, look at the negative block and outline how you would structure the first affirmative rebuttal. What are the key issues? How would you divide your time in the first affirmative rebuttal speech?

3. How can the first affirmative rebuttalist narrow the debate?

4. What is to be gained by keeping each speech in the debate organized?

5. Identify the strategies for each of the constructive speeches. How do these strategies change in the rebuttals?

The Affirmative Constructive

Objectives

After studying Chapter 6, you should be able
1. To explain how the affirmative decides which case area to offer in a debate.
2. To explain the process for defining the terms in the resolution.
3. To define the terms of the resolution.
4. To discuss the stock issues.

Key Terms

To effectively debate the affirmative, you will need to know the following terms:

definition by authority
operational definition
definition by example
should-would argument
structural inherency
fiat
attitudinal inherency
presumption
burden of proof
prima facie case
stock issues
topicality
harm
significance
solvency

In each debate the affirmative argues in favor of the resolution. The resolution identifies an area of public policy that has problems. As with any public policy, there are programs that are working, others that need modification or to be eliminated, and areas of need that are not being addressed. Because the affirmative is the advocate for the resolution, it is the affirmative's responsibility to identify the specific needs that are not being addressed or need modification and to outline ways to address those needs.

The affirmative case outlines the position to be developed by the affirmative throughout the debate. It includes a justification(s) for change, a plan, and the advantages (or solvency) of the plan. Because debate resolutions are written to include a wide variety of interpretations, the affirmative may choose to investigate and discuss any area of the resolution.

It is not unusual for novice debaters to prefer debating the affirmative position over the negative position. This is because on the affirmative, they begin the round knowing which area of the resolution will be debated and they also begin with one prepared speech. On the negative, they can only second-guess what cases other affirmative teams might run. Many novice debaters are scared to death of being caught with nothing to say!

The sense of security about the affirmative soon vanishes as debaters learn the responsibilities and obligations of the affirmative. In this chapter, you will examine the responsibilities facing the affirmative. First, you will look at the definition of terms, which sets the parameters for the debate. Second, you will examine presumption and the burden of proof as it applies to the affirmative. Finally, you will walk through the stock issues.

Definition of Terms

The playing field in any debate is determined by the affirmative's definition of terms and analysis of the resolution. The affirmative can choose any area of the resolution to debate, as long as it clearly maintains the spirit of the proposition. But how does the affirmative decide which area to debate and what case to offer?

The affirmative team starts by defining the terms in the resolution. This process begins by identifying the key terms in the resolution and exploring their various meanings in a number of sources. One of the first sources to consult are standard dictionaries, such as the following:

Webster's Third New International Dictionary

Funk & Wagnall's College Dictionary

The Oxford English Dictionary

The American Heritage Dictionary of the English Language

Chambers Twentieth Century Dictionary

Random House College Dictionary
The Scribner Bantam English Dictionary
The Living Webster Encyclopedic Dictionary of the English Language

After consulting standard dictionaries, you should also consult some more specialized dictionaries, such as the following:

Black's Law Dictionary
Penguin Dictionary of Economics
A Dictionary of Politics
Dictionary of Economics and Business
Dictionary of Political Science
Dictionary of Development Banking
Systematic Glossary of Selected Economic and Social Terms

These lists just scratch the surface of sources that can be used when you are trying to define terms. Depending on the resolution, there will be various specialized dictionaries and resource materials that you will want to use.

It is a good idea to always consult more than one source for each key term in the resolution. Not only does this give you a better idea of possible affirmative cases, but it will also help you anticipate which cases might be used by the opposition. In past years coaches and debaters alike have seen resolutions made almost meaningless by the unexpected definition of what appeared to be a harmless term.

A couple of past resolutions can illustrate this. For the resolution

"Resolved: That the federal government should establish minimum educational standards for elementary and secondary schools in the United States,"

one team defined *for* as "for the benefit of." This definition opened up the topic to include cases that *helped* elementary and secondary schools in any way. This meant that the affirmative could advance a case setting standards either for preschools or for education departments at the university level, since both could be said to have a beneficial effect on elementary and secondary schools. (Setting standards for preschools would affect the ability of the child entering kindergarten, thereby benefitting the elementary school system; setting standards for university education departments would upgrade the quality of teachers and thus benefit both elementary and secondary schools.)

Another example relates to the resolution

"Resolved: That the United States government should reduce worldwide pollution through its trade and/or aid policies."

Defining Terms

1. A definition should not be too broad.
2. A definition should not be too narrow.
3. A definition should apply only to that which is being defined.
4. When defining, only essential characteristics should be included.
5. Definitions should not be circular.
6. Definitions should be literal.
7. Definitions should not be vague, obscure, or ambiguous.

The term *aid* was defined as "to provide assistance." While the phrase "trade and/or aid policies" was intended to refer to foreign trade and assistance, the adjective *foreign* did not appear in the resolution. Thus, at least one affirmative team, using standard definitions from many common dictionaries, argued that a case that provided "aid" to utility companies in the United States with the intent to reduce pollution worldwide would be topical.

A third example relates to the resolution

"Resolved: That the federal government should guarantee comprehensive national health insurance to all United States citizens."

At first glance, the resolution would seem to require the affirmative to present a plan providing health insurance that covered all illnesses and medical procedures. However, an examination of the key term definitions would provide the affirmative with different options. For example, the key term *comprehensive* could be defined as follows: "covering completely or nearly completely; comprising many things, having a wide scope." Using this definition, the affirmative could limit the scope of the affirmative case to specific illnesses that are significant in scope and involve a significant number of individuals.

Using the definition above, the affirmative could also argue that they are providing "comprehensive" insurance for all citizens stricken with a particular illness. Thus, the affirmative could limit the scope of its plan to citizens with AIDS, the mentally ill, or the homeless. The affirmative would have covered a particular area comprehensively and health would be covered "more" completely than it had been before the affirmative case.

Generally, phrases or terms of the resolution are defined in one of three ways: by authority, by an operational definition, or by example.

Definition by Authority

When using **definition by authority**, debaters often go beyond standard dictionary definitions and include authorities in the field being debated. For example, when defining *aid* on the pollution topic, an affirmative might consult the *Dictionary of Development: Third World Economy, Environment, Society* or the Congressional Research Service Committee Print, *U.S. Foreign Aid in a Changing World*. Both of these sources would provide contextual definitions by authorities in the field. On the national health insurance topic, an affirmative might want to look at the *Glossary of Insurance Terms* or the *Dictionary of Insurance.*

If you use definition by authority, you should provide your definitions at the beginning of the first affirmative constructive. You need only define those terms that you consider crucial to your case—but you need to remember that the negative might offer definitions of other terms that may affect your own definitions. Always choose your definition carefully. If the affirmative is running a case that does not use the commonly accepted definition, it is strongly suggested that terms be defined to avoid any misunderstanding.

Operational Definitions

An **operational definition** is one that is implicit. Rather than defining the key terms through dictionary definitions or the testimony of experts, the affirmative presents a justification and plan that implicitly define the resolution. For example, on the comprehensive national health insurance topic, the affirmative plan would be offered as an example of what a comprehensive policy would look like.

If you use operational definitions, you will generally announce this at some point in the first affirmative constructive.

Definition by Example

Definition by example is similar to operational definitions. The affirmative relies on numerous examples to show how a term has been applied to similar policies, and then argues by analogy (comparison) that the definition is appropriate.

For example, if the phrase "environmental protection legislation" has been used to refer to land and water pollution but *not* to air pollution, then—if you are defining terms for a topic requiring environmental protection—you may legitimately leave air pollution out of your definition. You could argue that current legislation defines environmental protection as protecting the land and water from pollution, and therefore you are not obliged to consider air pollution. An affirmative proposal dealing with only land and water pollution could claim solvency and advantages with regard to environmental protection.

Definition by example can be a very powerful argument. If you choose to use it, you will need to make sure that you have researched and analyzed the relevant examples. Obviously, some negatives may challenge the topicality of a plan based on definition by example. Make sure the opposition cannot offer counterexamples that will undermine your case.

Unusual Definitions

Debaters have always been known for their creativity. No matter how carefully the topic committee words a resolution, there will be loopholes through which the affirmative might crawl. However, there is a distinction between the "unusual" case and the "squirrel" case.

The unusual case centers around an area of the topic few have thought of. For example, on the energy topic

Resolved: That the federal government should establish a comprehensive program to significantly increase the energy independence of the United States,

the MHD (magnetohydrodynamics) case would be considered unusual, because MHD, an energy alternative in the research stage, is not a recognizable term to the average person. The MHD case adhered to the intent of the resolution. That is, it provided a form of energy that would help to alleviate our dependence on other countries.

In contrast, a squirrel case involves a case idea that the affirmative tries to work into the topic. It usually involves searching for a definition that will incorporate the case idea. The energy topic provides a good example. The affirmative defines *energy* as a "source of power." This definition seems innocent enough, until the affirmative also defines *fire* as a source of power. Combining these two definitions, the affirmative then offers a case on fire prevention. Of course, such a case does not remedy the energy crisis, which was the intent of the resolution.

Another way to separate unusual definitions from a squirrel case is to test the definitions. Place the affirmative's definitions back into the resolution. Most of the time, when this is done the resolution will make no sense. The success of a squirrel case is usually short-lived. If it is successful at all, it is because the negative team panics and allows the affirmative to run the show.

In recent years debate resolutions have tended to be very broad. Without stretching their imagination, debaters have been able to think of dozens of possible cases. Usually, there are one or two key terms in the resolution that can have many definitions. In the resolutions that follow, the key terms have been underscored.

Resolved: That the federal government should implement a comprehensive program to guarantee retirement security in the United States.
Resolved: That the United States government should significantly increase space exploration.

Resolved: That the federal government should <u>significantly</u> increase <u>social services</u> to <u>homeless</u> individuals in the United States.
Resolved: That the federal government should guarantee <u>comprehensive national health insurance</u> to all United States citizens.

In an effort to limit the range of interpretations of the topic, the committee that develops topics provides "parameters of the resolution." This means that the committee provides a statement of what the committee had in mind when framing the resolution. Although this statement is not binding on debaters, it does help the negative to build a framework for a topicality argument against any off-the-wall definitions offered by the affirmative.

Should vs. *Would*

Debate resolutions almost always contain the word *should*. The focus of the debate is on whether the affirmative proposal *should* be enacted, not whether it *will* be enacted. In most debate contexts, the term *should* is used to mean "ought to, but not necessarily will." Because of the word *should* in the resolution, the affirmative only has to show that there is good reason to adopt the proposal but not that it will be adopted. Thus, the affirmative is not required to prove that Congress or the President would adopt the proposal, nor that the Supreme Court would uphold the constitutionality of the proposal.

Negative teams are often heard arguing absolute plan-meet-need arguments against the affirmative proposal. These usually focus on the claim that if the proposal were adopted it would soon be repealed, thereby negating any affirmative solvency or advantages. Such arguments are known as should-would arguments. In a **should-would argument**, the negative claims that the affirmative plan will never be adopted rather than discussing whether it should be adopted.

Consider the following example of a should-would argument on the comprehensive national health insurance topic, described by Rich Edwards in *The Forensic Quarterly*: Vol. 67, No. 1, 1993.

> The affirmative plan proposes that the United States adopt a single-payer national insurance system modeled after the program used in Canada. The negative team responds to this by reading evidence that Congress, given the current budget deficit, would never spend the amount of money necessary to fund the Canada plan; the negative evidence suggests that Congress would prefer a program which uses a managed competition approach to health care. The negative argument concludes that the affirmative plan could never be implemented; Congress would block it or repeal it. The proper affirmative response to this argument is that it is "should-would." The affirmative team is simply arguing that the government should shift its priorities to support for a single-payer system; whether this ever would happen is ir-

relevant to the debate. The affirmative team can simply make the priority shift to the Canada plan by using the power of fiat.

Although the affirmative needs to provide enough detail to show that its plan will work, the affirmative does *not* have to provide the kind of detail that would be found in an actual piece of congressional legislation. The affirmative is given the power to implement its plan. This is the power of **fiat.** However, the use of "affirmative fiat" is not the answer to all negative workability or plan-meet-need arguments. In the example of the single-payer affirmative plan, the negative would likely argue that the affirmative does not provide comprehensive national health insurance because not all citizens would have complete access to medical care. The negative would argue that cost and bureaucracy would result in the rationing of health care and might read evidence related to the Canadian plan that indicates people have been denied care because it was deemed unnecessary, or have been placed on long waiting lists to receive care or elective surgery. The negative would argue that unless all citizens receive comprehensive medical care, the affirmative does not have solvency.

In response to such an argument, the affirmative could not argue that this workability/solvency argument is should-would, since it would not be reasonable to argue that all the affirmative has to do is prove that access should be provided to all and not that all will receive access. Nor can the affirmative argue that affirmative fiat insures access, since the affirmative has proven access *should* be provided. To do either of these would be an abuse of affirmative fiat. If the affirmative chooses to fiat its proposal into existence, then it must prove the proposal will achieve the wanted results. The affirmative cannot fiat away any rationing of medical care; instead, it must show how the affirmative proposal overcomes rationing and provides access to all citizens.

The exception to all of this occurs when the affirmative utilizes **attitudinal inherency.** In such a case, the affirmative argues that present attitudes preclude the present system from adopting the affirmative plan. When arguing that attitudes are the barrier to adoption, the affirmative must also show how its proposal will overcome those attitudes. If it does not, then the negative can present a strong argument that the present system would not adopt the affirmative proposal, because the same attitudes that preclude the present system from taking this action will preclude the affirmative proposal from being adopted.

Once the affirmative has defined the terms for the debate it cannot simply take a position and argue for a change. The affirmative team has several obligations in the debate in order to assure a victory. The affirmative must overcome presumption, uphold the burden of proof, and present a prima facie case. The affirmative must also understand the stock issues which must be addressed in order to present a prima facie case. A discussion of these obligations follows.

Presumption

The present system is presumed to be adequate until and unless the affirmative fulfills its burden of proof by presenting a sufficient reason for adopting the resolution.

An affirmative debate team discusses using "affirmative fiat" as an answer to the negative's arguments.

Presumption is an initial understanding that, until proven otherwise, the present system should remain as it is and the resolution should be rejected.

In theory, if an affirmative and negative met for a debate but neither team made a speech, the judge would cast a ballot for the negative. In reality, both teams present their arguments and the judge rules that the debate is a tie (neither team presents a convincing reason to adopt or reject the resolution), the judge would still vote negative. The negative has presumption because—all things being equal—the present system should not be changed unless there is a good reason for doing so.

An example of presumption can be found in the American judicial system, in which a person is presumed innocent until proven guilty. In the judicial system, if the defense and the prosecuting attorney met before the judge and neither made an argument, the defendant would be freed: presumption would hold that the defendant is innocent until the prosecution proves otherwise. Similarly, if the arguments for both sides were equal or if the defense's arguments were enough to raise a doubt as to the defendant's guilt, presumption would hold that the defendant should be found innocent, because the prosecution has not upheld its burden of proof.

Does presumption always reside with the negative? Not always. In some situations, there is no present system policy, and the presumption resides with doing *something*, even if the proposed policy is of doubtful value. (This, of course, assumes no significant disadvantages.) In addition, if a present policy contradicts a deeply held value, then presumption arguably may reside *against* the present system.

For example, on the topic "*Resolved*: That the federal government should significantly increase social services to homeless individuals in the United States," the affirmative could argue a policy to provide Supplemental Security Income (SSI) benefits to the homeless. The affirmative could argue that the present system did not have a policy in place to provide these benefits to the homeless, while other needy Americans who were elderly, blind, and disabled could receive them. The affirmative policy put into place a program to identify homeless individuals who would otherwise be eligible for SSI benefits. The affirmative argument would be that presumption rested with the affirmative to take action since there was no policy in the present system and no disadvantages to adopting such a policy.

Since presumption need not always reside with the negative, affirmatives find there are times when it is desirable to argue for a **shift in presumption** so that it resides with the resolution. To do this, the affirmative argues that even if the debate is tied with regard to the reasons for change, it would be more prudent to implement the resolution and try a change than to continue on the same old path. The affirmative in essence argues that since there are no significant *disadvantages* to the proposal, it should be adopted and given a chance. The bottom line would be that a chance for a solution is better than staying with the present system, which has not worked. The negative, of course, is likely to contend the contrary.

In most rounds, judges will view the affirmative as having the burden of proof (needing to justify a reason for change). If this is not adequately proved, presumption will rule the day and the negative will win the debate.

Burden of Proof

In a debate, the affirmative must provide sufficient reason for adopting the proposition. This is called the **burden of proof**. The burden of proof always resides with the affirmative. (The exception would be when the negative presents disadvantages and/or a counterplan, in which case the burden of proof resides with the negative. This is discussed further in Chapters 8 and 9). The affirmative must provide sufficient reason and evidence to warrant the adoption of the resolution. Each debate begins with the premise that unless the affirmative can prove there is good reason to change, the present system should be maintained. In debate, change for change's sake is not viewed as a good thing.

In the debate round, each debater has the burden of proving any asserted argument with evidence (or, in some cases, with well thought-out reasoning). In most cases, merely asserting an argument is not considered a valid argument. However, in addition to this general burden of proof, the affirmative has a specific burden of proof relating to the affirmative case. If the affirmative does not fulfill this burden of proof, then the negative should expect to win the debate. It is not the negative's burden to prove that the resolution should be rejected, but the affirmative's burden to prove that it should be accepted.

What does it mean for the affirmative to have the burden of proof? Most debate theorists would argue that the affirmative must present an affirmative case sufficient to convince a reasonable and prudent person that the resolution merits acceptance. The affirmative must show that a change is needed in the present system (that a part of the system has failed or could be improved). The affirmative also must show that the plan is workable and will bring about the desired change. If the affirmative does not present a significant justification (or reason) for change, it does not fulfill its burden of proof, and the negative would win the debate.

The Prima Facie Case

To meet its burden of proof, the affirmative must present a case sufficient to warrant adoption, or a **prima facie case**. *Prima facie* is a term from Latin meaning "on face value" or "at first sight." Presenting a prima facie case involves more than stating a justification, describing a plan, and listing its advantages. For the affirmative case to be complete "at first sight," the affirmative also must support each of these issues with enough evidence and analysis to make a case both qualitatively and quantitatively. The affirmative case as presented in the first affirmative construction must be strong enough to stand alone until it is weakened or refuted by the negative.

A prima facie case must stem directly from the resolution and give good and sufficient reason for adopting the resolution. In the debate round, a prima facie case is the bare minimum in arguments (with support) required to support the resolution without refutation. Without a prima facie case, the affirmative team cannot win the debate: in fact, technically, if the affirmative does not establish a prima facie case, the negative does not even need to reply to the affirmative arguments, other than to point out why there is no prima facie case.

Most negative teams, however, will refute any case that appears to the average person to be prima facie. And, if the affirmative succeeds in presenting a prima facie case, then the negative has the burden of refuting it and convincing the judge not to accept the resolution. Just as the affirmative has the burden of proof with regard to the resolution, the negative has the burden of refutation with regard to the affirmative case.

Stock Issues

The affirmative has a great deal of latitude in deciding which area of the resolution to explore. However, once that decision has been made, there are issues that the affirmative case must address in order for the affirmative to present a prima facie case. These issues are commonly referred to as the **stock issues.** The stock issues that concern the affirmative include topicality, inherency, harm, and

Many judges consider stock issues the basis for evaluating a debate.

solvency. The final stock issue, disadvantages, concerns the negative. Disadvantages are problems or negative side effects that would result if the affirmative plan was put into effect.

Stock issues are the broad questions within a resolution. Debaters support each stock issue by identifying claims and providing proof for the claims. The analysis of these claims and proof form the major points of disagreement in the debate.

Many judges use the stock issues as their basis for evaluating the debate. When using the stock issues approach, a judge begins by assuming that the present system is dealing adequately with the problem area. To overcome this initial assumption, the affirmative uses the stock issues: it shows that there is a need to change the present system (harm); that the affirmative plan is the only way to achieve the best solution to the problem (inherency); that the affirmative plan (topicality) does what the resolution says it should; and that it works and solves the problem or it is desirable to make the change (solvency). If the affirmative does not prove all of these issues (or if the negative proves there are significant disadvantages to adopting the affirmative solution), then the assumption is that the present system should not be changed.

Affirmative Stock Issues

Topicality–Does the plan do what the resolution says it should?

Harm–Is there a problem in the present system that merits the attention of policymakers?

Inherency–Is there a law or attitude that prevents the present system from solving the harm?

Solvency–Will the affirmative plan solve the problem?

Topicality

Each year a new debate topic (resolution) is chosen. The resolution calls for a general course of action. For example, the 1993–94 resolution, "*Resolved*: That the federal government should guarantee comprehensive national health insurance for all United States citizens," opened up a broad area of debate within the medical care arena. It was the affirmative's responsibility to choose an area of concern and justify a change from the existing system; the negative's job was to defend the existing system. For there to be clash in any debate, there must be reasonable boundaries for what will be available for debate.

Since the affirmative sets the stage, it is vital that the affirmative's case fall within the bounds of the resolution. For example, on the comprehensive national health insurance resolution, an affirmative case arguing for limits on malpractice awards might be considered outside the bounds of the resolution. The question the negative might have addressed is, "How does controlling malpractice awards provide comprehensive national health insurance for everyone?" If the affirmative case does provide coverage for everyone, it happens only after several links have been made. The affirmative logic might have run as follows: malpractice suits increase the cost of medical care; high medical care costs drive up the price of health insurance; many people do not have health insurance because it is too costly; many companies do not provide health insurance due to cost; therefore, if the affirmative controls malpractice awards, then everyone will be able to afford health insurance. Chances are good most judges will find the links a bit far-fetched and rule that the affirmative case is not topical.

Topicality—making sure the affirmative case is within the bounds of the resolution—is the most basic of the stock issues. If the affirmative case is not topical, the affirmative cannot win the debate. However, despite its importance as a stock issue, topicality is rarely argued in a debate round with any impact. Although topicality is a key stock issue, the affirmative only needs to defend it if challenged by the negative.

Two terms which are often used by debaters when discussing topicality are **nontopicality** and **extratopicality**. While some debaters tend to interchange these two terms, they refer to separate issues of topicality. Nontopicality is used to refer to an affirmative case that fails to justify all terms included in the resolution. An affirmative case would be considered nontopical should it provide for health insurance but failed to provide comprehensive coverage. Extratopicality is a term used in reference to the affirmative plan and its advantages. An extratopical plank of the plan is one which does not support the resolution. For example, finance planks of the affirmative plan are extratopical. While they are necessary to the operation of the affirmative plan, the affirmative cannot claim any advantages from the particular type of financing used. Such an advantage would be labeled as an extratrapical advantage.

For example, suppose the affirmative funds national health insurance by an increased tax on cigarettes (one of the sources of funding). The result of such a tax would be decreased sales of cigarettes, leading to a decrease in the number of cigarettes smoked, which would result in a decrease in lung cancer. Such an advantage would be extratopical. The advantage comes form the funding plank of the plan and not from the implementation of national health insurance.

Harm

To justify a change from the present system, the affirmative must show that there is a problem. This problem(s) is known as the affirmative **harm.** The affirmative harm is caused by the presence or absence of one or more government policies.

Resolutions identify the general area of harm. For example, if a resolution identifies policy pertaining to health insurance, then the harm area must relate to the inadequacy of medical care coverage and the impacts of lack of coverage. If a resolution identifies policy pertaining to worldwide pollution, debaters can expect to discuss the problems of air, water, and land pollution around the world.

It is not enough for the affirmative just to identify or label the harms that are suggested by the resolution. To say "Millions of Americans are without health insurance and cannot get adequate medical care" means very little unless the effects of such a harm are spelled out. In many cases the effects of the harms are easy to document: for example, individuals who cannot get treatment for catastrophic illnesses due to the cost and a lack of health insurance are relatively easy to document. However, not all effects are so straightforward. A lack of health insurance may mean that individuals do not get yearly physical exams, with the result that illnesses and diseases that can be treated if caught early go undetected, and individuals die needlessly. Poor pollution policy may lead to unnecessary pollution by third-world countries, and that pollution may be a link to the threat of extinction. The affirmative should be sure to examine the wider aspects of the harm suggested by the resolution.

However, it is not enough for the affirmative to say there is a harm in the present system and to identify its effects. The affirmative also must show that the effects are significant enough to justify consideration. The issue is one of significance.

The **significance** of the harm can be demonstrated in one of two ways, qualitatively or quantitatively. If the affirmative chooses to document the harm *qualitatively*, it tries to show that present policy (or lack of policy) violates core values. When given a choice, most affirmatives would like to deal in the qualitative harms of death and suffering, since death and suffering hit people at their core values.

However, the affirmative may not always be able to claim a harm of death and suffering. In many cases the affirmative harm will deal with depriving individuals of their rights, liberty, the pursuit of happiness, the right to privacy, or the infringement of First Amendment freedoms. Each of these can be compelling evils and warrant change. The affirmative also might argue that basic rights extend to material freedoms—freedom from hunger, unemployment, inadequate housing, discrimination, or inadequate healthcare. To the extent that the affirmative can define core values and show that a policy (or lack of policy) violates what is important to a civilized society, it establishes the qualitative significance of a harm.

On the other hand, *quantitative* significance deals with the quantity of the harm (numbers or the body count). The affirmative looks to count the number of people that have been harmed or the amount of money that has been wasted. This is done by looking at empirical data, or statistics. For example, if the affirmative argues that children are harmed by a lack of immunizations, then the affirmative will want to link the number of deaths each year from childhood diseases to the lack of immunizations. Empirical evidence is important to establish that a harm is widespread. How many people suffer because they do not have health insurance? How many people die because they could not afford the medical treatment? How many children who have not been immunized die from measles or mumps? The affirmative may wish to introduce trend evidence to suggest that the number of individuals suffering and dying is increasing. Such evidence suggests that the problem will only get worse in the future and strengthens the affirmative's argument for change.

The ideal harm is one that is significant both qualitatively and quantitatively. For example, on the comprehensive national health insurance topic, an affirmative might choose a case area in which it can prove that a lack of health insurance costs lives. Life is the ultimate core value. Yet the affirmative case is strengthened when the affirmative can then show how many lives are lost due to a lack of health insurance. Not all harms can be proven both qualitatively and quantitatively. With each affirmative case, you will have to decide how much significance is needed to justify a change.

Inherency

The affirmative must do more than present a harm and prove that it is significant. The affirmative also must show that the present system cannot solve or minimize the harm that has been presented. That is, the affirmative must show that the problem is *inherent* within the present system. In a debate, the affirmative's inherency is often labeled as *structural inherency* or *attitudinal inherency.*

One of the easiest reasons that can be identified for **structural inherency** is a gap in the present system. From time to time, problems come up that the present system did not anticipate. Groups of people may have been left out, or a particular part of a problem left untouched. For example, the Environmental Protection Agency must designate a chemical as hazardous before the federal government can pass legislation to control its emissions or disposal. Even though scientists may know a chemical is harming the environment, nothing could be done about it due to a lack of legislation that would authorize the EPA to act.

On the other hand, structural inherency may be based on the existence of a barrier that prevents the present system from taking action. The barrier may be a law, a government policy, or a court decision. For example, federal law governing school financing requires federal dollars to be spent only for items specified in the original budget. The result can be that halfway through a school year, a school district may find its schools are running out of school supplies (paper, crayons) and money. Yet at the same time, the school district may have a surplus of funds in its building budget. By law the district cannot spend monies from the building fund to provide supplies for the classroom. Only a proposal that would change the law would alleviate the problem.

Attitudinal inherency deals with feelings as opposed to laws (or the lack of laws). When the affirmative argues attitudinal inherency, they claim that attitudes prevent action from being taken to solve a problem. The affirmative may even admit that there is a structure within the present system to solve the problem but that attitudes prevent that structure from being used to solve the problem.

Solvency

The last stock issue (for the affirmative) is solvency. **Solvency** encompasses the affirmative plan's ability to solve the harm or to bring about the advantages identified in the affirmative case.

How does the affirmative prove solvency? The affirmative presents an affirmative plan in the first affirmative constructive. Most affirmative plans are relatively simple. However, they must provide for a complete method of enacting the resolution. The plan must specify what action will be taken, what sources of funding will be provided, who will enforce the plan, and any circumstances that might prove sufficient for exemption from normal operation. The affirmative also must show that the plan will actually solve the harm(s) that has been identified.

If the affirmative has argued attitudinal inherency, the affirmative must demonstrate why the attitudes that prevent the present system from solving the problem will not stop the affirmative as well. For example, the affirmative might argue that current environmental legislation is failing because business lobbies influence conservative politicians. Unless the link between influence and enforcement can be broken, there is no reason to believe that the same problems would not exist under the new plan. If the link is not broken, the negative will argue circumvention. The circumvention argument shows how a law or policy will not work because of factors beyond the law's control. To avoid a circumvention argument, the affirmative would have to demonstrate that a new combination of punishments and rewards would significantly reduce or eliminate influence peddling. Incentives would thus bring about changes in attitudes.

Summary

The affirmative position involves a great deal of work and a number of critical choices. The affirmative team must explore the definitions of the terms of the resolution. From these definitions the affirmative begins to narrow the resolution down to a specific case area and to look at the stock issues. The development of the stock issues helps the affirmative team to build their case.

Most debaters enjoy being affirmative, for it is their chance to offer solutions to serious problems. Novices prefer the affirmative side of the resolution because they feel more secure on the affirmative. For many this is a false sense of security; only careful planning and continual research can help assure an affirmative victory.

Questions

1. What does *prima facie* mean? In order to present a prima facie case what must the affirmative do? What happens if the affirmative does not present a prima facie case?

2. In the stock issues form of debate analysis, a series of basic questions are raised about the affirmative case. What are these four basic questions? What is the fifth question that deals with the negative?

3. What is the difference between structural and attitudinal inherency?

4. What are the two types of significance and the difference between the two?

5. If the present system contains possible solutions to the problem, has the affirmative proven inherency? Why or why not?

6. What does it mean for the affirmative case to be topical?

Discussion Opportunities

1. In debate, the affirmative is said to have the "burden of proof." What does this mean? What is it that the affirmative must prove?

2. Why is it important to define the terms of the proposition before choosing a case idea and case structure?

3. Does the affirmative or negative begin the debate with presumption? Why?

4. Why must the harm be significant? What is the relationship between the affirmative harm and the negative disadvantages?

5. What are the two ways to establish inherency? Describe the differences between the two. Is one better than the other?

6. What are the drawbacks to using unusual definitions when defining terms?

Writing Opportunities

1. Identify a problem that exists in your school. What are some of the possible solutions? Why haven't any of these problems been solved? Are these reasons you cite structural or attitudinal?

2. Using the current debate resolution (or one determined by the teacher), identify the key words in the resolution. Provide a definition for each word from at least three different sources.

3. What are the three different types of definitions discussed in this chapter? Is one type preferable to another? Provide an example of each.

4. Using the harms outlined in Critical Thinking Opportunity 3 and the research from Critical Thinking Opportunity 4, write a short (three-minute) speech that develops a single harm contention.

5. Revise your speech that developed the harm contention to include inherency arguments. The speech should now be at least four minutes in length.

Critical Thinking Opportunities

1. Watch a segment of "60 Minutes," "Nightline," or a program similar in format. By academic debate standards, did the reporter meet the burden of proof when presenting the news story? Why or why not?

2. Using the current debate resolution, identify some possibly unusual definitions of key terms. Explain why such definitions would arise during a debate round.

3. On the national debate topic (or one provided by your teacher), outline the harms that might provide a justification for change.

4. Using the harms outlined in Critical Thinking Opportunity 3, begin research to document the harms and their significance. Bring the information to class.

5. Having developed a harm area with inherency in your four-minute speech, consider possible solutions to the problem. Outline a possible solution.

6. Using your outline of a possible solution, try to anticipate possible solvency arguments and outline answers to them. Now research the answers. Bring the arguments, answers, and research to class.

7. What is the purpose of using the term "should" in the debate resolution?

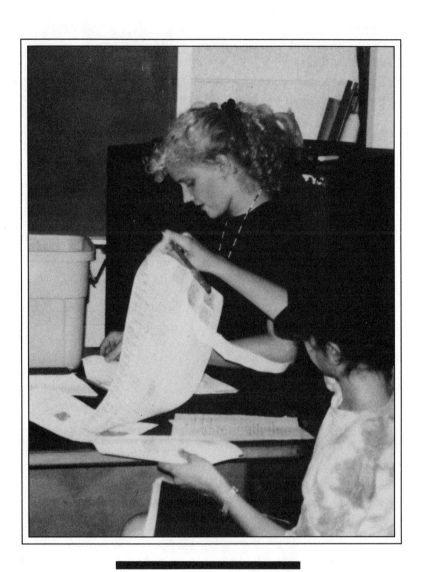

The Affirmative Case

Objectives

After studying Chapter 7, you should be able

1. To explain the essential characteristics of each type of affirmative case construction.

2. To explain how to decide which type of case construction to use.

3. To produce an affirmative case complete with evidence.

4. To construct an affirmative plan.

Key Terms

To effectively construct an affirmative case and plan, you will need to know the following terms:

traditional need case
comparative advantages
    case
goals case
net benefits case
systems analysis
alternative justifications
    case
affirmative plan
plan planks
plan spikes

The affirmative arguments for change can be structured in a variety of ways. This structuring is known as the affirmative case. This chapter examines five specific types of affirmative cases: traditional need, comparative advantages, goals, net benefits, and alternative justifications. Although these are not the only types of affirmative cases, they are the ones used most often. This chapter also discusses how to develop an affirmative plan.

At most tournaments teams debate both the affirmative and negative sides of the resolution. Since half of the rounds are on the affirmative, it makes sense for debate teams to put some time and effort into developing and structuring the affirmative case. A well thought out, researched, and organized affirmative case can deliver a high percentage of wins. If a debate team can win the majority of their affirmative rounds, then it would only take one or two wins on the negative for the team to consistently qualify for the elimination rounds.

To achieve this end, debate teams need to develop a plan of action. This plan of action should include selecting a case area, researching, choosing a case format, and finally writing the affirmative case.

Selecting a Case Area

The starting point for any affirmative team is selecting a case area. This decision is a very important one. It will determine what areas of the resolution will be explored and what the debaters will discuss half of the time. Given that both of these activities are quite time-consuming, debate teams should select a case area that interests them and that they feel they can believe in. If the case area is boring or one that is difficult to support, most debaters will find it difficult to spend the time necessary first to create a good affirmative case, and then to anticipate negative arguments and research answers.

In addition to choosing a case area of interest, debaters need to consider their level of experience. Beginning debaters might find it easier to defend an affirmative case that is right down the center of the topic such as the single payor system under the health topic. An affirmative case in the center of the topic makes it easier for novice debaters to anticipate and prepare for negative arguments.

More experienced debaters, on the other hand, might prefer a challenge. Experienced debaters may want to keep looking for an unusual approach to the resolution. This does not mean running a squirrel case (one that is likely to be challenged on topicality grounds), but it may mean exploring a case area that takes a little more research. On the other hand, experienced debaters may find it challenging to run a case that is in the center of the topic. Since the issues would be more predictable, the level of argumentation could be more complex.

A key factor in selecting an affirmative case area is time. How much time do you want to commit to researching the case area? A large, complicated case right down the center of the topic can take a great deal of time to support and maintain. Everyone can predict what will be run, and responses to negative attacks need to be consistently updated because everyone is hearing the same answers.

Selecting a case area may depend on the available library facilities. If debaters are not near a university library, it might be more practical to choose a case area that can be updated with periodicals and newspapers that are readily available. If debaters expect to continue to win on the affirmative, they must be able to update the research on the case. A case on a remote part of the topic may also be impractical if debaters are not near a university library or government depository.

Finally, debaters need to think about who will be judging the debates. Does the tournament use lay judges who are likely to know only the most basic information on any given resolution? Does the tournament use a large number of college debaters who are likely to have done research on the topic or who have worked at a summer institute? (College debaters tend to be more liberal as judges: they will often listen to unusual case areas and accept definitions on the outer edges of the resolution.) Debaters will want to select case areas that reflect the views of coaches in the area. If the coaches are more traditional in their judging philosophies, then a case towards the center of the topic is more likely to keep the judge's attention than one on the periphery. Remember it is the judge that votes affirmative or negative. It is the judge that must be convinced that the case is topical and justified.

Researching the Case Area

Once the case area has been chosen, the real research begins. Before choosing a case area, you will have done a significant amount of background reading. Based on your background reading, you should begin by analyzing the stock issues that will need to be researched. What ties this case area to the resolution? What are the harms and what is their significance? Why can't the present system solve the harms outlined? What action should be taken to solve the problem? Are there any negative side effects to solving the problem?

With these questions in mind, you can begin your research. Original research will be more helpful to your affirmative case than evidence found in a handbook or in briefs from a summer institute because it will always be more current than prepared materials. For example, most handbooks are printed in June, which means the research stopped by the middle of May. Since the first debate tournaments of the season occur in late September or early October, a great deal usually has happened in the four-month gap between when the handbooks were printed and when the tournament began.

Researching the affirmative case takes much the same process as researching the resolution. You should make lists of key words and create and update a bibliography. The most important thing is to never stop researching. The job is not finished just because the first affirmative constructive speech and the case and extension briefs have been written. To stay abreast of new developments concerning your case, you

A team reviews their debate flows to prepare for their next tournament.

must continue to research. Continued research will provide updated evidence as well as uncover new and sometimes better responses to negative arguments. Also remember to review your debate flows, determine which arguments were weak, and research and strengthen them for the next tournament.

Choosing a Case Format

Once you have selected and researched a case area, you will need to organize your arguments into a presentable form (the affirmative case). Chapter 6 discussed the requirements for the affirmative case and emphasized that the affirmative must present a prima facie case in the first affirmative constructive speech.

There are a number of ways to organize an affirmative case for presentation. Each of the following five case formats accentuates different elements of the affirmative case. You will need to look at each format and determine which will best suit your needs. Remember that no one case format is better than another or more difficult for the negative to attack. No matter which case format you choose, you still must include topicality, harm, inherency, and solvency arguments. What you want to do is pick a case format that will highlight the strengths of your particular case area.

Traditional Need Case

The **traditional need case,** as the name suggests, is a conservative case. It is built on the philosophy that there is no reason to change the status quo until it has been demonstrated that serious evils exist in the present system; the new proposal can correct the evils without generating new problems that would be worse.

For example, a debater supporting the affirmative side of the proposition "*Resolved*: That automobiles should be prohibited in Gotham City" might argue that automobiles are unattractive and that they destroy the aesthetic beauty of the city. It might be suggested that automobiles cause traffic jams that jangle the nerves of the citizens and create difficulties for the police. The negative, however, could respond to such arguments by saying that they do not meet the requirements of the traditional prima facie need case. If the beauty of the city is marred by the presence of cars, so what? Where is the serious problem? The advantages of having cars far outweigh the disadvantages. If traffic problems are caused, so what? Automobiles are so beneficial to Gotham City residents that everyone wants to drive, and some difficulties naturally follow.

It would be possible, however, to build a traditional need case on such a topic. The affirmative could argue that some change is necessary because there is a significant air pollution problem. The toxic content of the city's air is so high that the health of a large part of the citizenry is in danger. Children may die because of smog. In addition, people are leaving the city, and new businesses are not moving into Gotham City but are looking for new, clean locations. The affirmative could go on to demonstrate that the heavy automobile traffic of the city is the prime cause of the pollution problem. It could also show that, until cars are banned, the problem cannot be solved.

Having proved a need for a change, the affirmative would suggest that automobiles should be prohibited in Gotham City. It would show that banning cars would solve the problem and that many advantages would result. The health of the citizenry would no longer be in danger. People would no longer feel a need to move from the area, and new businesses could again be attracted. Finally, the affirmative might demonstrate that the disadvantages of not allowing automobiles in the city could easily be overcome by expanding the public transportation system—an added feature that would bring in more revenue, cut the accident rate, and settle the nerves of the citizens.

In the traditional need case, the affirmative begins the process of building a prima facie case by demonstrating that there is a need for a change—not, thus far, a need for the proposition but *a need for a change in the present system.* After demonstrating the need for change, the affirmative then says that it also has a *proposal* for change—

the affirmative plan—that corrects the problem and that also has several advantages. If the affirmative meets these basic arguments, it has met its burden of proof by presenting a prima facie case.

Most debaters feel that the most difficult phase in the traditional need case is establishing the need-for-a-change argument. What constitutes a need for a change? Generally, there are four elements to a sound need-for-a-change argument. The affirmative must demonstrate that:

1. The problem exists.
2. The problem is harmful.
3. The harm is significant and warrants change.
4. The problem is inherent.

Once the need for a change has been established, the affirmative must offer a solution and demonstrate the solvency and advantages of the plan.

Establishing the Need for Change

The first step in constructing a need-for-a-change argument is identifying a problem that clearly exists in the present system. This usual identification is not very difficult because of the way debate topics are framed. You will want to focus on problems in the system that currently exist but that, at the same time, could be remedied by the proposal implied in the proposition.

For example, for the resolution "*Resolved*: That the United States government should reduce worldwide pollution through its trade and/or aid policies," the problem identified by a number of teams was pollution caused by U.S. economic aid programs. These affirmative teams narrowed the area of pollution harms to toxic wastes and Alaskan oil. For the topic "*Resolved*: That the federal government should guarantee comprehensive national health insurance to all United States citizens," many debaters concentrated on a variety of health care issues, including the cost of health care, the ability of the health care system to deal with the costs of acute care, and the overutilization and underutilization of medical services.

In each of these examples, affirmative debaters researched the topic and combined their background knowledge and specific evidence to focus on a problem in the present system. Identifying the problem as a fact became the first step in justifying the first affirmative contention that a change was necessary in the present system.

As indicated, however, the need-for-a-change argument requires more than merely identifying the problem. To persuade the judge that it has presented a prima facie case, the affirmative must still establish that the problem is harmful, that it is significant enough to warrant change, and that it is inherent in the present system.

The next step is to demonstrate that the problem is compelling. In other words, the affirmative must show that the problem causes suffering, either economic or physical. Most affirmatives will try to identify a problem area that can be quantified by human death and suffering. If the harm cannot be shown quantitatively then the affirmative must look to prove the harm qualitatively.

Some topics, such as the comprehensive national health insurance topic, lends itself to both quantitative and qualitative arguments. For example, the affirmative could demonstrate that people suffer because they cannot afford health care. They could argue that each individual has a right to health care (qualitative) and that when high costs exclude some from the system (quantitative), those individuals are being denied a fundamental right.

Need-for-a-Change Argument

Topic	Problem	Harm
global pollution	export of toxic wastes	contamination of water
national health insurance	high cost of coverage and medical care	suffering and/or financial ruin

---

After establishing that there is a problem and that it is harmful either quantitatively or qualitatively, the affirmative must establish that the harm is significant and warrants change. The affirmative might argue that the exportation of toxic wastes overseas results in contaminated water. The negative could respond "So what? How many people are affected by this contaminated water?" If the affirmative can only show that a small number of people might contract cancer over the next 40 years, the negative could argue that while contaminated water is undesirable the harms are not significant enough to justify a change in the present system.

On the national health insurance topic, the affirmative would also need to be establish that the harm is significant and should be changed. If people cannot get medical care due to the high cost of insurance and the high cost of medical care, what are the harms? The affirmative might argue that people suffer needlessly or spend their way into poverty trying to get needed medical care. The affirmative would quantify the significance with studies that show the number of people suffering through illnesses because they cannot afford medical care. The affirmative would also document the number of people who are spent into poverty and then document the harms of poverty.

It is not enough for the affirmative to say there is a problem and it is harmful. The affirmative must go one step further and demonstrate that the harmful effects of the problem are so significant that they justify taking action to change the present system.

Need-for-a-Change Argument

Topic	Problem	Harm	Significance of Harm
global pollution	export of toxic wastes	contamination of water	cancer deaths
national health insurance	high cost of coverage and medical care	suffering and/or financial ruin	death from treatable diseases and poverty

---

The last element in establishing the need for a change is proving inherency. Most debate coaches feel that inherency is the key to the need argument. As discussed in Chapter 6, there are two types of inherency, structural inherency and attitudinal inherency. *Structural inherency* argues that the problem cannot be corrected until basic changes have been made in the structure of the present system. Generally, the affirmative will identify a particular law, set of regulations, or lack of legislation that stands in the way of the affirmative solution. *Attitudinal inherency* argues that the attitudes of the government or those of industry stand in the way of the present system solving the affirmative problem. For example, an affirmative might argue that profit motivation drives the prices of health care up, and that no action will be taken to control spiraling prices unless and until legislation is passed. Thus, the attitude of industry would preclude the provision of medical care to all citizens at a reasonable price.

Good affirmative teams always show that any problems they identify are inherent in the present system because of a structural or attitudinal defect in the present system. In each case, the argument is causal: there is something inherently wrong with the status quo that causes problems and prevents them from being resolved.

Need-for-a-Change Argument

Topic	Problem	Harm	Significance of Harm	Inherency
global pollution	export of toxic wastes	contamination of water	cancer deaths	EPA does govern exports
national health insurance	high cost of coverage and medical care	suffering and/or financial ruin	death from treatable diseases and poverty	profit orientation

Providing a Solution

After establishing the need for a change, the next contention in the affirmative case is a proposed solution, or plan. The plan must represent a basic change in the present system. The affirmative solution should, moreover, be inherently capable of correcting the faults, just as the present system is inherently incapable of solving the problem.

Over the years affirmative plans have changed significantly. They have moved from lengthy, detailed plans with great elaboration involving executive boards, oversight boards, enforcement boards, and financing to more modest proposals. Currently in debate, the affirmative plan is only a summary of a proposed solution, but it should be specific enough for the negative team and the judge to understand what changes the affirmative is advocating. A sample plan on the comprehensive national health insurance topic aiming to control skyrocketing medical costs might look like the following:

> *Plank One:* Mandates. Over a five-year phase-in period, the United States will implement a program of health care based on the Canadian model. All conflicting legislation will be superceded.
>
> *Plank Two:* Logistics. Enforcement and funding will be through normal means. Affirmative speeches shall serve as legislative intent.

The Forensic Quarterly, Vol. 67, No. 3, 1993, p. 33.

Once the affirmative has presented the proposed solution for change, the affirmative must also demonstrate how the plan eliminates the harms that have been presented. If the affirmative plan is modeled after a program that has been tried on a limited basis, the affirmative could prove solvency by reading evidence indicating the success of the trial program. If the affirmative is proposing a solution that has not been tried, then it will need to provide evidence indicating why experts think such a proposal will solve the identified harms.

Using the evidence, the affirmative needs to carefully explain why and how the proposal will eliminate the harmful effects of the structural or attitudinal defect in the present system. Then the affirmative should specify how the nation or the individuals involved would be helped after the problem has been corrected. This explanation brings the full affirmative case into focus for the judge. It provides the connecting material that ties the contentions into an appeal for the resolution.

Additional Advantages

It is often the case that an affirmative plan that solves an identified need will also generate additional advantages. Should the affirmative choose to present such advantages, they are presented as the last part of the traditional need case. The advantage contention gives focus to the entire affirmative argument, and it adds extra persuasive effects when the affirmative calls for the adoption of the debate resolution. Such advantages might include the economy of the proposal, its greater efficiency, and specific side advantages. When this phase of the case is finished, the affirmative team obviously has presented a prima facie case that meets the affirmative's burden of proof.

Traditional Need Case

Statement of the Resolution
  I. There is a need for change. (harm with significance)
  II. The present system will not solve the harm. (inherency)
Plan: Affirmative presents a proposal to solve.
  III. The plan will meet the need. (solvency)
  IV. The plan will result in additional advantages (optional).

Sample Traditional Need Case

Resolved: That the federal government should significantly increase social services to homeless individuals in the United States.
  I. Present system ignores the plight of runaway and homeless youths.
      A. Youth homelessness is pervasive.
      B. Present system youth programs are inadequate.
  II. Youth homelessness is harmful.
      A. Youth homelessness promotes victimization.
      B. Youth homelessness promotes the spread of AIDS.
Plan: 1. Mandates. Adopt Younger Americans Act and double funding of Runaway and Homeless Youth Act. Award grants to states and localities for long- and short-term shelters and other support services for youths. Alcohol and drug rehabilitation, health care screening and treatment, employment training and other social services provided. Testing for AIDS, counseling and treatment.
      2. Logistics. Funding by increasing the income tax rate paid by wealthy Americans; national sales tax; tax on gasoline, cigarettes and alcohol. Enforcement through existing means. Legislative intent.
  III. Expanded youth services solves.

Adapted from *The Forensic Quarterly*, Vol. 3, 1991, pp. 35–41.

Comparative Advantages Case

Up until the early 1960s, debaters used the traditional need case structure when developing affirmative cases. However, the sixties saw the birth of a new form of affirmative case— the **comparative advantages case.** This new case format turned from attempts to solve the problems of the present system to comparing new policies against those of the present system.

Although the comparative advantages case was initially greeted with resistance and hesitation, many debaters and critics argued that the comparative advantages case was more like the real world than the traditional need case. New government programs usually do not solve all of a problem, but legislators generally argue that the attempt at resolution is better than what existed before.

While the traditional need case identifies a problem that cannot be solved in the present system and *then* offers a solution, the comparative advantages case looks to compare the present system to the affirmative solution. Therefore, when developing a comparative advantages case, the affirmative begins with an observation about the nature of the present system. For example, on the resolution: *"Resolved*: That the federal government should guarantee comprehensive national health insurance to all United States citizens," the affirmative might argue that medical care should be affordable. The debate would then center around whether the present system or the affirmative proposal could best provide affordable medical care. The affirmative would argue that its proposal (say, adopting the Canada plan) would better provide affordable medical care than the present system.

Next, the affirmative outlines the proposed change (the plan). This change in structure from the traditional need case is a logical one. In order to compare the two systems, one must first know what the change is.

The plan is followed by the affirmative advantages. The affirmative must show that the advantages are significant and unique to the affirmative plan. Under the traditional need case, the affirmative has to show that there is a compelling need or reason for change; under the comparative advantages case, the affirmative must prove that the advantage is compelling or significant. The affirmative must show that the number of lives saved, money saved, or efficiency provided is significantly more than that provided by the present system.

Significance of the Advantage

The significance of an advantage is generally determined by the evidence provided. Support for significance can be of two types: quantitative and qualitative. Most of the time, debaters will provide quantitative proof to support an advantage. For example, on the topic *"Resolved*: That the federal government should establish uniform standards for testing and marketing all products with potentially carcinogenic effects on humans," teams arguing for the banning of cigarettes found it easy to provide data supporting the harms of smoking. It was also easy to provide quantitative support for an advantage of saving lives or saving money.

However, not all cases lend themselves to the use of quantitative evidence. The topic "*Resolved*: That the federal government should establish minimum educational standards for elementary and secondary schools in the United States" serves as a good example. Most cases dealing with educational standards are going to involve talking about beliefs and values. It would be difficult to provide quantitative evidence to support educational programs for the gifted. But there is *qualitative* evidence that indicates that there are advantages to be gained from such a program. Affirmatives should not fear such questions from the negative as "How many people die?" and "How much money will be lost to the economy?" The right of the individual to an education should be considered a significant advantage: in this case it is the value that is important, not a statistical entity.

After the evidence has been provided, it is still necessary to ascertain whether the advantage is significant. *Significance* is a term of comparison. The advantage must be shown to be significant when compared with what is offered by the present system (including minor repairs) and then shown to be significant as compared with the disadvantages presented by the second negative. An advantage that saves 1,000 lives but runs the risk of nuclear war would not be significant.

It is important to note that the comparison will not always be one of numbers against numbers or values against values. In many cases debaters compare the advantage of saving lives as opposed to the disadvantage of a loss of a value. The affirmative case that banned cigarette smoking serves as a good example. When the affirmative saves lives by eliminating cigarettes, it is also taking away a liberty of the individual—the right of free choice. In such a case, the affirmative must demonstrate why the advantage of saving lives *outweighs* the disadvantage of the loss of freedom of choice. The advantage is supported by quantitative evidence, while the disadvantage is supported by qualitative evidence. This kind of comparison is difficult, but one that will have to be made in many rounds. In the end the affirmative must be able to show that the advantages outweigh both what the present system can do and whatever disadvantages may result from the adoption of the affirmative proposal.

In addition, the affirmative must prove that the advantages are unique to the affirmative plan. In a traditional need case, there has to be some structural or attitudinal barrier preventing the present system from solving the affirmative problem, or inherency. In the comparative advantages case, the affirmative also must demonstrate a reason why the present system cannot do what the affirmative proposes. Most often the barrier will be an attitude. The affirmative will be required to show that the present system, even with minor repairs, is incapable of attaining the affirmative advantages.

Take, for example, the topic "*Resolved*: That the federal government should establish minimum educational standards for elementary and secondary schools in the United States." The affirmative could run a comparative advantages case on sex education. The advantage would be fewer teenage pregnancies. The negative might offer a minor repair with community-sponsored sex-education programs or information campaigns for parents. In order to win inherency (to show that the advantage is unique to the plan) in such a case, the affirmative would have to be able to show that, because of prevailing attitudes about sexual material, many teenagers would shy away from community programs and parents would continue to put off talking with their children about sex. The affirmative would thus argue that a program in the schools would better insure that the information got out and would result in a decrease in teenage pregnancy.

One important word about advantages. It is quite likely that the affirmative will claim more than one advantage. In such cases, it is a good idea to argue that each of the advantages is independent. That way, you need win only one advantage to win the debate.

In the end the affirmative advantages are compared to what the present system can do and then compared to the disadvantages presented by the negative. If there is still a significant advantage after these two comparisons, the affirmative will most likely win the debate. The following is an example of the structure of a comparative advantages case:

Comparative Advantages Case

Statement of the resolution.
Observation: Goal of the present system.
Plan: Specific proposal that will yield the following advantages while achieving
    the present system goal.

Advantage I. Specific Advantage produced by plan.
            A. Problem in the present system. (harm)
            B. Why present system cannot solve. (inherency)
            C. Solvency

Advantage II. Specific Advantage produced by plan.
            A. Problem in the present system. (harm)
            B. Why present system cannot solve. (inherency)
            C. Solvency

Adapted from *The Forensic Quarterly*, Vol. 66, No. 3, 1992, pp. 41–49.

A sample of a comparative advantages case is on page 198.

Goals Case

Another common case format is the **goals case,** illustrated on page 199, which focuses on the goals or values toward which a policy should be directed. The affirmative then demonstrates how its proposal best meets the goals. A goals case begins by

---

Sample Comparative Advantages Case

Resolved: That the United States government should reduce worldwide pollution through its trade and/or aid policies.

Observation: The U.S. lacks a worldwide air pollution policy.

Plan: 1. Mandates. U.S. enter a series of negotiations to ensure technology transfer of air pollution control devices. U.S. shall ensure transfer of technology is economically feasible. Use of advanced clean coal technologies in the U.S.

      2. Logistics. Enforcement through normal means. Funding through mix of effluent fees, gasoline tax, and general federal revenues. Affirmative speeches serve as legislative intent.

Advantage 1. Prevention of European air pollution deaths.

      A. Sulfur oxides cause death.

      B. Transfer of pollution technology solves.

Advantage 2. Adaptation to global warming.

      A. Carbon dioxide emissions assure global warming.

      B. Global warming is disastrous.

      C. Transfer of clean coal technologies averts warming disaster.

---

establishing the desirability of each goal and the inability of the present system in meeting the goal. Then the affirmative presents its proposal to meet the goal.

In essence, then, the goals case consists of two contentions. The first contention outlines the goals by which the affirmative proposal should be judged and shows how the present system cannot meet the goals. It is important to present goals that are significant and that can be readily agreed upon. To establish this contention, the affirmative must isolate an inherent barrier that prevents the present system from achieving the goals. The second contention of the goals case demonstrates how the affirmative proposal can better meet the goals. The affirmative must demonstrate how the affirmative plan will solve the problem.

For example, on the topic "*Resolved:* That the United States government should reduce worldwide pollution through its trade and/or aid policies," the affirmative might develop a goal of providing any energy source that is nonpolluting while still being affordable and technologically proved. The affirmative could argue in favor of energy sources that would help to free the environment of air pollution without financially straining industry or consumers. In the first contention the affirmative could show how current use of coal and nuclear power plants continues to increase air pollution and that technology for cleaning the air is not likely to help. In the second contention the affirmative could argue that hydrogen is a nonpolluting source of energy and could be used in power plants, homes, or automobiles, and that therefore its use would better meet the goal of clean air. This global environment topic lends itself very well to a goals case format; you will find that some topic areas are better suited to the goals case than others.

The strategic value of the goals case is found in how it enables affirmative debaters to refute negative counterproposals, minor repairs, or inherency arguments. Once it has been proved that the affirmative case meets the goals for clean air, the negative must show that its counterproposals or the present system alternatives can meet the goals equally well. This creates a problem for the negative. In the energy example, each energy source presented by the negative (whether current or alternative) must also be nonpolluting, affordable, and technically proved. The affirmative has established that coal and oil pollute the air and water; the negative must be able to overcome charges that more exotic alternatives, while they may be nonpolluting (and in some cases affordable), still are not technologically proved.

Thus, the strength of the goals case is that once the affirmative has a proposal that meets the outlined goals, the affirmative can use the goals to defeat virtually any policy that the negative presents. Even if the affirmative concedes that the negative position fulfills *some* of the goals, the fact that it does not fulfill all of them means the affirmative proposal alone is the superior alternative. A sample goals case is shown on page 200.

Goals Case

Goals: Goal of the present system or a desired goal for the present system.
Plan: Plan to meet the goal.
    I. The present system has not been able to meet the goal.
        A. Barriers which prevent the achievement of the goal (inherency)
        B. Results of not meeting the goal (harm)
    II. The affirmative plan can better meet the goal. (solvency)

Net Benefits Case

An innovative affirmative case idea is the net benefits case. The net benefits case did not evolve directly from existing debate theory, in that it is not grounded in the stock issues. To understand the net benefits case, you need to begin from a different frame of reference, one that involves systems analysis.

Sample Goals Case

Resolved: That the federal government should adopt a nationwide policy to decrease overcrowding in prisons and jails in the United States.

Goal: Laws should minimize harm to others.

Plan: 1. Legalize marijuana, heroin, and cocaine except for laws pertaining to children, restrictions in elementary/secondary schools, restrictions on public ads of drugs.

  2. Commercial drug sales will be taxed. Funds now used for enforcement used for drug education programs. Enforcement through existing means.

  I. Prohibitions on drug use increase harms to others.
   A. Present prohibits drug consumption.
   B. Prohibition increases criminality.
   C. Prohibition overwhelms the judicial system.

  II. Legalization prevents harms to others.
   A. Legalization minimizes the harms of drug abuse.
   B. Legalization better uses law enforcement resources.
   C. Legalization constitutes a better drug control policy.

Adapted from *The Forensic Quarterly*, Vol. 63, No. 3, 1989, pp. 48–54.

Systems analysis assumes that policy develops in an environment that is constantly changing because of growth in population, economic fluctuations, and demographic trends. Also, it assumes that policies already exist in all the problem areas considered by the current policymakers. Systems analysts argue that there is no need to debate whether a policy should be adopted, because policy has already been adopted. What is at issue instead is how existing policies can be adjusted to accommodate the continual changes that are occurring. Instead of assuming that policies should remain unchanged until a need is demonstrated to change them, under systems analysis what is debated is the degree and direction of changes that should be implemented.

Within this frame of reference, the net benefits case incorporates four steps: (1) the application of systems analysis to the problem area; (2) the determination of the components that make up the system and the rules governing how the components are interrelated; (3) the analysis of the differences that could be predicted following a change in policy governing these interrelationships; and (4) the determination of the most favorable ratio between the costs and the benefits of the proposed change in the system. In other words, the affirmative must not only show the advantages accruing from the plan, but also must demonstrate that the plan would result in the greatest net benefit possible, considering both the predicted advantages and the predicted disadvantages. When defending the affirmative proposal, you would demand that the negative not only refute the affirmative case, but also present a counterpolicy system that the judge could use to compare the negative and affirmative methods of controlling and guiding inevitable change.

Proponents of the net benefits approach believe that it more closely approximates how decisions are made in policy deliberations in government. Congressional committees and administrative agencies do not often debate whether the federal government should adopt a new policy (whether based on traditional need or comparative advantage); instead, they engage in a continuing process of amending, adjusting, and fine-tuning the laws already on the books. Real-world decision making appears to be based on the relative net benefits of making the proposed change in the overall system as compared with other proposals.

Systems analysis has many implications for debate. First, the affirmative team is able to admit that the proposed resolution has disadvantages as well as advantages. The basis for systematic decision making is the net benefits after taking into account the advantages *and* the disadvantages.

Second, the basis for decision in the debate cannot be simply the significance of the net benefits of the affirmative plan. Instead, there must be a comparison between the benefits of the affirmative plan and the benefits of an alternative system that might be proposed by the negative. If the negative team is not prepared to defend an alternative system, the affirmative system is then accepted, because the known risk of a system is preferable to the incalculable risk of having no system at all. This does not mean that the negative is obligated to present a counterplan. The defense of the present system is always an option. The important point is that the negative must be prepared to show that the benefits of continuing the present system—or any other system, for that matter—are greater than the net benefits of the affirmative plan.

Again, unlike the other cases discussed in this chapter, the net benefits case is not an evolutionary outgrowth of traditional debate theories and practices. Unlike other case formats, the net benefits case calls for the negative team to uphold a system of its own. The judge must then decide which competing policy system would produce the greatest benefits, taking into account the cost-benefit ratios of the two systems. In the net benefits case, neither the affirmative system nor the negative system carries presumption. Instead, this type of case argues that the *net* benefits of a proposal—considering both the advantages and disadvantages—is a better measure of the acceptability of a system than the advantages alone.

Net Benefits Case

Statement of the Resolution
Plan: Policy changes in the system.
Rationale:
  I. Net benefits of present system.
      A. Costs.
      B. Benefits.
 II. Net benefits of proposed affirmative plan.
      A. Costs.
      B. Benefits.
III. Relative cost-benefit ratios favor affirmative.

Sample Net Benefits Case

Resolved: That the United States government should significantly increase space exploration.

Plan: 1. Mandates. National objective of an advanced, human-occupied base on the moon. A) conduct preparatory exploration to determine site selections B) establish research outpost for short-range experiments C) establish permanently occupied base for longer-range missions D) establish advanced base for astronomical observations, long-range surface exploration, and resource mining.

2. Logistics. Funding through an optimal mix of raising tax for rich, 5% national sales tax, and increasing taxes on gas, cigarettes, and air travel. Enforcement through existing means. Legislative intent.

Rationale:
  I. Lunar exploration is not a priority in the present system.
      A. Research of moon has not advanced since Apollo 11.
      B. Plans for a lunar base have not been backed with funding.
 II. Lunar base would promote space development.
      A. Costs of space exploration would be cheaper from a lunar base.
      B. Lunar base would facilitate space exploration and development.
III. Net benefits of a lunar base.
      A. Cost effective.
      B. Development of space industries.
      C. Stepping stone for exploring Mars.
      D. Unless a lunar base is made a priority the benefits of a space program will be lost.

Alternative Justifications Case

The last case format is the alternative justifications case. The **alternative justifications case** can best be defined as an affirmative case that offers multiple justifications for the adoption of the resolution. The format evolved from the comparative advantages case. In a comparative advantages case, the affirmative will most likely claim more than one advantage from the adoption of the affirmative plan, and most affirmatives will argue that each of the advantages is independent—that is, each advantage is a separate unit and can result from the adoption of the affirmative plan with or without the other advantages. Thus, when offering independent advantages, the affirmative need win only one advantage to win the debate.

The alternative justifications case takes this concept a step further: it offers multiple independent *plans*, as well as advantages. For example, on the topic "*Resolved*: That the federal government should establish uniform standards for testing and marketing all products with potentially carcinogenic effects on humans," the affirmative might propose the banning of cigarettes, with the advantage of saving lives; the restriction of sugar-coated cereals, with the advantage of decreased dental decay in children; and mandating the installation of dual airbags in cars, with the advantage of decreased death and suffering. Each of these plan's planks and advantages is self-contained. Since each is self-contained, the affirmative will argue that it need win only one to warrant the adoption of the resolution.

This distinction between the comparative advantages case and the alternative justifications case is an important one. The comparative advantages case offers one proposal, or plan, that, if adopted, will result in one or more advantages. The alternative justifications case, on the other hand, offers two or more proposals, with one or more advantages stemming from each proposal. The following diagram illustrates this:

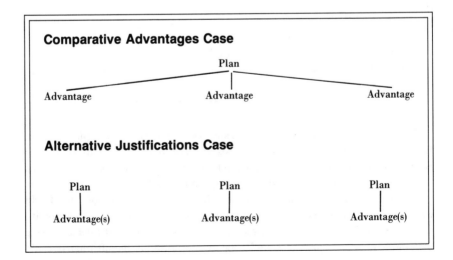

The key advantage of an alternative justifications case is that it offers the affirmative increased maneuverability. Negative debaters have long been able to choose from a variety of strategies. The negative might use straight refutation, minor repairs, a counterplan, and disadvantages all in the same debate round. By the end of the debate, the negative can pick and choose from all the arguments presented and go with its best arguments. The alternative justifications case enables affirmatives, too, to present more than one option for consideration and then narrow to one proposal.

However, while it offers greater maneuverability, the alternative justifications case is not an easy one to present. When presenting alternative justifications, the affirmative must meet all of the traditional burdens of proof. But instead of making a prima facie case for just one plan, the affirmative must now do this for two or three. Each alternative justification must be inherent, significant, and solvent. This approach can spread the first affirmative constructive speaker pretty thin: establishing all of this is a lot to do in an eight-minute constructive speech. However, once the case has been set up, the affirmative can strategically choose which advantages it will attempt to carry along in the debate round.

The alternative justifications case can be structured in one of two ways: an independent plans format or a unit plan format with independent planks. Each is illustrated below, and a sample unit plan follows.

Independent Plans Format

Statement of the resolution
Definition of terms
Affirmative Plan 1
Affirmative Plan 2
Affirmative Plan 3
Comparative Advantage 1
Comparative Advantage 2
Comparative Advantage 3

Because of time constraints, most affirmatives use the second, unit plan, format. By using this structure, the affirmative does not need to repeat portions of the plan common to each solution (such as administration, personnel, enforcement, or finance). The plan is presented as a unit, with planks specific to each alternative justification.

While the second format might save time, there is a drawback the debater should consider. Some critics argue that when the plan is presented as a unit, the affirmative does not have the option to drop a plank and advantage out of the debate. Using the sample plan from page 205, under the unit plan format the affirmative could

---

Unit Plan Format with Independent Planks

Statement of the resolution
Definition of terms
   I. Affirmative Plan
      A. Independent Plank 1
      B. Independent Plank 2
      C. Independent Plank 3
  II. Comparative Advantages
      A. Comparative Advantage 1
      B. Comparative Advantage 2
      C. Comparative Advantage 3

---

not simply drop banning cigarettes out of the debate. Instead, the disadvantages resulting from this portion of the plan would have to be weighed against the rest of the case to determine if there was a net advantage to the adoption of the resolution.

The reasoning behind this is fairly straightforward. In the traditional need or comparative advantages case, the affirmative would not be allowed to drop a plank out of the plan just because the negative presented a good disadvantage against it. Therefore, when the plan is presented as a unit, the affirmative cannot drop one of its alternatives. This is not to say that the affirmative must win all the alternatives in order to win the debate. As long as the advantage outweighs the disadvantages of all the alternatives presented, the affirmative could still carry only one alternative and win the debate.

A sample of an alternative justifications case that was run on the product safety topic is shown on page 206.

The Affirmative Plan

Regardless of which case format they use, every affirmative team must specify how they will implement the resolution. For example, once the affirmative has shown the need to control the high cost of medical care and to provide everyone access to that care, the affirmative must provide a way of accomplishing this goal. The method by which the affirmative accomplishes the goal is called the **affirmative plan.**

Over the years the affirmative plan has gone through a great deal of refinement. Originally, teams relied on the resolution to solve the problem outlined. Then the affirmative began to provide a skeleton outline of a solution. When the traditional need case was the only structure in use, the plan was presented in the second affirmative speech. When the comparative advantages case came along, affirmatives

Sample Alternative Justifications Case

Resolved: That the federal government should establish uniform standards for testing and marketing all products with potentially carcinogenic effects on humans.

Definitions: Operationally defined in the plan.

I. Regulation of lawn mowers would decrease needless death and suffering.
   A. The resale of lawnmowers is not regulated now.
   B. Used mowers hurt people.
   C. Solvency.

II. Cigarettes cause needless suffering through fires.
   A. Cigarettes cause fires.
   B. Self-extinguishing cigarettes would decrease fires.
   C. Cigarette manufacturers will not chemically treat tobacco, so a federal mandate is needed.

Plan 1

1. A safety board will be established to develop and oversee safety regulations for the sale and resale of lawnmowers. All necessary staff and funding will be provided.

2. Mandates
   A. All lawnmowers must be registered at the date of sale.
   B. All lawnmowers must be inspected and certified for safety before resale.
   C. The certificate of safety will be issued as a part of the bill of sale.

3. Funding will be provided by a 5% surcharge on the sale of lawn equipment.

4. Violations of the plan will be treated as follows:
   A. First violation will be fined $1,000 and treated as a misdemeanor.
   B. Any person involved in the sale of an uncertified used mower that is involved in an accident will be prosecuted for a felony.

Plan 2

1. An independent, self-perpetuating board will be established to implement the plan. All necessary staff and funding will be provided.

2. Mandates of the plan.
   A. All cigarette manufacturers will be required to manufacture self-extinguishing cigarettes.
   B. A 10% tax credit will be given to ease the cost of production.

3. Violations of the plan will be enforced with fines and/or imprisonment. Periodic spot checks will be made of cigarettes to verify compliance.

4. Funding will be provided by a 1% tax on insurance companies and the elimination of federal paper waste.

began to introduce the plan in the first affirmative constructive. With the comparative advantages case, it was necessary to present the plan in the first affirmative constructive in order to compare the affirmative solution against the present system. Now judges and debaters alike have come to expect the affirmative to present the plan in the first speech, no matter what case format is used.

Generally, judges feel that presenting the plan in the first speech promotes clash. If the affirmative waited until the second affirmative speech to present the plan, the first negative would not be in a position to choose the most appropriate strategy of attack against the entire affirmative case. The practice of presenting the plan in the first affirmative constructive speech has become so widespread that the debater who has no plan (and merely stands on the resolution) or waits until the second affirmative constructive speech risks losing the round.

All affirmative plans are constructed around plan planks. **Plan planks** are statements that authorize specific kinds of action in order to implement the resolution. Occasionally, a plan may need to have only one plank. For example, if a resolution called for the abolition of the Interstate Commerce Commission, a plan might simply contain one plank that directs the Congress of the United States to follow appropriate procedure to decommission this agency.

As this example suggests, resolutions that call for a reduction of government power generally have compact plans, because the affirmative can call upon the normal processes of government to implement the reduction of power. Most resolutions, however, do not invite such a simple plan of action. Typically, resolutions call for the creation of some kind of government action—a new agency or increasing the scope of responsibility of an old agency.

The affirmative plan doesn't have to be a solution created solely by the affirmative team. When the affirmative team is looking for evidence to support the contentions in the affirmative case, they should also look to see how the experts suggest the problem should be solved. The solutions proposed by experts in the field, who work regularly with the problem or who have spent a great deal of time studying the problem, are likely to be very good. The affirmative may also find solutions that have been tried on a small basis. These can be very valuable, since potential problems will already have been identified and remedies suggested.

As an affirmative, you should make a list of the possible solutions you come across, and evaluate each of the solutions in light of the specific affirmative case harms. You should also evaluate each solution from the negative perspective, asking what objections the negative might raise and how those objections can be answered or additional planks added to solve the harms.

The affirmative wants to avoid creating an entire new bureaucratic structure if possible—it is more desirable to integrate the affirmative plan into the present system. By using structures that already exist within the present system, the affirmative makes it more difficult for the negative to run disadvantages against those portions of the plan. For example, if there is a government agency that could implement the proposal, the affirmative should use that agency instead of creating a new one. This eliminates negative disadvantages against bureaucracy. These planks of the plan are often referred to as *operational planks*. They do not deal with the topical mandates of the plan; rather, they deal with the day-to-day operation of the plan.

Early on, affirmative plans were very detailed. They would take two to three minutes to present (often at a very rapid rate of speed), and debaters often acted as if they were presenting a piece of legislation before Congress that needed everything but the kitchen sink in it. This approach rapidly proved unrealistic and impractical. The affirmative was not presenting a bill before Congress but rather a framework of a solution to a problem.

Current debate practice dictates that the affirmative plan should be as simple as possible. Each plank of the plan should represent a mandate that describes the action that should be taken. (This action will usually have been documented in the affirmative solvency evidence.) Plan planks should be explained in a clear and straightforward manner. Each plan should explain the steps that must be taken to solve the harm. However, at the same time, the plan must provide enough detail so that the negative team and the judge can tell exactly what changes in the present system the affirmative is proposing.

In order to implement the proposal, the affirmative is allowed to include nontopical planks that help make the proposals. These might be called "housekeeping" planks. They include such things as who will administer the proposal, funding, or enforcement, all of which are provisions that would be necessary for any proposal to work. The only stipulation is that the affirmative cannot claim an advantage from these kinds of housekeeping planks. For example, the affirmative cannot claim a monetary advantage that might result from the mechanism used to finance the plan. Such an advantage would be extratopical and not a reason to adopt the affirmative proposal.

As the affirmative tries to anticipate negative challenges and disadvantages, they will want to draft provisions that would preclude those challenges or disadvantages. Such plan planks are called **plan spikes**. Most often these provisions are also nontopical and are used to head off disadvantages, and the affirmative is not allowed to claim an advantage from such a nontopical provision. For example, if the affirmative is worried that the negative will argue that the affirmative budget cuts to provide funding will result in cuts in AIDS research, they can specify in the plan that AIDS research will not be cut. However, the affirmative cannot claim any advantage from AIDS research.

When the affirmative decides to put a plank in the plan to help implement the proposal or to head off a disadvantage, it is not without some risks. The affirmative is responsible for each plank of the plan (whether topical or nontopical). If the negative develops a disadvantage against a nontopical plank of the plan, the affirmative must defend against it. If the disadvantage is proven significant and won by the negative, it could cost the affirmative the round. Plan spikes can prove to be very useful, but the affirmative must remember that they can be potentially dangerous.

Despite this risk most affirmatives find plan spikes to be a very good affirmative tactic.

Summary

Developing the affirmative case requires a great deal of work. Once the case area has been chosen, the debaters must decide what format to use—traditional need case, comparative advantages case, goals case, net benefits case, or alternative justifications case. To make this decision, the debaters must explore the options to see which will best fit the needs of their problem area. After the case area has been developed, a plan is devised. The plan must come with all parts in order to work. If a provision is overlooked, the plan either won't solve the need or it will create a potentially serious disadvantage.

Questions

1. Why is inherency the key to the need-for-a-change argument? What is the difference between structural and attitudinal inherency?

2. When developing the affirmative plan, how do you decide what to include?

3. What is the meaning of the following statement: the advantage is unique to the affirmative plan?

4. What are three important considerations in preparing a comparative advantages case?

5. When considering what case area to run, why is it important to consider who will be judging the debates?

6. What is the difference between the comparative advantages case and the goals case? What is the advantage of the goals case over a comparative advantages case? What is the strategic value of the goals case?

7. What are the four steps involved in the net benefits case?

8. What are nontopical plan planks? What is their purpose?

Discussion Opportunities

1. Discuss the essential differences between the five types of affirmative cases. Describe the advantages and disadvantages of each.

2. In the comparative advantages case, what constitutes a significant advantage?

3. What are the differences between the traditional need case and the comparative advantages case? What are the strategic reasons to choose one over the other?

4. Using one of the first affirmative constructive speeches presented in class, discuss the following questions:
   - Was the case significant?
   - Was inherency clearly established?
   - Was solvency provided?
   - Were the advantages inherent and significant?
5. What is the distinction between the comparative advantages case and the alternative justifications case? What is the advantages of the alternative justifications case?

Writing Opportunities

1. After having researched the area identified for the affirmative, choose a case format. Outline the issues for the case. Does your choice of format fit your case idea? Why or why not?
2. Assemble the research you have done on the case area. Draft a first affirmative constructive speech in which there is a single contention or advantage. This should be approximately two pages long or two to three minutes in length when presented.
3. Expand the constructive you wrote for the previous Writing Opportunity to include all contentions or advantages. This should now be approximately five to six pages in length; when delivered, it should run six minutes.
4. Using your affirmative case outline, draft a plan. Be prepared to defend your plan. Combine this plan with your expanded constructive speech to create a complete first affirmative constructive speech.

Critical Thinking Opportunities

1. Why is it important to define the terms of the proposition before choosing a case idea and case structure?
2. When looking at case types, what would be the advantage to the affirmative in using the net benefits format?
3. How would you decide how many harms or advantages to present in an affirmative case?
4. Listen to the affirmative speeches as they are delivered in class. Identify what type of case format was used. Was it appropriate for the case area? Why or why not?
5. Considering the first affirmative constructive speech you chose for Writing Opportunity 4, what are the most likely negative attacks against your case? How can the case be improved to answer these attacks?
6. What are the drawbacks to the alternative justifications case?

STRATEGIES IN ACTION

John just met with his academic adviser, Mr. Rochelle, to discuss the requirements for his Senior Honors Thesis. As he walked down the hall, the only thing John was sure of was the subject area he has chosen for his thesis: Freedom of Speech, Censorship, and the School Newspaper. John began to second-guess his ability to take on such a large project as a Senior Honors Thesis.

When he met with Mr. Rochelle later that day, John expressed his concerns and feelings of being in over his head. Mr. Rochelle listened patiently, but then asked John about debate and how the squad was doing. John began telling him about this great affirmative case he and his partner were running. Mr. Rochelle suggested that John might try developing his Senior Honors Thesis in the same way he and his partner developed their affirmative case. That night, John went over the steps for writing an affirmative case and then used the same process to develop his thesis. Take a look at the course of action John put together:

- Define the terms (or concepts) freedom of speech, censorship, and school newspaper. Do any of these terms have special restrictions?

- From your readings on the subject, outline the issues that appear to be important. Initially, be sure to balance the issues on both sides of the question.

- Having looked at the issues, what position do you want to defend? List the reasons for your position.

- Use the stock issues as a checklist for proving your position.

- Using the affirmative case format as an example, develop a structure for presenting your position in the thesis.

- Research, looking for evidence to support the issues you have identified.

The strategies John uses in developing, researching, and writing his affirmative case as a debater can also be used to construct a term paper or honors thesis. Each requires identifying what the subject area means, identifying issues, building a prima facie position, and using research as well as writing skills.

CHAPTER 8

Negative Argumentation

Objectives

After studying Chapter 8, you should be able
1. To explain how to conduct straight refutation.
2. To explain how to argue a defense of the status quo.
3. To develop indictments of an affirmative plan.
4. To build solvency, workability, and alternative causality objections.
5. To create several different kinds of disadvantages.
6. To explain how to indict topicality arguments.
7. To evaluate different standards for topicality.
8. To develop a negative position.

Key Terms

To effectively debate the negative position, you will need to understand the following terms:

running refutation
strategic refutation
negative position
defense of the present
   system
trend argument
minor repair
plan-meet-advantage
disadvantage
alternative causality
workability
circumvention
link
turnaround
impact
generic policy
   disadvantage
process disadvantage
topicality

The fortunes of affirmative and negative debaters have varied over the years. In the 1950s and early 1960s, negatives won most of the preliminary rounds, and it was rare for a team to choose the affirmative position in a round of debate. It was difficult to win on the affirmative side because judges required highly restrictive interpretations of topicality, and the need-plan case allocated stock issues in such a way as to obligate the affirmative to win nearly every argument to be successful.

However, beginning in the mid–1960s the pendulum began to swing the other way. While definitions of topicality were still highly restrictive, two changes in debate altered the competitive balance. The first was the comparative advantages case. As mentioned in the previous chapter, a comparative advantages case does not require that an affirmative solve some great problem in order to show cause for the resolution. Rather, the affirmative need only demonstrate that the case alleviates the *effects* of a problem. When teams discovered that advantages stemming from a common plan could be independent of one character, the affirmative was put in a much better tactical situation.

Throughout the late 1970s and 1980s, the pendulum swung back and forth. For a while, developments in topicality attacks, counterplans, and disadvantages favored the negative. However, the overall trend in the 1990s has been to make debating the affirmative side of the issue easier. Therefore, it is especially important to master negative strategy. Since you will be debating negative approximately 50 percent of the time, make certain you can carry as many negative points as possible.

Negative strategy is divided into two chapters. This chapter analyzes all negative strategies except counterplan argumentation. Chapter 9 focuses on counterplans. Before you can run an effective counterplan, it is necessary to master fundamental negative strategies.

Stock Issues and Negative Argumentation

Policy debate evolved from classical courtroom argumentation. In a courtroom the prosecuting attorney affirms the guilt of the accused and asks for appropriate punishment. The prosecutor maintains that the defendant was seen committing an act, that the act could be defined as a crime, that the crime had pernicious consequences, and that the court has a duty to punish the defendant. Together, these stock issues make a case that establishes the guilt and proper punishment in a trial.

The defense has several choices. The defense attorney could question the reliability or reasonableness of the evidence presented by the prosecutor on all counts. Thus, the defense would argue:

1. There is not enough evidence to show that my client committed the alleged act.
2. There is not enough evidence to show that the alleged act is a crime.
3. There is not enough proof to establish that the consequences of the deed were pernicious.

Using the same strategies as a defense attorney, the debater may use a combination of running and strategic refutation.

4. There is not enough evidence to secure the jurisdiction of the court on this case.

The defense attorney's strategy is one of **running refutation**, or indicting the prosecution's evidence at each and every point. By questioning every statement made by the prosecutor, the defense hopes to come across a weakly developed stock issue. Should one stock issue fall, then there is no prima facie case for punishment.

Another strategy available to the defense attorney would be to combine running refutation with **strategic refutation**. Strategic refutation requires spending a good deal of time to disestablish, that is show false, an important claim. For example, the defense attorney might argue that the defendant has an alibi and could not have committed the act in question. Strategic refutation has the advantage that if just one important stock issue is disestablished, then the others do not matter. If the client did not do the act, then it does not matter if the alleged action can be defined as a crime, is wrong, and is punishable. Strategic refutation proceeds by (1) casting doubt on the opponent's evidence, (2) introducing contrary evidence, and (3) stating the importance that winning the argument in question has for the other stock issues.

Prima Facie Requirements, Presumption, and Topicality

The issues of prima facie requirements, presumption, and topicality apply to any round of debate, whether it focuses on the need, the plan, or some other type of affirmative rationale for change. Since stock issue arguments enter in at the decision point of a debate, the negative will want to make their choices for strategies.

Prima Facie Requirements

As discussed at the beginning of this chapter, prima facie simply means that a case must be proven on its face. A negative makes a successful prima facie indictment when it points out that one could accept everything argued by the affirmative case as true and still not have a sufficient reason to adopt a change in policy and accept the resolution. If an affirmative team has forgotten to specify a plan of action, or if there is no evidence to show that the action will have intended results, then the case may be judged not prima facie. However, since most advocates develop complete cases, or if there are defects, the constructives give them time to complete their case development, prima facie arguments rarely win rounds of debate for the negative.

Presumption

Traditionally, presumption rests with the negative. Presumption argues that, absent a clear rationale for change, the status quo should be maintained. Presumption is valuable as a decision rule. When there is substantial confusion or uncertainty about the wisdom of both sides, the judge needs a way to decide the round. If the negative has presumption, then a default exists for the decision.

Occasionally, however, affirmatives will try to claim that presumption supports the resolution. In situations where the status quo has no policy, some action may be better than no action. Indeed, in some cases of uncertainty the only way to learn is to try and see the results. If the status quo is undergoing a period of substantial turbulence and indecision in a given area, then even a rather significant plan of action might be presumed better than nothing.

Therefore, it is in the interest of the negative to defend or even enhance presumption. Presumption is defended by showing that the affirmative plan adds to uncertainty, rather than decreasing it, thus multiplying the risks inherent in an unsettled state of affairs. Alternatively, presumption is enhanced by showing that the comparative merits of an affirmative policy are so small or pertain to so few people that presumption is not overcome.

Topicality Arguments

Perhaps more important than prima facie requirements and presumption is the stock issue of topicality. The reason that topicality is a crucial issue is that the most

---

Practicum: Sample Topicality Argument*

The affirmative plan does not *significantly* increase social services for the homeless.
  A. The resolution requires that the affirmative team *significantly* increase social services for the homeless.
  B. A significant increase must be an important increase.
       Words and Phrases, Vol. 39, 1989 supplement, p. 100.
       "Standard 'significantly affecting the quality of the human environment' can be construed as having an important or meaningful effect, direct or indirect."
       This definition requires that the affirmative cannot simply increase social services; it must be an important increase, based on the amount of money spent, or the number of homeless involved.
  C. The affirmative case is not "important."
       The affirmative team neither spends a significant amount of money for its plan, nor significantly increases the number of homeless that receive social services.
  D. The affirmative definition is unreasonable.
       It makes the word "significantly" irrelevant, since any case that helps the homeless would be topical.
  E. Topicality is a voting issue.
       1. The tournament invitation acts as a contract; attending this tournament indicates that teams agree to debate the resolution.
       2. Traditionally, topicality is a voting issue.

---

basic duty of affirmative debaters is to establish that they support the resolution. If the affirmative fails to support the topic, then it has not fulfilled its burden to advocate the resolution. If the affirmative case does not fall within the area of change outlined by the resolution, then the plan is not authorized by the topic.

As these steps suggest, topicality has become a very elaborate issue. The stakes are high, and it therefore pays to be prepared to argue topicality extensively. Unfortunately, there are conflicting views of what constitutes a reasonable definition of terms.

From the affirmative standpoint, advocates should be able to present *a* reasonable definitions of terms—not *the* only reasonable definition of terms, or even one more reasonable than that presented by the negative. Since the affirmative has the burden of presenting a case, it should be able to at least set out the terms upon which the debate is argued. From the negative standpoint, such a view is unfair, because it destroys the comparative nature of topicality debate. Since anything is "reasonable" from some perspective, the loose topicality requirement virtually guarantees that any misconstrual of the topic will be adequate to justify the affirmative plan. The negative argues that like any other argument in the round, the better job of debating should determine the outcome, and no team should be privileged.

But then the question arises, what is a more reasonable definition of terms? There are some guides to answering this question. First, when there are two different definitions, the one that is in line with state-of-the-art use in public policy is more authoritative. Not only do such terms serve as legal precedent for securing the plan, they also reflect common concerns of policymakers.

Second, when there are competing definitions, the one that fits within the grammatical context of the resolution is superior. Context in this sense is determined by the relationships among agents of action, the plan or directed activity, and the object or outcome of policy.

Third, when there are competing definitions, the one that most evenly divides affirmative and negative ground is preferred. For example, for the topic that stipulates that "a program of comprehensive health care should be adopted for all American citizens," it would be equally reasonable to determine that the topic means either *for* in the sense of "for the benefit of" or *for* as "extended to." The first interpretation would license any specialized plan pertaining to medical practice, since a benefit for one is in some sense a benefit for all. The second interpretation would require a more well-rounded plan. Clearly the second interpretation is more reasonable since it more evenly divides ground.

It is not entirely clear what happens if *part* of an affirmative plan resides beyond the scope of a topic. For instance, a national health care policy does not require any particular form of financing, but a progressive tax might be useful to prevent the more harmful effects of a consumption or transportation tax. The affirmative is usually allowed some leeway in choosing the means of implementation.

However, suppose that a crucial link to an advantage was brought about by an extratopical plan provision, one that lies outside the scope of the topic. While extended geriatric day care may not be part of "medical care" per se, a significant portion of advantages for extending comprehensive care to the elderly may rest on just such long-term collective residences. From the affirmative point of view, extratopical parts of the plan are simply deleted as rationales for decision. From the negative point of view, the plan ought to be rejected as a whole and tested in another round.

One key element of topicality arguments is justification, or the requirement that the affirmative come up with a unique reason for each term in the topic. If the affirmative does not present a rationale for a specific term, it falls short of the duty of advocacy. For example, even if the affirmative can show that more medical care is needed for many, unless it can show why a "comprehensive system" is warranted, it does not meet its burden of defending the topic. The justification argument strengthens the negative's hand by increasing the proof burdens on the affirmative.

These are some basic approaches to topicality. Other strategies continue to develop. As a strategic debater, you should be alert to such developments, acquire more evidence, and strive for reasonable definitions.

The Negative Position

Just as a defense attorney can defeat the procecution's case by destroying one of the stock issues in the case against the defendant, so too the negative can defeat the affirmative's case against the status quo by showing (1) that there is no harm, (2) that the harm is not inherent, (3) that the affirmative has provided no effective remedy for the harm, or (4) that the resolution of the harm has significant disadvantages. In addition, just as the strongest position in a court of law flows from a conclusive demonstration that the indictment of the defendant is not true, so too the strongest negative position is a demonstration that the indictment of the status quo is not true.

Whenever a negative team engages in strategic refutation, the negative argument coalesces into a **negative position** in the debate. This position offers a complete picture of why the affirmative case is wrong. The negative position requires proof and consistency in establishing what is the probable truth, and it enhances the power of the negative by increasing its focus on its strongest argument. For the negative to develop a position it must (1) assume a burden of proof, and (2) make arguments that consistently reinforce one another.

While the strongest negative position is one that refutes all of the stock issues, in some situations a negative might argue a hinged or *contingent* position. In a courtroom, an attorney might put forward a contingent position by claiming:

1. My client did not do the deed.
2. If he did, it cannot by law be defined as a crime.
3. If it could be defined as a crime, it is only a technical definition and does not deserve punishment.
4. The court has no jurisdiction anyway.

In debate, a contingent position has the strategic advantage of permitting a number of independent voting issues. However, because such a position diffuses the focus of the negative attack, even if it is logically consistent, it is often less persuasive than a coherent, sharply defined and narrowed defense. The essence of the negative strategy, whether in courtroom policy or debate, seems to rest on the choice between presenting a large number of issues that are partially developed and loosely related on the one hand, and presenting a smaller number of tightly integrated, well-established arguments on the other. There are risks to both strategies. The following sections will focus on how these strategies can be applied to different affirmative case formats. By understanding the advantages and risks involved with these strategies, you will be prepared to employ them effectively in your debate rounds.

Traditional Need Cases and Case-Side Arguments

For many years, in arguing traditional need cases, negative debaters gave little thought to plan-meet-need arguments and almost none to disadvantages. All the action was on the "case side." While there are few pure need-plan cases left, negative debaters still have a tendency to draw "indictments" against status quo policies. The following section, then, explains traditional negative strategies of argument against a need-plan case. The tactics presented here should be useful against any team that describes the present system as less than it could be. More importantly, however, these basic negative arguments will prepare you for sophisticated elaboration and development of arguments later on.

Running Refutation Strategies

As suggested at the beginning of this chapter, running refutation depends on methodically casting doubt on each of the affirmative's arguments. Imagine yourself listening to a round of debate. The first affirmative speaker presents a reasonably complete case, structured around several contentions and many subpoints. The first negative speaker stands up and makes the same three responses to every affirmative statement: (1) there is not enough proof to know that the affirmative statement is true; (2) there is some evidence to indicate that the affirmative contention is probably false; and (3) even if the statement were true, it has no bearing on the question of whether or not the resolution ought to be adopted.

Imagine further that the second affirmative speaker is quite inept and cannot answer any of the negative charges. The debate continues like this throughout all the speeches. How would you vote? Negative, of course. Presumption rests with the negative unless or until the affirmative can demonstrate a reason to change.

Under presumption, the negative argues that there should be no change just for the sake of change—there must be a net benefit. By employing three basic proof challenges, negative debaters can uphold presumption.

First, the negative can establish that there is not enough proof. In some debates key arguments are not supported by evidence. There may be no empirical studies that measure a harm, no pilot programs that show the efficacy of a particular approach to solving a problem. There may be no authoritative sources that concur in the opponents' assessment of the gravity of a harm. When running refutation, the negative must look for such assertions, identify them as unsupported or weakly supported, and demonstrate why it is important that the affirmative prove the statement.

For example, suppose the affirmative were debating the resolution "*Resolved*: That the federal government should establish a program to provide for aging American citizens." Unless the affirmative can demonstrate some pilot program or other kinds of studies that has provided the same protection for older Americans, the affirmative probably will not be able to prove with evidence how the affirmative plan will bring about the advantage claimed.

Of course, there are more subtle analytical problems. The affirmative may have general evidence claiming that the problem can be solved but may only assert that the solution is similar to the one used in the plan. Consequently, the negative must look for implied premises that are assumed to be true but actually need to be proved before a warrant for the resolution can be said to have been established.

In the previous example, the affirmative may refer to a program in England or Canada that provided for its aging citizens, outline the advantages that had been gained under such programs, and claim that under the affirmative plan, the same will come about in the United States. The negative would have to look for differences between the English and Canadian systems (or ways of life) and the system in the United States. The argument would be that unless all underlying assumptions are the same, there is no reason to assume that the affirmative plan would gain the same advantages.

The second negative strategy when running refutation is to establish that the affirmative statement is probably false. The adequacy of the proof is always a comparative question. Unless each side explains why its evidence is superior, a judge is left in a quandary. Merely entering contrary evidence in the round does not negate a point. The key tactic is to explain the comparative merits of the proof.

The process of explaining tests of evidence can become quite complicated. However, a key consideration is source credibility. It is not enough to state qualifications of the source: you must indicate *why* those qualifications are superior to those of the source used by the opposition. It is important to demonstrate why greater expertise should be accepted over another source's bias, or why having more experts agree with a source is more valuable than the date of the evidence. To win the evidence challenge, negative debaters must be prepared to make the ultimate extension, proving why their criteria for credibility are superior to the criteria of the opponents. If this is not done, the judge has no way to evaluate the argument.

The third step in running refutation is to establish that even if the affirmative's statement were true, it has no bearing. It is important to test the coherence and relevance of the affirmative contentions. The affirmative may have a lot of irrelevant verbiage in the first constructive speech.

Basic proof challenges

1. There is not enough proof.
2. The affirmative statement is probably false.
3. Even if the statement were true, it has no bearing.

Although establishing a lack of proof, reversing the weight of evidence, and pointing out irrelevant or meaningless arguments are the basis of running refutation, it is important to stay alert to other possible strategies. Many affirmative teams hedge their bets by claiming that several subpoints of a contention are independent. For example, in showing that the present system can't solve poverty, the affirmative might claim that the failure of current efforts is caused by lack of coordination, by lack of personnel, and by conflicting jurisdictions. The net effect of this structure is to make it possible for the affirmative to lose two out of three of the subpoints and still be left with a reason why the present system programs fail. Thus, in the second affirmative rebuttal, the latitude of strategic choice is greater. Whichever subpoint the negative attacks with the least strength is featured as the determinant inherency argument.

The negative should be prepared for the strategy just described. Whenever the affirmative claims reasons to be independent or whenever a case is structured in such a way that later in the debate the affirmative may bring up claims to independence, the negative should collapse (combine) the independent subpoints into a single argument. In the example given, the negative could argue that it is really the problem of jurisdiction that causes personnel shortages and coordination problems, and, further, that the jurisdiction question can or will be resolved without the affirmative plan. By collapsing the independent subpoints to a single issue, the negative reduces the likelihood that the affirmative can merely pick and choose arguments.

Running refutation is an important element, but not the sole one, in the preparation of almost any negative position. Although it may be true that some affirmative teams will be overwhelmed by questions, challenges, and demands made of every contention, this strategy alone is not likely to be successful in the long run—because teams will continue to research their own cases and gather evidence.

Defense of the Present System

One way to augment running refutation is to offer a defense of the present system. A **defense of the present system** always involves two arguments: first, refuting the affirmative claim that life under the present system will be worse in the future; and, second, that the future looks promising in respect to the harm area isolated by the affirmative. There are three ways to defend the present system. You may use any or all of them, depending on the available evidence.

Defense of the Present System Arguments

1. Affirmative does not prove a harm.
2. The harm no longer exists and is not likely to recur.
3. The harms isolated by the affirmative will soon abate.

The first way to defend the present system is to establish that the affirmative does not prove a harm. This defense argues that the features the affirmative claims to be undesirable in the present system are either necessary evils or do not exist. The debate turns on the question of values.

For instance, an affirmative case may claim that the CIA violates individual privacy by wiretapping and eavesdropping. It may even prove that such intrusion upon important civil rights is likely to continue into the future. The negative would defend the present system by justifying such violations for the greater good, namely collective security. This might be a difficult position to uphold, because the negative assumes the burden of proving that such vital information could be gathered in no other manner. But the "necessary evil" is always a possible option.

Another method of redefining a harm is to prove that the affirmative's value structure is not acceptable. It is virtually undeniable that lives are saved when mandatory seatbelt laws are enforced. Moreover, it is probably difficult to prove that not wearing seatbelts is a necessary evil, serving some greater good. But it could be argued that even though saving lives is an important duty of government, the government has no right to intervene in instances where individuals choose knowingly and willingly to take risks at their own expense; that such action would be the very essence of tyranny. In this example, the defense of the present system centers on the argument that the value of liberty outweighs the value of saving a number of lives.

Most affirmatives identify harms that are usually agreed on as being unnecessary and susceptible to some social or government action. Therefore, a negative position arguing that the harm is not really a harm—all things considered—is typically quite rare. However, in some topic areas, especially those touching on civil liberties, the argument may become more common.

The second way to defend the present system is to argue that the harm no longer exists and is not likely to recur. This position may appear silly with regard to some topics. It would be news indeed if war were eliminated or air pollution had migrated to another planet or the poor were no longer with us. However, in other instances this position becomes much more defensible.

It may be argued that some social problems are products of a unique confluence of circumstances or climate of opinion. If the circumstances change or if the opinions are reshaped, the problem may be unlikely to recur. For example, in arguing that the power of the President of the U.S. should be restricted, advocates might point to Vietnam as an example of an unwarranted, disastrous intervention brought about by misuse of executive discretion. Of course, the negative would be hard-pressed to refute this point. But the implication of the argument—that future interventions would be unwarranted and equally as disastrous—may successfully be refuted by referring to the disastrous nature of the war in Vietnam itself. It could be maintained that since our involvement in Vietnam was so disastrous, no president would risk the political consequences of entering into such a conflict without consulting the Congress.

You could argue that the reaction of the American public to Vietnam had the effect of limiting the power of the president and no further restrictions are needed. Where cases depend on historical example to prove the potential significance of a recurrent harm, the negative can defend the present system by arguing that measures have been taken to assure that past mistakes will not be repeated.

In the Vietnam example, the negative would argue that the test of presidential power came in 1991 with Operation Desert Storm (Gulf War). In this conflict, the options were placed before the Congress and debated in an open forum. The actions then taken by President Bush were done so with the consent of Congress. The negative could also provide the example of military action in Somalia (1992–93), where the President used executive discretion to send in troops for humanitarian reasons. Even when pressured to step up troop involvement, President Clinton resisted.

Also, civil war is being waged in Bosnia in Eastern Europe. Many have called for the United States to send in troops. In Vietnam, U.S. involvement began with the sending of political advisers and then presidential power (granted by the Gulf of Tonkin resolution) was used to escalate involvement without step-by-step approval from Congress. In Bosnia, no military action has been taken at this time, nor is it likely to be without an open debate in Congress. The negative would argue that these examples prove that measures have been taken to insure that history does not repeat itself.

The defense of the present system in this manner must always be carefully staged. Proving that circumstances have changed may magnify the possibility of a harm recurring. For example, the sentiment of the American public to avoid another Vietnam might lead to warlike actions by belligerents in other countries, who calculate that the United States will not respond. The negative would look for examples where the United States had been tested and the belligerents backed off or action was taken. For example, it might be argued that Saddam Hussein (Iraq) invaded Kuwait because he was convinced that the United States might threaten Iraq but would not take action. President Bush proved him wrong and the independence of Kuwait was restored.

The third way to defend the present system is to suggest that the harms isolated by the affirmative will soon abate. This position is the most common defense of the present system, although it is becoming less useful. Combined with running refutation, the negative argues that the harm is not growing, and that new programs or measures have been designed to solve the problem as much as possible. This is called a **trend argument**, meaning that the direction of programs into the present system is to solve the affirmative harm. The negative further maintains that additional efforts would be premature—perhaps even making the situation worse. The logic behind this position is that trends in the multifaceted present system are better than the single approach suggested by the affirmative.

The utility of this approach is limited by the notion of comparative advantages, since the affirmative could admit that even though the present system may eventually solve a problem, the affirmative's plan offers a better way of reaching a solution. Many affirmatives prepare for "trends of the present system" arguments by arguing that each trend that has proven hopeful in resolving the problem either makes the problem worse or results in some other effect that is less desirable than what the affirmative plan would achieve.

Another limitation of the trend argument is that it doesn't always constitute a true defense of the status quo. Although it is not logically inconsistent to argue that the present system is moving to solve a problem in a way similar to the affirmative proposal and that this movement is disadvantageous, many judges expect the negative to defend the present system and show that it is doing something good. What is the point of arguing disadvantages to a policy if the present system will adopt the policy in any case? The negative must be prepared to show the differences between the movement of the present system and the resolution, and that the method of movement supported by the resolution is what constitutes the harm.

Defense of the present system can often be a complicated task. Because the status quo is imperfect, you should not expect that a defense of the present system can be conducted with unwavering success. In most debates a defense of the present system is combined with an attack on the affirmative plan. Nevertheless, as a negative debater you should carefully consider how such a defense can support your position.

Minor Repairs

Minor repairs in the present system is a variation on the trend argument. A **minor repair** is a change advocated in the present system that falls short of the resolution. It gains the advantages that the affirmative claims as justification for voting for the resolution. A minor repair is often used in conjunction with a trend argument, because no matter how promising the trends of the present system, they will always fall short of an ideal affirmative plan.

For example, when debating the resolution "*Resolved*: That the federal government should guarantee comprehensive national health insurance to all United States citizens," the affirmative might argue that the present system of private health insurance does not provide all individuals with comprehensive coverage. The affirmative could argue that, while it is true that private insurance does cover a variety of illnesses and services, the affirmative case is still warranted because it sets up a system by which all medical needs are met. Furthermore, the affirmative could argue that this saves the individual from having to search for the "right" insurer before knowing what the insured might need in the future. Unless the negative can counter this claim, the affirmative would win because its system is still superior to the present system.

The negative might counter with a minor repair: namely, setting up standards for health insurance and a system for adjudicating health care claims. This is certainly not the same thing as a national health insurance plan, and it mitigates the only reason for adopting the affirmative case.

Typically, a minor repair consists of isolating small problem areas in the present system, stipulating the desired change, pointing out how this action is not tantamount to enacting the resolution, and establishing that the minor repair can solve the problem identified in the affirmative analysis.

Minor repair arguments are not used very extensively at present. The weakness of the minor repair argument is that it assumes the same burdens as the counterplan. Moreover, if a repair moves to resolve a problem in the same direction as the affirmative, it has the added problem of affirming the topic.

Not all arguments against traditional cases have to do with indicting the reasons given for change. Sometimes, negatives actually find reasons that the plan would not meet the need or that disadvantages would result. But clearly the major argumentative action centers on the attack and defense of the status quo. To a large extent, debate

A negative debater plans her defense of the present system—the status quo.

has shifted to a comparative advantages format, where the debate centers on the merits of the affirmative plan, rather than the affirmative case. The next section focuses on "plan side" arguments and the development of strategic positions against comparative advantages cases.

Comparative Advantages Cases and Plan-Side Arguments

As discussed in Chapter 7, a comparative advantages case enacts a plan that illustrates one or more of the actions authorized by the resolution. The plan is said to produce certain advantages, which may be independent of one another. Comparative advantages cases are developed in a number of ways, but in their simplest form they all argue that: (1) the plan produces a certain effect; (2) the effect is qualitatively beneficial; (3) the benefits are significant; and (4) the present system does not or cannot garner the same degree or kind of advantage.

For example, in the case of a plan that would ban smoking, the affirmative might argue:

I. Advantage: Banning smoking produces significant life savings.
  A. A ban reduces the number of smokers.
  B. Reducing the number of smokers reduces the chance of lung cancer.
  C. Lung cancer results in a high death rate.
  D. Voluntary smoking cessation programs will not reduce smoking and lung cancer rates as well.
II. Advantage: Banning smoking reduces an unnecessary drain on medical resources.
  A. A ban reduces the number of smokers.
  B. Reducing the number of smokers reduces the risks of respiratory illnesses.
  C. Respiratory illnesses create a high demand for hospital resources that could be eliminated.
  D. Smoking is increasing in the status quo and it is unlikely that hospital demand will decrease.

Note that the advantages in this case are relatively independent of one another. One emphasizes the reduction of deaths, the other of illness and hospital resources. The advantages are only dependent at the level that both presume a similar plan-meet-advantage causality argument; namely, that the proposal will reduce smoking. Note also that the plans do not offer solutions to the problems of cancer deaths or hospital overcrowding. Rather, both simply make social conditions better. It is in the nature of the comparative advantages case to ameliorate social problems rather than reach resolution. What options are open to the negative with such a case development?

Two options previously discussed under case-side arguments are useful, with some adaptation. The negative could utilize the strategy of straight refutation to simply deny the truth value of the affirmative claims; that is, the negative could question the accuracy, authoritativeness, and timeliness of affirmative proof. Additionally, the negative might wish to defend the present system by showing trends of decreased smoking, reduced cancer deaths, and decreased hospital utilization for respiratory disease. But these arguments, by themselves, are not likely to be very effective. However, well the present system is doing, there is always room for improvement. And it is the notion of room for improvement that the comparative advantages case sells.

Additional arguments are needed: "plan-side" arguments. Traditionally, the first negative handled the case-side arguments, and the second negative developed indictments, a division of labor that produced clear organizational responsibilities. However, since the advent of the comparative advantages case, the division of labor is less clear, and plan arguments are usually sketched in their entirety in the first negative constructive, with extensions coming later in the debate.

This section presents a few of the most typical plan indictments. Alternative causality and workability are typically **plan-meet-advantage** arguments. In effect, they maintain that—for different reasons—the affirmative cannot obtain either the kind or degree of advantages it purports to produce. **Disadvantages** suggest that whatever effects the plan will have, such consequences are not benign, may be significantly harmful, and are a unique product of an affirmative action.

Alternative Causality

Alternative causality means that there are causes for the problem other than those dealt with by the affirmative. The negative team approaches alternative causality with the following strategy: first, point out that a problem has more than one cause and isolate a number of reasons why the problem exists; second, indicate that the amount of the problem that will be eliminated by the affirmative plan will be small, because the affirmative has misanalyzed the root causes of the problem; third, establish that the cause isolated is the major cause, and most importantly, will persist even though the affirmative plan is adopted.

For example, on the resolution "*Resolved*: That the United States government should reduce worldwide pollution through its trade and/or aid policies," affirmative teams argued that lesser-developed countries used high-sulfur coal to supply power, resulting in high levels of air pollution since these countries did not have the technology to control the pollution. The plan proposed that the technology be supplied to these countries and that its use be encouraged. If a country did not take advantage of the technology, their trade status with the United States would be affected.

Negatives were able to reduce the effectiveness of the plan by pointing out that the lesser-developed countries were not the only countries who did not use the available technology. The negative pointed out that many industries in the United States, as well as those in other developed countries, were not using the latest technology because of the high cost of that technology. Therefore, even if the lesser-developed countries used the technology that they were given in exchange for good trade relations, there would be no guarantee that air pollution from high-sulfur coal would decrease because the developed countries would still be polluting.

If the negative team can quantify the significance of the alternate causality, their argument is much stronger. In the air pollution example, the negative could read evidence indicating how much pollution was generated by the coal-fired plants in the United States. The evidence would demonstrate the significance of this pollution and then show what is being done in other developed countries. The negative would argue that while the affirmative might decrease air pollution generated by industries in lesser-developed countries, the problem would still be significant due to pollution generated in the developed countries.

Using the worldwide pollution resolution, consider another approach the negative might take. The affirmative still argues that lesser-developed countries use high-sulfur coal to provide their energy. The affirmative harm is death and suffering from lung cancer. The affirmative supplies the technology to reduce pollution and, thereby, reduce death and suffering. The negative argues that people will still die of lung cancer because the rate of cigarette smoking is high in these countries. The negative then reads the evidence on lung cancer caused by smoking. However, in this example, the negative cannot provide a study that differentiates the degree of responsibility of lung cancer caused by cigarette smoking and that caused by air pollution from coal-fired plants. Thus, the affirmative could argue that since there were direct, known links between the sulfur dioxide pollution from coal and lung cancer, some degree of effectiveness could be shown. Unless the judge is quite strict and demands that the plan completely meet the need, the negative does not make as great an inroad on the argument as it might.

Workability

When presenting workability as it relates to the affirmative, the obligation is to present a plan that is feasible. On the negative, a **workability argument** is one that claims the plan is *not* feasible because it lacks a crucial internal step that the affirmative did not anticipate, or it depends upon resources that are not available, or requires actions that are impratical. Sometimes even experienced advocates will have a flaw in their plans. A funding plank will be left out, no enforcement provided, or no topical action mandated. In such cases the plan will not work and ought to be rejected. Few judges will allow the affirmative the luxury of amending the plan. Like a bill called to a final vote before Congress, the resolution is voted up or down as it is presented in the first affirmative constructive.

Most **workability** arguments do not come from obvious errors in the plan. Rather, workability emerges from matching the mandates of the plan to the external environmental factors that limit the objectives of the plan. For example, a plan to make doctors work in a ghetto for five years would not work if such a mandate caused all doctors to go into research in order to avoid the injunction. A plan to control wages and prices would not work if all goods were sold illegally on the black market, despite government laws. To discover workability arguments, it is necessary to ask, "Why hasn't this plan been tried before?" There are often many good reasons.

Workability is a fundamental requirement for a plan to be successful. If it does not work, then there is no reason for adopting it. On the other hand, it is difficult to prove absolutely that there is no prospect for a plan to work, unless the affirmative has made a careless mistake. For this reason, workability is usually presented with other arguments.

Circumvention

One form of plan-meet-advantage argument frequently employed by negatives is that countermeasures will arise that circumvent the objectives of the affirmative plan. This area of analysis becomes particularly fertile when the case depends on the attitudes of interest groups or social agencies (attitudinal inherency). The essence of this position is that unless the attitudes that continue the problem are changed, the old object will simply reappear in a new form. One can remove guns, it may be argued, but thrill-seekers will merely turn to knives. The plan-meet-advantage argument can be expanded into a disadvantage if the new manifestation of the attitude is more harmful than the old one. If knives are more lethal than guns, then the net effect of the plan is to worsen needless suffering and death.

A **circumvention** argument always has two parts: the motive and the means. The *motive* for circumvention usually can be isolated from the inherency presented by the affirmative. Certain social groups or institutions often perpetuate problems because they benefit in some way from preventing the greater good. Unless the affirmative changes the structure of social incentives, giving these groups a motive for doing good, the ultimate reason for the problem will continue to exist. If the affirmative does not buy off, break up, or ship out the wrongdoers, then the motive remains. In contrast with the motive, the *means* for circumvention are as various as the negative speaker's imagination is fertile.

However, circumvention arguments aren't always easy to establish. There are several means by which the affirmative can argue attitudinal inherency and not open itself up to circumvention attacks. The most prevalent method is to argue that the motives of people under the present system are unknown or passive. People perpetuate the problem by bad habits, inertia, or poor coordination. Given no strong attitude one way or the other, they are not likely to circumvent the plan.

In practice, the negative rarely reads evidence on circumvention; most of it is provided by the affirmative. The first negative might argue inherency and claim that the motives in the present system are not so adamantly evil as portrayed by the affirmative. This would not preclude the second negative from arguing plan circumvention, as long as the argument is prefaced by the phrase "To the extent you accept what the affirmative says is true, then . . ." Otherwise, a circumvention argument might contradict inherency.

In such a circumstance, the negative must press for a motive, a way in which the plan may overcome inertia and challenge people to action. For example, under the topic "*Resolved*: That the United States should ban military aid to Central America." A plan under this resolution would ban the sending of arms and munitions to regimes in Central America. Note that there is a natural avenue for circumvention of the affirmative intent to reduce military conflict in Central America. The negative could argue that Congress might send financial or food aid to Central America. This would free up resources that could be spent on weapons and the regimes in Central America would simply buy these weapons form Europe or Asia. The affirmative could declare such attempts illegal under this plan, but these efforts might be viewed as beyond the scope of the resolution. On the other hand, it would appear that economic assistance is a form of military aid, although indirect, and could be banned under this resolution. Whether the plan could be expanded to involve indirect or extratopical efforts to stop circumvention will vary by debate district.

Assessing Plan-Meet-Advantage Arguments

Alternate causality, workability, and circumvention arguments all point to the same conclusion: the affirmative advantage will not come about. The basic idea behind plan-meet-advantage arguments is to show that the plan efforts will be no better than the status quo. When combined with running refutation that casts doubt on the affirmative's own proof, plan-meet-need arguments yield a lower net benefit to adopting the affirmative proposal.

However, a lower net benefit is not a *zero* net benefit. Unless there is some clear reason to reject the affirmative proposal, many judges might be willing to give the proposal a try. In any given round of debate, the likelihood that the negative will establish complete failure of the plan to achieve its advantages is very low, especially when the affirmative has multiple, independent advantages to the plan. Therefore, in debating comparative advantages cases, it is necessary to develop disadvantages.

Disadvantages

Disadvantages are the potentially bad consequences implied by the specific affirmative case. Disadvantages are the fifth stock issue (voting issue). The first four are affirmative issues discussed in Chapter 6. Disadvantages are a stock issue argued by the negative, much the same as the stock issue of topicality. For example, a case that justifies socialized medicine may result in a doctors' strike, harming the quality of medical care. Socialized medicine might also discourage students from pursuing a career in medicine, thus worsening the quality of the delivery system. When raising disadvantage arguments, the negative claims that to gain an advantage in one area of the topic will only make things worse overall. The disadvantage has the effect of turning the case—making a problem worse rather than better. Disadvantages are a powerful argument in most rounds. If they are won by the negative, the affirmative cannot win. *Uniqueness* is an important element of the negative argument. If the disadvantage is not unique to the affirmative plan, the affirmative could argue that the disadvantage is not a reason to vote negative, because it is possible for the disadvantage to occur under the present system.

Any disadvantage is composed of two parts: the links and the impacts. The **link** can be defined as the "why" part of the disadvantage. It is the proof that explains *why* the affirmative plan will cause an undesirable effect and *why* that effect is unique to the affirmative plan. A link may be either direct or indirect. In the disadvantages to socialized medicine, the strike argument would be a *direct* link to the affirmative plan. A doctors' strike is not likely under the present system, but the negative would attempt to prove that it is certain to occur under the affirmative plan. The disadvantage of a future doctor shortage would be an example of an *indirect* link, because it must first be established that socialized medicine as proposed by the affirmative would reduce doctor profits, thereby reducing the incentive to pursue a medical career.

In either case, the negative must be certain that the disadvantage does not occur under the present system *and* that the affirmative plan is not effective in offsetting the harm. If the affirmative could prove that the number of doctors under current conditions were declining and that the affirmative plan provided greater incentives that would offset the problems of socialized medicine, then the disadvantage would be turned around—it would be a net reason to vote for the affirmative. The negative disadvantage must be unique to the affirmative plan. For the disadvantage to be unique, it must result solely form the affirmative plan.

Since **turnaround** arguments are popular, when you are debating negative you will want to take them into account and preempt potential responses when structuring your initial disadvantage. The first step in discovering a potential turnaround is to answer the question "Why would this disadvantage not occur within the present system?" Or, alternatively, "Why is the disadvantage unique under the affirmative policy system?" The second step is to look at the affirmative plan to see if there are special plan provisions that might arguably offset the harmful side effects of the policy system.

As discussed in Chapter 7, these special plan provisions are sometimes referred to as *plan spikes*. A plan spike is usually an ingenious means of implementing a resolution to avoid the ordinary objections made against the resolution. For example, in arguing socialized medicine, the affirmative could predict that a recurrent negative objection will be the effect of the plan on doctors. In anticipation of this objection, the affirmative would take measures in the plan to offset the potential harm. The affirmative would then be prepared to demonstrate that these measures are an improvement over the present system, thus turning the disadvantage around. For example, the affirmative could provide salaries that are competitive with private practice, or the affirmative might pay for a doctor's education. The net effect would be to restore the economic incentive to entering the medical profession while guaranteeing medical care for all citizens.

The negative should be prepared to defeat the viability of these plan spikes. For example, in the case of socialized medicine, the negative could argue that pay is not the primary factor in determining a medical career. Rather, it is entrepreneurial freedom—a core feature of socialized medicine that cannot be offset by any plan spike to increase salaries.

Negative teams typically argue several independent links to the harm, and they should be prepared to rebut three possible affirmative responses. First, the affirmative may argue that any or all of the links are not unique to the affirmative plan. Second, the affirmative could turn around the link, thus adding another advantage to the affirmative case. Finally, the affirmative could argue that the significance of the causal relationship between the link and harm is not established.

What should the negative do if the affirmative argues all three positions against a single disadvantage? First, the negative must decide if it wants to extend the disadvantage or concede it and concentrate on another one. If the negative decides not to extend the disadvantage, it could concede the affirmative significance argument. This could be done by admitting that the negative has not presented sufficient evidence to relate the link to the harm.

The result of the negative's conceding the affirmative significance argument would be that the affirmative could not claim a turnaround; if the link is not sufficient to cause the impact, then there is no disadvantage for the affirmative to turn. An advantage that is turned around may count for the affirmative, if the affirmative can show that adopting the resolution would not make the harm (identified by the negative) worse, but would actually reduce the risk of the harm that may occur.

While the link in a disadvantage explains why the disadvantage will occur, the **impact** is the end result or outcome of the disadvantage. In the socialized medicine disadvantage, the doctors' strike argument tells why the quality of medical care will decline. The death and suffering that will result when people have inadequate medical care due to a shortage of doctors is the impact of the disadvantage.

The impact may be quantitative or qualitative. The *quantitative* disadvantage argues that adopting the affirmative proposal would result in a large number of deaths, a widespread increase in unemployment, or a substantial decrease in the gross national product. When arguing a quantitative disadvantage, the debate focuses on the relatively simple question of which policy system will have the greater lifesaving benefits.

On the other hand, the negative could argue a disadvantage with a *qualitative* harm or impact. For example, the negative might argue that the plan will significantly restrict liberty. This type of disadvantage can be very difficult to compare with the affirmative advantages, particularly if the affirmative is arguing *quantitative* advantages.

The difficulty lies in comparing two different values, quantity versus quality. When the impacts flow from different value areas, the negative should be prepared to argue the superiority of one value over another. Unless this is done, the judge is left to pick between apples and oranges.

Common disadvantages are discovered by looking to subject matter related to the topic. If the area is foreign policy, for example, and the traditional areas for advantages are security, stability, prestige, peace, cooperation, and prosperity, then the negative should search for the unique ways in which the resolution will create a decrease in safety and increase international tensions, conventional or nuclear conflict, arms racing, and possible world collapse. Moreover, the negative should be able to select its own disadvantages, compare the possible impacts, and be prepared to argue for their importance as compared with the affirmative advantage. This selection process should take into account whether the present system will be subject to the same harm without the affirmative plan and whether the affirmative plan has unique measures that might offset the disadvantage.

Generic Policy Disadvantages

One type of disadvantages that negatives frequently identify are generic policy disadvantages. **Generic policy disadvantages** involve the affirmative case and its impact on society as a whole. They deal with policy in general and not with the specific action of the affirmative plan.

Policy disadvantages stem from the notion that there is no such thing as a discrete action or a delimited area: all policies are interrelated to some extent. Thus, in looking at possible disadvantage areas, negatives first examine possible higher-order impacts—earth-ending threats.

Links are important in generic policy disadvantages to the extent that the policy effects are *directed* toward making the catastrophe more or less likely. When devel-

oping the disadvantages the negative will often use the term **threshold** or **brink**.
A threshold is a point in time when conditions are ripe for change. A brink means
approximately the same thing. An example of a brink situation is just before World
War I, there were enough armaments and animosity in Europe to create the conditions
for war. The assassination of Archduke Ferdinand in Sarajevo in 1914 was all it
took to start the war. In many cases, the threshold (the point at which the disadvantage
would occur) could not be precisely known, but any policy that pushes the affirmative
in the direction of a looming catastrophe would be viewed as unwise (or a reason
not to adopt the plan).

Of course, it would be very difficult for a negative team to prove, say, that
increasing arms sales to Iraq would result in the final catastrophe of nuclear war.
But the negative could argue that given the disastrous consequences of such a war,
it would be foolish to take the risk unless there were very significant advantages.

A typical example of a generic policy disadvantage is the "social spending," or
cost, disadvantage. As soon as the affirmative spends money to accrue an advantage
or solve a harm, the negative can argue that money will not be available for other
societal needs. It does not matter whether the affirmative case is energy conservation,
socialized medicine, ocean mining, minimum educational standards for gifted students, agricultural subsidies, pollution control, control of illegal drug smuggling, or
military intervention into countries fighting for "democracy." If the plan spends
money, social spending can be argued.

Sample Social Spending Disadvantage

   I. The affirmative will spend x$ to implement the plan.
  II. Congressional budget restrictions will not allow increased spending, so
     existing programs will need to be cut to fund the affirmative plan.
 III. Those programs with the weakest political constituencies will be cut first.
     These are often the programs that help the most people.
    A. Foreign aid will be cut.
       1. Money spent for foreign aid is more effective than money spent
         for the affirmative plan.
       2. Example of benefits of foreign aid (with evidence).
    B. Welfare programs would be cut.
       1. Traditionally, food stamps have been targets of budget cuts.
       2. Only a few dollars a year would save a life.
       3. Illustration of number of people currently receiving food stamps.
         Outline what is currently spent on food stamps vs. the money to
         be spent on the affirmative plan.

In the sample social spending disadvantage the negative would argue as follows. The affirmative claims that its plan will cost x dollars; of course, it will cost more because of inflation, cost overruns, corruption, and so forth. In addition, congressional budget restrictions are such that any new spending will come about only at the expense of existing programs. The programs that will be cut are the ones with weak political constituencies, such as foreign aid and welfare programs. Ideally, the negative would be able to establish that the programs being cut would jeopardize more individuals than the affirmative plan would benefit.

There are many policy disadvantages: trade wars, pollution, Malthusianism, or nuclear war, to name just a few. Debate handbooks are filled with evidence related to these issues, largely because of their popularity and cross-applicability among topics. These rather common disadvantages should be explored by all teams. The key is to remember that almost all debaters will be thoroughly familiar with these areas, so careful preparation of generic disadvantages is essential.

Process Disadvantages

Another type of common disadvantage is the process disadvantage. A **process disadvantage** focuses on flaws in the affirmative method of producing results. A process disadvantage relates neither to the particular content area of the topic nor to the policy's effect. The judge is asked to reject the affirmative case because the plan is an inappropriate method of achieving any advantage.

For example, a case that isolates harms in advertisements directed toward children could focus on the negative effects of television commercials for violent video games. It could be argued that children become desensitized to violence because of the onslaught of commercials for violent video games. These advertisements are colorful and action-packed, showing the player (child) firing at characters on the screen. The affirmative could propose that, first, video games should be rated for parental control, much the same as movies are; second, that television commercials for any video game containing violence should not be aired during children's programming on Saturday mornings.

A process argument may be launched against this plan, substantiating the importance of freedom of speech. The net effect of this position is to show that, even it is proved that banning commercials for violent video games is desirable and effective, the result would be interference with the right of freedom of speech, an earlier and superior social value. Thus, even if there are some unique probabilities of sparing the children, the process by which the affirmative plan achieves this goal is not worth the advantage.

Of course, there are answers to this position, but it should be noted that there is a low probability of a turnaround. The affirmative does nothing in the area to enhance free speech, and thus the negative is not debating on affirmative ground.

Assessing Benefits and Risks of Plan Arguments

Now that you know the possible negative plan arguments, it is time to begin the complicated task of putting together a complete negative position. In one sense, the negative strategy for plan-side arguments is rather simple. The negative merely aims to show that the disadvantages to the plan outweigh the advantages to the plan. However, the parts that go into the equation are rather complicated. At the end of a round, a judge has to figure out what are the remaining, unique advantages to adopting the affirmative plan and weigh them against the intrinsic, unique disadvantages to the plan.

On the advantages side of the equation, the judge subtracts out those advantages that will not occur due to alternative causalities, workability, or circumvention. Further, if the status quo is in the process of already garnering some of the advantage, then there is no unique justification for the affirmative case. On the disadvantages side, the judge has to subtract out the likelihood that the disadvantage will occur whether or not the plan is adopted and assess how well the plan is linked as a unique cause of a harm, or as a unique additional increment of risk in an unstable situation. The situation is further complicated by turnarounds. Because the situation is so complicated, it is a good idea to carefully frame your overall assessment of issues in your team's final rebuttal.

Summary

Constructives offer the negative an opportunity to refute the first affirmative position and to develop an extended position on the affirmative plan. In earlier years, the division of responsibilities largely compelled the first negative constructive speaker to engage in refuting the first affirmative, while the second negative speaker launched new plan attacks for consideration. However, as plan arguments became more important, the first negative's role became less certain.

Contemporary debate practice allows the first negative to offer a variety of arguments, including disadvantages, plan-meet-need indictments, and workability. The task of the first negative is to explain why these arguments warrant rejection of the affirmative positions. Thus, the coherence of the negative position depends upon how successfully the negative focuses its attack. In a case where there are multiple advantages, for instance, a first negative might argue that the first advantage does not fall within the resolution and so cannot be considered; the second will not accrue from the plan due to workability problems; the third is not really all that important in light of status quo efforts; and the fourth will produce results but the harms attendant to it are worse than the benefits. Thus, the position of the negative is geared to different opportunities for discussion and debate.

The second negative is in a good position to pick and choose arguments for development. The second negative may concede ineffective arguments or explain why they are not relevant to the other more successful position. On the other hand,

Stock Issues and Negative Strategies

   I. *Topicality*. The affirmative has not met its argumentative burdens.

     A. Are affirmative definitions of terms reasonable? Do they make grammatical sense, stem from authoritative definitions, and fairly divide argumentative ground?

     B. Are there superior definitions of terms that could be argued as alternatives? What are the implications for the plan if definitions are proven unreasonable?

  II. *Prima Facie Arguments*. the affirmative has not met its burden to present a complete case.

     A. Has the affirmative failed to develop a key stock issue that would establish harm, significance, inherency, or plan efficacy?

     B. If one accepted everything the affirmative said as true, would the resolution or plan remain unwarranted?

 III. *Presumption*. The decision should rest with the negative.

     A. Are there good reasons to have presumption rest with the status quo, given comparative degrees of change between the plan and the evolving status quo policy?

     B. Is the concern of the affirmative so small as not to overcome a presumption threshold?

 IV. *Straight Refutation*. There is no truth to or proof of the affirmative contents.

     A. Is the evidence for the affirmative contentions weak?

     B. Is there strong contrary evidence to affirmative claims?

     C. Are there key claims that, if denied, substantially weaken the affirmative rationale for change?

  V. *Defense of the Present System*. The present system does not need to be changed to resolve a problem or gain an advantage. (Traditionally called an inherency argument.)

     A. Is a problem or concern being reduced? Can a trend line be shown?

     B. Are there factors in the status quo that assure a former problem will not recur, or that a current one grow worse?

     C. Are there measures short of the affirmative that might be advocated as minor changes, without incurring the burdens of counterplanning?

 VI. *Plan-Meet-Need or Plan-Meet-Advantage Arguments*. The affirmative plan will not bring about the desirable state of affairs it claims to bring about.

     A. Are there reasons to believe the plan will not work?

Continued

Continued from page 237

Stock Issues and Negative Strategies

      B. Are there reasons to believe the plan will be circumvented?

      C. Are alternative causalities at work that vitiate plan effectiveness?

 VII. *Disadvantages.* The plan brings about unique events or actions that leads to significant harms.

      A. Does the plan lead to harmful, unanticipated consequences?

      B. Are these consequences the unique result of the affirmative plan and unlikely to be achieved successfully by the status quo?

      C. Are there multiple links to the harms, each of which is sufficient to bring about the disadvantage?

      D. Is there any possibility that the plan will result in a greater likelihood of resolving the harm not less (turnaround arguments)?

VIII. *Comparative Assessment Argumentation.*

      A. Do the disadvantages outweigh the advantages of the case?

      B. If the plan-meet-advantage and straight refutation objections are subtracted, do the disadvantages outweigh the advantages?

      C. What is the likelihood that the present system could mitigate some of the adverse effects of the plan or that the plan could turn negative consequences of its effects in a positive direction?

if an argument is working very well, then a good deal of time might be spent reading supporting evidence and refuting affirmative assertions. This movement back and forth between jettisoning losing arguments and expanding winning positions is the essence of strategic negative debate.

Questions

1. What are some strategies of straight refutation?
2. How does a workability argument differ from a circumvention argument?
3. In what instances does the negative shoulder the burden of proof?
4. How can the negative bolster its claim to presumption?

Discussion Opportunities

1. What are the limits of straight refutation in grappling with an affirmative case?

2. In what way is debating a need-plan case different from debating a comparative advantages case?

3. Must a negative always win a disadvantage in order to win a debate (assuming the case is topical)? Why or why not?

4. When does a turnaround of a disadvantage count as an affirmative reason for change?

Writing Opportunities

1. Write a brief introduction to a negative position. Be sure to identify why the position is a strong one for the round.

2. Script a disadvantage. Make sure your reasoning is complete and persuasive.

Critical Thinking Opportunities

1. Why is alternative causality a key issue in debates?

2. What is the basis for requiring a reasonable definition of terms? How can the comparative reasonability of definitions be determined?

CHAPTER 9

The Negative Counterplan

Objectives

After studying Chapter 9, you should be able

1. To construct and present a counterplan.
2. To understand how a debate resolution invites certain types of counterplan development and issues.
3. To grapple with topicality issues in counterplan argument.
4. To develop argumentation over competitiveness requirements.
5. To select refutation strategies in conjunction with counterplan argument.
6. To deal with issues of fiat.
7. To deal with problems of presentation and strategy in counterplan rounds.

Key Terms

To effectively present counterplans, you will need to understand the following terms:

counterplan
fiat
means
mandates
risks
processes
policy direction
philosophical
    competitiveness
mutual exclusivity
net benefits
permutations
presumption

An important negative strategy that has grown in popularity in recent years is the counterplan. A **counterplan** is an alternative to the affirmative proposal. The negative team presents a specific, detailed policy that they feel would be more desirable than the affirmative plan.

The counterplan should meet two requirements. First, it should not be topical. If the negative team defends a topical policy, it violates the common assumptions about the role of the resolution, which is to divide the debates between both teams. Second, the counterplan must compete with the affirmative policy. Generally, the negative team should demonstrate that the plan and the counterplan cannot or should not exist simultaneously.

A counterplan requires that the negative (1) shoulder the burden of proof in establishing the desirability of a workable proposal, (2) establish that its proposal does not fall within the grounds of the resolution as established by the affirmative, and (3) demonstrate that the counterplan is a genuine alternative to the affirmative plan. Despite these relatively straightforward requirements, the counterplan is the most challenging form of argument in contemporary debate. Mastering the counterplan is not easy, because it adds many layers of complexity to traditional debate.

This chapter addresses counterplan debating and strategy in detail. There are few issues in counterplan theory and strategy that are not controversial. Counterplan requirements are still evolving, and so far there is no consensus. Because fashions in counterplanning go in and out of favor, local practices and expectations vary a good deal. Although you will want to adjust your strategies to meet local practices, this chapter will explain the structure of counterplans, the development of counterplan theory, and the general considerations that go into the strategic assessment of such proposals.

Counterplan Structure

Generally, the first negative presents the counterplan. After the second affirmative presents refutation, the negative team uses the negative block to select and divide up pertinent issues. There are no hard-and-fast rules about how to write a counterplan. However, most counterplans follow a standard format.

First, the negative should present a detailed description of the counterplan they wish to defend. This counterplan should be just as detailed as the affirmative plan.

It is generally desirable for a negative team to explain how they meet their theoretical burdens—competitiveness and topicality. Even if this explanation is not offered when the counterplan is initially presented, the negative should be prepared to defend these burdens.

Once the groundwork is laid, the negative should explain why their counterplan is not topical—why it does not meet the requirements of the resolution. If the negative counterplan fails to meet any individual word in the resolution, then the negative can establish nontopicality. In addition, the negative should explain why the counterplan is competitive with the affirmative policy and why the plan and the counterplan cannot (or should not) simultaneously coexist.

An optional part of presenting a counterplan is to explain why the counterplan does not abuse fiat. **Fiat** is the power to establish policy by decree or executive order. If the negative is defending a controversial type of counterplan (such as anarchy, world government, or socialism), they may wish to explain why their plan is legitimate.

After presenting the counterplan, the negative should explain why their counterplan is advantageous. Any counterplan advantages should be developed in a similar manner to affirmative plan advantages.

This standard format is the most straightforward way to present a counterplan, but beneath the apparent simplicity is some complex reasoning, especially in the area of advantage development. In general, the essence of counterplanning is the argument that the negative plan is comparatively better than that presented by the affirmative. Some judges like to think of such debate as comparing two different options or policy systems. Thus, the development of advantages comes down to looking at the comparative strengths and weaknesses of two proposals. There are five basic options for conducting such comparisons.

Means

The first option for comparing advantages is to compare **means**. The negative argues that the counterplan meets the affirmative goal better than the affirmative plan does, because the counterplan enacts superior means.

In this instance, the negative focuses on comparative plan-meet-advantage or plan-meet-need kinds of argumentation. The negative shows that the means adopted by the affirmative for the resolution of some problem for garnering some advantages have intrinsic defects that are not duplicated by the alternative counterplan.

The negative need not utilize all of the subpoint developments suggested in the sample outline. A debate may turn on circumvention, workability, or causal analysis alone. For example, in a debate in which the comparative merits of cash versus in-kind services are competing with the common goal of mitigating poverty, a negative might contend that increases in the amount of cash will not have the desired effects of mitigating poverty. The negative might argue that (1) income increases are likely to be offset by price rises, especially in low-income communities, (2) the consumer power that is not eaten up by increased inflation will be wasted because of poor purchasing strategies, and (3) money is not likely to get to those poor who need it the most, the children. On the other hand, the provision of in-kind services (food, clothing, shelter) meets the goals of reducing poverty more effectively because such services (1) come out of surpluses and are not subject to inflationary limits, (2) are not dependent on the purchasing habits of any consumer group, and (3) can be distributed directly to those who need them the most. As this example illustrates, the

---

Comparing Means

Advantage: The negative more effectively meets the goals stipulated by the
affirmative.
A. Affirmative selection of means has substantial defects.
   1. Problems with circumvention
   2. Problems with workability
   3. Problems with eliminating causal barriers to effective garnering of
      advantage
B. Negative selection of means accomplishes affirmative goals.
   1. Fewer problems with circumvention
   2. Fewer problems with workability
   3. Causal obstacles to garnering an advantage more easily overcome

---

limits to the affirmative policy in meeting its goal are argued as strengths of the
counterplan in pursuing its strategy.

Such counterplan development has the merit of addressing a problem area similar
to that outlined by the affirmative, and thus promotes clash. The strategic weakness
of an alternative means approach is that the affirmative might ask, why not do both?
In the example, cash could help offset some poverty problems; in-kind services could
offset others.

Mandates

The second option for conducting a comparison of the affirmative plan and the
negative counterplan is to compare **mandates**. In this option, the negative argues
that the counterplan meets most of the affirmative goals, but stops short so as not
to encounter significant disadvantages to a comprehensive mandate.

In this kind of strategy, the negative accepts the basic efficacy of the affirmative
plan. Comparative workability arguments or circumvention arguments, for example,
are not at issue. Rather, the focus of the debate is on the *extent* to which efforts must
be made to resolve a problem.

Suppose the resolution calls for comprehensive health insurance to be guaranteed
to all American citizens. Suppose also that as a requirement of the affirmative plan,
all citizens would be guaranteed health benefits including cosmetic surgery. The
negative might argue that their own plan would include most health benefits, but

A negative team prepares a counterplan that effectively meets the goals stated by the affirmative.

exempt cosmetic surgery. The development of the advantage, then, would involve two steps: first, to establish that the exemption of cosmetic surgery would not significantly impair health benefits, and second, to show that the inclusion of cosmetic surgery would drive up costs and have serious and undesirable economic effects, perhaps even impairing the effectiveness of the medical industry. The negative would argue that sometimes doing less is doing more.

Risks

The next negative strategy is to offer a counterplan that offers a system with less **risk** than the affirmative proposal. A comparative risks counterplan aims at making a subset of disadvantages unique. It is often deployed where the affirmative offers a plan that relieves or improves a dangerous situation by incremental action. The negative response is to eliminate the dangerous situation altogether, thereby reducing policy risk even more effectively than the affirmative.

Comparing Mandates

Advantage: The negative team garners most of the affirmative advantage
without encountering significant disadvantages.
A. The negative adopts the measures advocated by the affirmative plan, with
specific exceptions.
   1. The specific exceptions do not bar the general working of the affirmative
   plan.
   2. The specific exceptions do not result in a significant loss of advantage.
B. By adopting a more wide-ranging plan, the affirmative creates significant
problems.
   1. The extended coverage of the affirmative plan brings about certain
   harms.
   2. The harms generated by the extended coverage do not outweigh the
   benefits.

Comparing Risks

Advantage: The negative bans any and all activity in the policy area addressed
by the affirmative.
A. The policy area addressed by the affirmative has substantial, irremediable
risks.
   1. Risks in the policy area are extremely difficult to mitigate.
   2. Risks in the policy area have potentially catastrophic results that
   outweigh any relative benefits.
B. The counterplan eliminates risks in the affirmative policy area.
   1. The affirmative plan still is subject to risk.
   2. The counterplan encounters fewer or no risks.

Consider the example of genetic engineering. An affirmative team may wish to
reduce the problems attached to genetic engineering by increasing federal regulation
of laboratory testing, by restricting the kinds of crops that can be genetically manipulated, or by lengthening the testing process before field application. This incremental

plan would preserve the benefits of genetic engineering while reducing the area of potential harms. The plan thus introduces greater increments of safety. A negative may disagree that this is a desirable goal, because the policy of genetic engineering per se is so potentially harmful and its likelihood of long-term successful containment of harms so small that any incremental policy is undesirable. The negative counterplan would therefore ban genetic engineering, show how such a ban would be feasible, and show that the loss of any possible benefits are outweighed by the risk of catastrophic harms.

The strategic thrust of this counterplan is to concede and *magnify* the affirmative harm area, stating that the potential problems are even *worse* and *more difficult* to resolve than the affirmative imagined. By magnifying the problems, the negative can argue that the alternative requires a much more radical and far-reaching solution than is offered by the affirmative. This type of counterplan removes a potential area of contradiction with the traditional duty of the negative to defend the status quo. While the affirmative might develop a case that shows how genetic engineering is presently evolving without regulations and that any safety advantage comes from the imposition of the affirmative plan, the negative instead offers a counterplan banning *all* genetic engineering. The negative thus does not have to be held accountable for the defects of any of the current regulatory processes.

Comparing Processes

The fourth option for counterplans is **comparing processes.** In this option, the counterplan enacts a superior process of addressing the affirmative concerns.

Occasionally, a resolution will bring the question of process into view. The question posed by the resolution will lead to debate that focuses not so much on comparative efficacy or risks but on what agents or agencies of change are most appropriate. There are many versions of counterplans that require different levels of decision making or different kinds of decision makers operating within alternative guidelines or contexts. Two representative examples of process counterplans are study and agent-of-change counterplans.

Study Counterplan

The *study counterplan* includes all approaches that involve a delayed commitment to action. Sometimes negatives will argue that a policy should be submitted to referendum, court decisions, extended public debate, and so on. The idea is that no decision should be reached at this moment because there is sufficient uncertainty about the nature and solution of the present problem. It is important in such debates to show (1) that the situation does not require immediate attention, and (2) that taking action now will foreclose important options in the future. The more prudent action, then, is to wait and see.

Study Counterplan

Advantage: The negative opts for a policy of superior flexibility in regard to the affirmative goal.

A. The present stature of a problem is uncertain.
   1. Some experts agree with the affirmative assessment; some do not. There is no consensus.
   2. Data for an informed consensus require more scientific measurement and evaluation.
B. Waiting to enact policy is a prudent choice at this time.
   1. Waiting will not significantly impair timely action.
   2. Taking immediate action will impair an adequate response.

One example of a topic that might prompt study counterplans has to do with climate change. Since experts disagree about whether the world will end in fire or ice, environmental policies could be developed to augment climatological change in either direction. If the negative can demonstrate significant uncertainty about which policy to pursue, the negative burden of proof is lessened. The negative does not have to show that the affirmative is *mistaken*, merely that there is enough doubt to make policy action unwise at the present. The negative could argue that there is time to gather more data, and that it would be better to set out on the right foot than gamble on a policy. The study counterplan would result in better-informed action in the future.

Note, though, that with a study counterplan, the affirmative has significant room for rejoinder. If there is no choice but to act at the present, or if the consequences of action can be reversed later in the event of additional data, then there is less of a reason to delay action now in the interests of acquiring more information.

Agent-of-Change Counterplan

Some resolutions specify an agent of change that may or may not be appropriate. Many resolutions, for example, stipulate that the "federal government" should take some action or other. An alternative way of addressing a problem might be to locate the agent of change at either a more global or a more local level. Such *agent-of-change* process arguments range from advocating the action of a world government or international alliances, to state action, to private foundation or industry action.

Agent-of-Change Counterplan

Advantage: The counterplan employs a superior agent of change in addressing affirmative concerns.
A. The agent of change stipulated by the resolution is inappropriate.
   1. The agent of change does not have sufficient jurisdictional requirements.
   2. The agent of change has limited means to resolve a problem or gain an advantage.
   3. The agent of change incurs disadvantages unique to its position.
B. The agent of change stipulated by the counterplan is more appropriate.
   1. The counterplan agent has sufficient jurisdiction.
   2. The counterplan agent has access to better means.
   3. The agent of change does not incur disadvantages.

For example, in debating the question of whether the United States should significantly increase its commitments to outer space exploration, some negatives presented as an alternative the creation of an international space agency. Such an agency, it was argued, would have better access to the world scientific community, thereby increasing space efforts to a greater degree. Moreover, the funding for such efforts would be more in line with the degree of resources necessary for serious development. Finally, a consortium would not be subject to the disadvantages involved in unilateral efforts: if all nations were engaged in a joint venture, then there would be less risk of starting a space arms race.

In some cases, agent-of-change counterplans have problems with competitiveness. Affirmatives might respond that it is possible to have action at both or many policy levels. This is a valid argument and a substantial indictment of the counterplan. The negative must be prepared to explain why running both plans at the same time would be undesirable. In the example, this negative might argue that by running both the affirmative plan and the negative counterplan, any unilateral efforts taken by the United States would result in arms race problems and undermine the benefits of an international process.

Policy Direction

The last form of counterplan involves comparing **policy direction**. This form of counterplan mandates that action be taken in a direction opposite to the outcome stipulated by the resolution.

In many resolutions, the linchpin of action is an injunction to "increase" or "decrease" activity in a certain area. For example: *Resolved*: That the United States should increase foreign aid to Eastern Europe, or *Resolved*: That the federal government should decrease deficit spending. A negative might argue a counterplan that basically accepts the mandates of the affirmative plan and requires that other actions be taken that are antithetical to the direction of the resolution. This is sometimes called an *offset counterplan*.

Comparing Policy Direction

Advantage: The negative shows that overall adoption of the resolution is undesirable.
A. The counterplan adopts the affirmative proposal in its entirety, while taking additional measures that are anti-resolutional.
  1. The proposal does not result in a "significant increase" of the resolutionally specified action.
  2. The proposal does result in a significant decrease of the resolutionally specified action.
B. The resolution is unwarranted.
  1. General action taken in the direction of the resolution is unnecessary.
  2. General action taken in the direction of the resolution is undesirable.

For example, on the Eastern Europe topic, the affirmative may choose to argue that increasing aid to Bosnia is an important duty. Supplies are low, the winter is approaching, and medicine, food, and energy aid would save lives. Therefore, aid to at least one country in Eastern Europe is justified. The negative team would encounter great difficulty in denying these claims. However, they may argue that just because it is desirable to increase aid to one country in Eastern Europe, it does not mean that aid to *all* countries in Eastern Europe should be increased. Therefore, the negative might develop a counterplan that permits some aid to increase, but that decreases the overall amount. Further, the negative would argue that the rationale for undertaking such a policy is demonstrated by the fact that all the nations of Eastern Europe, save Bosnia, do not need aid, and that increasing aid will only delay self-reliance, independence, and a general move toward economic self-determination.

In this example, a likely affirmative response would be to question why both of these proposals cannot be enacted at the same time. The answer is that they *could* both be done at the same time, but that the judge would have to vote for the negative because it has been shown that the resolution is unwarranted. This may seem unfair,

A debate team checks with their coach about a regional tournament's rules on offset counterplans.

because the affirmative was supposed to be able to define the interpretation of the resolution. However, the negative could counter that the affirmative definition unreasonably narrowed the requirements of defending the topic.

As the example suggests, the strategy behind an offset counterplan is to refocus attention away from the affirmative plan, which wishes to use the resolution only as an authorizing statement for a specific area, and toward justification of the resolution as a whole. The negative contends that it is the affirmative obligation to establish the overall desirability of the resolution. Whether such argumentation be labeled as *justification* arguments, *counterwarrants*, or *offset* counterplans (different terms for roughly the same idea), the acceptability of such a strategy is still highly controversial. If the offset counterplan is acceptable, the negative is able to widen affirmative case obligations. If the offset counterplan is found unacceptable, then the affirmative is able to narrow its own obligations to tiny case areas. You will need to assess the practices in your debate district or region before deciding to run this type of counterplan.

Choosing a Counterplan Structure

There are many different kinds of counterplans and many variations on the counterplans that have just been discussed. In addition, counterplans continue to evolve and remain controversial. There are some clues in the previous discussion that will enable you to participate in the ongoing development of counterplans.

It is important to note that the kind of counterplan popular in any given debate season depends on the kind of resolution under discussion. If you want to prepare a counterplan—or if you are debating affirmative and want to anticipate the likely counterplans that may come against you—you will need to carefully analyze the type of resolution being debated.

If a resolution emphasizes a change in the *means* of resolving some commonly accepted problem, then you should prepare a counterplan that offers alternative methods of resolving some social issue.

If a resolution emphasizes a change in the *scope* of coverage, by universalizing or guaranteeing comprehensive policy or a uniform approach, then you should prepare negative proposals that specify important exceptions while admitting most of the mandated action.

If a resolution emphasizes a change in the *process* by which problems are resolved, then you should prepare negative proposals that locate action in different contexts. For example, you might utilize either more global or more local agents of change, or require different sorts of participatory criteria.

If a resolution calls for greater certainty by reducing *risk*, then you will want to develop counterplans that offer radical risk reduction alternatives to incremental regulations and improvements over the status quo.

If a resolution emphasizes a change in the *direction* of policy, then you should prepare negative proposals that push overall policy in the opposite direction, especially if affirmative cases splinter into a number of small examples and leave open the question of overall direction.

No matter what the resolution is, though, you will need to remember that all resolutions are subject to interpretation. Any given policy resolution may invite more than one kind of policy argument. You may want to develop several kinds of counterplans and test them.

Strategic Considerations and Counterplan Development

Counterplan debating remains controversial. In addition to the actual issues under contention, there are a number of theoretical concerns that inevitably come under discussion. The reason that theory is contested is because a round of debate can be determined by which side demonstrates most appropriately the requisite burdens. This section discusses a variety of theoretical arguments surrounding counterplans, moving from more traditional considerations to the outer limits of debate theory.

Presumption and Burden of Proof

The traditional counterplan was a response to an affirmative need-plan case. The counterplan was deployed when the affirmative case area was so strong that it could not be refuted, or when the likelihood of successful refutation was limited. Thus, to offer a counterplan was to basically concede the affirmative harm as both significant and inherent. The debate then focused mainly around the comparative efficacy (workability, solvency, circumvention) of both plans. In such cases, the negative was required to show that their plan was not topical and was better than the affirmative proposal.

For a long time, counterplans were neither popular nor successful. There are probably two main reasons for this. First, when a negative had to concede that a problem existed and that it could not be solved, it granted the affirmative a large amount of territory that it could subject to critical cross-questioning. Second, by conceding the case area, the negative lost presumption and shouldered the burden of proof. Advocacy of a counterplan required that the negative establish that its plan would work and not have disadvantages. The additional burden of having to show cause for a negative ballot seemed to reduce chances of success.

However, with the development of comparative advantages cases and the liberalization of affirmative topicality requirements, counterplans became more successful and popular. The comparative advantages case altered the focus of debate from justification of the resolution to a discussion of the merits of a plan of action. Such an alteration, while apparently subtle, had far-reaching effects. No longer was the basic question whether the resolution should be adopted but, rather, whether the affirmative version of the resolution was desirable.

Securing presumption in a counterplan round is difficult. Does the counterplan team abandon its advantage of presumption when it argues a counterpolicy? If presumption is abandoned by the negative, does it then reside with the affirmative team? And if presumption goes nowhere, what does the poor judge do in case of a tie? All these questions need careful answers.

Recall the reason why the negative has presumption on its side. The status quo is not said to be the best system, or even a good one. Presumption is located with a defense of the status quo because it at least exists, whereas the affirmative must demonstrate that its plan is feasible. Presumption in debate reflects the fact that the greater the measure of change, the greater the risk involved.

The results of this reasoning for counterplans are rather straightforward. In a counterplan round, the team that can demonstrate that it deviates less from the status quo is said to have presumption. Thus, presumption does *not* naturally reside with one side or another, but with the advocates who can show that a policy has a less degree of risk, that it embodies a more cautious change, than the opposition.

Topicality

A counterplan must not support the resolution. If a counterplan supports the resolution, then the negative has failed to do its job. If this requirement were not in place, then there would be no common grounds for debate, as each team would simply advocate the topic. But what version of the resolution must the negative *not* uphold?

The negative has two choices: it can argue either (1) that the counterplan is not topical under the affirmative's own definition of terms, or (2) that the affirmative definition is unreasonable and, hence, that the counterplan is not topical under a more reasonable definition of terms. The latter strategy has the effect of reducing the debate to a topicality discussion. In this situation, the counterplan functions to underscore the unreasonableness of the affirmative definition.

Many affirmative teams do not define terms in the first affirmative constructive. Those that do most often choose an operational definition or a definition by example. For example, they may state that an increase in trade with the Pacific Rim will mean an increase in trade with Japan. From the affirmative point of view, such definitions are not exclusive. Just because one interpretation of the resolution focuses on a particular area, that does not mean that there could not be other cases that are equally topical. Indeed, most if not all policy topics support a variety of cases.

This means that the negative must propose counterplans that are not only outside the area of the affirmative case, but also outside any reasonable definition of the topic—even if such definitions are not made clear at the outset of discussion. From the negative point of view, the affirmative should not be allowed to expand definitions of the topic once it has chosen its own particular ground. The affirmative job of advocacy includes taking responsibility for its own definition of terms.

From a strategic perspective, definition of terms should be clarified in the first cross-examination period. If no definitions are given in the first affirmative constructive, the negative should begin the cross-examination by asking what specific terms mean in the round. Otherwise, a counterplan becomes subject to shifting definitional standards.

What happens if the counterplan is found to be partially or wholly in support of the topic? From the affirmative perspective, a counterplan that is found to be topical and desirable may be argued as an additional rationale for the resolution. Victory in the topicality area therefore mandates an affirmative win. Realizing that such a perspective makes counterplanning a strategy of some risk, negatives traditionally seek to minimize this burden.

There are two strategies available. One strategy is to place a condition in the plan itself so that decision makers are directed not to adopt any plans determined to be topical by the judge. Therefore, the net effect of the counterplan is zero, and if there are disadvantages that outweigh the affirmative plan, then a negative ballot would still be warranted. The second strategy is to claim that all counterplans are conditional or hypothetical (hypothesis testing). Such counterplans stipulate that an action *could* be taken, not that it is necessarily desirable. If action could be taken short of

Counterplans play a significant role in public debate, such as that surrounding the health care reforms proposed by President Clinton. Here, U.S. Senator Robert Dole speaks to the National Governors' Conference on alternative plans.

the resolution, then it should be. The negative can argue that its policy positions should be adopted.

Both strategies are controversial. The attempt to discard either part or the whole counterplan, if found to be topical, undercuts or makes "artificial" the policy comparison. Rather than defending a system, the negative is merely multiplying its options. The same indictment is leveled against conditional counterplans. Both strategies are criticized because they are said to reduce clash. However, both strategies can be defended as fair. Just as an affirmative might argue that parts of their proposal can be dropped without voting against the entire affirmative plan, so too the negative should be able to preserve flexibility in its own plan.

Competitiveness

In reference to counterplans, *competition* simply means whether the counterplan is a genuine alternative to the affirmative plan. Ideally, if a counterplan is competitive, then it is nontopical. In some cases, however, competition and topicality are not the same. There are various ways to develop and test competitiveness. Some of the more popular approaches include philosophical competitiveness, mutual exclusivity, net benefits, and permutations.

Philosophical competitiveness is perhaps the weakest means of testing competitiveness. The argument goes that there are two different value approaches to a case area and that the values are not commensurable; that is, they do not stem from the same outlook or general set of social purposes. For example, medical care could be increased either by voluntary charity work on the behalf of doctors and hospitals, or it could be enhanced by more money from the federal government. A state approach is philosophically different from a private approach. The reason that this competitiveness standard is weak is that in a pluralistic society different value positions can be brought together to work for the same end. If *both* state and private interests in medical care were enhanced, then even more could be done.

The second means of testing competitiveness is mutual exclusivity. **Mutual exclusivity** refers to the impossibility of adopting both the plan and counterplan at the same time. There are several conditions under which this might evolve. First, if there are opposing legal mandates, then policymakers could not undertake opposing actions at the same time. Second, if there were a limited, nonexpandable pool of resources, then resources such as trained personnel, raw materials, and so on could not be used for two different purposes.

The third competitiveness test is net benefits. **Net benefits** lays down a decision rule for the judge: for a negative decision, the net benefits of the plan plus the counterplan must be less than the benefits of the counterplan alone. To put it differently, if one could do both what the affirmative wants and what the negative wants, would this be better than what the negative advocates alone? This kind of competitiveness standard is used when the negative is advocating policies that help garner the affirmative advantage.

The basic logic behind the affirmative position is that if one could have a resolutional and a nonresolutional policy at the same time, then both working together would be beneficial, further reducing risks to the status quo. For instance, if an affirmative wished to expand private health insurance coverage and a negative counterplan offered increased government medical programs, both would effectively reduce health risks. Moreover, since neither impedes the other, it is desirable to have both, since neither may work perfectly and the harm of poor health coverage is great. A negative might argue that multiple approaches involve a degree of redundancy, but so what? Redundancy is sometimes a good thing, especially in an area of significant policy risk.

The last competitiveness standard is permutation. **Permutations** simply mean the rearrangement or reordering of things. A permutation as a standard of competitiveness substantially favors the affirmative. Using this standard, the affirmative argues that any parts of the counterplan that could be done at the same time as the affirmative plan become reasonable additions in a world where the plan is affirmed.

For example, suppose that a health care counterplan argued that spending on health care should be reduced, not increased, because of the harmful effects of government spending; further, to assure this reduction would not result in disadvantages, certain social activities would be banned: smoking, drinking, and marketing of high-fat foods. The affirmative might engage in permutations of its own proposal to reorganize the health care system for more efficient (albeit costly), comprehensive coverage by saying that the social restrictions called for by the negative counterplan could be adopted in combination with the affirmative plan to reduce costs, offset its disadvantages, and result in a better world. The negative proposal, even if clearly beyond the boundaries of the topic, can nonetheless be partially combined with the affirmative plan to produce a better world.

Permutations are useful in a number of ways. It might make sense to first undertake the affirmative plan and then engage the counterplan; thus, the resolution is enacted at least once. For example, for a resolution advocating increased exploration of outer space, it might be useful to launch a new system of weather geo-satellites and then ban further development.

Responding to Affirmative Case Arguments

In a counterplan round, the negative response to affirmative case arguments generally takes one of three directions. Which alternative to choose depends on the kinds of policy being developed in the round.

The first possibility is for the negative to concede case issues. If the negative adopts different means to reach an objective similar to the affirmative, then it may make little sense for the negative to argue against any affirmative arguments. The strategy then merely requires that the negative admit affirmative contentions, but show why they do not matter to the outcome of the debate. This strategy focuses the clash on narrow comparative policy rationales and de-emphasizes affirmative contentions.

The second negative option is to make partial concessions. In many counterplan rounds, the negative opts both to attack the affirmative contentions and to advance counterplan arguments. The reason for this strategy most often is that the desirability of the counterplan is enhanced by reducing the efficacy of the affirmative plan.

For example, an affirmative plan may seek to relieve the effects of poverty by giving cash grants to the needy. If a negative can show that giving the poor a greater cash income will not result in decreased hunger, enhanced health care, or better housing, then a counterplan that features vouchers for in-kind services will look that much better. Further, if the negative can show that the problems of hunger, health care, and housing are overstated, then even if in-kind services are not as desirable as cash, the comparative consequences of any disadvantage that may come about due to the increased spending of the affirmative plan are still enhanced. Thus, an important part of the negative strategy is reducing the net benefits of the affirmative plan.

Note that there is an important caveat to the strategy of partial concession.

The negative should make sure that the solvency, workability, and significance indictments launched against the affirmative plan do not apply to the counterplan as well. The negative also should guard against those indictments that apply even more to the counterplan than to the affirmative. The most effective affirmative strategy against counterplans is to show that solvency arguments are more telling on the negative side.

Finally, the negative could choose to make no concessions. In some instances, a counterplan debate proceeds like a traditional round, except that the counterplan, competitiveness, and topicality arguments are presented in the first negative constructive. The first negative then proceeds to make whatever additional indictments that are appropriate: case arguments, plan arguments, or topicality arguments. The major extension or explanation of the significance of the counterplan is left for the second negative to explain.

This strategy works because in some cases counterplans are viewed as only hypothetical commitments. Therefore, the negatives wait to assess the affirmative responses before developing the counterplan. In the earlier poverty example, it makes a great difference to the negative strategy if the affirmative is going to argue that in-kind services meet the definition of the resolution and are a good policy, or if in-kind services are competitive and disadvantageous. The negative time investment in counterplan development depends on which line of attack becomes operational. Whatever the standing of case arguments, negatives running counterplans should be careful to selectively engage discussion and to explain *why* certain arguments matter and others do not.

Fiat

Every policy resolution uses the troublesome word *should*. This term frames the ultimate question of the round. It also distributes affirmative and negative burdens: the affirmative must prove that the resolution (plan) *should* be adopted, not that it will; and the negative must demonstrate either that the resolution should not be adopted *or* that there is not enough information to decide either way.

Fiat, in its literal sense, means simply "let there be." When a debater says that a plan is "fiated," what is meant is that one should be willing to imagine that the plan will in fact go into effect. The reason for this requirement is to blunt negative arguments that it is fruitless to consider a proposition because that proposition is unpopular, unlikely to be adopted, or opposed by many people. Although some debaters think of fiat as a power, it is not. No policy is really made in a debate round—only critical testing of ideas and issues occurs.

The key question with fiat is how far the imagination can be taken. Negative fiat asks that, just as the judge would grant the plan in effect for purposes of critical testing, so too the counterplan should be granted a license of imagination. The negative might ask the judge to imagine a world where there is anarchy, disarmament, or a socialist system—and then consider what becomes of the necessity or desirability of the affirmative arguments.

Many judges think such a request is unreasonable, because it diverts attention away from clash over substantive issues. Others see such negative counterplans as imaginative and expansive—a sign of critical thinking freed from more limited, mundane concerns. What is important to remember is that the dividing line is far from secure, and will probably shift with each new topic.

This section concludes on an advisory note. Counterplan debate is a tempting strategy for the negative. After all, there are many different kinds of affirmative cases licensed by debate resolutions. When a counterplan is run, the negative is on grounds of debate that may be better prepared and more easily practiced than those involved in debating against a new affirmative. Moreover, the strategy of a counterplan round, if well designed, keeps the focus off issues where the negative has the least chance of winning and narrows clash to those issues where the affirmative is most vulnerable. For these reasons counterplans appear as popular options.

Summary

To successfully engage in counterplan debate, debaters need to be as careful and experienced with the counterplan as they are with the development of an affirmative case. Introducing a counterplan creates unique proof burdens for the negative team. If a disadvantage applies equally well to the counterplan as to the plan, then the disadvantage does not become a net reason to favor the negative. Moreover, if a counterplan works and gains an effect in a given area better than the affirmative plan, but the effect turns out to be undesirable, then even an effective counterplan may produce a net voting reason against the negative. Finally, the counterplan is not an elegant tool of debate. Counterplan theory is still evolving, and there are few neat ways to draw comparisons when two or more systems and related permutations are under discussion. While complexity might be intellectually stimulating, such uncertainty does not lend itself well to sound strategic planning and execution.

Counterplans are likely to be with debate for a long time to come, and counterplan theory undoubtedly will continue to evolve. Remember that each resolution will tend toward different sorts of counterplan development, depending on how the resolution is constructed, and how affirmative and negative ground are divided.

Questions

1. What are the two most basic requirements for arguing a counterplan?
2. What are the differences between a study and an offset counterplan?
3. What are the different kinds of competitiveness arguments?
4. What is the nature of fiat?

Discussion Opportunities

1. In a counterplan round, why does the negative shoulder the burden of proof?
2. Explain the strategic strengths and weaknesses of counterplans that: (a) share affirmative goals but use different means of accomplishing the goal; (b) share affirmative means and goals generally, but require specific plan exemptions; (c) are designed to reduce risks of action in a given policy area; and (d) emphasize a different process of enactment.
3. Why has counterplanning become a popular negative strategy? What are the strengths and weaknesses of counterplanning from a presentational standpoint in debate?

Writing Opportunities

1. Write two counterplans for this season's topic. The first counterplan should involve a rather dramatic change from most standard affirmative approaches; the second one should involve a change less risky than this year's approach. Compare the strategic merits of each counterplan.
2. Write a competitiveness argument for your counterplan from the negative point of view.
3. Anticipate responses and write a counterargument supporting your own understanding of competitiveness.

Critical Thinking Opportunities

1. Why must counterplans be nontopical in order to fulfill the negative obligations in a debate? What would happen if topical counterplans were acceptable?
2. What are the criteria for deciding to concede opposing arguments in a debate? In what situations would concessions be wise or unwise?

STRATEGIES IN ACTION

Julie's debate teacher had just announced the annual debate topic: *Resolved:* That the United States government should adopt a policy to increase political stability in Eastern Europe. That night Julie turned on the news and heard President Z being interviewed again about possible military intervention in Nation X. The President stated several possible reasons why such intervention might be considered, as follows:

- United States nationals are at risk and there is a need to protect American business interests in that country.

- The volatile situation in that country is threatening national security because it is destabilizing other regimes in that part of the world.

- There is needless chaos, bloodshed, and oppression within Nation X because the current regime is in disarray.

- There is a hint that the military within that country is contemplating the development of a nuclear arsenal and may already have chemical and biological weapons.

The next day during debate class, the annual debate topic was discussed in terms of the direction of the policy to be taken. (The only thing the class could agree on was that the direction was ambiguous.) Julie and her colleague began to prepare their debate for the negative. They both knew that the affirmative might introduce a plan that would either prohibit the President from a planned intervention or compel the President to take action immediately. Either way, the debate team was well aware that a significant argument—the Vietnam syndrome—always seemed to come up during debates over military intervention.

Thinking about the topic, the class discussion, and what the President had recently said, Julie and her colleague decided to research and write briefs on both sides of the issue, those being—

- The Vietnam syndrome is a myth, because it is a historically unique incident of an intervention misadventure and is unlikely to be repeated.

- The U.S. experience in Vietnam is a paradigm case of the risks of a military intervention, which have grown far greater in the post-Cold War era.

Consider Julie's use of strategy in negative argumentation. Looking at how ambiguous the direction of the resolution was and remembering what she had heard on the news, Julie decided to prepare arguments on both sides of the issue. This strategy was implemented in terms of negative briefs preparation.

Cross-Examination Strategies and Tactics

Objectives

After studying Chapter 10, you should be able
1. To explain the obligations of each speaker in a cross-examination debate round.
2. To explain and demonstrate the objectives of cross-examination in debate, both as the examiner and witness.
3. To participate effectively in a round of cross-examination debate on both the affirmative and negative sides.

Key Terms

To participate effectively in cross-examination, you will need to understand the following terms:

clarification
admissions
obtaining data

The use of cross-examination can be traced to ancient Greece in the fifth century B.C. Aristotle outlined the value of cross-examination when he noted that raising questions about both sides of an issue would help thinkers more easily detect the strengths and weaknesses of points that arose. This notion of the value of cross-examination was carried through various legal systems and used in trials. In England, the right of cross-examination was first introduced into common law in the eighteenth century. In the United States, the right of confrontation is included in the Sixth Amendment to the Constitution, which states that "the accused shall enjoy the right . . . to be confronted with the witness against him." The right of confrontation is another way of saying people have the right to cross-examine witnesses against them.

While many people think of cross-examination in terms of Perry Mason or Ben Matlock questioning witnesses until they break down and confess to the crime, cross-examination in debate is a little less dramatic. Since the concept of cross-examination in academic debate was first proposed in 1926 and adopted by the National Forensic League in 1952, cross-examination has become one of the most common formats for debate tournaments. It offers debaters many challenges and opportunities, both educationally and competitively.

The Value of Cross-Examination

Cross-examination offers some benefits over standard debate. First, the use of cross-examination makes debate more interesting to an audience. Just as in the courtroom, cross-examination opens debate to the unexpected. Because debaters deal more directly with each other, cross-examination opens up debate to a more informal conversational style of clash. Therefore, debaters as well as audiences seem to have more fun in cross-examination debate.

Second, the use of cross-examination forces more adaptation in the round. Debaters must fine-tune their analytical skills. Because questions and answers occur instantaneously, debaters must learn to think ahead, take advantage of the opportunities presented, think through questions before answering, maintain a good speaking manner under pressure, and keep the process moving.

Third, cross-examination debate pushes debaters to prepare thoroughly. Knowing that the opposition will be given an opportunity to ask questions about arguments motivates most debaters to take greater care in preparing their arguments. Weak spots are not as likely to be left glaring.

Fourth, cross-examination debate focuses the issues more clearly. The use of questions enables debaters to provide greater in-depth analysis and extensions of important arguments. Evidence that does not prove significant will be pointed out, and meaningless challenges will be exposed.

Finally, cross-examination debate provides good experience for those considering careers in law, teaching, journalism, the media, or any profession where the dialectic method is used. Debaters become practical in posing and answering clear, direct questions.

The Nature of Cross-Examination Debate

In standard debate format, the two debate teams never talk directly to each other. Instead, they discuss the other team and its arguments in the third person, directing all of their comments to the judge. In cross-examination debate, however, each of the constructive speeches is followed by question-and-answer periods, in which the speaker is questioned by a member of the opposing team. (In cross-examination debate, this means four question periods; in Lincoln-Douglas, this means two cross-examination periods.) Cross-examination solves one of the common problems of standard debate, the lack of clash between individuals. It becomes more difficult for one team to ask a question in a speech, and then have the other team ignore, misinterpret, or fail to answer that question.

Cross-examination thus heightens the clash of ideas and arguments, giving each team a chance to penetrate even deeper into the ideas and analysis of the opposition. For this reason, many coaches prefer good cross-examination debating to good traditional debating. Nobody, however, seems to enjoy cross-examination debate when the debaters do not know how to handle cross-examination. The rest of this chapter will provide a few strategies for effective cross-examination debate.

Goals of Cross-Examination

Even though debaters are given much freedom during the cross-examination period, there are basically three purposes for asking direct questions of the opponent. The questions should be designed to (1) provide clarification, (2) gain an admission from the opponent, or (3) obtain data for later speeches.

Clarification

One of the great advantages of cross-examination debating is that debaters have the opportunity to clarify and define their opponent's position. At the simplest level, **clarification** may involve asking for information that the debater did not hear or that may have been misunderstood. The questioner can ask for points or evidence to be repeated, or he or she can ask for something to be explained. These types of questions should be asked directly and quickly, so that the opponent doesn't have a chance to provide more information than that which was specifically requested.

In most cases, however, the questioner will be looking for clarification of a *position* that was not clear. It may be that the opposition structured the argument so that it could be extended in a number of different ways, depending on the responses. The cross-examination period can be used to force the opposition to take a stand. For example, if the opposition outlines more than one proposal from which to choose, questions should be asked to try and determine which proposal is the most likely to be used.

Admissions

The second goal of cross-examination is to gain **admissions.** Although it is difficult to get a debater to admit anything—especially that something might be wrong with his or her logic—skilled examiners can often use the opposition's arguments as evidence against them. Logicians have suggested for more than two thousand years that evidence from a reluctant witness is very good evidence for an advocate. If one side can get the other to admit flaws in its own case, little additional evidence will be needed to prove the debater's points. One of the purposes of cross-examination, therefore, is to gain an admission from the opponent that will damage its case.

Obtaining Data

The goal of using cross-examination to **obtain data** obviously overlaps the goals of providing clarification or gaining admissions. Debaters must remember that cross-examination does not take place in a vacuum. The main purpose of examining the opponent is to get material that will be useful in subsequent constructive and rebuttal speeches.

For example, if only portions of your arguments have been attacked in the opponent's constructive speech, it might be useful to use the cross-examination period to identify areas that were not touched. Affirmatives often use this process to help break up the negative block. By focusing clearly and quickly on the disadvantages presented in the second negative constructive, the affirmative questioner can ask questions that identify whether the links apply to the affirmative plan, as well as questions that examine the brink evidence (brink cards), proof that demonstrates at what point something will occur—the threshold of the disadvantage. The questioner can also ask questions that assess the actual level of impact from the affirmative plan. Breaking these questions in the middle of the negative block, the affirmative is positioned to use the negative's answers in the first affirmative rebuttal (sometimes eliminating the need to read evidence to answer the disadvantage). Of course, the key to this strategy is following up on the answer. One of the things that irritates judges in poor cross-examination debating is that debaters rarely follow through on the answers they get; in fact, the questions often seem totally unrelated to the debate.

Cross-examination can also be used to identify areas in which your opponent has agreed with your assumptions. For example, suppose that the affirmative has argued that the lack of health insurance is harmful to individuals. The negative does not argue that there is no harm in a lack of health insurance, but instead argues that the present system is working to provide options for those individuals without health insurance. By arguing that the present system is working to solve the problem, the negative has tacitly agreed that there is a harm. The exchange might go something like this:

Q: Now, the first affirmative argued that the lack of health insurance is a serious problem. Do you agree with that?

A: I argued that the present system is working to provide alternatives for those without insurance.

Q: But is the lack of insurance a serious problem?

A: I did not argue whether it was or wasn't.

Q: But you argued that the present system is working to get people covered. Right?

A: Yes. There are alternatives available.

Q: Why would the present system provide alternatives to insurance if to be without it wasn't a problem?

A: I guess the assumption would be that it is a problem.

Again, the important thing to remember is that the answers must not be dropped. The second affirmative constructive speaker would want to draw this negative admission through into his or her speech, reminding the judge that the negative agrees to the harms of a lack of health insurance. Debaters must realize that many judges feel that admission or points won during cross-examination do not apply to the decision unless they are mentioned during a formal debate speech.

Cross-Examination Tactics

Tactics for the Examiner

There are a number of tried-and-true tactics used by examiners and witnesses in cross-examination. These tactics help debaters acquire useful information or answer questions without damaging their cases.

The first tactic for the examiner is to begin with careful, analytical preparation. Anyone who is even slightly familiar with legal strategy knows that cross-examination is a vital part of the trial. Legal cross-examination is not an unplanned, extemporaneous affair, but a carefully prepared and reasoned approach to witnesses. Good attorneys avoid asking questions of a witness if they are uncertain about how the witness will answer. The same is true of cross-examination in debate.

As an examiner, then, your first tactic is to carefully analyze the case you expect to hear. Once you are ready to account for what the opposition actually says in the debate, you should prepare specific questions that contribute to your attack. Each question should lead to a point of clarification or of admission. You should be fairly certain of the answer that will be given to the question being asked—few things are more damaging than a surprise answer that helps the opponent.

The second tactic is to develop simple questions. The purpose of the question is to get an answer, not to confuse the opponent. Each question should be direct and

A debater from the negative team is questioned about brink evidence during the cross-examination period.

simple, so that the witness cannot fail to understand it. If the witness then tries to be evasive by pretending to misunderstand, the judge will quickly see through this ploy.

As an examiner, you should be particularly careful not to ask complex or negative questions. A complex question is one that requires two answers. A negative question is characterized by "Is it not true that. . . ?" and is too difficult to understand and answer.

The third tactic for an examiner is to develop limited questions. Because the witness knows the purpose of cross-examination, the examiner can be sure that the witness will be on guard. No debater will make large admissions that will damage the case. However, skillful debaters can lead witnesses in little steps that do not *seem* dangerous.

For example, the following exchange took place in a debate on the censorship of books. The witness was on the affirmative side, in favor of eliminating all censorship, and the examiner wanted the witness to contradict his argument that no book is a corrupting influence. The examiner knew that the whole affirmative case rested on this argument, and that the witness would be very careful in his answers.

By using limited questions, the examiner prevented the witness from seeing the implications of the questions.

Q: Are you a religious person?

A: Well, yes.

Q: Would you recommend the Bible to people who want to become more religious?

A: Yes.

Q: Would you recommend it, say, to a children's Sunday school class?

A: Of course.

Q: Do you think the Bible might make the children more religious?

A: Yes.

Q: Now turning to a different subject, do you believe in education?

A: Yes.

Q: Do you believe in using textbooks and movies to supplement class work?

A: Yes.

Q: Why?

A: Well, because they help the student. This seems like a waste of time. What's your point?

Q: My point is this. If children can be influenced religiously by the Bible and educationally by books and movies, how can you argue that pornographic books have no influence?

A: Well . . . .

Another tactic is to ask worthwhile questions. There is no rule in debate that says the examiner must use all of the cross-examination time (or all of the speaking time for that matter). Each question should be worthwhile, or it should not be asked. Debaters who use cross-examination poorly often ask a question just to hear the opponent say yes. The answer may never be used for any purpose, or the question may not even pertain to the debate.

As an examiner, be sure to direct your questions at topics that are most important to the opponent's case. Questions of clarification are about relevant items, not unimportant details. Questions to gain admission often focus on the points of the opponent's case that bear heavily on the burden of proof or presumption.

This leads to the next tactic for examiners, which is to use the answer in later speeches. This point has already been made but it should be stressed again. Skillful debaters refer to the questions and answers at the first opportunity during a constructive or rebuttal speech. This guarantees that the judge will see the relevance of the cross-examination period to the debate.

Finally, examiners should ask questions fairly and honestly. This, in many ways, is the most important point of all. Although examiners are in control of the question period and have a great deal of latitude in what they do, examiners should be honest with and considerate of their opponents. It should be remembered that the witness is *not* required to give yes or no answers, has the right to ask for clarification of the questions, and can be expected to avoid dangerous admissions. Debaters who remain honest and cool-headed can expect to be successful at cross-examination debating.

Tactics for the Witness

Like examiners, witnesses can employ a set of tactics to improve their ability to answer questions without being afraid of destroying their own cases. The first tactic is to carefully analyze and prepare for questions. Thinking debaters prepare for the role of witness as carefully as they prepare to ask questions. The case should be carefully analyzed, both affirmative and negative, to see what questions would be most likely for the opponent to ask. Answers should be carefully prepared or the case adjusted so that the questions are no longer relevant.

Many debaters take advantage of intensive practice to sharpen their ability to answer questions, and practice debates with fellow squad members can be very useful. Also, colleagues should practice questioning each other. Because they are very familiar with the strengths and weaknesses of the case, their questions will likely be better than those any opponent can be expected to ask.

The second tactic for witnesses is to think ahead. In answering each question, witnesses should carefully think of the implications of the answers. The witness in the censorship example should have seen where the examiner was leading him. He could have avoided the trap by saying that the Bible could make children more religious only if they were already religious, that books and movies could help students learn only if they were ready to learn. Correspondingly, he could have argued that pornographic books could influence only those who were already predisposed to be influenced.

Finally, witnesses should answer questions honestly and fairly. The credibility of a debater often is a major element in his or her effectiveness. Only by answering questions fairly and honestly can debaters maintain their credibility. Judges evaluate debaters who avoid answering questions or who fill up time with long answers as harshly as they evaluate unethical examiners.

Keeping Cross-Examination in Perspective

It is important to keep cross-examination in perspective. Cross-examination periods are a time to clarify points, gain admissions, and obtain data. They are not intended for grandstanding or trickery. One key point to remember is that cross-examination is not a time to present arguments. One of the rules of cross-examination debating is that the cross-examination period consists of questions and answers. Judges are usually very severe in enforcing this requirement, and they watch carefully for violations, such as questions that begin "Are you aware of the fact that . . . ?"

Cross-examination also is not a time to perform. One of the reasons that many people become disenchanted with cross-examination debating is that for some strange reason debaters think the examination period is a time to show off their skills as fledgling attorneys. Doing poor imitations of Perry Mason, performing debaters will shout at their opponents and strut back and forth. Such behavior, clearly, is to be avoided.

Most important, cross-examination is not a place for trickery. The best way to handle cross-examination is honestly and fairly. However, a number of immature debaters look to gimmicks for getting the best of their opponents. There are two reasons for not trying to trick your opponent during cross-examination. First, trickery is unethical and inconsistent with debate, which is formal argumentation based on reasoning and evidence. Second, *there are no effective tricks!* Inexperienced debaters often think that the only difference between themselves and champion debaters is that the latter know the "tricks of the trade." They soon find out that the only "trick" that really works is taking the path of most resistance to achieve superior research, organizational, and competitive skills. Debaters who try to use other tactics soon find that they lose more debates than they win.

Summary

Cross-examination debate is an excellent way to learn the skills of argument. The introduction of cross-examination into academic debate provides debaters the opportunity to question one another and learn the skills of public defense and attack. The value of the cross-examination periods is only as great as the questions are good. Gains are made only by drawing answers into the formal speeches of the debate round. With experience and some practice, debaters should be able to do quite well in the cross-examination periods.

Questions

1. What is the value of cross-examination in debate?
2. What is the purpose of cross-examination periods in debate?
3. What should you do with the information you obtain in the cross-examination period?
4. Why is preparation important for the cross-examination periods?

Discussion Opportunities

1. Because the negative gains a tremendous advantage during the negative block, how can the cross-examination of the second negative speaker be used to help the first affirmative rebuttalist?
2. When questioning the opposition, why is it important not to ask open-ended questions?
3. When you are being questioned, why shouldn't you volunteer information?
4. What makes the cross-examination periods in debate exciting?

Writing Opportunities

1. In the last few chapters you have been outlining affirmative and negative arguments. Take these arguments and work out some possible cross-examination questions.
2. Using the questions from the previous exercise, provide answers to the questions.
3. After examining your cross-examination periods in the critical thinking activities, rework your questions and answers.

Critical Thinking Opportunities

1. Using the flow of a debate, determine where the negative fell short in its questioning of the affirmative. Was there evidence that could have been challenged? Was the affirmative harm linked to the inherency?
2. Using the flow of a debate, determine where would have been good places for the negative to have asked questions. What questions would you have asked?

3. Using the flow of a debate, focus on the negative block. Was the questioning of the second negative speaker effective? Did it help the first affirmative rebuttalist? What could have been done to get more mileage out of this questioning period?

4. After having participated in a cross-examination debate, go back and review the debate. What questions or answers served you well? What were the problems?

CHAPTER 11

Refutation and Rebuttal

Objectives

After studying Chapter 11, you should be able
1. To recognize logical fallacies of argumentation, including both fallacies of arguments and analytical fallacies.
2. To anticipate possible arguments and prepare for actual arguments.
3. To explain the strategies of refutation and rebuttal during the debate round.
4. To analyze and answer an argument in a debate round.

Key Terms

In order to effectively refute and rebut arguments in debate, you will need to understand the following terms:

clash
logical fallacies
non sequitur fallacy
post hoc fallacy
analytical fallacies
begging the question
ad hominem attack
inferences
slippery-slope argument

Debate consists of much more than doing research, developing a strategy, and laying out constructive arguments. Although such work is extremely important in preparing to meet the opposition and developing the best position to advocate change or defend the status quo, more important still is engaging in clash. **Clash** occurs in the process of refutation and rebuttal: the act of attacking opposing arguments and casting doubt on them, and the act of answering charges, dispersing doubt, and defending, developing, or modifying initial arguments to meet opposing challenges.

The more clash becomes focused and contested in a round of debate, the better the debate becomes. Debaters learn more about the art of debate by meeting the strongest challenges to their positions and by engaging in a vigorous exchange of evidence and ideas. It is quite important, therefore, to develop and practice skilled techniques of refutation and rebuttal.

Refutation and rebuttal, the practices of exposing flaws in opponents' arguments and re-explaining your previous speeches, emerge from the process of logically developing arguments. If an argument is soundly constructed, it will contain the best available evidence, the evidence will support the claim in a straightforward and complete manner, and the claim will be made in a measured way, taking into consideration reservations and rebuttals. Any argument that has faulty evidence, a faulty link between data and claim, or an ill-considered statement of what purports to be true is said to be *fallacious*. Thus, refutation centers on the process of demonstrating that an opponent's argument is badly constructed—that it depends on fallacious reasoning. Rebuttal argues either (1) that the fallacy is only *apparent*, not actual, or (2) that further evidence and argument can secure the reasoning.

Many argumentation books contain discussions of the general fallacies of argument. While interesting, these descriptions are not always helpful to debaters, because debate involves certain characteristic problems of evidence and reasoning. There are special, recurrent weaknesses in the ways arguments are made, and there are certain tests that always seem to be important in policy debate because of the way stock issues are generally framed.

To be a strategic debater, you must become familiar with the kinds of fallacies that are typical in policy discussions. In addition, you also need to learn to quickly identify the specific kinds of uncertainties that characterize different topics. For example, the kinds of refutation and rebuttal that are important for a foreign policy topic are not identical to those important for a domestic policy topic, and even within the scope of a domestic topic, you will want to apply different tests of evidence depending on the nature of the problem addressed and solutions suggested.

This chapter looks at fallacies of argument and then lays out the most frequently employed tactics of refutation and rebuttal. Some of these tactics may seem familiar; others, more exotic. You will need to pick and choose your strategies, practicing and developing a variety of refutation and rebuttal techniques until you have mastered them and can apply them effectively. In a way, learning to argue is like learning to play music: generally speaking, the wider the musical range, the stronger the musician. But remember that there is a trade-off between learning to play one piece well and spending time on a number of different tunes. As a debater you should be aware of all the argument tactics available to you, but you should learn to adapt and use those that seem to work best for you.

Logical Fallacies

Logical fallacies, or breakdowns in the connections between evidence and argument, can be divided into three main categories: those relating to factual arguments, those relating to value arguments, and those relating to causal arguments. Whether you are debating affirmative or negative, you should be alert for logical fallacies in your opponent's arguments and be prepared to challenge and overcome such fallacious arguments.

Factual Arguments

As discussed in Chapter 1, a factual argument has as its conclusion a statement of fact. The debater maintains that something exists or does not exist or is or is not true. Further, there are three general sources of evidence for factual arguments: experiences that the debater and judge have had in common, reliable statistics, or authoritative opinion. Each of these sources of evidence can lead debaters to create fallacious arguments.

When using personal experience to demonstrate that a factual argument is true, debaters risk creating a fallacious argument on at least two levels. Personal experience may simply be invalid, or one's generalizations from that experience may be faulty.

For example, a debater once argued that no poverty existed in his hometown, Colorado Springs. The student suggested that he had lived there all his life and had never seen a poor person; certainly, some people had more money than others, but nobody was really poor. The debater hoped that his argument would stand as an example of one place in which a general poverty program would be unnecessary, but his argument could be regarded as fallacious on either of the two levels mentioned above.

On the one hand, the debater's report of his experience might not be based on accurate observation of his surroundings—as a young man from an upper middle-class home, he might not recognize poverty. On the other hand, his generalization might be faulty—one student's experience may not justify a generalization about an entire city. In either case, the opposing team was right to point out the possible limitations of this debater's argument.

Compared to personal experience, it might seem that statistics would be a reliable basis for forming arguments. However, as a nineteenth-century British Prime Minister, Benjamin Disraeli, put it, "There are three kinds of lies: lies, damned lies, and statistics." This cynical comment does not mean that statistics should always be distrusted, but it does suggest that statistics can lead to logical fallacies.

Strictly speaking, a statistic is a tool that allows a researcher to make inferences about the nature of reality. Figures are manipulated through mathematical procedures to yield more data than are already known. For instance, "average" is a statistic that yields more information than a long column of figures. Sophisticated statistical techniques can tell us a good deal about the nature of reality.

A statistical argument can be fallacious for many different reasons, but three problems are most common: a fallacious sample, the nature of material that is left out of the statistical report, and the nature of the process of reasoning from statistics to conclusion (the non sequitur).

Fallacious samples involve statistics that aren't truly representative. Many of the statistics that debaters use are sampling statistics. The principle involved in sampling is that looking at one part of the population will yield information about the population as a whole. For example, to determine the average class size at a particular school, you might determine the average size of ten classes chosen at random. If the sample was valid, it could be assumed that the average obtained was valid for the school. As you probably know, most public opinion polls are based on sampling. Rather than interviewing everyone in the country, pollsters carefully sample a few thousand persons and use their responses to predict the outcome of an election.

While many such samples result in accurate predictions, the sampling process can go astray if, for instance, the sample does not represent the whole. This was the case in a 1936 presidential poll conducted by the *Literary Digest*, which assumed that a sample of telephone subscribers was representative of the electorate. What they overlooked was the fact that many people—in this case Democrats—couldn't afford telephones during the Depression. The *Literary Digest*'s results turned out to be way off of the mark. A more recent example can be found in the 1980 presidential election. The weekend before the election, the race was being described as "extremely close." Yet, on election day Ronald Reagan won by one of the largest landslides ever.

Even if the sample is legitimate, other problems can arise. Statistics frequently are gathered through questionnaires, but researchers know that only 10 to 15 percent of those who receive questionnaires can be expected to answer them. For example, a poll of a sample of police chiefs that tried to determine police effectiveness received answers only from those who were satisfied with their departments. Those who weren't satisfied were reluctant to admit it. Furthermore, people sometimes lie to interviewers. A famous study revealed that *Harper's Magazine* was one of the most popular in the United States, but the number of subscribers, as projected by the poll, was several million more than the circulation figures *Harper's* reported. Because they wanted to appear "cultured" to the interviewers, many people simply lied about the magazines they read.

A second problem with statistics is that material may be left out of a report. Debaters should be very careful of unlabeled graphs and statistical tables that do not detail the methods used to compile them and the kinds of statistics being reported.

For example, by not reporting the *kind* of average in a study, researchers can leave their readers in the position of accepting an argument that may be fallacious.

There are three kinds of averages: the mean, the median, and the mode. The *mean* is the arithmetic average, the total divided by the number of scores. The *median* is the point below and above which 50 percent of the scores fall. The *mode* is simply the score that appears most frequently.

The following table shows how using a different kind of average changes the appearance of the statistics.

Income in Subdivision

Family A earns $60,000 per year	
Family B earns $45,000 per year	Mean = $35,857
Family C earns $36,000 per year	
Family D earns $32,000 per year	Median = $32,000
Family E earns $26,000 per year	
Family F earns $26,000 per year	Mode = $26,000
Family G earns $26,000 per year	

By not explaining which system of averaging was used, an unscrupulous person could manipulate these averages to suit a particular cause. For example, in an effort to attract new business, one might say that the average (mean) family income in the subdivision is $35,857.00 per year. Or one could quote the median, $32,000, to show that the subdivision is the "average American city." On the other hand, it could be argued that the poor citizens of the subdivision just can't afford to pay taxes: their average income is only $26,000 per year (mode). Using the mode would make a stronger argument against high property taxes than, say, the mean.

Researchers who are ethical carefully label their statistics so that readers can see what the statistics actually mean. Fallacies can be expected, especially in unlabeled statistics and in statistics that are provided by sources with vested interests.

The third kind of fallacy associated with statistics is the non sequitur. **Non sequitur** stands for "does not follow" and is used by logicians to describe any fallacious argument in which the conclusion does not follow from the evidence. Non sequitur arguments are heard every day. A petulant sweetheart might say, "You never give me presents! You don't love me!" A debater might say, "I'm due to win; I've lost three debates in a row." Or a debater might argue, "The public schools no longer need to spend large sums of money on sex education in secondary schools because teenage pregnancy has dropped by 50 percent."

Statistical non sequiturs usually take the form of the last example: the statistics are valid, but the evidence and the conclusion pertain to two different things.

Therefore, one cannot say that the conclusion follows from the evidence, even if the evidence and the conclusion separately are valid.

Many non sequiturs are easy to identify. If a debater suggests that poverty is disappearing in the United States because the gross national product has reached more than $700 billion, it should be obvious that the conclusion does not follow from the data. However, some non sequitur fallacies are more subtle. If crime statistics seem to indicate that crime is on the increase, but the definition of crime has changed from one year to the next, the crime rate may not be increasing. Similarly, one could argue that the incidence of cancer has increased in the last fifty years, but the argument would be fallacious simply because doctors did not readily identify the disease until fairly recently.

In addition to fallacies associated with personal experience or statistics, fallacies of factual arguments can also involve authoritative opinion. The opinion quotation is the most common form of support for factual arguments in debate. If a debater cites an expert who offers the opinion that something exists or does not exist, one or two common fallacies may exist. The individual author may be suspect, which is a matter of external criticism, or the "facts" reported may simply be untrue, which is a matter of internal criticism.

The most common fallacy associated with opinion involves a biased authority who reports something to support his or her cause. For example, a person who opposes a foreign aid program may present evidence to prove that the program is ineffective, while the opposition may select the available information to validate a counterstand. One might say that the program is a failure 30 percent of the time, while the other might argue that it is 70 percent effective. As discussed in the chapters on evaluating evidence, it is very important to test the external and internal values of evidence and reject any evidence that does not meet the highest standards.

Value Arguments

A value argument is one in which debaters want the audience to agree that a positive or a negative value should be attached to a particular situation. After showing that poverty exists, for instance, a debater will want the judge to agree that poverty is bad. Or after proving that crime is increasing, an advocate may want the judge to decide that such a situation is a social evil.

Value arguments usually are established either from criteria or from authority. Criteria arguments are based on standards that have been officially established, on examples, or on the debater's personal experience. Authoritative arguments are based on reading quotations from experts who have expressed their value judgments about the issue. The fallacies that are connected with each of these forms of argument arise from inadequate support.

In searching for recorded criteria, debaters look for written statements of the goals and interests of the principal parties in the debate topic. For example, you might turn to the Charter of the United Nations, the Constitution of the United States, or policy statements issued by the President. Fallacious arguments arise when a written statement does not agree with actual practice or when the statement has been misinterpreted.

For example, one might argue against war and for peace because the policy of almost every country is said to be peace-loving. But if such criteria represented the real interests of all nations, there could be no war. In practice, ideology and sovereignty seem to be more important than high-sounding policy statements. Another kind of criteria argument is an argument from example. The validity of such an argument clearly depends on a very high degree of similarity between two situations.

For example, when socialized medicine was debated, negative teams were fond of pointing to difficulties in Great Britain to show why the affirmative's proposal would be bad. The affirmative countered by pointing with pride to elements of the system that worked well in Great Britain.

In fact, both arguments were likely to be fallacious. There are many more differences than similarities between the United States and Great Britain, and usually there were significant differences between the proposal the affirmative suggested and the British system of national health care. Unless an example compares very favorably in every important way with the situation to which it is being compared, the argument from example probably is fallacious.

The discussion of faulty authoritative arguments related to factual arguments also applies to values judgments. A value argument probably will be fallacious if the authority does not meet the criteria. The source must be an expert and should not be biased. The information should have been gathered carefully and should be recent enough that the debater can be sure that no new developments have affected the validity of the argument.

Causal Arguments

The third kind of logical fallacy involves causal arguments. Causal arguments have already been identified as the most difficult arguments to prove, and because of this it is very easy to show that a causal argument is fallacious. Three major fallacies of causal arguments are the post hoc fallacy, the fallacy of the hidden cause, and—again—the fallacy of inadequate authority.

The **post hoc fallacy** is so common that some logicians feel if they could just educate people about its dangers, they would have done all they need do in the way of logical training. The phrase *post hoc* is short for the Latin phrase *post hoc ergo propter hoc*, or "after this, therefore because of this." Because one event is closely followed by another event, the first is assumed to have been the cause of the second.

Superstitions usually are based on post hoc reasoning. Someone, a long time ago, had bad luck just after walking under a ladder. Somebody had trouble all day on Friday the 13th. A baseball player noticed that he got a hit just after he touched his right hand to his left heel. From then on, the first person avoided the ladders, the second stayed home in bed on Friday the 13th, and the baseball player always touched his left heel before going to bat.

Such fallacies, however, also appear in less frivolous kinds of thinking. The stock may fall if the President is slightly ill, because investors remember that the last time the President had a serious illness a recession followed. Reformers say that Rome fell because it experienced the same faults the reformers were trying to remedy.

Logicians counter such reasoning by pointing out that *correlation is not causality.* Just because two events change simultaneously or are close to each other in time does not mean that one caused the other.

The best test for the post hoc fallacy is to ask if the second event would have occurred if the first had not occurred. For example, even if you could prove that the salaries of Baptist ministers had a high correlation with Puerto Rican rum prices, few people would argue that the rum prices wouldn't have gone up if the ministers hadn't been given a raise. There is no logical, causal relationship between the two events.

The second kind of causal argument fallacy involves the hidden cause. Teachers—including the authors—are fond of selling the values of education to students. One of the most common arguments they make is that the longer students remain in school the more money they will make later. People with an eighth-grade education can expect to make, say, $675,000 during a lifetime; high-school graduates might make $900,000; and college graduates might make $1,350,000. The cause may be good, but the argument is fallacious.

While it may be true that a degree or a diploma is required for many positions, it doesn't appear true that education is necessarily the cause of higher salaries for the more educated citizens. Hidden causes probably result in both a higher level of education and higher salaries. For example, highly motivated and intelligent persons are more likely to go farther in school and are more likely to be highly regarded in their work. To see that a hidden cause probably is more important in such cases, one need only look at the self-made millionaire who went no farther than the second grade or at the Ph.D. who makes less than the millionaire, even after obtaining a great deal of formal education.

Often hidden cause fallacies are very difficult to uncover. The tests of post hoc fallacies can also be helpful to point out hidden cause fallacies.

Finally, causal arguments can also be fallacious due to improper use of authorities. Many debaters find it easy to turn to the opinion of an expert to "prove" that causal relationships exist. Experts, however, are not immune to fallacious thinking. Critical debaters should carefully examine what experts say to discover post hoc thinking and hidden causes. If such fallacies seem to be operating, or if the authorities fail to meet the criteria for establishing their expertise, any argument that is based on their opinions will be fallacious.

Analytical Fallacies

Besides looking for specific logical fallacies, debaters should examine case constructions and presentations for **analytical fallacies**. Analytical fallacies involve basing a case on faulty interpretations or assumptions. Frequently, debaters overlook larger

Many debaters rely on opinions of experts, as stored in their evidence files, for "proof" that causal relationships exist.

problems in case construction when searching for specific points of attack. Analytical fallacies include begging the question, faulty assumptions, non sequiturs, inconsistencies and emotional appeals, and ad hominem attacks. Identifying such fallacies is an important strategy for refutation.

Begging the Question

Begging the question is basically a fallacy of the affirmative constructive argument. It involves unreasonably expanding or narrowing the grounds of debate. Although the affirmative has the right to its own analysis of the resolution, it is obligated to interpret it within reasonable limits. Some teams try to narrow or expand their analyses, thus misinterpreting the proposition, so that their opposition has a much more difficult time attacking their case.

Limiting the question is the most common form of begging the question. For example, on the topic "*Resolved*: That the United States should substantially reduce its foreign policy commitment," one team felt that it could not support a substantial reduction; therefore, it advocated withdrawing the United States' commitment to import goods from Monaco. Few negative teams could argue with this, but every judge who heard the team felt that it was begging the question.

Another team, which was debating the same topic, suggested world disarmament as the solution to the world's problems. The case was so general and philosophical that it was very difficult for negative teams to defeat it. Again, most judges felt that the affirmative had expanded the proposal so that it wouldn't have to debate the real issues. It was begging the question.

Even though begging the question is primarily an affirmative fallacy, negative debaters also can be guilty of this fallacy. Any time a debater answers an argument of the other team by limiting or expanding its implications, it is committing the fallacy of begging the question.

Faulty Assumptions

Wise debaters carefully examine the assumptions that underlie the opponent's case. They try to discover the premises on which the case is built. If the argument derives from a faulty assumption, the whole case may be one large fallacy.

For instance, on the topic *"Resolved:* That the federal government should establish minimal educational standards for elementary and secondary schools in the United States," several affirmative teams advocated that minimum competency testing should be instituted in secondary schools to guarantee future increases in college enrollments. However, the case was based on the assumption that minimum competency testing would increase college enrollment. Negative teams who could show that the assumption was faulty could readily defeat the case.

Non Sequiturs

Non sequiturs can appear as part of a number of analytical fallacies. The first is the non sequitur need for change. In the traditional need case, there are usually four arguments underlying the affirmative claim that the present system should be changed: a problem exists in the present system, and the problem is inherent, harmful, and sufficiently widespread to justify a change. Occasionally, though, the conclusion does not follow from the specific contentions that the affirmative develops.

For instance, does the existence of minor waste in the foreign aid program justify a structural change in the present system? Perhaps the problem calls for adjustments to eliminate waste, but it does not necessarily follow that the program should be discontinued.

The second type of fallacy involves the non sequitur proposal. Negative teams should always ask themselves whether the affirmative's proposal follows from the need-for-a-change argument. One team, for example, argued for free trade in the western hemisphere because of the growth of communism in Latin America. If such a problem exists, a change certainly may be warranted, but does this analysis justify free trade between Canada and the United States? Does it even follow that the United States should engage in free trade with Latin America?

The third type of fallacy involves non sequitur advantages. This analytical fallacy arises when the affirmative's advantages do not follow from its analysis of the present system and from its proposal. In the free trade example, does it follow that the affirmative can claim the advantage of being able to stop the communist menace? Could it even argue that free trade would help the poorest Latin American nations? If they are underdeveloped nations with little to trade, lower tariff barriers would do little good.

Inconsistencies and Emotional Appeals

Two other kinds of analytical fallacies involve inconsistent attacks and emotional appeals.

In a debate, each team is responsible not only for its specific arguments, but for the way these arguments relate to each other. It is on this level that many teams commit the inconsistency fallacy. Experienced debaters watch carefully for inconsistent argumentation.

On the affirmative side, many teams want to maximize their need-for-a-change argument while minimizing the cost of their proposal. If they go too far in either direction, the case can become inconsistent. For example, in a debate on compulsory health insurance, the affirmative said there was dramatic need for a change because 7 million elderly persons were without adequate medical attention every year. Clearly, this was a serious problem, but the same team said that its plan would cost only $50 million a year to operate. This sounds good, but was it consistent? Does it seem reasonable that $7.00 per person is adequate for solving such a drastic problem? Or perhaps the $50 million figure was accurate, and the need argument was exaggerated. Through such inconsistency the affirmative worked itself into a very common affirmative dilemma.

A common negative fallacy, on the other hand, is to argue first that the present system is working beautifully and that the affirmative's proposal is terrible, and then to turn and argue that the affirmative hasn't met its obligation because the plan it proposes is just like the present system. Such reasoning causes a judge to question the entire negative analysis.

Nearly as common as inconsistencies, and just as problematic, are emotional appeals. In most kinds of public speaking, emotional appeals are acceptable and even desirable as evidence. However, they are not acceptable in competitive policy debate. An argument that is based on religious or patriotic appeals—however heartfelt and persuasively delivered—is considered fallacious by most debate judges. More subtle, but just as fallacious, are arguments that discuss a "spreading, cancerous growth" in the present system or that compare the affirmative's case with communism. Such arguments are too emotionally charged for effective policy debate.

Ad Hominem Attacks

The last type of analytical fallacy involves the **ad hominem** (literally, Latin for "to the man") **attack**, an old standby of propagandists and unscrupulous advocates. Instead of attacking a person's arguments, the debater attacks her or him personally. Although such arguments may make entertaining politics, they are not considered legitimate in debate.

Although debaters rarely call each other names, they should be very cautious of giving critiques of their opposition's debating skill. Some experienced but not especially wise debaters seem to enjoy pointing out how illogical their opponents are, how poorly they have developed their case, and even what poor speakers they are. This is simply a form of the ad hominem fallacy.

It is, of course, perfectly legitimate for debaters to point out weaknesses in their opponent's case. They must not, however, criticize the other team members as individuals. Debaters must attack the arguments, not the people who present them.

Questions of Authority

Much of refutation and rebuttal comes down to whom you believe. As a process, policy debate is different than political debate because decisions are supposed to be made on the stronger evidence, not on the stronger image or personality. As the discussion of logical and analytical fallacies suggests, one key to presenting strong evidence is to choose sources who offer better opinions, observations, and conclusions than those chosen by an opponent. Debating often comes down to a contest of whose authorities are better situated to offer testimony in support of a claim.

Refuting Authority Arguments

In contests over authority, you can refute your opponent's argument by attacking the authority's qualifications, relation to consensus viewpoints, right to express views, consistency, or currency. Any of these strategies can be used in combination.

The first refutational strategy is to claim that the authority has *little or no qualification.* If a debater cites evidence without stating who has said what, then the evidence is no more credible than if a stranger had made the conclusion. Unqualified evidence is untrustworthy because it has no rational basis for belief. Sometimes, there is a modicum of credibility given a source because it is reported as a *Law Review* article or a magazine article by a journalist. To the extent that such observations reflect common sense or a consensus, the use of such minimal qualifications or claims to expertise may be sufficient. However, to the extent evidence is likely to become contested, then better sources are needed.

The second refutational strategy is to claim that the authority *does not reflect a consensus point of view.* There are experts who make all sorts of claims, and some of the best "evidence" on a topic may come from sources who make really outrageous claims, magnifying social problems in order to get action on a cause. Such claims can be refuted by showing that the evidence resides outside mainstream consensus. For example, an affirmative might cite evidence from an ecological activist who argues that human rights have to be abandoned if ecological policy is to be successful. If the negative can establish that no other person takes such a position, the negative can undermine the credibility of an authority's claim to a consensus position.

Another refutational strategy is to point out that the authority is not in a position to advance the claim being made. One of the key questions to ask is whether the authority is making a statement that she or he has a right to make; that is, whether the opinion requires some sort of empirical evidence before it can be certified as being true, and whether such evidence can in fact be gathered. On some legal topics, evidence abounds from conservative think tanks to the effect that 90 percent of criminals get off on legal technicalities, and that therefore the justice system is a failure. However, since trial is the only way we have found to determine guilt or innocence, the number of "criminals" who get off on technicalities is actually unknowable, and it can be concluded that the source has no way of making such a conclusion.

Another effective refutational strategy is to show that the cited authority has inconsistent views. One of the key tests of evidence is whether a particular source has been quoted in context: that the opinion taken as a whole tends to support the argument an advocate wishes to make. Some authorities will say that gun crimes are getting out of hand, but their solution to the problem is more guns, not fewer. Debaters should be careful not to use such evidence to support a conclusion contrary to the opinion of the source.

The last strategy for refuting evidence based on authority is to establish that the authority's views are dated. Opinions change as times change. What was once a consensus on the magnitude of a problem or the advisability of a solution may change as social conditions and knowledge are altered. The unimportant can become important and the impossible possible. A good way to refute an opinion is to show that altered conditions have changed the situation, rendering past observations mute. For example, there once was a lot of debate over whether health maintenance organizations or fee-for-service medicine would be the best. There has been enough recent evidence to dismiss speculations that HMOs would not work.

Rebutting Authority Arguments

Rebuttal tactics require the strategic use of time, so you should be careful to pinpoint exactly where major clash has occurred. As a rule, arguments that can be conceded without fatal damage or significant harm to a position ought to be let go. Instead, spend your time and energy on those indictments that can be effectively rebutted and that are crucial to the success of your position.

Many advocates will quibble relentlessly with the source qualifications of an opponent, but when it comes to defining their own sources they will not offer any better credentials or conclusive testimonials. Source qualifications are always a matter of comparative assessment, and it is essential to establish why your own sources are more credible than your opponent's. When rebutting challenges to your sources' qualifications, the more evidence from the greater variety of sources the better. If you can find agreement among representatives from different fields and from different political points of view, then you can demonstrate consensus.

However, it is important to note that sometimes consensus positions need to be carefully studied. For example, it may be the case that there is consensus that privacy is an important value, but there may *not* be consensus that what an advocate claims to be a violation of privacy (say wiretapping, or automatic dialing telephone sales) constitute significant violations of privacy. If a claim is backed by a consensus of authorities, then the advocate must establish a rebuttal by refining the context in which the claim becomes important. On the other hand, if a valid consensus backs an opponent's position, it may be best to abandon an attempt to question authority.

The position of an authority to make a statement is very important. The more important the evidence to the case, the more well-qualified and substantiated the source. Blue-ribbon commissions, government advisory reports, prestigious Senate investigating committees, consortia of university researchers—all these sources delve into and investigate social problems and solutions. Preparing the best evidence on key issues is necessary to win the debate, and you should be ready to reestablish the value of your evidence in rebuttal.

Part of rebuttal consists in giving reasons why certain authorities are not trustworthy, either by demonstrating that they have a bad track record or that their opinions are self-interested. Moreover, there often creeps into debate subtle inconsistencies between the strength of a claim and the strength of the opinion experts, who often qualify their evidence and hedge on its conclusiveness. To discount opposing authorities, you must be able to account for discrepancies.

For example, some experts say that low-level radiation from atomic reactors is harmful, while others say that radioactive waste produces no greater harm than does background radiation. Even if there is no way to tell who is right, you may be able to argue that it is better not to take the risk, given that people who are experts on both sides disagree. Note that even in the absence of clear-cut consensus of opinion, you can use rebuttals to further advance your position.

Finally, it is possible to rebut potential problems with dated opinions and observations by asking whether newer evidence is always better evidence. More recent evidence only makes a significant difference if conditions have changed to a degree to warrant a fresh assessment, or if observation techniques have improved in completeness or accuracy. Just because someone claims to have newer evidence does not mean that any headway is being made in refutation, especially if the evidence has some other weakness. In rebutting the latest evidence, you might wish to affirm that your own observational evidence was gathered across a sufficiently lengthy time period to impart confidence in the durability of your claim.

In sum, when it comes to the question of authority, refutation and rebuttal is at the heart of most debates. While debating qualifications of sources and quality of opinions is not as exciting as some other arguments in debate, nevertheless when it comes to contesting key issues it is important to know how to defend your choices. It is best to have good sources at the outset and to prepare even better sources for rebuttal. Also, when preparing refutation, remember that people in glass houses generally should not throw stones: if your own evidence won't hold up to challenges, you may want to plan another line of attack.

Questions of Fact

Debating questions of fact comes down to the basic decision of whether something is or is not true. If reliable experts witness a phenomenon, then a question of fact may not be subject to debate. Facts become contestable only when they can be measured and observed indirectly, that is, when one is extrapolating from a few cases to a general condition. Debating questions of fact, then, gets into determinations of measure and degree.

Refuting Factual Arguments

In contests over facts, you have several refutational strategies available to you. You can question definitions, assess the comparative importance of facts, or examine the measurement technique.

The definition of a fact is an index of what needs to be known. Sometimes definitions are manipulated to make facts appear to be greater or lesser. For example, the Reagan administration redefined a "small farm" by including relatively large corporate farms in the same category as small family-owned farms. The administration presumably changed the definitions of what constituted a small farm so that they could show that the number of small farms and concomitant income was not dropping, even though Reagan policies had created a farm crisis. To refute the status of facts, be sure to examine whether definitions are used consistently and are not changed to recolor the problem.

The second refutational strategy is to assess the comparative importance of facts. For debaters, facts by themselves are relatively unimportant. Facts only achieve importance when they are used in comparative fashion to indicate states of threat or opportunity that require action. Refutation usually consists of putting facts into a different frame of reference than represented by an opponent.

One way of framing the importance of facts is to develop a trend line. The trend line can establish that a problem is getting better, or worse. For example, if more and more people are leaving welfare and gaining employment, then one might see even the relatively large number of poor people in an optimistic way. Facts presented in this light suggest confidence that the system is working and that poverty can be eliminated without a substantial change in the present system.

Assuming that a trend line can be demonstrated, two avenues of rebuttal are suggested. First, there may be factors that limit the continuation of any trend. For example, the facts may suggest that poverty has been substantially reduced, but there are substantial reasons to believe that the rate of reduction will not continue and that a limited number of people will remain who cannot be helped by the addition of more employment. Thus, the importance of a trend is blunted, even if established.

Second, trends are subject to reversal. It may be the case that poverty does decrease for a while, but that when the business cycle creates recession, many people are thrown out of work and poverty returns. By widening the perspective on a trend to include a broader perspective on cycles, facts are put into a different kind of perspective.

Another way of framing the importance of facts is to develop comparative standards. For example, many people who wish to demonstrate the need for gun control show how the United States is ranked highly in violent death due to handguns when compared with other nations. Similarly, many advocates who wish to demonstrate the need for government prenatal care will cite evidence of how the United States compares with other, presumably less developed, nations in infant mortality. Facts put into such comparative frameworks achieve significance because they show that others can do better and that our own policies are doing worse.

Refutation of such comparative analysis is quite difficult. One way to blunt such comparisons is to show that the facts are really not comparable on a similar scale. For instance, it may be true that the United States has far more deaths by handguns than Great Britain, but the United States is a much larger country.

The rebuttal to this argument maintains, of course, that the percentage of deaths due to handgun violence is still greater in the United States per capita, that is accounting for differences in population. But even when the data are put in a comparative framework, it is important to present reasons that make the data unique. In this case, it might be argued that the United States is a more violent society than Great Britain. Handguns, knives, or shotguns, it does not matter: crime will continue. Notice, though, that the refutation here forces the advocate to shift the rebuttal on to weaker grounds, grounds that cannot deny the comparative desirability of the British system (at least insofar as handguns are concerned), but merely argues that the goals are not attainable in the United States. While the latter position is less satisfying, sometimes it is the only one available.

The third refutational strategy is to ask whether the measurement techniques are appropriate. The kind of general social facts that are discussed in policy arguments are usually based on the process of measurement and extrapolation. *Measurement* requires the identification and sampling of a population whose factual makeup is being determined. *Extrapolation* requires making a generalization from the specific group being observed to the whole population. The larger the number of observations and the more representative the sample, the greater the confidence one can place in the extrapolation. Both refutation and rebuttal are directed at the confidence that ought to be placed in measurement.

Some facts simply cannot be measured because there are inadequate sampling techniques or instruments of observation. For example, one cannot know precisely how many homeless there are in the United States because the homeless by definition do not stay at home to be counted. At best, one can guess from indirect clues: soup kitchen attendance, homeless shelter occupancy rates, and welfare questionnaires. However, even though homelessness is a dire condition and its harms to individuals cannot be underestimated, because of the problem of measurement, the number of the homeless in the United States has never been established as significant.

To refute factual arguments

1. Question definitions.
2. Assess comparative importance of facts.
3. Examine the measurement technique.

Rebutting Factual Arguments

As with authority arguments, it is important to allocate your time wisely when rebutting factual arguments. Rebutting the definition of facts generally involves reestablishing the value of your own definitions. Rebutting the comparative importance of facts and the appropriateness of measurement techniques involves other strategies.

There are two ways to rebut charges related to measurement techniques. One way is to establish a *range of measurement*. There are conservative estimates that establish a minimum number of facts necessary to prove that a problem is quantitatively significant. Even if the minimum number is small, the existence of such facts may still warrant policy change. For example, since homelessness is a dire condition, you could argue that it really doesn't matter how many homeless there are to warrant government action.

Another way to rebut measurement arguments is to establish *criteria for measurement* as part of a program of action. If established measurement techniques are uncertain, then part of any plan of action could include putting in place mechanisms that could accurately assess the problem and rationally administer solutions. Such plans can work for both the affirmative and the negative, either as resolutional alternatives or as study counterplans.

Facts are at the center of debate. Questions of definition, extrapolation, and measurement are bound up with debate over the dimensions of a problem, whether it will grow worse or better in the future, and the reliability with which a solution can be fashioned. However, attention to questions of fact are important only insofar as a call for better or more precise quantification and definition is reasonable.

Steps in Rebuttal

1. Reestablish the value of definitions.
2. Establish a range of measurement.
3. Establish criteria for measurement.

Competitive debaters have developed their strategies, knowing which line of refutation to take—and when.

Questions of Inference

Debating **inferences** requires investigating whether one can logically move from examining specific evidence to forming a general conclusion based on that evidence. There are three main ways of forming inferences in debate: (1) extrapolating from examples to a conclusion, (2) extrapolating from analogous (similar) situations, and (3) reasoning from cause to effect. Each type of inference involves particular refutation and rebuttal strategies.

Refuting Inferential Arguments

In some policy debate, debates take place within a relatively well-defined domain of examples. For instance, in discussing the issue of U.S. intervention into the affairs of other countries, an affirmative might claim that the examples of U.S. intervention in the twentieth century show that such actions are likely to meet with success and have a relatively low risk of failure. There are approximately a hundred examples of U.S. intervention, and the affirmative could choose from a variety to show that goals have been accomplished with modest loss of life. Such examples, then, would permit the affirmative to move to the claim that intervention in Somalia, Bosnia, or Haiti is warranted.

There are a number of lines of refutation that are applicable to these kinds of inferences. The first question is whether the interventions chosen are typical of *all* interventions. If it were the case that only three or four interventions had been successful, then the negative could demonstrate that a false inference had been made. If the majority of interventions had turned out badly, then intervention as a policy could be shown to be inherently risky.

The second question is whether there are significant counterexamples that show there are substantial risks—even if the majority of examples have gone a similar way. For example, on the intervention issue, the negative could point to examples in which interventions have gone substantially awry. Korea and Vietnam, for instance, cost a lot in terms of American lives and dollars. Thus, it could be argued that the mere chance that an intervention could turn out badly, even if the majority had turned out well, would be enough to call into question the inference of safety.

A third question is whether the examples cited cover a relevant time period. It may be the case that interventions were more risky during the time of United States–Soviet confrontation, because intervention into an opponent's sphere of influence risked escalation to a global conflict. Debaters could argue that such risks are presently absent, so interventions could be more successful: the United States would not need to restrict the force brought to bear in order to be successful. For example, the Gulf War could be cited as evidence that when American force is focused, it can win against even well-armed and supplied opponents.

A second kind of inference draws a comparison between two like situations, and makes the argument that what is true or appropriate for one is true or appropriate for another. Often, an analogical inference is used to establish the viability of a proposal. If a proposal worked in one time and place, then there is evidence to suggest that it will work in another. If a policy worked successfully on a local scale, then that success can be extrapolated to a national scale. The strategy of refutation in such cases is to show that there are critical differences that should dissuade against parallel treatment.

The key refutational strategy is to point out that there may be unique factors in one place and time that would be lost by shifting the place or scale of a policy. For example, school programs that seem to work as experimental projects are often indicted on this score. The very status of such programs as "experimental" attracts dedicated and highly motivated personnel. A debater could argue that one cannot assume that such efforts would be duplicated if programs became status quo efforts.

Finally, questions of cause and effect are important to debate in two ways: first, for an affirmative to identify a solution to a problem, the causes of a problem must be identified, and second, for a negative to show that a plan is undesirable, it must demonstrate that the plan will cause certain undesirable conditions. Cause-and-effect reasoning frequently becomes the focus of considerable clash.

Part of the clash occurs around the question of whether there is only one main cause or a number of important, independent causalities that bring about a problem. For example, poverty seems to have one main cause, a lack of money; hence, the simple way to cure poverty is to bring the income of the poor above the poverty line. To refute such a simple, linear causal argument you can begin by expanding the causal frame of reference. You might argue that there are a number of causes of poverty: that the poor do not know how to get employment, to keep a job, to spend money, to avoid dependencies, to get access to reasonably priced goods, and so on. By establishing multiple causality, you would open up an opportunity to develop plan-meet-need arguments. If the causes of a problem persist, then the likelihood of an effective solution is diminished.

Another kind of causal reasoning involves the development of scenarios. A *scenario* is a picture of future conditions, should a sequence of cause and effects play out. The types of fallacious scenario reasoning are well known. One type is the **slippery-slope argument** in which one thing leads to another and to another, and pretty soon, we are down the slippery slope to perdition. This type of argument is relatively easy to refute. For example, just because there is now a short waiting period before one can get a handgun, the Bill of Rights has not necessarily been repealed. However, not all scenario reasoning is so easily refuted.

Scenario reasoning usually occurs with the development of disadvantages. A disadvantage uses causal reasoning to say that the plan will bring about undesirable conditions. Sometimes the undesirable conditions are claimed to increase the very harm that the affirmative team claims to be solving. In the poverty example, increasing taxes to help the poor might depress business activity, throwing more people out of work and thereby forcing more families down to the poverty line. Pointing out the "reverse causality" of the disadvantage is a very effective refutational strategy, because it shows that the affirmative is making the problem worse rather than better.

At other times, scenario reasoning is built on a series of more far-reaching conditions. To continue the above line of thinking, the negative might argue that if taxes are raised, the United States might face a recession; if the United States faces a recession, then it might lead the world into a depression; if the world is in a depression, then the hard-liners in the former Soviet Union would gain political support and the Cold War would come back to plague the globe. Is this an unlikely scenario? Yes. There are a number of causal links that have to be established. Is this a plausible scenario? Yes. It could happen. Since risk analysis deals in probabilities, and prudence dictates that one deal with a causal sequence (even if relative probabilities are hard to establish), the negative could argue persuasively that the risk is simply too great to be ignored.

Rebutting Inferential Arguments

The most successful strategy for rebutting inferential arguments is to turn around the arguments by offering counterexamples or reversing the causality of the arguments.

For example, in order to rebut counterexamples, you should try to isolate the unique conditions that isolate those counterexamples. For instance, the affirmative might argue that the reason Korea and Vietnam got out of hand is that they were contiguous with a major communist state that could supply the insurgents with weapons and troops. Absent these conditions, not a single United States intervention has been unsuccessful. By restricting the counterexample to its atypical conditions, it is possible to rebut the refuted extrapolation.

In order to rebut indictments based on analogous situations, it is necessary to anticipate that there will be differences between a pilot program, a local effort, or a previous policy and the one that is advocated—and to make the most of those differences. For instance, it may be the case that windpower can generate energy on a local scale, but it would be unreasonable to extrapolate its energy savings nationally, because the wind does not blow with the same intensity everywhere in the United States. An affirmative could concede this point, and in a plan developing energy alternatives add solar, geothermal, and hydroelectric power efforts to windpower. Thus, a limited analogy can be admitted, while the rest of the plan adds components that offset the restricted extrapolation.

In order to rebut objections that raise the specter of multiple causality, affirmative debaters usually show how the plan provides mitigating strategies or effects that get at adjacent causes. For example, an affirmative might argue that if the poor had money, they would have time to invest in education, to increase discrimination of purchases, to engage in activities that reduce dependency, and so on. According to this argument, one cause cures many ills. Another alternative is to admit to multiple causality, but to develop a plan with an equal number of solutions; in this case, the affirmative might offer worker retraining, drug rehabilitation, rent controls, spending help, and more.

In order to rebut causal scenarios, a successful strategy is to locate the points at which the direction of causality is reversed. To continue the poverty example, a tax increase only leads to recession if it is not coupled with a spending increase. The affirmative could argue that spending on poverty programs has a good effect in increasing economic growth, so if the judge is worried about the return of the Cold War, he or she should vote for the side that helps the economy. By co-opting the causal sequence, debaters rebut arguments by showing that the reasoning actually supports their own side.

Refutation as Oral Advocacy

So far, this chapter has discussed many of the techniques and strategies of refutation in terms of being logical and tactical responses to weaknesses in argumentation. The chapter also has suggested how to reestablish the strength of an argument. As you no doubt have observed, the processes of refutation and rebuttal can get very complicated very fast, and this is part of what makes debating challenging and fun. However, advocacy is more than an intellectual game. It also involves persuasion. Thus, it is important to devote the same degree of attention to the persuasive requirements of refutation and rebuttal as is given to the rhetorical situation.

Remember, above all, that in debate it is not enough to know what the best argument is on a given position; rather, in addition to knowing a good argument, you must be able to express it in a timely, understandable, and convincing manner. Below are some "do's" and "don'ts" that may help you to master refutation and rebuttal as an art of persuasion.

RULES OF ORAL ADVOCACY

Do

★ Summarize an opponent's arguments.

★ State objections to a contention.

★ Consider what will happen if neither side wins a particular argument.

★ Deal with opposing arguments in a calm, efficient, and respectful tone.

Don't

★ Practice refutation with the childlike "Yes, it is, No, it isn't, Yes, it is. . ." argumentation strategy.

★ Employ shallow tactics such as overwhelming your opponent with a flood of questions. (This tactic may come back to haunt you.)

★ Get in a rut. (Reassess your strategies periodically. Change tactics occasionally.)

★ Forget to be critical of your own constructive arguments.

Persuasive Strategies

One helpful strategy is to practice the skill of summarizing an opponent's argument. Refutation requires that you identify exactly what an opponent wishes to prove how the proof is established. The more concisely and convincingly this can be done, the better. Concise explanation decreases the time you have to spend reminding the judge of the argument in contention, and increases the time you can spend building refutation. Also, if you state the argument in a precise way, you can emphasize its flaws very succinctly. To practice concision, try to make complex arguments and reduce them to a central point with main arteries of proof.

Another strategy is to practice the skill of stating objections to a contention. In stating an objection, there are two steps: first, establish why the opponent's claim is doubtful; and second, suggest why a weak claim counts against your opponent.

Debaters often do the former but neglect the latter, since in many cases the inference appears self-evident. For example, if the resolution calls for enhancing the space program, your opponent claims that the funding for NASA is decreasing, and you can show that funding is up—you have won a victory.

But often it is not immediately apparent why it matters to win a particular argument. If your opponent claims funding for the space shuttle is decreasing, and you can show that funding for NASA is up overall, then the argument only matters if you can demonstrate that the space shuttle should be reduced as a priority while other means of exploration ought to be increased; in other words, that the status quo is making the right set of priority decisions. It is not enough merely to fire off an objection. To do damage, the objection has to be properly aimed at a vital argument supporting the opposing side.

Another strategy is to ask yourself the question, "what happens if neither my opponent's argument nor my own refutation can be conclusively proved?" In many debates key points are in contention, and frequently there are so many points of refutation and rebuttal on both sides of the issue that the judge may think of the issue as a draw.

For example, in debates over global climate concerns, some scientists say the world is about to end in fire; others say that the world is about to end in ice. Who is right? The fact that an issue cannot be demonstrated conclusively for one side or the other does not mean that it is without consequence. Strategic refutation considers the possibility of a draw on an issue and then asks what the most prudent policy would be in the face of uncertainty. Even if global warming might not be conclusively demonstrated, reducing certain pollutants may not hurt, even if the results would not be as spectacular as originally maintained.

Finally, a useful strategy is to practice dealing with opposing arguments in a calm, efficient, and respectful tone. Good arguments are exciting; good argumentation, however, requires a civil tongue. The strength of an argument should be a product of the quality of evidence, and therefore it is useful to find evidence from prestigious sources who can frame an issue clearly in a moving way. The literate quality of the evidence adds to the persuasiveness of a speech.

Strategies to Avoid

While some of these strategies to avoid may seem obvious, a surprising number of even experienced debaters occasionally falls into them. To argue persuasively, you should strive to avoid these common strategic errors.

First, don't practice refutation as small children argue: yes it is; no it isn't; yes it is; no it isn't. By challenging everything the opponent says, by claiming that *everything* is doubtful, untrustworthy, and suspicious, you can fall into the trap of quibbling. There are so many objections that the judge can't tell the important ones from the trivial ones. If a substantial amount of evidence supports a point, why not concede it? If there is little evidence that supports a point, but the point is really not crucial to the determination of the acceptability of the resolution, why not simply point this out rather than trying to refute the point as well? Good refutation means knowing when to say no.

Second, don't practice a double standard. Some debaters think of refutation as merely asking a bunch of questions: "What is the significance? Who is the source? How do we know the source is truthful? Why is the evidence old?" The logic behind such questioning seems to be that by raising so many questions, the other side will be overwhelmed by sheer dint of numbers and will be unable to recover and present convincing evidence. However, debaters that employ this tactic usually spend little time establishing the reliability of their own proof, and they are vulnerable to getting back the same shallow tactics in kind. Powerful refutation needs to be focused, and you should be prepared to meet the same standards of acceptable evidence and proof that you establish for an opponent.

Next, don't get into a rut. Plan refutation, and evaluate what works and what doesn't. In debate, as in battle, tactics change as the unexpected happens and arguments shift back and forth. Just as the "fog of war" clouds the best strategies of a battle, so actual debate is different than strategic planning. Reassess what refutation goes well and what doesn't. As a rule of thumb, try to eliminate the weakest arguments and find newer ones. Weaker arguments will be those where the preponderance of evidence goes against your position, or where the use of some arguments precludes others due to the risk of contradiction.

Finally, don't fail to be critical of your own constructive arguments. There have been debaters who believed that all the arguments they authored could not be wrong, for if they were bad arguments they would not have authored them. Such circular reasoning belies the fact that all policy argument has strengths and weaknesses, and that debate is a learning process where an advocate can become self-critical. The process involves anticipating the strongest objections to a position and assessing whether answers will be sufficiently strong to overcome objections. Just as one develops one's own refutation skills over the course of a debate season, so too constructives will improve by imagining the latest extension or development of an issue. Such critical introspection is crucial.

Summary

Although attack and defense tactics of refutation and rebuttal require practice, they are fairly easy processes. The debaters need only understand the logical and analytical fallacies and develop sound strategies for attack and defense.

Refutation and rebuttal skills, however, are much easier to talk about than to learn and practice. This, probably, is why many good public speakers have difficulty speaking fluently when they first learn to debate. Only after hard and careful practice can they become proficient debaters.

Questions

1. What is a fallacy?
2. Why is authority so important in a debate? What are the common means of refutation over authority?
3. Differentiate between begging the question and a faulty assumption.
4. What role does a non sequitur play in refutation and rebuttal?
5. What are the four traps to avoid when preparing for persuasive advocacy?

Discussion Opportunities

1. How do you detect fallacies in factual arguments?
2. How do you detect fallacies in value arguments?
3. How do you detect fallacies in causal arguments?
4. What role does refutation play in debate?
5. Describe the typical problems with inference that characterize policy debate. How might these be avoided?

Writing Opportunities

1. Make a list of arguments that embody the fallacies listed in the chapter. Have your colleagues guess which fallacy the argument illustrates. Work to create good or valid versions of the same arguments.
2. Take the current debate resolution and predict what are likely to be important affirmative cases. Prepare a set of arguments that can be used to refute these cases. Outline the strategic merits of the position you construct.
3. Attend a tournament and flow elimination round debates. Using the flows, identify the problems in refutation and rebuttal for the affirmative. Then look at the negative. How might these problems have been corrected?
4. Using the flow from the previous activity, look for and outline any analytical fallacies in the affirmative constructive arguments. Construct a negative position based on the fallacy. Then do the same with the negative constructive arguments.

Critical Thinking Opportunities

1. What happens to an argument when it is found to be inconsistent with another argument advocated by the same team?

2. How does the fallacy of emotional appeal differ from that of ad hominem attacks?

3. How should a debater select arguments for refutation?

4. Using the flow of a debate, identify the areas of clash in the debate. Are there places where the negative could have clashed with the affirmative and chose not to? Was this a good choice?

5. Using the current resolution, identify arguments that can be used on the negative. Look for studies or statistics that would support one of these arguments. Review the study or statistics in light of the fallacies listed in this chapter. Are there problems? Would this evidence be usable in a debate round?

6. What is the value of practicing rebuttals?

STRATEGIES IN ACTION

Dan and Bill have developed a very strong affirmative case on the debate topic on the national situation with the homeless. They show that the way the United States has dealt with the homeless has resulted in a significant increase in the number of homeless people. Also, Dan and Bill's case demonstrates how community treatment programs for the mentally ill, favored by recent Supreme Court decisions—as compared with commitment to asylums, have not been adequately developed. Having built a fairly strong case, Dan and Bill had won several rounds in previous competition.

It's the quarter-final round and Dan and Bill are up against a very good team. This team talks fast, makes a lot of vociferous challenges, and rolls up a victory. Dan and Bill wonder what hit them. Their coach suggests that they listen to the tape of the round and figure out what went wrong. While listening to the tape, they discover that their opponents talk very fast, but use the same arguments over and over again.

Their standard lines are:

- What's the date of the evidence?
- How do we know the source is authoritative?
- What is the significance?
- How do we know the cause is linked to the effect?
- Quantify the advantage. What are the exact figures?
- Why *can't* we spend money on other programs?

Dan and Bill have to admit that some of these questions are hard to answer, perhaps some are even unanswerable. For instance, since the homeless drift from one place to another, no one really knows how many there are.

Consider how Dan and Bill could improve their case and restructure their first affirmative constructive speech by answering the following questions:

- How can they anticipate unanswerable questions and discount challenges for specific and unreasonable demands for quantification?
- Would it be feasible to develop a line of analysis which argues what is typically negative ground—that most of the homeless are being helped at present?
- Which arguments are likely to need reexplaining as well as additional documentation?
- How can Dan and Bill respond effectively to rapid-fire questions?

The strategy of reviewing a loss and determining what went wrong during a round, then reworking the first affirmative constructive speech as well as the plan and extension brief, makes a loss like Dan and Bill's a learning experience—not just a defeat.

CHAPTER 12

Fundamentals of Lincoln-Douglas Debate

Objectives

After studying Chapter 12, you should be able
1. To explain the differences between Lincoln-Douglas debate and policy debate, including the differences between debating a proposition of policy versus debating a proposition of value.
2. To identify the stock issues in Lincoln-Douglas debate.
3. To identify the differences between value comparison and value assertion debates.
4. To explain value exclusivity, on-balance judgment, and value premise.
5. To research a value proposition.
6. To plan a strategy for cross-examination.
7. To explain the basis for judging Lincoln-Douglas debate.

Key Terms

To participate in Lincoln-Douglas debate, you will need to understand the following terms:

value comparison
value assertion
value exclusivity
residues case
on-balance judgment
criteria
value premise
value hierarchy

One strength of contemporary debate is the variety of formats available. Lincoln-Douglas is a format of increasing popularity among students. Like individual speech events, Lincoln-Douglas debate offers an opportunity for persuasive speaking and competition on a one-to-one basis. Like team debating, it offers an opportunity to demonstrate analytical skills. While all the material concerning argumentation and debate discussed in earlier chapters is relevant to Lincoln-Douglas debating, there are some key differences.

Abraham Lincoln is shown here during one of his debates with Stephen Douglas which focused on the slavery issue.

History of Lincoln-Douglas Debate

Lincoln-Douglas debate can be traced directly to the seven historic debates between Stephen Douglas and Abraham Lincoln, who ran against each other in Illinois for the U.S. Senate in 1858. The format was simple: the debates were limited to three hours each, with the first speaker given one hour, followed by an hour and a half of negative speaking, and concluding with a thirty-minute rebuttal speech from the first speaker. Most critics agree that the debates themselves were even. While Lincoln did not win the Senate race, these debates were significant in building Lincoln's reputation and played a significant role in his later success in the presidential race of 1860.

Since 1858 there have been many debates between various political candidates. The role of such debates became very visible in the Kennedy-Nixon Presidential debates of 1960. Over the years the time constraints and the rules have been modified to fit a variety of formats, but each debate has focused on the same central question: who is the better candidate? Such debates are no longer limited to presidential candidates. You have probably witnessed local candidates debating for seats in the state legislature, for mayor, or even for alderman. But whatever the purpose, this format has long served the needs for the exchange of ideas on important issues of the day.

It was not until the 1980 National Forensic League Speech Tournament that high-school students were able to use the Lincoln-Douglas (sometimes referred to as value debate) format in national competition. Since that time, thousands of students have competed at local, state, and national tournaments. At first, comparisons to team debate were the most understandable and appropriate methods for studying Lincoln-Douglas debate. But now, theory unique to value debate in general and Lincoln-Douglas in particular is developing.

Although Lincoln-Douglas debate formats may vary somewhat, standard practice includes the following allocation of time:

Affirmative Constructive	6 minutes
Negative Cross-Examination	3 minutes
Negative Constructive	7 minutes
Affirmative Cross-Examination	3 minutes
Affirmative Rebuttal	4 minutes
Negative Rebuttal	6 minutes
Affirmative Rebuttal	3 minutes

You may notice that there are some similarities with cross-examination debate. The affirmative speaker has the first and last opportunity to plead the case. The negative has more interior speeches, including a block of eleven minutes that is interrupted by only three minutes of affirmative questioning and a short rebuttal. Notice, too, that the total time allocated to each side is equal. This undoubtedly is a fairness condition for the debate.

However, the dissimilarities between Lincoln-Douglas and cross-examination debate are significant enough to alter strategic considerations. The first dissimilarity is that the burden of debating is placed on the single speaker. Whereas in two-person debate an advocate can specialize in case or plan, depending on the speaker position, in Lincoln-Douglas debate the speaker must be acquainted with all facets of the proposition under consideration. Note, too, that the participants are involved throughout the debate and cannot take a rebuttal break when their speeches are finished.

On the affirmative side of the ledger, such a format has significant implications for constructing the opening position. Because the first affirmative constructive speech is considerably shorter than in either standard or cross-examination debate, the speech must emphasize core evidence and arguments. Yet, it must permit room for the expansion of ideas throughout the discussion. The affirmative gets only one constructive speech. Consequently, the constructive should have as many well-developed independent subissues as possible. Although it is vital to craft a strong first affirmative, it is also important for the affirmative to develop flexible rebuttal skills because the affirmative speaker has more time and opportunity at the end of the debate.

On the negative side, it should be noted that there are fewer speeches, but more time is given to each speech. Negative speakers have a great opportunity, if they are prepared to carry the debate into areas not identified by the affirmative but relevant to the value questions at hand. Even if the negative spends as much time talking about the affirmative case as the affirmative did in the first constructive, the negative still has a minute more constructive speaking time. And even if the negative talks about all the issues that the affirmative covered in its four-minute first rebuttal, the negative still has two additional minutes to extend the discussion. Thus, the negative has the opportunity to widen the ground of argument. Of course, the affirmative still speaks last and can use the opportunity to point out why the negative considerations are not relevant. Still, it would seem that as long as negative speakers are inventive and relevant, they should be able to use their time advantage to its maximum strategic value.

In Lincoln-Douglas debate, both the affirmative and negative are more involved in cross-examination than they are in other debate formats. Cross-examination becomes a more significant feature, to the extent that it is useful in generating positions, testing evidence, and separating relevant from irrelevant considerations. Even more significant, because the debate is between only two people, the rapport established in cross-examination influences the tone and style of the activity. Unlike team debate, which has a corporate or legal style, Lincoln-Douglas debate depends on social grace, friendliness, and appropriate behavior—that is, on the character of the individuals involved—to create an interesting, productive dispute. While cross-examination should still be pointed, it also needs to be reasonable and interesting.

Propositions of Value

One of the reasons for the creation of Lincoln-Douglas debate was to offer an alternative to team debate. Because of this, Lincoln-Douglas debaters only discuss propositions of value. The *Oxford English Dictionary* defines *value* as "something of worth, to be highly regarded or held in great esteem." In terms of debate, a value is a belief. That is, a proposition of value asserts that some individual, belief, institution, or object possesses or lacks a certain desirable or undesirable characteristic.

Perhaps the best way to understand the nature of a debatable value question is to contrast propositions of value to propositions of policy. A proposition of policy always states a question of future conduct that is being proposed. Presumption resides with the negative because the proposal is, on its face, a request to do something different. The result is that the affirmative has the burden to show cause—a significant harm that cannot be remedied by the present system but that can be remedied, or at least minimized, by an alternative system.

The primary similarity between both policy and value propositions is that opinion in each type is unsettled on a matter of some concern. If everyone agreed that a policy was good or, alternatively, that a value was an absolute norm, then there would be no reason for discussion. In every proposition of policy is a statement of fact (a statement of a perception of reality) and a value claim (a statement that achieving that reality is desirable). Indeed, the value claim is at the heart of the proposition of policy, because if we support the value claim the next step would be to advocate a policy of action.

However, beyond this similarity the responsibilities for discussion are quite different for value and policy debate. A value question does not call for the advocates to debate possible futures that will be influenced by present choices of conduct. Rather, a value question focuses exclusively on the present. The debaters must try to resolve how the community (represented by the judge) feels about a question of common concern. Thus, the value proposition asks the debaters to place a concern in a context of appreciation or understanding.

There are many different ways of doing this, and the way the value question is framed will determine what the affirmative's and negative's contextual obligations will be.

Value Comparisons

Some propositions feature a **value comparison**. A comparative value proposition is structured along the lines of the statement "x is better than y." Such values can be abstract (for example, freedom is better than equality), or they can be concrete (for example, Latin Americans are better trading partners than Europeans). A good comparative value proposition is one that involves two values that are of relatively equal strength but clearly different and asks for support.

When debating a comparative value proposition, the affirmative has to show that under most or all circumstances the proposition is true. If the values under consideration are abstract, the affirmative needs to develop concrete examples that demonstrate the truth of the statement. For example, for the proposition "Competition is of greater value than cooperation," the affirmative might show that the resources necessary for a society to operate are maximized only to the extent that individuals are motivated, and that motivation depends on competition. The affirmative might also say that artistic and intellectual competition moves people to think harder and perform better than does a cooperative system, which breeds complacency and inspires an excessive concern for fairness.

Note that the examples are developed by (1) stating why the value of competition is a positive good, and (2) stating that the good is better because it precedes or trades off favorably with its competitor. If competition is not proved valuable per se, then there is no reason to think that it is a good value in the first place. If competition is proved to be good, but it is *not* shown that it trades off favorably with cooperation, then there is no reason to think that it is better than cooperation.

Comparative propositions are often concrete rather than abstract. For example, a proposition might say, "It is better to cut government spending than it is to raise taxes." Note that the implied time frame is the present. Neither the negative nor the affirmative has the right to assume that the word *always* is implied in a value proposition. When debating propositions that involve concrete comparisons, the affirmative examines current circumstances and evaluates the alternatives available. In many instances, concrete comparisons may have implications for policy. For example, if it is unwise to raise taxes, then a plan of action could require a balanced federal budget. But in value debate the affirmative does *not* have to defend alternative, future policies. Rather, the affirmative burden is limited to evaluating the options put under consideration by the resolution. Still, such a debate involves policy issues insofar as one is looking to the consequences or outcomes of choices. In such cases, the affirmative and negative argue much as they do in counterplan debate, by comparing the merits of policy.

The negative position in a compromise value argument may be constructed on one of three grounds. The first option is to argue the opposite of the affirmative. For example, if the affirmative contends that duty is better than pursuit of private happiness, the negative argues that pursuit of private happiness is a higher value than performance of duty. If the affirmative argues that privately funded retirement plans are better than forced contributions to social security, the negative defends the reverse. In such instances, the negative must not only object to the affirmative's argument that it offers the superior value, the negative also must advance constructive arguments defending the worth of its own position.

The second negative option is to argue that the two values are equivalent. For example, the negative might argue that William Faulkner and Saul Bellow are both fine authors and that while each is different, neither is necessarily better. The negative could advance this position by demonstrating the unique context that makes a comparative evaluation inappropriate. For instance, the negative might argue that although Faulkner deals with Southern culture and Bellow represents Chicago, both are regional writers who did the most with their material. The negative would claim that there are no reasonable grounds on which to assign a value of comparative merit. To win this argument, the negative must undermine the affirmative standards of comparison—in this particular example, the status of absolute artistic quality.

The third option available to the negative is to argue that not enough is known about the question to make a decision at this time. The negative claims that any evaluation would be the product of ignorance, prejudice, or parochialism. Such an attack would (1) emphasize all the possible areas of value comparison that must be resolved before a well-founded judgment can be rendered, and (2) point to the fact that the affirmative has either failed to consider all the values in question or that no answer is possible because of limiting factors on research at the present time. In the comparison of Faulkner and Bellow, the negative might point out that literary criticism is itself in a state of disagreement over what constitutes a good work or a significant contribution. It is important to note that if the negative takes this third position, it cannot also argue the first and second positions. If not enough appropriate information exists at this time, then the reverse of the proposition cannot be asserted.

Value Assertions

Another kind of value proposition features **value assertions.** A value assertion proposition is a categorical judgment stated in positive or negative terms. A *positive* value assertion states that some person, belief, custom, practice, event, or instrument is good. "Good" can be variously described by the proposition as right, just, valuable, beneficial, or beautiful. A *negative* value assertion states the opposite, depicting "bad" as unjust, worthless, detrimental, or harmful. Thus, unlike a policy proposition, which must be stated in positive terms, a value assertion may be either positive or negative.

Like value comparisons, value assertions may be either concrete or abstract. A concrete value assertion identifies a person, thing, event, or custom to be evaluated. The value assertion may refer to a class or a specific event. For instance, a value assertion referring to a class would state, "The Olympic movement has been worthwhile for sports." If the value statement refers to a class, then the affirmative case is constructed first by showing examples chosen from the class and then by drawing a generalization.

In the example, the affirmative might argue that the Olympics in Atlanta, Los Angeles, Seoul, Sydney, and Athens were good for sports. The burden of the affirmative analysis is to show that all members of the class have the same essential qualities—such as stimulating competition, drawing publicity, and featuring fair play. The affirmative must be prepared to show why counterexamples—that is, Olympic events that were unsuccessful—were atypical. Moreover, the affirmative must be prepared to show why the harmful consequences of Olympics for sports (say, in giving a stage for nationalism or terrorism) are either accidental qualities of only some Olympics or do not outweigh the good features.

If a value assertion refers to a specific person, event, or custom, the affirmative must be thoroughly acquainted with the unique qualities of the instance in question. For example, when debating a specific proposition such as "The Los Angeles Olympics were worthwhile for sports," the affirmative might point out that the free enterprise system of sponsoring events made that particular event a success. Whereas other Olympics burdened cities and left large debts, the Los Angeles games helped the city by generating revenue and increasing civic spiritedness and showed that large sporting events could help the public, thereby making international sports more viable. Note that the burden of the affirmative here is a bit different. The affirmative must show why a member of a class has unique features that make it noteworthy.

The negative position in a debate over value assertions is variable. The negative may wish simply to deny the proposition. In that case the negative has two options. The first option is to say that the link between the valued instance and class is simply not true. For example, consider the abstract proposition, "The two-party system is detrimental to democratic ideals." The affirmative might argue that what is detrimental is that the two parties do not reflect the range of public sentiment, monopolize office, and provide inadequate choices. The negative might respond that the parties are diverse, that choices exist within the range of party opinion, and that such a system guarantees discussion and debate. Here the negative simply argues the reverse of the affirmative.

On the other hand, the negative might choose to say that the value as defined by the affirmative is misrepresented. Here the negative would show that democracy does not mean fragmented, diverse, chaotic speech but requires organized, meaningful representation of government by the people. If the negative takes this position, it might agree with the characterization of the party system advanced by the affirmative but show that the value in question has been inappropriately represented. Strategically, it might make sense to argue that the affirmative has inappropriately characterized the class or thing in question *and* has misdefined the value that is being applied as a criterion. However, the negative must first make sure that no contradiction appears. In the above example, the negative position would be inconsistent if the negative argued both the value of representative democracy and the nonrepresentative nature of the party system.

In addition to straight refutation, the negative has the option of maintaining that there is not enough certainty or evidence to suggest that a judgment can be made. Suppose a proposition was stated thus: "United States defense spending is excessive." Certainly, there have been a lot of arguments pro and con on this issue. But it may be the case that in the present situation, when terrorists have boldly attacked major American cities, a judgment cannot be made.

By balancing conflicting signals, the negative can set up a context that implies that no judgment can be rendered at this time. To the extent that the negative can show that there is substantial uncertainty about the proposition—that there are equal reasons for a favorable or unfavorable judgment—it undercuts the affirmative rationale.

Value Exclusivity

Just as adjectives permit people to make routine judgments about the good, the better, and the best, value propositions enable debaters to refine their thinking and to move toward refined judgments of discrimination. The third kind of value propositions are those that call for **value exclusivity.** These kinds of propositions ask that a certain person, event, thing, custom, belief, practice, or class be judged above all competitors.

Sometimes such propositions put an unfair burden on the affirmative, especially when there are a number of near competitors. For instance, if a proposition stated that Billy Graham was the best preacher in the United States, the affirmative would not have a hard time defending the fact that his work is good, important, or even outstanding. But given that the United States contains many good preachers, it would be hard to defend one against the many alternatives that could be advanced by the negative.

On the other hand, questions of value exclusivity can be fairly advanced when there is a small group of options. A proposition can be worded so as to provide the context for judgment. For example, a proposition might read, "The St. Louis Cardinals are the best professional baseball team." Because there are only a limited number of professional baseball teams, the exclusivity of the proposition does not put an unfair burden on the affirmative.

An affirmative case that argues for an exclusive value judgment often proceeds by process of elimination. The technical term for this case structure is a **residues case**. A residues case is one that eliminates all alternatives except for the one that the affirmative desires. For example, an affirmative debating the St. Louis Cardinals proposition might argue that teams that have not been to the World Series cannot be considered as good because they lost in the early rounds of competition. Of those teams that have been to the World Series in recent years, only the New York Yankees might be a legitimate challenger. Because there is a relatively small class for comparison, this case structure is relatively easy to define. However, the affirmative should be prepared to argue that other examples offered by the negative are not appropriate or adequate competitors.

The negative has several options when debating value exclusivity. The first option is straight refutation. The negative might choose to say that one or all of the class in question are superior or equal to that defended by the affirmative. If the negative chooses one example, the debate evolves into a straight comparison. If the negative chooses to defend multiple examples, the debate focuses on how those examples are better in different ways than the affirmative example. The strategic advantage of arguing a single example is that the negative can focus in depth on a single comparison; multiple examples make the round more complex but also permit the negative some latitude in concentrating rebuttal arguments.

When running refutation, the negative might wish to expand the pool of examples. Expanding the grounds for argument is a useful negative strategy because the affirmative is likely to pick the strongest value criterion to define its judgment. If the negative expands the grounds of debate, however, it must show why its criteria are relevant, important, and superior to others for assessing the proposition. In the above example, the affirmative obviously would want to discuss the team's record, while the negative might want to move beyond records to an alternative criterion—present prospects. The negative must be able to clash at the level of criteria for evaluation, or it cannot reasonably widen the grounds of debate.

The final option for the negative is to show that there is not enough information to make a judgment. Here the negative might suggest that all competitors for the superlative status are relatively equal, that the differences are not decisive, or that conditions are in a state of flux.

On-Balance Judgments

Value propositions usually involve decisions about what is good, better, or best. However, another kind of value argument centers on questions that are less easily resolved. Such propositions involve issues that are not clearly good or bad, but that have a checkered past. The clash in such debates centers on how the person, event, situation, custom, or belief can be evaluated as a whole. Such debates thus depend on **on-balance judgments**: the affirmative and negative are asked to weigh the issue or instance and convince the judge that, on balance, the proposition should be accepted or rejected.

For example, consider the following proposition: "On the whole, television has been good for society." Note that this proposition implicitly acknowledges that television has been criticized and even that it may have done some harm. The affirmative is not expected to prove that television has always been good, that it is better than other media, or that it is the best thing that could have filled the public airwaves. Rather, the proposition permits the affirmative to acknowledge that television has not always worked well. It asks the affirmative to take the good and bad into consideration and to show how the former offsets the latter.

For instance, it may be the case that television creates bad health habits by advertising unwholesome food to children. But it is also the case that television alerts the public to health hazards, provides aerobics and exercise shows, and informs the public about new medical advances. The affirmative might argue that studies of television's negative influence on nutrition are unreliable or that TV's positive influences are better for the nation as a whole or in the long run. The affirmative also may argue that despite claims that television diverts attention from studying and encourages sedentary habits, expansion of cable TV gives people access to arts and sciences that are not otherwise available. Seen this way, television makes worthwhile viewing available, and the responsibility for mindlessly watching bad programming is the viewers'. The affirmative asks the judge to vote affirmative on the grounds that the possibilities offered by TV as a whole outweigh the disadvantages.

Affirmative cases that depend on an on-balance judgement must have two components. The first component establishes the **criteria** for rendering the judgment. In the television case, the criteria might be based on either actual effects (the health example) or potential consequences (such as consumer habits). The affirmative must be prepared to defend its choice of criteria and to clash with the criteria that the negative might advance.

The second component of the case shows why the criteria demonstrate the affirmative's claim. In the above example, by showing that the arts, sciences, and other events are made uniquely accessible by television, the affirmative demonstrates that television has a positive benefit. By showing that greater numbers of people are attending to quality programs and that people who watch bad television probably would waste their time anyway, the positive impact of such potential is demonstrated on the whole to be better for society.

The negative has a complex task in debating on-balance values. The negative first must choose either to accept, deny, or amend the affirmative's criteria. If the criteria are accepted, then the debate focuses on whether the affirmative proves its case. If the criteria are denied, then the negative must show why the affirmative criteria are wrong.

In the above example, the negative might say the issue is not whether television itself has been or can be good, but whether it has interacted appropriately with other artistic, educational, and cultural institutions. The negative might argue that television has displaced traditional lines of authority, minimized individual creative opportunity and talent, disrupted family life, and undermined real, human interaction. The criteria of social value and displacement open up another line of thinking about the resolution. However, it is not enough to open up alternative criteria—the negative must show why its own criteria are superior to those of the affirmative.

One strategy that may make the negative task a bit easier is to distinguish between true and false instances of the value in question. In the above case, because the core of the affirmative's argument depends on the special services that cable TV has offered, the negative might wish to separate cable television from television per se. It could be argued that TV offered little variety in programming beyond police shows, news and weather, talk, and game shows before cable. Therefore, though cable TV might have future potential, the on-balance judgment ought to refer to network television. By distinguishing between a true and a false representative of the class, the negative undercuts affirmative ground.

Debates that call for on-balance judgments are certainly the most complex value discussions, as many value questions do require factoring in the good and bad. On the other hand, if criteria are not clearly defined and discussed, these kinds of debates can evolve into mere assertions of opposing points of view. When that happens, the side that has the most clearly articulated presumption should win.

Unlike policy debate, Lincoln-Douglas offers no natural position for presumption. A judge could assign presumption to the negative simply because he or she believes that all statements are not presumed true until proved so. Or a judge could assign presumption to the affirmative simply because the affirmative offers a clearly defined position while the negative spreads confusion without being clear about anything. Presumption also could be assigned to the position that is closest to other precedents and values held by society. As a strategic Lincoln-Douglas debater, you will want to build your case so that you can persuade the judge that presumption rests with your side.

Democratic presidential nominee John Kerry makes a point while U.S. President George W. Bush looks on during their debate at the University of Miami in Coral Gables, Florida, in September 2004.

Lincoln-Douglas Stock Issues

Just as the stock issues in policy debate evolved around the need for change and the plan for solving the harm, value propositions are also evaluated through stock issues that include the object or idea being evaluated and the evaluation term. There are four stock issues involved in debating a proposition of value:

1. Defining the object of evaluation.
2. Identifying the key evaluative term in the debate.
3. Establishing the criteria or standards for evaluation.
4. Establishing and justifying a value hierarchy.

As in policy debate, stock issues constitute the burden of proof that rests with the affirmative. The affirmative must present a prima facie case supporting the resolution. Failure to address any one of the stock issues means the affirmative has failed to uphold its burden of proof.

Also as in policy debate, the negative has the burden of rejoinder. It is the responsibility of the negative to clash with the affirmative case and arguments. This means the negative must deny the relationship between the affirmative object of evaluation and the criteria used in defining the evaluative and introduce a competitive, independent value. If the negative does not deny the affirmative value or present a competitive value, it has failed to uphold its burden of rejoinder.

In his book *The Value Handbook*, Lee Polk, Chair of the Communications Studies Department at Baylor University, states the prima facie case

> "defines the object of evaluation and the evaluative term in the resolution. The central theme in the debate is the values and the value hierarchies used to evaluate the object of evaluation contained in the topic."

Defining the object of evaluation, or definition of terms, is the first stock issue in Lincoln-Douglas debate. This stock issue is important because it helps to minimize misunderstandings of how the important terms in the resolution are being used in the debate. Defining the terms means clarifying the meaning of the important words in the resolution. This is done by the affirmative but may be challenged by the negative. The definitions provide the boundaries for analysis in the debate by placing limits on the interpretation of the resolution.

The second stock issue, identifying the key evaluative term in the debate or the value premise, is important in understanding and accepting the resolution. The **value premise** identifies the affirmative's highest value. As discussed in the next chapter, the negative presents a countervalue to the affirmative's value premise. Then the judge is placed in the position of choosing between the affirmative's value premise or the negative's countervalue.

The third stock issue, establishing the criteria for evaluation, provides the mechanism for choosing between the affirmative's value premise and the negative's countervalue. People have many different ways of evaluating values, and the criteria provide a guide for the judge when choosing between competing values. The affirmative and negative may disagree about the criteria that should be used to evaluate the values. The outcome of this disagreement would depend on which of the two criteria the judge accepts.

Finally, the affirmative moves to show how the values and criteria fit the problem area of the resolution. This involves establishing and justifying the value hierarchies, the final stock issue. The function of this stock issue is to justify why the affirmative value premises and criteria should be accepted by the judge in support of the resolution. The **value hierarchy** provides the method for comparing the values presented in the case with other competing values. Sometimes the resolution will provide the hierarchy (setting out two values to be compared); other times resolutions will give the affirmative considerable leeway. Once the hierarchy has been established, the affirmative must justify that value hierarchy by discussing it in the context of the subject area of the resolution.

These are the stock issues most commonly used in Lincoln-Douglas debate. As you develop your understanding of these stock issues, you will learn how to apply them in your interpretation of the resolution.

Research and Evidence

To begin research for Lincoln-Douglas debate, you must know what to look for. At least in the first few steps, research for value debate is much the same as for policy debate. The first step is to brainstorm and analyze the resolution. Brainstorming is best when done as a group activity. The group can pool ideas about the resolution and prioritize the areas for research.

A useful way to begin is to examine the terms of the resolution and determine which terms will guide the process of identifying the value premises, criteria, and value hierarchies in the debate. These are the terms whose implications will need to be explored. For example, for the resolution, "The American criminal justice system ought to place a higher priority on retribution than on rehabilitation," the key terms would be *criminal justice system, retribution,* and *rehabilitation.* The definitions of these key terms will determine the direction of the debate.

After examining the key terms, you should consider the potential value premises and criteria that might be used. In the sample resolution, the key terms *criminal justice system, retribution,* and *rehabilitation* can each be characterized as values. You will want to ask why they are values; what criteria could be used to measure the values; what the hierarchy of the values should be; and how you could justify the hierarchy. Even before seriously beginning your research, you will need to consider why one particular value is superior to another.

The next step in research is to define the key terms through the use of dictionaries and encyclopedias. These sources provide the most precise definitions possible. You will want to begin with a general reference, such as the *American Heritage Dictionary* or *Webster's Third International Dictionary,* and then move on to more specialized dictionaries. The more specialized dictionaries will provide definitions as they are used by experts in the field. Encyclopedias also help provide an understanding of the resolution and provide general background information. Encyclopedias, too, can be general or specific. General-use encyclopedias would include *Encyclopedia Britannica* or *World Book;* subject-specific encyclopedias would include the *Encyclopedia of American Foreign Policy,* the *Encyclopedia of Philosophy,* or the *International Encyclopedia of Education, Black's Law Dictionary,* or the *Dictionary of the History of Ideas.* Which subject-specific encyclopedia you would want to consult will depend on the actual resolution to be debated.

The next step would be to create a bibliography of key sources on the topic. This will tell you what is available on the topic, so that you can narrow and focus your research. An effective research plan would enable you to gather information from a wide variety of sources, and a good bibliography should provide that variety.

After you have completed your bibliography and begun to read books and articles, you will need to identify materials that can be used as evidence. This is where the research strategies for policy and value debate begin to diverge. Both forms of debate require quite a bit of evidence, but the evidence is fundamentally different.

First, in Lincoln-Douglas debate proof depends much more on the character of the speaker. Statements of value are always personal to some extent. They represent who you are, what you believe, and what you feel is reasonable and important enough to encourage others to agree with. Therefore, you must find the right means of expressing your feelings about a question, rather than merely rattling off objective evidence. Careful word choice and well-articulated arguments are essential to linking the character of your own concern with the quality of proof.

Second, because questions of value move people into concerns beyond the immediate, the quality of opinion is important. One of the tests of quality is the opinion's ability to endure over time. Since values are the product of human opinion, predilection, or a feeling for the infinite, it stands to reason that those thinkers or leaders who have been time-honored should be given some deference. In policy debate, Plato, Frederick Douglass, or Susan B. Anthony may be judged out of date, but in value debate, they can provide relevant proof. This is not to say that contemporary opinion is not prized where appropriate. However, it is to say that the range of potential evidence is greater.

As in policy debate, you will need to be able to locate any piece of evidence easily and quickly during the debate round. To do this, you will need to develop an evidence filing system. (See Chapter 4 for details about how to record and file evidence.) In Lincoln-Douglas debate, it is usually possible to divide your evidence between affirmative and negative issues. After separating the evidence between the two sides, you should look for natural categories. For example, on the topic "That secondary education in the United States ought to be a privilege, not a right," divisions might include "Current Laws," "Survival Skills," and "Dropouts." As your files grow, subheadings would become necessary.

Briefs

As discussed in Chapter 4, another way of organizing evidence is through affirmative and negative briefs. Using briefs allows debaters to think about arguments and put evidence into place before the actual debate. This provides more time in the actual round to listen for arguments that had not been anticipated and to pull together responses and evidence on these.

Briefs in Lincoln-Douglas debate are developed in much the same way as they are in policy debate. The key difference is that they typically are not as extensive. For example, you will not find solvency, disadvantage, and extension briefs in Lincoln-Douglas debate. Briefs should be developed so that they help you organize your arguments. They must present your arguments in a clear and persuasive manner, identifying each argument with a label. If the labels are short but still understandable, they will help you organize your speeches for the judge.

The evidence for each brief should support your assertions and be as specific as possible. General, vague evidence is not appropriate for briefs: you should only use on-point evidence.

Cross-Examination

In Lincoln-Douglas debate, there are two cross-examination periods. The first is conducted by the negative; the second is conducted by the affirmative. There are many similarities between the cross-examination periods in cross-examination debate and Lincoln-Douglas debate. Both are used to (1) clarify arguments, (2) establish common ground, and (3) identify weak points.

One of the purposes of the cross-examination periods is to clarify arguments. Even in Lincoln-Douglas debate, arguments are not always clear, the evidence doesn't always quite make sense, or debaters might miss part of the speech while pulling evidence for the upcoming speech. The cross-examination period is an ideal opportunity to clarify points, ask to see a piece of evidence, or even to have the speaker repeat a particular argument. Using the cross-examination period to clarify arguments makes for better refutation in the following speeches.

Another purpose of the cross-examination periods is to establish common ground. Sometimes what the opposition has said sets up an argument you want to make. Rather than having to repeat the same common arguments, you can use the cross-examination period to identify for the judge the points of agreement and disagreement with the opposition. This acknowledgment of common arguments can then be referred to in your speech, and you can then spend your constructive or rebuttal time developing the rest of the argument. Another advantage of using the cross-examination period for this purpose is that you may also find that what you thought was common ground actually is not. This will help you avoid wasting time developing an argument that can be dismissed by a single statement of disagreement.

Finally, cross-examination can be used to expose weaknesses. After filling in any missing data and identifying areas of commonality, you will want to begin exposing weaknesses in the opposition's arguments. Weaknesses can range from poor use of evidence, illogical analysis, or no response to weaknesses in the opponent's position. When used to expose weaknesses, the cross-examination period is a form of refutation—provided you carry through with any information you gain in your subsequent speeches.

A Sample Affirmative Brief (Lincoln-Douglas Debate)

```
                        DEBATE BRIEF
                        by Nate Austin


           R.  When called upon by one's government individuals are
               morally obligated to risk their lives for their country.


Primary argument:  Where does the moral obligation lie, and how is it defined?

I.    John Stuart Mill

      A.  Societal and individual morality

          1.  Individual morality is subjective.

              a.  When evaluating things that will affect only the individual

          2.  Societal morality is objective the evaluated by utilitarianism

              a.  When evaluating things that will affect society

              b.  Utilitarianism is comparable to a universal morality.

              c.  Individual is obligated to consider the interests of others
                  when making decisions that will affect society.

              d.  Obligation also exists due to the benefits that an individual
                  receives from society.

              (Rousseau also agrees with this point.)

II.   Moral obligation derived from laws

      A.  Government will generally act for the benefit of society.

          1.  Without the society, government would have no purpose.

      B.  Moral obligation to follow the laws of that government

          1.  Laws are how the government secures rights.

              a.  Contradictory to disobey what protects you
```

Courtesy of the Lincoln High School (Lincoln, Nebraska) Debate Team.

A Sample Negative Brief (Lincoln-Douglas Debate)

DEBATE BRIEF
by Nate Austin

R. When called upon by one's government individuals are
morally obligated to risk their lives for their country.

Primary argument: Who determines moral obligation, and to what extent?

I.   Thomas Hobbes

A. Natural rights

1. Government has moral obligation to make laws that protect natural
rights.

a. The most important right is the right of life.

2. Individuals' moral obligation to follow laws unless they inflict on
natural rights

a. Individuals' ultimate appeal to the preservation of their lives

b. Individuals are inherently selfish (will consider own rights
before others).

B. Social contract

1. Without social contract, life is "nasty, brutish and short."

a. National rights not protected

2. The purpose of the social contract is to protect natural rights.

a. Primarily life

C. The resolution

1. Asking individuals to risk their lives

a. Life not being protected, as in state of nature

b. No obligation to government, because social contract has failed
in protecting an individuals natural right of life

Strategies for the Examiner

There are a number of strategies you can use to help facilitate the value of the cross-examination period. The first is to develop series of questions when possible. The single question is of little value and is often soon forgotten. However, a series of questions leading to a conclusion can have a lasting impression. The judge will begin to see where the argument is going and is likely to recall the exchange when the argument is developed in a later speech.

To be successful at this takes planning and organization. The questions cannot be haphazard—the sequence must make sense. The first question should identify the issue of concern, and subsequent questions should then be used to explore the issue in greater depth. The final question should bring closure to the issue. A word of caution, however; each series of questions needs to be reasonable in number, generally not exceeding five questions in a series. If a series involves more than five questions, the train of thought will get lost. You may know what is going on, but it is likely no one else will.

A second strategy is to emphasize closed- rather than open-ended questions. A closed-ended question is one that requires only a "yes" or "no" answer. For example, on the resolution "The principle of majority rule ought to be valued above the principle of minority rights," a closed-ended question might be "Was it your contention that democracy is based on majority rule?" On the other hand, an open-ended question on this resolution would be "Why do you think minority rights have a lower priority in a democracy?" The first question gives the examiner better control of the cross-examination; the second question invites the witness to provide a lengthy explanation and waste the examiner's time. This does not mean that the respondent cannot qualify the "yes" or "no" answer, but it does mean that the qualification must be brief and responsive to the question asked.

A third strategy is to ask concise questions. You should concentrate on asking questions and gaining as much information as possible, not on making speeches. Asking a lengthy question that begins with an explanation of an argument wastes time. Odds are the witness will ask you to repeat the question, wasting still more time, and then not provide the answer you were looking for.

Finally, be professional during the cross-examination period. Browbeating the witness does not look good. Being rude or obnoxious only detracts from the questions. If your behavior during the cross-examination period is poor, the judge is more likely to remember the behavior and not the information. This is not to say there won't be times when the witness dodges questions or talks endlessly. The temptation will be to get angry and lose your cool. However, remember that the judge also can recognize when the witness is dodging a question or rambling; such behavior will count against the witness. Your opponent is not likely to concede the key points in the cross-examination period, but the purpose of "cross-x" is to obtain information and clarify information, not to force confessions out of the opposition.

Strategies for the Witness

As a witness, you will want to come out of the cross-examination period without having made any damaging mistakes. The goal is to hold your own while being open and cooperative.

This does not mean to give away the store when a question is asked. You should think carefully before answering a question. If a closed-ended question is asked, stop to think if an explanation is needed to qualify the answer. If it is, then the qualifier should be given before saying "yes" or "no." If you do not understand a question, you should ask for it to be repeated or explained. Chances are, if you didn't understand the question, the judge didn't understand it either.

Above all, as a witness you want to create the impression that you have nothing to hide and are very willing to cooperate and answer questions. If you do not know the answer to a question, it is acceptable to say, "I don't know." This is better than trying to put together an answer to a question you do not know, as the answer may create whole new lines of argument for the opposition. Above all, you want to avoid having to come back and say, "That's not what I meant." The cross-examination periods are an excellent opportunity to explore arguments and highlight the weaknesses of the opposition. They are also a good opportunity for debaters to appear competent and cooperative. This is part of what makes cross-examination fun.

Flowing Lincoln-Douglas Debate

In principle, taking a flow in Lincoln-Douglas debate is the same as in policy debate. The main difference is that there are no solvency and disadvantage arguments. In their place, though, the negative may argue a counterwarrant, or the negative's interpretation of the resolution.

In Lincoln-Douglas debate, there are five speeches. The flowsheet is divided so that arguments can be traced through all five speeches. Many debaters use two sheets of paper divided into columns. The first sheet is divided into five columns, representing all five speeches, and used to track the arguments that correspond to those presented in the first affirmative constructive speech. The second sheet is divided into four columns and used to track arguments that correspond to the negative counterwarrant. The strategies for flowing arguments are basically the same as presented in Chapter 4. An example of a Lincoln-Douglas debate flowsheet follows.

In his textbook *Lincoln-Douglas Debate: Preparing for Value Argumentation*, David A. Frank, Director of Forensics at the University of Oregon, cites a number of strategies for flowsheeting, as shown on page 324.

Affirmative Constructive	Negative Refutation	1st Affirmative Rebuttal	Negative Rebuttal	2nd Affirmative Rebuttal

Negative Case	1st Affirmative Rebuttal	Negative Rebuttal	2nd Affirmative Rebuttal

Flowing a debate can be done efficiently by following the strategies below.

1. Use a lot of paper; always leave plenty of room.
2. Consider using two different-colored pens, black for affirmative and red for negative.
3. Develop an abbreviation system and update it as the season progresses.
4. Flow evidence and arguments as well as labels.
5. Be neat so you can follow the arguments across the flow.
6. Flow all speeches, including the arguments you plan to use in your own speeches.

For an example of a flowsheet from an actual Lincoln-Douglas debate, see Appendix B.

Judging Lincoln-Douglas Debate

The more you compete in Lincoln-Douglas debate, the more you will understand particular judges. Generally, you will encounter three different types of judges in competition: lay judges, college judges, and coach judges.

Lay judges are very common at smaller, more local tournaments. Though they are genuinely conscientious, they may not be as well versed in debate theory as the debaters. Because of this, they may not be able to flow as quickly (if at all) or be as familiar with a specific topic. The lay judge will not understand debate jargon. Therefore, if an issue is important, you must be sure to explain it clearly. For example, lay judges may have no idea what it means to say the negative wins because the affirmative did not present a prima facie case. If this is the case in your round, you may need to explain it. It is also very important to be organized and signpost your arguments in each speech. Even if the judge is not taking notes, hearing a label repeated throughout the debate will make the impression that this is an important issue in the round.

College judges are generally quite skilled in public speaking and may even be members of college forensic teams, or former Lincoln-Douglas debaters. Chances are good a college judge will flow the round. But this does not mean anything goes. You will still need to observe how the judge is responding and whether the judge seems to have a background in debate theory. When an argument is presented, does the judge appear to understand it right away? Don't assume the college judge is an expert, will take notes, and will miraculously put it together at the end of the round. It is your responsibility to guide the judge through the round, explaining why arguments are important.

Finally, debate coach judges are certainly well aware of the topic, as well as the arguments and perhaps even the evidence. Often, at large tournaments, coaches are required to judge. But remember that the debate coach is also a teacher. Such a judge may be especially interested in evaluating the round in terms of how well it exemplifies what "good" debate involves, what an "articulate" speaker sounds like, or even how debate theory develops.

What does this all mean? Debaters have to be able to adapt to the judges in the round. This means learning how to persuade the actual judge critiquing the round, and not the "ideal" judge. The key is to find out what you can about a judge ahead of time, and then observe the judge's reactions during the round and adapt.

While standards for Lincoln-Douglas debate vary somewhat by region, there are some generally accepted guidelines for judging Lincoln-Douglas debate. You will want to follow these guidelines and adapt your strategic arguments to meet these goals.

Generally, a decision should be based on:

1. Clear use of values argumentation throughout the round.
   a. Establishment of a values premise to support the debater's position in the round.
   b. Establishment of values criteria based on the values premise.
   c. Clash in the debate, based on the values criteria and the values premise.

2. Application of the values presented to the specific topic at hand.
   a. Validity of logic in relation to the values.
   b. Logical chain of reasoning, using the values, that leads to the conclusions of the affirmative or negative position.
   c. Clear explanation of the relation of the values to the specific topic, with adequate explanation and a moderate degree of authoritative opinion for support.

3. Crystallization and condensation of the issues.

4. Presentation of contextual definitions by both debaters, with justification presented by the negative if he or she challenges the affirmative definitions.

5. Debating of the resolution in its entirety. Neither the affirmative nor the negative are to debate their positions from the standpoint of isolated examples.

6. Effectiveness of delivery, using oral communication skills to persuade the listener with logic, analysis, and mode of delivery.

7. Overall presentation. Isolated dropped arguments are not enough to give a speaker a loss in the round.

8. Persuasiveness and logic should be the primary considerations. Analysts of values agree that values cannot be proved through factual, statistical evidence nor through isolated examples. Lincoln-Douglas debaters should be encouraged to develop the use of authoritative opinion as evidence when needed.

9. Both sides should present the judge with a basic value position that is applied throughout the round and used to refute the resolution. There are no prescribed burdens in Lincoln-Douglas. Neither the affirmative nor the negative has presumption or burden of proof. There is no status quo.

These are generally the kinds of issues judges will be considering when judging a Lincoln-Douglas debate. A sample ballot follows.

Summary

Lincoln-Douglas debate offers students a unique opportunity for one-on-one competition. Debating propositions of value requires a special approach and the development of skills not often used in policy debate. Lincoln-Douglas debate is also judged by a somewhat different set of criteria. Debaters should familiarize themselves with these criteria as part of their preparation for competition.

LINCOLN-DOUGLAS DEBATE BALLOT

ROUND _____ ROOM _____ TIME _____ DATE _____ JUDGE _____

Affirmative (name and code) _____

Negative (name and code) _____

INSTRUCTIONS TO JUDGES

1. Unlike team debate, the resolution to be debated will be a proposition of value, rather than a proposition of policy. Thus debaters are encouraged to develop argumentation on conflicting underlying principles to support their positions. To that end, they are not responsible for practical applications. There is no need for a plan (or for plan attacks).
2. The burdens on the affirmative and negative positions are not prescribed as they may be in debates on propositions of policy; therefore decision rules are fair issues to be argued in the round.
3. In making your decision, you might ask yourself the following questions:
   a. Which of the debaters persuaded you that their position was more valid? (Which debater communicated more effectively?)
   b. Did the debaters support their position appropriately, using logical argumentation throughout, and evidence where necessary?
4. Remember, there should be clash in the debate.

CIRCLE THE APPROPRIATE NUMBER

	SUPERIOR	EXCELLENT	GOOD	AVERAGE
Affirmative	50-49-48-47	46-45-44-43	42-41-40-39	38-37-36-35
Negative	50-49-48-47	46-45-44-43	42-41-40-39	38-37-36-35

AFFIRMATIVE	NEGATIVE
Case & Analysis	**Case & Analysis**
Support of Issues Through Evidence and Reasoning	**Support of Issues Through Evidence and Reasoning**
Delivery	**Delivery**

Reason for Decision

In my opinion the better debating was done by _____
                                                (affirmative or negative)   code

Critic's Signature _____

FORMAT

Affirmative	6-minute constructive	Affirmative	3-minute cross examination
Negative	3-minute cross examination	Affirmative	4-minute rebuttal
Negative	7-minute constructive	Negative	6-minute rebuttal
		Affirmative	3-minute rebuttal

Questions

1. What is required to debate value comparisons?
2. What is required to debate value extensions?
3. What is value exclusivity?
4. What constitutes an on-balance judgment about values?
5. How do the stock issues in Lincoln-Douglas debate differ from those of policy debate?

Discussion Opportunities

1. What are the differences between Lincoln-Douglas debate and policy debate?
2. How does debating a proposition of policy differ from debating a value proposition?
3. What are some of the reasons for the creation of Lincoln-Douglas debate? What opportunities does it provide?

Writing Opportunities

1. Develop three or four examples of the different types of value propositions and evaluate the debatability of each of the propositions.
2. Using the criteria for evaluation developed in the previous activity, construct an affirmative brief.
3. Using the current Lincoln-Douglas debate resolution, divide into groups and brainstorm a list of arguments and ideas that are expressed in the resolution. Next, separate out the arguments and ideas that should be pursued through research.
4. From the brainstorming session in the previous activity, develop a list of key terms and find definitions for them. Include general as well as specific definitions.
5. Based on the brainstorming session, develop some questions you would ask and practice cross-examination.

Critical Thinking Opportunities

1. Using the current Lincoln-Douglas topic, find the value term; decide what type of value proposition it is; identify the criteria for evaluation; and identify the value hierarchy.

2. Listen to a sample debate and identify the four stock issues in the debate.

3. Identify some values you think are important. Why are these values important to you? Place them in a value hierarchy.

4. Using the current Lincoln-Douglas debate topic, identify an area you would like to explore for an affirmative. Begin your research and collect five articles on the area.

CHAPTER 13

Lincoln-Douglas Strategies and Tactics

Object

After studying Chapter 13, you should be able

1. To research and write a Lincoln-Douglas affirmative case.
2. To explain and demonstrate negative case strategies in Lincoln-Douglas debate.
3. To explain the affirmative and negative responsibilities in Lincoln-Douglas rebuttals.

Key Terms

To effectively argue affirmative and negative positions in Lincoln-Douglas debate, you will need to understand the following terms:

defining terms
value premise (value
 term)
criteria for evaluation
value hierarchy
justification
counterdefinition
countercriteria
value implications

Lincoln-Douglas debate focuses on value propositions, which require debaters to argue about the merits of particular value statements. Compared to policy debate, Lincoln-Douglas debate places less emphasis on evidence and more on analysis. To that end, it is usually more communication-oriented than policy debate. The rules and practices of Lincoln-Douglas debate are designed to create a style of debate that emphasizes good communication. This means persuasive speaking, more analysis, and the development of abstract ideas.

Delivery is a very important component of Lincoln-Douglas debate. Constructive speeches should receive substantial polishing. Speeches ought to be concise, vivid, and worded with care. Although there is always pressure to speak faster and say more, debaters instead ought to practice clearing out irrelevant arguments, so that those that remain receive greater explanation, support, and careful delivery. Lincoln-Douglas debaters should take time to organize arguments and practice them frequently.

This chapter explores affirmative and negative case construction in Lincoln-Douglas debate. While the information provided here should prove useful in most instances, you should keep in mind that theory in Lincoln-Douglas debate is still evolving. What is written here is not the only approach to Lincoln-Douglas debate. Your own coach will have suggestions about which strategies are appropriate for your part of the country and about new theories that you should take into account.

Developing the Affirmative Case

In the first affirmative constructive speech, the affirmative must present a prima facie case, one that will stand on its own when first presented. In order for the case to be prima facie, the case should include the following stock issues: 1) definition of terms; 2) value premise; 3) criteria for evaluation; and 4) value hierarchy and justification. The burden of proof is considered to rest with the affirmative, just as it does in policy debate. However, in Lincoln-Douglas debate it is possible for the affirmative to actually lose one of the stock issues and still win the debate.

For example, suppose the negative were to present a counterwarrant to the affirmative criterion for evaluation. The negative might be able to prove that the counterwarrant is a better measuring stick by which to weigh the truth of the resolution. This does not necessarily mean that the affirmative should lose the debate, even though it has lost one of the stock issues. The affirmative could still win if it could show that even if the negative counterwarrant is used as the measuring stick, the evaluation inherent in the resolution is true.

The following sections examine each of the stock issues as a part of the affirmative case in Lincoln-Douglas debate.

Defining Terms

The first stock issue to be covered in affirmative case construction is the **definition of terms**. The affirmative will want to define the meanings of the important words in the resolution in order to assure that everyone will be talking about the same thing. It is not unusual for key terms in a resolution to have more than one meaning. There are three ways in which the affirmative might define the terms: formal, contextual, and operational.

Formal definitions are found in dictionaries, encyclopedias, almanacs, or other sources that give specific meanings for words. For example, a key term in the resolution "When in conflict, the spirit of the law ought to take priority over the letter of the law," is *conflict*. The *American Heritage Dictionary* defines conflict as the "clash of opposing ideas," but this is just one of many definitions listed by the dictionary.

Second are *contextual definitions*. Contextual definitions may be found in books written by experts on the subject matter of the resolution. Experts often define a term by using it with other terms. In the sample resolution, the contextual definition of *conflict* might be found in a book on constitutional law. The legal experts would define *conflict* in reference to the U.S. Constitution.

Finally, a term may be defined *operationally*. That is, the term would be defined by its usage. Operational definitions need to be employed carefully, as it is possible for an affirmative to employ definitions that are off base. For example, suppose the affirmative attempted to define *conflict* operationally by classifying the Vietnam War as a conflict. While such a definition might be true operationally, it would not hold with the contextual definition or when placed in conjunction with other key terms in the resolution, such as "spirit of the law" and "letter of the law."

Which type of definition should be used? It will vary depending on the resolution being debated. The best rule of thumb is to always use the definition that gives the clearest, most precise meaning to the terms. Such affirmative definitions are more likely to hold up when challenged by the negative.

Value Premises

The **value premise**, or **value term**, is the particular value that the affirmative believes is most important in understanding and accepting the resolution. In debating the resolution "Laws protecting citizens from themselves are justified," the terms *laws, protecting, citizens,* and *justified* would need to be defined. The first three terms help limit the debate. They enable the debaters to focus on the most important aspects of the topic.

The next term, *justified*, is the value term. The value term is a major part of the value criterion. Its function is to enable the opposition and the judge to evaluate what the affirmative believes the topic is all about. Therefore, the definition of the value term should be as precise as possible. Defining *justified* as "accepted" does not help the opposition or the judge understand what the affirmative believes to be the best measurement of the topic.

The precise definition of the value term is considered part of the stock issues because it is essential to a prima facie case. Without it, the judge may not be able to evaluate the debate objectively. Because Lincoln-Douglas debate involves debating

---

Defining Terms of the Resolution

The United States government ought to provide for the medical care of its citizens.
Key Terms: *ought, provide, medical care*

The principle of majority rule ought to be valued above the principle of minority rights.
Key Terms: *ought, principle, majority rule, minority rights*

That secondary education in the United States ought to be a privilege, not a right.
Key Terms: *ought, secondary education, privilege, right*

An individual's freedom of expression is of greater value than political correctness.
Key Terms: *freedom of expression, political correctness*

---

values that people hold dear, if the affirmative does not tell the judge how two competing values should be compared, the affirmative is gambling that the judge's feelings will be the same as the affirmative's.

Criteria for Evaluation

The **criteria** for evaluation are the means by which the values in the resolution are measured. The criteria for evaluation are very important to the outcome of the debate. For example, in the resolution "That secondary education in the United States ought to be a privilege, not a right," two possible criteria for evaluation come to mind: money and knowledge. If the affirmative applied the criterion of money, the affirmative could argue that secondary education is a right, since each citizen has a right to earn a living and education is a prerequisite to earning a decent living. On the other hand, if the affirmative argued that knowledge for knowledge's sake was the criterion, the affirmative would designate secondary education as a privilege and not a right.

When exploring possible criteria for evaluation, Lincoln-Douglas debaters should include research into philosophy. Debaters will probably want to read the works of philosophers such as John Stuart Mill or Jean Jacques Rousseau. Books, philosophy texts, and articles are all good sources for philosophical theories that reveal possible criteria for applying values. When researching various philosophers, debaters should set up a notebook to collect information that could be used for more than one topic.

A Sample Statement of Philosophy

Communitarianism: Won't You Be My Neighbor

by Kris Stanley

Communitarianism can be seen indirectly addressed throughout many philosophies; from Aristotle's concept that moral and political virtue could only be achieved within the context of the polis, to Hegel's perception on the importance of various forms of community as a means to fully realize the moral and political capacities of human beings. However the full realization of communitarianism developed out of the critique of two separate philosophies: Utilitarianism and Kantianism.

Utilitarianism, many communitarians say, reduces rationality to the "instrumental calculation of costs and benefits," and views the individual as a maximizer of utility. Communitarians on the other hand, would view rationality with an added emphasis on the role of reflection, deliberation, and evaluation. Kantianism conceives rationality in purely formal and procedural terms, separated from any solid social or communal context. Communitarians would place individuals in a concrete political and moral context where rationality would be found within those restraints. Because it is such a contemporary philosophy, communitarianism has many different interpretations on the role of the community, therefore this is just a basic foundation, and not a specific look at the ideals of communitarianism. The concept of communitarianism has four central issues: conception of the self, conception of the community, nature and scope of distributive justice, and the priority of the right over the good. . . .

Communitarians argue that the search for a single overarching principle of distributive justice, applicable to different societal goods and across different spheres, appears possible to contemporary liberals only because they start from the perspective of the autonomous self as bearer of rights, and proceed to place the issue of distributive justice in terms of the conflicting rights claim of individuals separate from the social structure of a community. If instead you look at distributive justice from a social conception of the individual and from the acknowledgement of the primacy of community, then it is possible to argue that principles of distributive justice must be open to different conceptions of the good and different understandings of the value of human association. Communitarians challenge the primacy of justice over the claims of the community in saying that this outlook fails to account for the constitutive role of our communal aims and attachments. Taking this into account allows that we may be governed by the common good rather than by the principles of right and justice. By not acknowledging the diversities of separate communities, and their values, a common good cannot be attained. Thus the claims of justice would still have a limited application, but they would no longer have primacy over the values of community or the requirements of the common good.

One of the central claims of liberal philosophy is that of priority or the right over the good. They say that a just society does not seek to promote any specific conception of good, but provides instead, a neutral framework of basic rights and liberties within which individuals can pursue their own values and life-plans, this still being consistent with a similar liberty for others. Therefore, according to this belief, a just society must therefore be governed by principles that do not presuppose any particular concept of the good. However, communitarians believe that every conception of the right and of justice presupposes a conception of the human good and of the good of human association. Thus the concept of "the priority of right" cannot be valid, since it is itself based on a prior conception of the human good, and the good of human association. Every conception of justice is located within a tradition and makes evident its specific conception of the good. Thus, the good is always prior to the right because the right is derived from the good.

Bibliography

Byron, J. William. "Linking the New Communitarians," *America*, March 20, 1993

Foster, Lawrence. *Women, Family and Utopia.* Syracuse University Press: 1991

Levitas, Ruth. *The Concept of Utopia.* Syracuse University Press: 1990

Rasmussen, David. *Universalism vs. Communitarianism.* MIT Press: 1990

Sandel, Michael. *Liberalism and the Limits of Justice.* Cambridge University Press: 1982

Adapted from a statement created for the NHSI Philosophy Project 1993, Lincoln-Douglas Debate Division, National High School Institute, Northwestern University. Division Director, Steve Foral. Note that in the original (full) brief, the four central issues of communitarianism were fully developed.

To explore possible criteria for evaluation of the resolution, Lincoln-Douglas debaters often research the works of philosophers.

Value Hierarchy and Justification

The final stock issue involves establishing and justifying the **value hierarchies**. Which specific values and criteria are used will depend on the debate resolution. Sometimes the resolution may include a comparison of terms that make up the value hierarchy. For example, the resolution "Protecting an adolescent's privacy is more important than allowing a parent to invade that privacy" establishes the hierarchy of an adolescent's privacy over parental rights. When the hierarchy is not specified in the resolution, the affirmative must establish it.

Next, the affirmative must justify that hierarchy. **Justification** involves discussing the hierarchy in the context of the subject area of the resolution. In the resolution on adolescents' privacy, this would involve developing arguments about why an adolescent's privacy is more important than the rights of parents. Another example can be found in the resolution "That the American criminal justice system ought to place a higher priority on retribution than on rehabilitation." For this resolution, the affirmative would be expected to show why retribution should be ranked as a higher value. The affirmative might accomplish this by making two arguments: (1) retribution benefits society, and (2) punishment is the most just way to treat criminals.

Sample Value Justification Argument

  I. Retribution benefits society.
     A. Retribution tells criminals crime will not be tolerated.
     B. Retribution is superior to rehabilitation.

  II. Punishment is the most just way to treat criminals.
     A. Retributive justice is founded on the principle of fairness.
     B. Rehabilitation cannot be just because it is not fair.
     C. Retribution is legitimate, and is thus just.

In Lincoln-Douglas debate the affirmative does not present a plan or solution to the problems presented in the affirmative case. This does not mean the affirmative is off the hook with regard to any negative implications of the values and criteria. The negative may introduce value objections or implications and the affirmative will need to respond.

The support of the value justification can take many forms. The affirmative might use evidence from magazines, newspapers, books, interviews, television, or any other authoritative source. The affirmative also might choose to use analogies or comparisons. Even when the debaters do not use a great deal of evidence, they still will have read a great deal on the resolution. It is not unusual for Lincoln-Douglas debaters to refer to ideas and issues from their reading without using specific pieces of evidence.

Organization

Lincoln-Douglas debate has yet to develop a rigid, standard form of presentation. This is good insofar as it permits greater creativity for debaters. However, most affirmative constructives follow an outline similar to the following:

  I. Statement of Proposition

  II. Definition of Terms
     A. Define what is being evaluated by either a formal definition if the term is abstract (*good, bad, liberty, justice*) or a contextual or operational definition if the term is concrete (*military spending, health benefits, rock and roll*).

    B. State criteria for reaching a judgment about the proposition in the round (calling for a comparative, exclusive, assertive, or on-balance judgment). State how such a judgment can be reached in the round of debate.

III. Value Link Contention
    A. Show how an abstract value is related to a concrete value.
    B. Show support for the link.
       1. Historical precedent.
       2. Public opinion consensus.
       3. Expert or experienced opinion.

IV. Example Contentions
    A. Show how the example pertains to the general value.
    B. Show that the example is important.

 V. Offset Contentions
    A. Show how alternative links are untrue.
    B. Show how alternative opinion is wrong or misdirected.
    C. Show how counterexamples are unimportant.

In the sample case on page 339, the affirmative chose to offset negative contentions. Although such offsets may give the impression of defensiveness to the judge, sometimes they are desirable—especially when the affirmative is able to predict likely negative objections.

Developing the Negative Position

As in policy debate, the negative has the basic responsibility of clash, whether directly with the affirmative's interpretation of the topic or with the topic itself. If the negative does not clash with the affirmative's position, the affirmative can argue that the negative has not fulfilled its obligations and should lose.

How can the negative go about clashing with the affirmative? There are three options open to the negative: (1) directly refute the affirmative, (2) present the negative case, or (3) combine refutation and a negative case. In most debate rounds the negative will choose option three, a combination of refutation and a negative case.

Overview of Negative Position

The first task before the negative is to provide an overview of the negative position. Before launching into the actual arguments of the round the negative will want to give the judge (and the affirmative) an idea of the negative position against the resolution and the affirmative case. The overview allows the judge to anticipate the negative's arguments against the resolution and the arguments against the affirmative case.

Sample Affirmative Constructive

   I. Proposition: "The American space program is a success."

  II. Definitions.

     A. *space program:* NASA space effort from inception to present; *success:* ability to accomplish substantial, important goals.

     B. Criteria: Success should be measured by achievement, and in the context of a space program, achievement is measured in terms of making the best of scientific research in the pursuit of exploration.

  III. Value Link Contention: NASA has made significant achievements.

     A. NASA accomplishments have significantly increased humankind's ability to travel into and explore outer space. We can travel farther, see more, and understand more about the universe.

     B. Support: examples, testimony.

  IV. Offset Contention: *Challenger* disaster is not a sign of failure.

     A. Risk is an inherent feature of scientific research. Such a failure should not tarnish the program, given the complexity of bringing about success.

     B. *Challenger* was atypical.

     C. NASA will continue to be supported, and space exploration will proceed.

Presumption

Presumption is the position or attitude taken by individuals toward a particular issue. The issue is assumed to be true until arguments to the contrary are presented. For example, it could be said "I presume you have all the information you need unless I hear otherwise from you." In a court of law the defendant is presumed to be innocent until proved otherwise. The prosecution has the obligation to prove that the defendant committed the crime. It is not the obligation of the defendant to prove he or she did not commit the crime. In Lincoln-Douglas debate, presumption rests with the negative. This means that presumption rests against the resolution being presented. Once the affirmative has presented reasons for adopting the resolution, then the negative has the burden of rejoinder. This means that the negative has the responsibility to respond to the affirmative case once it has been presented.

Refutation

When directly refuting the affirmative case, negative debaters will find it advantageous to attack all the arguments one at a time, as they were presented. It is always important to tell the judge where in the affirmative case one is by signposting. For example, stating "On the affirmative's first contention of adolescent's rights . . ." will help the judge immediately identify where and what one is arguing.

When refuting the affirmative case, there are two lines of arguments open to the negative. The first is the affirmative's definition of terms. The negative may choose to reject the affirmative value term or criterion and offer its own value term. The negative can offer new definitions of any of the terms in the resolution or can offer a different value criterion—an alternative way to measure the values in conflict. When presenting **counterdefinitions** or **countercriteria**, the negative must be sure these new definitions are better than those offered by the affirmative. The claim of superiority must be supported by proof.

On the other hand, the negative may decide to accept the affirmative definitions and criterion. However, once the definitions and criterion have been accepted, both sides are bound by them for the rest of the debate. The negative cannot decide to offer a counterdefinition in the rebuttals.

The second line of argument open to the negative is to directly attack the affirmative's arguments or value justification. If the negative can show that the value justification does not support the value, the affirmative will have a very difficult time winning the debate.

The Negative Case

The negative case offers several interesting attack opportunities. First, the negative case can be used to directly attack the topic. If the topic is worded so that presumption is with the negative, as in "No political action is justifiable that is morally wrong," the negative can simply defend the present system. If presumption is not clear, as in the resolution "The public's right to know is of greater value than the right of privacy of candidates for public office," then the negative can argue the reverse of the proposition—in this case, that the right of privacy is actually greater than the public's right to know.

In either circumstance, when presenting a negative case the negative has the same responsibilities as the affirmative. The negative must define the terms, establish the value criterion, and provide the value justification, or the reason why the negative interpretation is better than the affirmative's. Just as the affirmative has the burden of proof when presenting its case, the negative has the burden of proof when presenting the negative case.

The second use of the negative case applies primarily to resolutions that imply a course of action. The negative would attack the implied plan. The first way to do this is to examine what might happen if the affirmative value case were accepted. For example, under the resolution "That public safety supersedes the individual's right to bear arms," the affirmative might establish the value criterion of "protecting individuals" as the most important value for the debate. To respond, the negative would attempt to show the potential harms of the affirmative's case. Such an argument may be called **value implications**, because the negative is examining what may occur if the affirmative case is accepted. For example, the negative might argue: (1) individuals will not be protected because the criminals will still have guns, and (2) denying individuals the right to bear arms violates the Constitution. The negative would then explain that the value of the Constitution is more important than the value of individual safety.

Negative cases usually run three to four minutes. This allows time for the negative to argue against the affirmative case as well as presenting a negative case. The organization of the negative usually works best when the negative first refutes the affirmative and ends the speech with the negative case. This leaves the judge with the negative interpretation of the topic as opposed to the affirmative's.

It is important to listen carefully to the affirmative case to hear exactly what is begin advocated in terms of a value. The negative can prepare briefs by thinking of all the possible interpretations of the topic. The negative would then be able to apply these briefs to the specific affirmative arguments.

Organization

As with the affirmative constructive, the negative constructive in Lincoln-Douglas debate is not yet completely formalized. Generally, however, there are several options for the negative constructive speech. It can focus its attack on the definition of terms, criteria for evaluation, link contention, or offsets. It also can advance alternative constructive arguments. The following outline delineates negative options:

I. Definition of Terms: Accept or debate the affirmative definition. If debated, show why the affirmative definition is on the whole unreasonable or why it needs to be significantly amended so that discussion centers on the proposition at hand and not on side issues.

II. Value Criteria: Either accept, dispute, or amend the criteria. If the latter two choices are made, then show why the negative criteria for assessing value are superior.

III. Value Link Disagreement

    A. Show that the instances of value advanced by the affirmative are not linked to criteria for judgment; that the qualities of the instance under evaluation are not in line with the affirmative evaluation; and that the examples are not relevant, complete, or as the affirmative represents.

    B. Show that supporting opinion is unreasonably prejudiced, unqualified, or irrelevant to the discussion at hand.

IV. Value Offset Argument
   A. Advance counterexamples that weigh into consideration.
   B. Show an alternative example that meets the negative criteria for making an evaluation of the proposition.
   C. Either refute or ignore, as appropriate, affirmative offset arguments.

Consider how these arguments might apply to the following sample case, which support the proposition "The American space program is a success." Note that the negative tried to make the *Challenger* example relevant and indicative of the present state of collapse for NASA. The affirmative, on the other hand, tried to minimize the example and in further extension of the argument would likely point to the necessity for manned space explorations. This argument would be supported by plans for a space station. The affirmative would wish to show its feasibility and value.

Sample Negative Case

   I. Definitions: The space program is equal to the NASA effort, but program goals are not necessarily the only determinants of success. A successful public policy is one that contributes to the welfare of the citizenry in proportion to its costs.

   II. Criteria: Although success equals achievement, that achievement must be evaluated in terms of contribution to society over the long term. Any program has small achievements. The criterion for making a judgment on NASA should be its overall contribution.

   III. Value Link Contention: NASA has made modest achievements in recent years.
   A. The early part of the space program was a success (putting men and women in orbit, landing on the moon, launching deep exploration vehicles).
   B. The more recent part of the program has been a failure. The commitment to space vehicles rather than rockets is counterproductive. The shuttle system is expensive, unreliable, and more of a public relations program than a scientific mission.
   C. Deviation from the original intentions of NASA has left it a failure in terms of future prospects for scientific achievement.

   IV. Offset Arguments
   A. The *Challenger* was an unnecessary disaster.
   B. The *Challenger* weakened political support for NASA and has blocked further scientific research.

A debater prepares for her rebuttal.

Rebuttals

Lincoln-Douglas rebuttal periods are similar to those in policy debate. The aim of rebuttals is to narrow the number of arguments to those that are the most relevant and crucial to the debate. Each side must resupport its own position on the appropriate criteria by which to assess the proposition. In clashing on criteria, debaters uncover value premises, the supporting assumptions on which the criteria for evaluation are based.

In the space program example, a value assumption that underlies the negative position is that the quality of a program must be based on its current state of contribution and its future potential. The affirmative could identify this as a premise and make the counterargument that a program can be a success if it makes a unique, outstanding contribution—and that NASA has done so. The negative might respond that the value premise on which this argument is based is that a program is considered worthwhile even if its history ultimately ends up leaving the situation worse off rather than better. Thus, the negative might say that public policy ought to be judged on the pragmatic grounds of continuing contribution.

First Affirmative Rebuttal

In this first rebuttal, the objective should be to cover as many negative arguments as possible and then to cover as many of the affirmative arguments as possible. Careful attention should be paid to the value term, making sure to defend against any negative attacks. In this rebuttal any damage to the affirmative should be repaired. This may be nothing more than answering a question, reading more evidence, restating, or reaffirming. If the negative only questioned the affirmative evidence, a simple response would be enough. It is important when researching the affirmative case to uncover enough new evidence for rebuttals. This provides backup support should the evidence from the constructive be attacked as biased or incomplete.

In this rebuttal, you do not want to forget to restate and reaffirm contentions that have not been attached. Restating untouched contentions helps the judge to know exactly the status of the affirmative case.

Negative Rebuttal

The negative has only one rebuttal in Lincoln-Douglas debate. In this last speech, the negative will want to be sure to respond to the affirmative attacks but also to stress what the negative believes to be the key issues of the debate. The rebuttal should begin with the affirmative case. A four-step approach can be used for each argument:

1. State where you are in the debate.
2. Restate your opponent's response.
3. State your response.
4. Summarize the impact of the argument on the debate.

If there are a great number of arguments still in the debate, the negative will need to choose from a couple of strategies. First, if the affirmative case has several contentions and each one has three to four pieces of evidence, the negative may not have time to respond to each piece of evidence. When this is the case, the negative should try to focus on the basic analysis behind each contention. Since Lincoln-Douglas debate stresses the communicative factor, the negative's first concern should be to debate the affirmative clearly and intelligibly.

Second, if the affirmative case is very shallow or has very little detail, the negative may have time to respond to each separate point and piece of evidence. However, the negative must remember that it still has its own case to rebuild. No more than three to four minutes should be spent on the affirmative case. As in the constructive speech, the negative wants to end the debate on the negative case.

Second Affirmative Rebuttal

This last affirmative rebuttal is only three minutes in length. This does not leave the affirmative much time to cover all the arguments, particularly in light of the fact that the negative has just spent six minutes covering affirmative and negative issues. The affirmative will also find the four-step pattern of restatement helpful:

1. State where you are in the debate.

2. Restate your opponent's response.

3. State your response.

4. Summarize the impact of the argument on the debate.

This pattern of response allows the affirmative rebuttalist to focus on the case issues the affirmative is winning while pointing out where the affirmative has beaten the negative. Such attention to organization is very important, because it is a means of making sure the affirmative has adequately responded to all attacks and has reasonably extended the affirmative case throughout the debate. It is also important because it greatly improves the debater's speaking style. Style can be a key factor in some debates. The affirmative wants to leave an impression with the judge of being organized, confident, and knowledgeable.

Summary

The first step toward becoming an accomplished Lincoln-Douglas debater is to learn all you can about the form. The next step is to practice. Through practice you will find Lincoln-Douglas a challenging and exciting activity that will allow you an opportunity to develop communication and critical-thinking skills.

Questions

1. What are the parts of the affirmative case? What is the importance of each?
2. What are the responsibilities of the negative speaker in the debate? Do some appear to be easier than others?
3. What approaches can the negative use in the constructive speech?
4. How should the negative approach the rebuttal in the debate? What should be the strategies?
5. What should be the affirmative strategy in rebuttal?

Discussion Opportunities

1. Discuss the debatability of value questions pertaining to the arts, the sciences, history, education, and the common welfare. Which areas do you think are most productive for debate?
2. What is the strategic advantage for the negative in presenting the negative case in the debate?
3. Discuss the suggestions on pages 325-326 for judging Lincoln-Douglas debate. How do these suggestions influence the development of argument strategy?

Writing Opportunities

1. Develop an affirmative case outline, using the resolution provided by your teacher.
2. Write an affirmative constructive speech defending a value proposition.
3. Outline the possible negative arguments to the affirmative case in activity 2 above.
4. Using an affirmative speech delivered in class, prepare a negative speech that includes a negative case.

Critical Thinking Opportunities

1. Develop two different negative strategies against a case supporting a value proposition. Evaluate the strategic strengths and weaknesses of each approach.
2. Choose a prominent person and conduct a values debate over that individual's contribution to a specific field.
3. Deliver your affirmative case as a speech in class. While other students are delivering their speeches, use the time to practice flowing the arguments.
4. Deliver your negative speech in class. Practice flowing the negative speeches of other students.

STRATEGIES IN ACTION

Katherine knew as they drove home from the tournament that the next two weeks would be busy ones. The tournament at Hillside High School would be the first tournament on the new topic *"Resolved*: Terminally ill patients have the right to die when and how they choose.*"* Every year, the new topic was challenging and exciting, but it required a great deal of work to get ready in so short a timeframe.

Katherine set out her game plan as follows, and began to work.

- Define the object of evaluation—the rights of the terminally ill.

- Identify the key value terms—terminally ill, right, choose.

- Establish the criteria for evaluation—moral and ethical standards.

- Establish and justify a value hierarchy—why do moral and ethical standards rank above individual choice?

To define the value terms, to establish the criteria for evaluation, and to justify the value priorities would require some background reading. Katherine went to the library and found several books to get her started. The strategies or tactics she used were as follows:

- Copy pages from medical books with pertinent definitions. Also copy pertinent pages from *Black's Law Dictionary*.

- Refer to—*An Introduction to Ethics* and *Moral Problems* for definitions and criteria.

- Refer to—*Philosophy of Law* and *A Theory of Justice* for material on legal theory.

- Pull information on Locke, Hume, and Rawls from her philosophy notebook.

Armed with these resources, Katherine set to work. From the medical and legal dictionaries she gathered the definitions needed to define the value terms. Using the books on ethics and morals, she developed framework for building a negative, but was going to need to do some more digging to justify an individual's right to die. From the legal books she found a negative criteria for evaluation and justification. Using her previous work on philosophers stored in her notebook, she found she had enough information to support both sides of the right to die issue.

Using her research and having developed a plan, Katherine was ready to sit down and outline a position on both sides of the resolution.

Persuasion in Debate

Objectives

After studying Chapter 14, you should be able
1. To demonstrate the difference between performance and communication.
2. To provide examples of different judging criteria.
3. To understand the nature of the debate speech.
4. To explain how debaters can develop high source credibility.
5. To demonstrate the tactics of effective communication.
6. To understand the nature of ethics in debate.

Key Terms

To communicate persuasively, you will need to understand the following terms:

balance of arguments
   judge
better job of debating
   judge
maverick judge
rate of delivery
vocal inflection
highlighting
forecasting
signposting
summarizing
word choice
credibility
ethics

It should be clear by now that debate is a complex activity. Debaters must be theoreticians thoroughly familiar with the fundamentals of debate and the logic of formal argument. They also must be researchers who are capable of doing intensive research on a broad question. They must know how to combine analysis and research to build sound constructive cases. They must be tacticians who study the best strategies and tactics of competitive presentation. Finally, they must be good public speakers.

No matter how effective debaters are at other tasks, success ultimately depends on the ability to communicate ideas and evidence to a neutral but critical party: the judge. Everyone today is deeply concerned about communication, and a large number of scholars have been studying communication theory, trying to find out what goes wrong in human communication and what can be done about it. Debaters are doing something about it.

Throughout the season, debaters work hard to overcome tremendous communication problems as they try to communicate a host of very complicated ideas to their critics. While others may read about how to improve communication, debaters actively engage in improving their communication skills. Strategic debaters constantly reevaluate and adjust their techniques to make themselves more effective communicators.

As you proceed through your debate career, you will learn the techniques of communication on a very practical and personal level. You will find that there are specific things you can do to be an effective public speaker. In fact, while you can benefit from the wisdom and experience of others, you must develop your own theories about how you can be effective. Fortunately, as a debater, you can practice before qualified judges who will provide feedback on the effectiveness of your communication skills. As a strategic debater, you will want to take full advantage of this feedback. Through feedback from judges, coaches, opponents, and colleagues, you can refine your skills to make yourself as effective a communicator as possible.

This chapter does not offer an absolute formula for being a persuasive communicator. The formula is different for each debater. Instead, this chapter offers a compilation of observations and generalizations about how debaters can communicate more effectively. This chapter discusses debate as a setting for effective communication and offers strategies for persuasive debating.

Elements of Communication

The basic strategy for effective communication in the debate setting is to remember debate is in fact *communication*, not performance. There are many speech events, such as oral interpretation contests, in which students might be said to be performing. On these occasions they will be graded on the quality of their performance. While some debaters carry this attitude over to debate, this is a great mistake. The decision in a debate most often rests on the debater's ability to communicate, rarely on the ability to perform as a debater.

A persuasive speaker knows how to communicate with an audience.

Almost every communication setting, including debate, can be broken down into four parts: audience, occasion, material, and speaker. The primary *audience* in debate is usually just one person: the judge. The *occasion* is the competitive setting, which includes everything from the debate room itself to the speakers on the other team. The *material* is the set of arguments and ideas that the debater wishes to communicate to the judge. The *speaker* is the debater, who must adjust to the other three elements in the most appropriate manner. These are the four elements that debaters must consider as they prepare for each debate. Debaters who keep these four elements in mind have already gone a long way toward becoming effective as speakers in the debate setting.

Audience: The Judge

It would be helpful if debate judges were like computers, able to take in all the ideas they hear, process them, and make decisions. It would be wonderful if judges were always objective, always attentive, and always correct in their decisions. As most experienced debaters know, however, this is not always the case.

Judges are just human beings—trained human beings, to be sure, but not machines. Judges may not always be objective; in fact, they can be very subjective if a debater angers them. They may not always be attentive; even though every speaker's ideas are fascinating to the speaker, a judge can be bored, tired, or even uninterested. And, sad to say, the judge's decision will not always please the debaters.

Strategic debaters know that they must adapt to their audiences. They must provide objective and subjective data that will help the judge understand their case. They must keep the judge's interest and attention. If a debater feels that the judge has voted incorrectly, it is the debater's fault, because only the debater can provide the data that will enable a judge to make the "correct decision."

Now the question becomes: how can a debater manage the data to win the debate in the mind of the judge? The first step is to understand something about how most judges reach their decisions in the debate. Although no one can read a judge's mind, debaters can make some fairly accurate predictions about the kinds of judges they will have and how those judges are likely to evaluate the debate. The starting point is the place on the ballot where the judge is asked to fill in the space in the sentence: "In my opinion the _____ team did the better job of debating." How does the judge decide whether to write *affirmative* or *negative*?

Judging criteria vary, but common criteria are (1) the balance of arguments, and (2) who did the better job of debating. These two criteria cover the majority of debate judges. Knowing which kind of judge you are facing will enable you to adjust your debating style.

Balance of Arguments Judge

Many judges base their decisions on which team best established its arguments during the debate. These **balance of arguments judges** listen carefully to the debate and usually take copious notes on their flowsheets. As the debate progresses, a balance of arguments judge analyzes the basic issues and the arguments and evidence that support them. The decision is based on the judge's determination as to which team did the better job of meeting its basic responsibilities.

For the affirmative, this means that the judge weighs the affirmative's issues. If the affirmative presents a traditional need case, the judge considers whether the affirmative established the need for a change, whether the affirmative's proposal was shown to be capable of solving the problems of the present system, and whether the advantages were maintained throughout the round. The balance of arguments judge may well award a loss to the affirmative team if any of these basic issues was significantly damaged.

If the affirmative presents a comparative advantages, net benefits, or alternative justifications case, the judge considers whether the affirmative has established its advantages. The judge also carefully evaluates how the affirmative responds to the negative's plan objections, to see if serious disadvantages still remain at the end of the debate.

If the affirmative presents a goals case, the balance of arguments judge considers whether the affirmative has done a better job of meeting the stated goals than the present system. The judge also considers any advantages claimed by the affirmative when meeting the goals. Finally the judge looks at whether any negative disadvantages remain, and whether they outweigh the goals or affirmative advantages gained by the affirmative plan.

The major concern of the balance of arguments judge is whether the affirmative has met its burden of proof. The judge looks closely at the negative arguments. Did the negative adequately defend the present system? Did its arguments and evidence penetrate the affirmative's case? Did the negative establish the disadvantages to the affirmative's proposal?

The decision, then, may well boil down to a single issue and to which side seemed to win it. Balance of arguments judges are likely to indicate on the ballot the points that decided the debate in their minds. These judges are likely to be much more content-analysis–oriented than other judges. They may well award the decision to a less articulate team that won a really significant issue, even though the other team was more persuasive.

Better Job of Debating Judge

Many debaters are disturbed if their judges do not take detailed notes during the debate. Some judges just sit back and listen to the round, without seeming to care about the specific arguments and evidence the debaters use. It is not unusual for a lay judge to not take a flow or even notes. Such judges are not incompetent; they are using different standards for judging the debate.

Better job of debating judges do not weigh the arguments to determine which team was more effective in the round. Instead, they base their decisions solely on which team did the better job of debating. While in some cases decisions may be totally subjective or even impressionistic, it is more likely that these judges use specific criteria to evaluate a round. Despite appearances, chances are that such judges will gauge the debaters' effectiveness on the criteria that are listed on the debate ballot.

Typically, a ballot asks the judge to consider five criteria: analysis, reasoning, evidence, refutation, and delivery. *Analysis* involves how well a team analyzes the issues of the proposition and the debate. *Reasoning* involves the debaters' logic, whether their conclusions were reasonable on the basis of the evidence they provided. *Evidence* involves how good that evidence was. *Refutation* is based on how well the debaters responded to arguments. And *delivery* ratings are based on the debaters' overall effectiveness as speakers—whether their delivery facilitated their case or detracted from it.

While balance of arguments judges view the ballot as a means of providing feedback to the student, not as a guide to decision making, better job of debating judges take the statement on the ballot literally, and attempt to answer who did the better job of debating. They generally interpret the criteria on the ballot as guides in deciding who won the debate.

Clearly, these two styles of debate judging overlap considerably. The general skill of a debater significantly affects the balance of arguments, and the balance of arguments is a significant factor in deciding which team did the better job of debating. Chances are, if a balance of arguments judge and a better job of debating judge are both listening to the same debate, they would come up with identical decisions. Nevertheless, debaters should be aware of the differences between these judges, both to help them develop their communication skills and to relieve their frustration over some decisions.

Many debaters seem to prefer balance of arguments judging. These debaters are frequently upset if they feel they have won an important issue in a debate, but the judge hasn't given them the decision. The chances are that the judge based the decision on general effectiveness and felt that the other team had the better debaters, even though they may have lost one or two issues. Strategic debaters know that it is necessary to win the decision of *both* types of judges in order to succeed in competitive debate.

Maverick Judge

Probably the most frustrating thing about debating is to occasionally get what feels like a bad decision. A common refrain among many debaters is the old line, "I've never lost a debate, but I sure get a lot of bad decisions." In the vast majority of cases, however, this is just a rationalization. Because debate is an intellectual activity, some participants feel a strong urge to excuse their defeats because they feel their intelligence is somehow at stake.

Even though the old rationalization may contribute to the mental health of some debaters, it is one of the major barriers to improving as a speaker. Debaters do not become really good until they admit that most of the time the judge is correct. Until they admit this, they have no real reason to improve: in their own mind they're always right, and the judge is always wrong. These debaters figure that if they could just get perfect judging every round, they would be the undefeated national champions.

However, while the vast majority of losses are due to the weakness of a team, it is important to acknowledge that all judges are not perfect. Indeed, a few judges consistently deviate from the decisions of other judges, even in rounds that have several judges. Such judges are not necessarily "wrong" in their decisions, but they are unpredictable.

The expression **maverick judge** was coined by Otto F. Bauer and C. William Colburn in 1966 to describe these judges. Whether they are debate coaches, speech teachers, or newcomers to debate circles, there is really no way to tell how or why they vote the way they do.

What can debaters do about this? Nothing. They must simply get used to the fact that they will occasionally draw a maverick judge. Debaters can take solace, however, from three things. First, maverick judges are a rare breed; in all likelihood, more than 90 percent of all judges will be balance of arguments or better job of debating judges. Instead of losing sleep over maverick judges, debaters should concentrate on the other kinds. Second, individual debaters should realize that they are not the only ones who will occasionally be judged by a maverick: everyone else runs the same risk. Therefore, if a team wins many debates, this does not mean it was lucky in avoiding maverick judges; it means the team members are good debaters. Finally, and most importantly, debaters should remember that a maverick judge is just as likely to vote *for* them as *against* them. If debaters want to excuse their losses by blaming maverick judges, they would have to regret some of their victories.

Occasion: The Competitive Setting

Debaters' communication behavior is conditioned by more than just the judge. The speaking occasion itself is an important influence on both speaker and the judge. It should, therefore, affect each debater's communicative approach.

There are several common elements about debate settings. Debates usually take place in school classrooms, on weekends, with only a few persons present to hear each round. Also, debates usually take place as part of a series of rounds that make up a debate tournament. This setting affects the communication situation in several ways.

The main effect is that the debate is not a unique experience for anyone. The judge has already heard many debates and is likely to hear many more—often as many as four or five debates in one day. Therefore, the occasion forces debaters to be more conscious of their communication than most other kinds of public speakers. Chances are, the judge is likely to be tired and not very interested in the debate. Indeed, one of the first and major surprises for the debater-turned-judge is how long a debate seems from the back of the room and how short it seems from the speaker's stand.

Naturally, the debate occasion is likely to change as debaters approach the final elimination rounds at tournaments. Suddenly, there is a large audience of debaters and a crowd of interested spectators; there are several judges instead of one. Tension is high and people are very interested in hearing exactly what the debaters say. Debaters must be able to adjust to this new situation. They need to speak to the large audience as well as to the panel of judges, keeping the audience interested but concentrating on defeating the opposition.

Material: The Debate Speech

Debaters, like any other speakers, must adjust their speaking material to their audiences and to the time allotted for presenting it. Debate material has several distinctive characteristics. First of all, there is a lot of it! Debaters must prepare and present tremendous amounts of arguments and evidence just to meet their basic obligations. This leads to a common criticism of debaters that the **rate of delivery**, or speaking speed, is uncommunicative, too hurried, and not enjoyable to hear. Such criticism may be just at times, but there is a reason for the accelerated delivery common to policy debate. The material in the first affirmative rebuttal alone would take much longer to cover if it were presented at an orator's rate of delivery, and the debater doesn't have that much time. No one wants to sit through an all-night debate just so each speaker can speak at the rate and with the distinctness appropriate to other speaking situations.

Second, most debate material is objective in nature, and debaters typically do not use flowery phrases or emotional appeals. Almost everything must be documented, down to the page numbers on important material, and debaters must present a great deal of statistical material. Even with more elegant turns of phrase, much of this material would not make good listening or provide the pure entertainment value of a popular television or radio show.

Finally, a great deal of debaters' material is delivered extemporaneously, some of it thought of during the speech, or as the debate progresses, or during a discussion of other points. The nature of the material is such that debaters are forced to standardize much of what they say, so that they can think better while talking. Among poor debaters this means that many clichés are used to facilitate debating. With better debaters it means that students develop their own standardized language so that they do not have to think of each new word as they argue.

Some listeners—speech teachers and others—may be taken aback by the way debate material is delivered. However, debaters who increase their rate of delivery and standardize their language are doing what all good speakers should do; adapting to the nature of the material they are trying to communicate. Debaters would be poor communicators if they did *not* adjust. However, there is a danger in *over*adjusting. Debaters who talk so fast that the judge can't understand them or who carry their debate style into other speaking situations are poor public speakers.

Speaker: The Debater

Just as debaters must know the strengths and weaknesses of their cases, they also must know their strong and weak points as speakers. Although debaters tend to have the same general style because of the situation and the material, each individual must develop a personal style of delivery. This style should be based on sound self-evaluation. Speakers should cultivate their favorable points and minimize the factors that detract from their persuasive communication.

A key element in speaking style is rate of delivery, which was discussed earlier. Debaters need to discover for themselves what is an appropriate rate of speed. Practicing the delivery of your prepared arguments will help you determine an appropriate rate of speed, but you need to be able to vary your base rate according to the type of judge in the round. A shotgun approach will be of little value if the round is being evaluated by a lay judge or a maverick. If the judge does not seem to be following most of what is being said, it's time to slow down.

Another key factor is **vocal inflection**. Even when speed is appropriate, you

A master of persuasive communication and debate, former Texas representative Barbara Jordan was the keynote speaker at two Democratic Party national conventions.

should try to avoid speaking in a monotone. Just as you should vary your rate of delivery, there should be some inflections in the tone of your voice.

Strategies of Persuasive Communication

Knowing something of the nature of the judge, the debate setting, debate material, and your own strengths as a speaker, you next need to develop some communication strategies that will help you persuade a judge. These strategies should not be designed for the perfect judge—always attentive, always objective—but for the average judge. Strategic debaters do not have to have the perfect judge to win a debate. They develop their ability to transmit their ideas to another person.

Strategic debaters know that many factors influence the judge's decision in a debate. As discussed in the previous section, many judges objectively weigh the arguments and issues in the round to arrive at their decisions. Others base their opinions on subjective impressions of the debaters' effectiveness. But most judges use a combination of objective and subjective factors.

Some debaters are the kind that a judge would like to see win: good, pleasant communicators who favorably impress the judge with their competence and command of the situation. Others are the kind a judge would like to see lose: they are ineffective, sarcastic, and perhaps even rude in their approach to the other team. The majority of debaters fall in the middle, and the judge is relatively neutral toward them. The basic persuasive debate strategy should be built on communicating arguments so effectively that the judge will *know*, objectively, why the debaters think their arguments are valid. At the same time, the debaters want the judge to *feel* that they should win the debate.

The work you have done thus far has concentrated on developing strategies for winning debates on objective terms. Now that you have mastered those strategies, you can refine your debating skills by concentrating on the more subjective aspects of debate. To be a persuasive communicator, you will need to control strategies of formal speaking, language, and style.

Formal Speech Strategies

Once debaters know what they are going to say, they must decide what formal devices they will use to facilitate communication with the judge. Debaters work in a very difficult communication situation. What they have to say is not easy for anyone to understand because often the material they use is technical, and the logic they use is subtle and complex. In addition, debaters have a great deal to say and very little time in which to say it. There are a number of formal speech strategies that help listeners better follow and understand the material. Some of the most useful formal strategies for debate include highlighting, forecasting, signposting, and summarizing.

The first step that debaters can take to facilitate communication is to arrange their materials in a form that makes the most important points stand out from the material that is less important. This is known as **highlighting**. When highlighting, debaters use well-written statements of their major issues, so that the issues will be easy to remember. Highlighted contentions should be short, clear, and worded in an interesting way. For example, one debater described the entire affirmative analysis by saying, "Ladies and gentlemen, we are going to argue today that it is time to take the dollar sign out of medicine."

By highlighting in such a manner, debaters can be fairly certain that at the end of the round the judge will remember the team's basic philosophy and major contentions so that the important parts of the case stand out. Some negative debaters develop "points of clash" that they can state early in the debate, to help the judge remember the negative position. These might include statements such as: "The affirmative has misanalyzed the present system," or "There are several compelling reasons for rejecting the affirmative proposal."

A second speech strategy is **forecasting**. Speakers know that if the audience is made aware beforehand of what is going to be said, it will be easier for the audience to understand it. Surprise is generally not a good strategy in debate: while you may want to surprise your opponent, you don't want to risk losing the judge. Forecasting enables debaters to ensure that the judge will be ready for what is to come.

When forecasting, you should begin each major argumentative development with a short statement of what is to come. First affirmative speakers, for instance, might begin with an overview of what they are about to do and might indicate the major divisions of their need-for-a-change argument before going into subpoints and evidence. The essence of forecasting is to clear away the trees to show the judge the forest—to forget about evidence and arguments for a moment and let the judge see the highlights of the logical development.

A third speech strategy is **signposting**. Just as forecasting tells the judge where the debate is going, the signposts tell the judge where the debater is at a particular time. After developing an argument, all the debater has to do is provide the judge with a brief perspective. Signposting lets the judge see what an argument means in terms of a particular segment of the case, or what else has to be done to finish the analysis.

Finally, a key speech strategy is **summarizing**. After telling the judge where you are going (forecasting) and where you are at each step of the case (signposting), you will want to remind the judge of what has come before. Most logical units of your presentation (such as major contentions) should be capped with a very short summary of your argument. In addition, most experienced debaters know that a one- or two-sentence summary at the end of a speech can help solidify the major ideas in the mind of the judge.

The four strategies described here can do much to improve your persuasive communication during a debate. While there is nothing new about these techniques, they remain very useful. Unfortunately, however, because they have been used so long, these strategies have become part of nonthinking debate. These strategies should be used thoughtfully. Employ them only when they help you communicate your material. Using them without thinking will not help you communicate, and it may waste much valuable time.

Language Strategies

In addition to speech strategies, debaters should employ language strategies that help them communicate effectively with the judge. The key here is to develop language habits that will help you explain what you mean and will hold the judge's attention. Some useful language strategies include carefully choosing your words and avoiding redundancy.

Judging some debates is like watching the fiftieth rerun of a very dull movie. The debaters seem to be saying what all the other speakers have said, and in just the same way the others said it. It is difficult for a judge merely to listen to such speakers—much less try to understand them. The basic problem is that many debaters "learn" the language of argument simply by listening to other debaters. As a result, they sound like everyone else; everyone chooses the same words to describe the same things.

Word choice is a key language strategy. Successful debaters know how dull a routine debate can be, and they carefully choose their words. They look for descriptive phrases, use words that will keep the attention of the judge, and avoid the terminology that everyone else seems to be using.

One danger in debate is language fads. If a good debater wins a major tournament or otherwise gains the respect of other debaters, many debaters will want to emulate that person and try out their turns of phrase. Unfortunately, however, by the time a fad has filtered down to most debaters, the terms will have lost their freshness. Strategic debaters avoid all debate clichés and choose the words that are most appropriate for their own cases and arguments.

Skillful repetition is another language strategy used by successful debaters. Such debaters deliberately describe a difficult concept two or three times, perhaps using different words each time. They know that very few persons understand everything the first time they hear it, and therefore they are not afraid to repeat themselves.

However, the difference between thinking and nonthinking debaters is shown in what they repeat. While thinking debaters repeat what needs repeating, in order to keep key ideas and arguments in the judge's mind, nonthinking debaters repeat because everyone else does. They fall into the trap of **redundancy,** or stating what doesn't need to be repeated. For example, there is no point in repeating something like "Therefore, there is a need for a change." What would be more helpful in the debate would be to repeat the reasons *why* there is a need for change—and to say it several ways so that the judge will fully appreciate your logic.

Style Strategies

It is partly through their style of delivery that debaters convey many ideas and attitudes and develop credibility. While individuals should find the delivery style that is best for them, there are four techniques that most debaters can use to become more effective: using conversational style, developing extemporaneous skills, using gestures, and analyzing past performance.

First, debaters should deliver their speeches as if they are speaking directly to each individual. They should convey the impression that they are persons, not computers. Debaters should try to be conversational and relatively casual, although without losing the formality of the public speaking situation.

Second, debaters should develop their extemporaneous speaking skills. The judge should feel that the speakers are tailoring the ideas to the specific debate and to the specific judge, not that they are simply delivering memorized speeches, reading only prepared briefs, or reciting long sets of debate clichés.

Third, debaters should use gestures, facial expressions, and body movements to help emphasize the arguments and keep the interest of the judge. They also should avoid any movements that detract from their communication. Distracting movements include everything from the obvious things, such as playing with a pencil or twisting one's hair to the subtly distracting habit of doing what everyone else is doing, which is apt to lull the judge into inattention.

Finally, debaters should carefully analyze their general effectiveness. With the help of their coach and by scrutinizing ballots, debaters should seek to eliminate anything that seems to detract from their speeches. They should eliminate any tics, mannerisms, or speaking habits that seem to adversely affect their listeners. Instead, debaters should cultivate habits that contribute to their general effectiveness as speakers.

Credibility

Credibility is a major factor in effective, persuasive communication. **Credibility** refers to the judgment an audience makes about the believability of a source of information. An important part of developing an effective speaking style is learning how to establish your credibility as a source.

Source credibility can be affected by such seemingly unimportant things as introduction and dress. For example, experimenters who wanted to test credibility used the same speaker, the same speech, and several similar audiences. They introduced the same person as a "major authority" at one time and as an "interested layperson" at another time. Audiences believed the speaker when he was "an expert" but not when he was a "layperson." The same speaker also appeared before one audience in army fatigues and before another audience in a business suit. The audience found the speaker more "believable" when he wore the suit.

Thus, the total impression or image that a speaker creates makes an important difference in how persuasive the speaker is. Image can even influence a judge's decision about whether an argument is valid, a decision that is supposedly based solely on the evidence the speaker presents. Therefore, as a strategic debater you want to develop high source credibility.

The best way to have high source credibility is to be truly credible. If debaters are honest in their research and development of ideas, judges are likely to believe them. If, on the other hand, they are not credible, judges are likely to see through the smoothest exterior.

Since most debaters are not perceived as actual experts on the topic, no matter how much research they do, they need to use the prestige of their sources to lend credibility to their arguments. Extensive, careful research is the most important factor in establishing credibility. The best debaters use the highest-quality evidence they have in a competent, fair way to show they know what they are doing.

The next element in credibility is character, and many decisions turn on this issue. Good character cannot be faked. Therefore, honesty and reliability are important not only for ethical reasons but for tactical ones! Good debaters are aware that even superficial things can arouse suspicion in an audience, and they study themselves to work toward a positive image. They know that dress and eye contact have a direct impact on how they are perceived. More importantly, they treat their opponents fairly and honestly and do not attempt to gain ground by distorting their opponents' arguments or key evidence.

Another element in establishing credibility is being a dynamic speaker. Unfortunately, far too many debaters seem to throw this asset away. Many debaters sound like talking machines, using too much jargon and too many clichés. The best debaters develop styles that are their own. They let their own personality come through and even smile. Audiences respond to the human qualities of a speaker. If the person is warm, likable, and extemporaneous, credibility will tend to be high.

Knowing all this, effective debaters develop strategies that will produce positive impressions of credibility. They work hard to be experts. They have strong values about honesty. And they develop speaking styles that are natural to them, extemporaneous, and dynamic.

Ethics in Debate

As a debater, ethical behavior is as essential as any other argumentation strategy, skill, or tactic. The concern with **ethics**—the practice of being ethical or moral in one's actions—encompasses the meaning and heart of academic debate. The authors believe that for debate to be truly meaningful, one must practice an ethic of recognition and respect for all participants, no matter how difficult the situation. The following Code of Ethics for debaters is recommended.

Code of Ethics

- Respect your colleague. Divide responsibilities fairly and be supportive, work as a team, and be supportive during a debate round—no matter what.

- Maintain high standards in developing arguments and preparing evidence. Quote accurately and note sources exactly. Do not deliberately misconstrue or manipulate evidence during preparation or during a round.

- Treat your opponents with respect. Avoid rude behavior. If you discover a problem with the opposition's evidence, do not embarrass that team during a round. Bring it to your coach's or the team's attention before the round.

- Develop an ethic of argument in terms of your judge. Prepare your arguments to enhance communication and facilitate judgment. Take care to adhere to tournament rules regarding talking with your judge(s) about a decision.

- Respect your debate coach—the decisions made and the advice given.

- Respect yourself as a debater. Make ethical choices that you can be proud of.

Summary

Debaters learn the principles of persuasive communication in a way that no other students of communication theory can. Debaters are faced, again and again, with a tremendously difficult persuasive communication task. While experience is valuable in itself, debaters also have the advantage of having a different judge almost every time they speak. The judges listen to the debaters and provide the speakers with feedback on their own communication skills. Debaters can improve their persuasive communication skills by employing speech, language, and style strategies.

Questions

1. What role does source credibility play in the persuasive setting?
2. What role does the choice of language play in a debate?
3. What is the difference between performance and communication?
4. Why is feedback important in communication?
5. Identify the four parts of the communication setting.
6. What role does ethics play in debate?

Discussion Opportunities

1. Listen and flow a debate paying particular attention to the use of highlighting, forecasting, signposting, and summaries. Discuss each debater's use of these four strategies.
2. How should a debater determine if it is necessary to speed up the delivery rate during a round? What strategies can the debater use to avoid frustrating judges during a speedy delivery?
3. What is wrong with this statement: "I've never lost a debate, but I sure get a lot of bad decisions"? How does such a statement impede the debater's improvement in debate?
4. If a debater or team chooses to use ethical strategies, what do you think the short- and long-term consequences will be?

Writing Opportunities

1. As you listen to debates, make a list of any debate clichés you notice. Also, note any mannerisms, gestures, or other elements of stereotypical delivery that you find negative or distracting. Write suggestions on how the debaters could reduce or eliminate the use of such clichés and mannerisms.
2. After each of your debate rounds in class, outline several ways you could improve your rebuttal speech.
3. Tape one of your debate rounds. Go back through the rebuttal speech, outlining arguments again, and examine your choices of arguments and evidence. Prepare a new rebuttal speech.

Critical Thinking Opportunities

1. It was once said that a debate takes place in the mind of the judge. What does this mean to you?

2. If you were debating before a "balance of arguments" judge, what criteria would you assume the judge is using?

3. Using an audio- or videotape of a debate, analyze one of the constructive speeches. Reconstruct the speech using different strategies for highlighting, forecasting, signposting, and summarizing.

4. Using the same tape, identify ways in which the first affirmative rebuttal could be presented differently. Rework the first affirmative rebuttal. Is this new rebuttal better than the original?

5. Using your first affirmative or one of the speeches you have prepared for a previous activity, work on varying your rate of delivery. Begin by delivering the speech very slowly, then increasing your speech speed until you find a rate that is both speedy enough for you and understandable for others.

6. Observe a town meeting, a public debate, or student government meeting. What ethical standards were demonstrated?

STRATEGIES IN ACTION

Recently, Doug and Jane, colleagues on their debate team, watched an elimination round where a team from a rival school (upholding the negative) came up with a novel argument: Nuclear war is good! This seemed at first to be an argument with poor credibility, especially since the anti-nuclear movement has gained momentum and most people dread the thought of nuclear war.

In the elimination round Doug and Jane observed, the argument was strategically powerful because the affirmative team was not expecting this unusual attack; its whole advantage was in creating conditions of stability that reduced the risk of nuclear war. Moreover, the solvency and significance of the case was hard to deny, because the affirmative was good at debating the issues which supported the case structure. The decision in the round was 3-2 for the negative. Doug and Jane begin to discuss the issue:

Doug: I know how to improve the argument. Nuclear war as a whole may be bad, but a regional nuclear war would serve as an example that would lead to world disarmament. It is better to have a small nuclear war now than suffer a complete catastrophe in the future. I would run the argument.

Jane: I am opposed to the argument on ethical grounds. Supporting a policy that knowingly leads to increased human suffering and death is wrong. It is a position that could justify a holocaust, and it is immoral to engage in or support that kind of reasoning.

Doug: You are being narrow-minded. Policymakers have to make life and death decisions all the time. You are simply refusing to choose. This argument is no different than making the argument that economic growth is bad because it leads to environmental harms.

Jane: Your reasoning equivocates. To take the conscious action of promoting conditions that start a nuclear war is to embrace deliberatively a morally repugnant policy. While it is true that we should control economic growth to reduce harms to the environment, we should also redistribute essential medical resources and cut back on nonessential production of luxuries.

Doug: You're splitting hairs, and you know that we cannot beat this team on other grounds. Besides, the value of debate is in arguing both sides of the proposition thoroughly. You are making an *a priori* judgment which is harmful to the process and your own education. You certainly don't believe every argument that you run, or else you could never debate both sides of the proposition.

Jane: Look, there are limits in debate. Intellectual honesty requires that you do not make arguments that are patently absurd on face value. Indeed, it is the strategic drive that turns debate into a game that limits its value.

This exchange took place in front of the debate coach. The coach turned to intervene in the discussion. After listening to the two positions, what do you think the coach said—not only about whether to run the "Nuclear war is good" argument but also about the purpose of debate in the context of communication ethics? Would you make the same choice? How do you know if the choice is the ethical one?

Debate
Tournaments

Objectives

After studying Chapter 15, you should be able
1. To prepare for a debate tournament.
2. To anticipate the types of judges used at tournaments.
3. To organize your materials for competition.
4. To understand the work of hosting a tournament.

Key Terms

To successfully participate in a debate tournament, you will need to understand the following terms:

preliminary round
preset match
power-matched rounds
elimination round
coach judge
expert judge
lay judge
student judge
ballot
pairing
tabulation room

One of the most enjoyable aspects of debate is competing in tournaments. Each year hundreds of debate tournaments are held across the United States. Some are hosted by national organizations like the National Forensic League and the National Federation of State High School Associations. Others are held by universities, either by special invitation or as part of a summer institute program. Still others are sponsored by local high schools as part of a season of debate activities. In most areas of the United States, high-school debaters have a range of tournament choices.

The key element that makes tournaments exciting is competition. When you enter a tournament, you will be competing against students from other schools and perhaps other parts of the country. Such a situation allows you to test your skill and preparation. Tournaments are designed so that participants encounter increasingly difficult levels of competition as they continue competing. There are few more intense or exciting moments than awaiting the results of a close quarterfinal round of competition. Debate tournaments always provides an intense, memorable experience. Competition can bring out the best of your abilities.

This chapter covers the basics of tournament competitions and will help you get the most out of the tournaments you attend. Every tournament can be an exciting, motivating learning experience. If you master tournament competition, you will gain skills that will help you handle other pressure activities as well.

Tournament Fundamentals

No two debate tournaments are exactly alike. A tournament is always an expression of how the hosts see the values of debate. Hence, each tournament has different schedules, rules for participation, and practices governing judging and the matching of teams. Generally, such diversity is a good idea. If all tournaments were alike, the activities might become routine and dull. Diversity encourages debaters to adapt to the situation at hand, a useful skill for all public speakers.

Debaters and coaches should carefully read each tournament invitation to see what special rules or procedures operate at a tournament they wish to attend. Fortunately, most tournaments have several features in common, including levels of competition, how rounds are set up, what kinds of judges participate, and what kinds of awards are presented.

Types of Competitive Events

A debate tournament involves a variety of different levels of competition—novice, junior varsity, and varsity. Novice divisions are for beginning debaters who enter a tournament for the first time. Generally, a beginning debater may debate in the novice division for all or part of one debate season, depending on the rules of the state or individual tournament. Some tournaments have a junior varsity division. This division is intended for students in their second year of competition or for debaters who are still in their first year but have progressed past the beginning stage.

Varsity debate is for those who are more experienced or have debated two or more years in high school.

Sometimes a tournament will have an open division that mixes all three levels of experience. The level of competition should be determined by the degree of readiness a debater has achieved before the tournament. If you have been able to conduct research, have practice rounds, and prepare a number of briefs, then you are ready to compete. If you have had two or more years of debate, then you are ready to compete at a varsity level. Early entrance into varsity debate is not always beneficial. You may not understand the arguments well enough to challenge another team successfully. On the other hand, staying too long at novice or junior varsity is not wise either. When competition becomes too easy, there is little to be learned.

Some tournaments offer both debate and individual speech events. In such a case, you might want to consider entering an individual event—such as oral interpretation or extemporaneous speaking—as well as debate. The first thing you will need to do is check the tournament schedule to see which events would be open to you and to make sure that you don't enter an individual event that runs at the same time as a debate round. Some debaters like a break from round after round of debate and see extemporaneous speaking as a way to add to their understanding of current affairs. It is also a way to improve speaking skills. Other debaters enjoy writing speeches and choose original oratory as a way to talk about issues of a broader and more elevated nature than those that come up during a debate round. Still other debaters like to do something that has no connection to debate. These might include after-dinner speaking, poetry, humorous interpretation, or dramatic interpretation.

If the schedule permits it can be fun to enter an individual event. On the other hand, if you find worrying about another event to be stressful and distracting, then stick to debate alone. Before you decide to enter an individual event, be sure to talk with your coach.

Rounds

Debate tournaments usually divide activities into preliminary and elimination rounds. A **preliminary round** matches competitors randomly or through some preassigned system. Typically, preliminary rounds are divided into preset matches and power matches. A **preset match** randomly assigns two teams to debate each other—one on the affirmative and the other on the negative. All or more of the preliminary rounds in a tournament may be preset.

Power-matched rounds are based on the accumulated record of teams at the tournament. For example, if you have won all of your preset rounds, you will meet another team that has won all of its rounds. If you have lost one round, then you will meet a team that also has one loss. Whether preset or power-matched, preliminary rounds usually consist of four, six, or eight matches per team, with each team alternating sides between affirmative and negative. The teams with the best record advance to the elimination rounds.

Elimination rounds in debate match teams with the best records in a bracket. Depending on tournament size, the bracket could begin with octofinals, quarterfinals, or even semifinal rounds. A single loss in a tournament elimination round eliminates a team from the tournament, while the winner goes on to the next higher level of competition. While there is usually only one judge in preliminary rounds, in elimination rounds, there are usually multiple judges. The team that wins persuades the majority of judges of its position.

Elimination rounds sometimes create some unexpected matches. If the teams meeting are from the same school and the tournament has chosen not to rearrange the bracket to accommodate such a circumstance, a particular round may not be held. In this case, the team with the better record typically advances.

Judges

Debate tournaments always involve judges who make decisions concerning the outcome and quality of the debates. The judge is the person who stands in for a larger audience and who renders a decision in accordance with tournament custom and good educational practices. As in any speaking situation, it is up to the debater to adapt to the level of expertise and needs of a judge. The kinds of judges you can expect vary from tournament to tournament, but generally you can anticipate that the judges will be either coaches, experts, lay judges, or students.

In many parts of the country, the coaches of participating schools will be asked to judge. **Coaches** make good judges because they are trained in debate and know the issues. They also have the objectivity necessary to see how arguments develop on their own terms. It is important to remember that while a coach appreciates the issues involved in a debate, she or he may also wish to see signs of good public presentation. After all, the larger purpose of debate is to enable students to become skilled advocates.

Tournament events are often judged by former debaters who have recently graduated from high school, are currently in college, or have graduated from college. Because these former debaters are familiar with the latest debate theory and practice, they are regarded as experts for the purpose of judging debate rounds. **Expert judges** require less explanation in order to comprehend the nature and weight of an argument. They also should be less prone to generally persuasive rhetoric (in place of argument and proof), since they understand and are concerned with the technical issues involved in debate.

However, expert judges also may wish to intervene more in the round because they know the material and may see implications in arguments that the debater misses. College debaters who serve as judges at high-school tournaments sometimes have a problem remaining objective. They tend to debate the issues along with the debaters in the round, rather than remaining neutral and rendering a decision based on what the debaters argued in the round. Fortunately, though, most former debaters make good judges.

Some tournaments invite **lay judges** from the community. These judges are not specialists in debate theory or in the topic under discussion, but they are interested in current affairs and have various levels of intellectual accomplishment. Sometimes people agree to judge as a favor to someone in the school or on the debate squad. Chaperoning parents, other teachers, and even bus drivers have been known to pitch in and help judge rounds.

These people can be good judges as long as the debaters remember to take into account that lay judges have no previous debate experience. Debaters need to explain issues in greater detail and show why particular issues are important to the outcome of the round. Debaters also should avoid jargon, since lay judges will not know what "T," "DA," "brink," "turn," and "counterplan" mean. However, if the arguments and their implications are explained clearly, the lay judge can and will vote on these issues.

Although most debaters tend to prefer expert judges, lay judges provide valuable opportunities for persuasive communication. Remember that if you try a case before a jury in later life, the outcome will depend not on your ability to use legal jargon (or, in many cases, to convince the judge), but on your ability to persuade people of good sense (a jury of one's peers) that your position is correct.

Finally, a few tournaments use students in the judging process. If you are asked to be a **student judge,** remember that you must be absolutely fair in rendering a decision. No real friend would ask you to play favorites. Also, when you write a ballot, remember that the purpose of commenting on a debate ballot is to be constructive—to help another person improve. Just as you want to learn from ballots that are written for you, you should want to help other people learn from the ballots that you write. See page 380 for an example of a NFL debate ballot.

Awards

Tournaments often formally recognize outstanding individual and collective efforts. Debate tournaments offer speaker awards, which are granted to contestants who have accumulated the greatest number of quality points during the preliminary rounds. Ties for speaker awards are often broken by comparing ranks.

While debaters should welcome official recognition of their achievement, they should not lose sight of the importance of team effort in winning debates. Many debate tournaments offer sweepstakes awards for the schools that have had the best overall performance at a tournament. The tournament invitation will indicate how the winners of special awards are determined.

Tournament Preparation

Once you have an idea of the rules, regulations, and nature of an upcoming tournament and have assessed the kind of judging and competition that will be available, you can begin preparing for a tournament. Preparation falls into four stages: discussion, practice, organization, and scheduling.

The first stage of preparation involves *discussing* your goals for the tournament. If you approach a tournament by simply saying that you need to do everything you possibly can do to get ready, you will raise your state of anxiety but will not get much accomplished. No one is ever fully prepared for a tournament. The debate topics are so broad as to involve, potentially, a career of research and thinking. Moreover, you will inevitably be working under time constraints. Given a great number of competing time demands, you need to establish a set of minimum goals that you want to accomplish in preparing for the tournament.

Your first goal should be based on the kind of personal achievement you want to strive for at the tournament. One kind of achievement might be developing a new idea that you think is worth testing or introducing to the debate community. Another kind of goal is developing a particular skill. For instance, cross-examination requires careful planning and can be an exciting activity. Perhaps a tournament could be a testing ground for a novel use of questioning. Whether you are thinking about substantive ideas, skills, or special strategies, it is important to agree with your coach and colleague on a set of productive goals for a tournament and to use the tournament as a way of achieving those goals.

Another kind of goal involves looking at the minimum number of activities you must perform to get ready for a tournament. All debate teams should have completed and practiced a first affirmative constructive. Some second-line affirmative arguments also are needed to defend the case. These should be the highest priority. On the negative side of the ledger, it is essential that a team develop one or two disadvantages against the general thrust of the topic. These can be adapted to suit specific cases. As the season progresses and you attend more tournaments, these minimum goals will be divided between repairing the arguments that need more evidence and developing new positions. Keep adding to your repertoire over the year.

The second stage of preparation involves *practicing* the material you have prepared. It does little good to research a lot of evidence or write many arguments if you are unfamiliar with them when you reach the tournament. Rather, it is necessary to speak—and speak again—before the tournament. If you can engage in practice debates with your colleagues on the debate squad, you can try out arguments and repair them. This way you can avoid making costly mistakes in the debate round.

Preparation is important at this stage because it enables you to simulate the debate round experience. Often debaters who do not practice speaking find themselves rusty at the beginning of a tournament. If you read your speech or practice arguing from briefs before the tournament, you will be able to spend more energy thinking up arguments on the spot at the tournament. Do not be discouraged if the arguments do not sound brilliant. It is difficult to capture the excitement of tournament competition when you are speaking in front of your squad members who doubtless have heard the arguments before. But such practice speaking is vital to a good tournament experience.

The third stage of preparation involves *organizing* materials for the tournament competition. It does little good to have the best evidence, briefs, and arguments if you can't find them at the tournament. Debaters who do the best usually have an efficient filing and flowing system that permits them to lay their hands on appropriate materials at the right time.

One way to organize your material is to color-code your briefs. For example, if you use blue paper for all speeches and briefs pertaining to the affirmative case, then you can easily sort out what is relevant to an affirmative debate. Different colors also can be used for different sets of negative arguments. Another way to organize material is to distinguish high-priority evidence, which is likely to be used in every round of debate, from low-priority material, which will be held in reserve. High-priority evidence should be kept together, while backup material can be sorted out by topic, each placed in separate folders. (Incidentally, it is a good idea to leave a photocopy of your affirmative case and briefs with your coach. Many debaters have lost rounds because this vital information was misplaced.)

The final stage of preparation for the tournament involves *setting up a schedule* for the tournament itself. At any tournament, there will be times of intense competition and times for socializing with friends. Strategic debaters use some of the socializing time to make adjustments in arguments. Work out a schedule with your colleague so that after a given round you can go over the debate and determine what worked and what did not. Given that a tournament is an intense experience, you will have to schedule such work sessions carefully. Otherwise, on-the-spot adjustments will be difficult. However, if you and the rest of the squad develop a working rhythm at tournaments, such coordination will be invaluable.

Tournament Preparation

1. Discuss the goals for the tournament.
2. Practice the material you have prepared.
3. Sort out materials for the tournament competition.
4. Set up your schedule for the tournament itself.

The Tournament Experience

Tournaments offer a complex set of experiences. Like any other event, a tournament involves people with whom you are very close and people who seem indifferent or even a bit unfriendly. Especially when competition is keen, feelings can run high. For this reason it is important to keep the tournament experience in perspective. If you can learn to keep your cool at debate tournaments and perform with grace and style under pressure there, you should be able to keep your head in difficult argumentative situations later in life. While you will have to decide on the meaning

Working cooperatively with your colleague during a tournament is essential.

of the experience and your own values, the following are some suggestions for developing a perspective on the activity.

The primary requirement for gaining a perspective on tournament experiences is to remember that your work is being evaluated—not you. When someone criticizes your work negatively, it is difficult not to take such a criticism personally. Some debaters get depressed when they lose, because they think that the loss means they have failed and that they are not as smart as their opponents. Others get angry and want to blame the judge or their colleagues for a loss. Neither attitude is very productive. Indeed, viewing a loss as a matter of blame undercuts your ability to see arguments objectively and to search for improvement. So, too, a win does not mean that you are smarter than another person; indeed, it is possible that a win deserves criticism because the arguments on both sides could have been better.

You should try to develop a perspective that permits you to evaluate your own arguments and the criticisms of others objectively. Pay attention to critiques. After a tournament, go through the arguments that you made and try to assess the strongest and the weakest and decide on new strategies. Only by maintaining an orientation to the arguments themselves will you be able to improve.

While tournaments are held to advance the quality of argument, they are also intended to help you understand how conflict is conducted and resolved with other people. If a debater wins a round by tricking the other side with an unusual affirmative or a strange strategy, the question must be raised as to whether that is a good thing to do to opponents who are also friends in a way. Remember, argument takes cooperation. Tournaments are held because people are dedicated to a process of learning through conflict and clash. Certainly, clever strategies are part of debating, but a debater needs to develop personal standards of fairness and scholarship. These standards are based on recognizing that competitors deserve the best ideas and evidence to consider rather than strategic guile.

One of the key features of a tournament is cooperation with your fellow squad members. Tournaments are pressure situations. In each round choices have to be made, and not all the choices will be under your control. Given that slight mistakes sometimes have consequences for the outcome of a round, there is a tendency for debaters to debate their own colleagues—before, during, and after rounds—about the arguments to be used. At a tournament, you need to find a way to develop reciprocal trust and keep communication open. When things are going well, it is easy to be on good terms with a colleague. When things are tense or a disappointing loss has been incurred, it is more difficult. In such situations it is very important to find a way to work out differences, to continue a give-and-take in planning new positions, to find a way to maximize cooperation. Just as you will be asked to work with colleagues in future life, you will be well served by learning how to work in tense situations with colleagues in debate.

Finally, the tournament experience is a social experience. Occasionally, debaters use the excuse of intense competition to justify rude behavior. However, politeness is important. If you are debating inexperienced debaters, it does no good to make fun of them. You were once inexperienced. If you dislike a judge or think a tournament is poorly administered, it does little good to complain. Few people will listen willingly to a debater's rendition of how she or he thought a debate was unfairly decided. Although it is understandable that you wish to talk with friends, exclusive cliques simply make the experience less than it would be if you knew people from other programs. Debate tournaments require civility. Precisely because they are so intensely competitive they require mature, polite, and deferential behavior. The best debaters are in complete self-control at all times.

Post-Tournament Work

As strange as it may seem, the most important work of the tournament begins after you have been eliminated from a tournament!

Debaters often underestimate the value of watching elimination rounds. Tired, discouraged, and ready to go home, debaters conclude that once they have been eliminated there is no need for further participation. But watching events can be extremely valuable. When you are debating, it is difficult to get the perspective of

---

Keeping Tournaments in Perspective

1. Remember that it is your work and not you that is being evaluated. Don't take the criticism personally.

2. While tournaments are held to advance the quality of argument, they are also intended to help you understand how conflict is conducted and resolved with other people.

3. Learn to cooperate with your fellow squad members, even in the pressure and tension of the tournament. Work to stay on good terms even when things are not going well.

4. Debate tournaments require civility. They require mature, polite, and deferential behavior. You need to be in complete self-control at all times.

---

a judge who hears all the arguments and who has to sort out the significance of each issue. By watching a round and carefully flowing arguments, you will be able to develop a judge's perspective. Listening to a round enables you to hear ideas that you have not thought of, record new sources for evidence, and analyze extensions to arguments different from your own. More important, if you try to resolve the arguments, you will see how difficult it is to sort out competing claims and put all the arguments into perspective. Once you have listened to a round, think of what could have been done differently or try to guess how the decision will come out (and for what reasons). Such analysis will aid your efforts to be persuasive in future tournaments.

When you return from a tournament, you, your colleagues, and coach should conduct a debriefing. Go over the tournament round by round. You may wish to redeliver some speeches. In this exercise, drop out the weakest arguments and concentrate on what you think were the most important. Do this with arguments you lost and arguments you won. Both deserve strengthening.

After assessing your tournament performance, take a look at your affirmative case and most often used briefs. Try to reach an agreement with your colleagues as to the likely direction that developments will take. For arguments that are strong, see if there are ways to make them even stronger. Your opponents are more likely to work on arguments they lost than on arguments they won. Perhaps updating your evidence will provide an edge the next time. Perhaps you will want to narrow a claim so that there is less ground to attack. In any event, constant improvement is necessary to make sure that a strong argument remains competitive.

Weak arguments should be either strengthened or eliminated. Some arguments are so weak that they do not merit further research. It is difficult to give up on an

Participating in a debate tournament can be rewarding—literally and figuratively.

argument once time has been spent researching it. However, if an argument is not successful and judges see either a consistent flaw or a different flaw every time, then there may be little value in putting in further time on the issue.

A final post-tournament activity should be looking for new ideas or arguments. Judges tire of hearing the same kind of argument, tournament after tournament. Moreover, the issue grows stale and too complicated for clear decision. Debaters should look for new sources of evidence, new variations on old arguments, or entirely new ideas on a topic. While not all of your time can be spent in this pursuit, often a new idea can make all the difference at a future tournament.

Hosting a Tournament

At some point, your school may wish to host a debate tournament. If so, examine a calendar of events in your area and see if there is an available weekend. Examine the tournament invitations for last year to determine what local customs govern participation rules and the appropriate kind and range of events. Contact programs in the area to see if they would be interested in attending the tournament at your school.

The following is a checklist of activities necessary for putting together a tournament:

1. *Facilities.* Tournament planners should get a list of open rooms, including an auditorium or central meeting area, and reserve these facilities. The number of events and tournament entries and schedule will depend on what facilities the school can make available.

2. *Schedule.* Get your tournament on the local schedule of tournaments. Send out invitations that specify rules, regulations, dates, and times of events. Set entry fees and judges' fees so that you will be able to cover the costs of hosting and of hiring appropriate judges.

3. *Judges.* Require coaches to judge, at one per every two teams. Look to school service organizations for guest judges. Hire limited numbers of guest judges if coaches are not available.

4. *Pairing.* Preset tournament preliminary rounds and assign rooms and judges to individual events sections and debates. Type a schedule for distribution to tournament participants.

5. *Tabulation room.* Set up a tabulation room that will keep track of results during the tournament for late power matching and elimination round selection. The tabulation room should also keep track of ballots and distribute results at the end of the tournament.

6. *Special events.* A tournament may have one or more assemblies at appropriate times to announce changes in preset rounds or elimination round results. The tournament might also wish to sponsor special seminars for the participants.

Needless to say, hosting a good tournament takes time and patience. Excellent tournaments are run efficiently, fairly, and graciously.

Summary

Competition is the final stage of debate preparation. Debaters spend many hours researching a topic and formulating affirmative cases and negative positions. Strategic thought goes into the selection of arguments. The process is not complete until debate is taken beyond the classroom and practice rounds and put to the test in a tournament setting.

Participation in tournament competition is a unique opportunity for you to try out new ideas, refine arguments, polish critical listening skills, and speak. Beyond the performance aspects of debate, the tournament also affords you an opportunity to make friends. The skills you cultivate will help you win in competition; the ability to test yourself under fire will last a lifetime.

Through competition you learn to persuade others, sometimes contrary to their initial prejudices. You will sometimes find yourself being required to argue positions not exactly in line with your own personal beliefs. This should help you learn the values and beliefs of others. Over time, debate competition will give you the opportunity to serve as both participant and judge. The first tournament is exciting, often scary. While the fear diminishes after experience, the thrill of exciting competition continues.

Questions

1. In the tournament setting there are several types of rounds. Explain the following: preliminary rounds, preset rounds, power-matched rounds, elimination rounds.
2. What is the best way to prepare for tournament competition?
3. Why should you observe debate rounds when you are not participating in competition?

Discussion Opportunities

1. After learning the basics of debate, why should you consider participating in a debate tournament?
2. How do debaters decide which level of competition is appropriate? Evaluate your own debating skills and those of your colleagues. What level of competition should you participate in? Why?

Writing Opportunities

1. Once you have been eliminated at your next tournament, choose a round to observe. Keep a flow of the round and find out which team the judges voted for. Do you agree with the judges' decision? If you disagree, on what issues do you think the judges would have voted? Why?
2. Attend a local tournament. There analyze your flow and the judge's ballot from one of your preliminary rounds. Explain why you won or lost the round and what arguments could have been developed differently.
3. Using the same flow and ballot from activity 2, rework the arguments the judge outlined as the reasons for his or her decision. This may involve researching new evidence, developing the link to a disadvantage, or reworking an affirmative or negative brief.
4. Outline your goals for the next tournament you plan to attend.

Critical Thinking Opportunities

1. What are the differences among the several categories of judges described in this chapter? How should debaters adapt to those differences?

2. Using a flow from one of your negative debate rounds, imagine that you have a lay judge. How would you change the type and number of arguments presented?

3. Look at the possible individual events that are offered at tournaments in your area. Which ones would be of interest to you? Why?

4. Using a flow from a previous affirmative debate, rework your rebuttal answers to one of the disadvantages. Practice regiving that portion of your rebuttal.

Sample Debate Ballot (Cross-Examination Debate)

NATIONAL FORENSIC LEAGUE DEBATE BALLOT

ROUND _____ DIVISION _____ DATE _____ ROOM_____ JUDGE_____

AFFIRMATIVE _____ CODE _____ | NEGATIVE _____ CODE _____

NAME   POINTS (0-30) RANK (1-4) | NAME   POINTS (0-30) RANK (1-4)

_____ _____ (   ) | _____ _____ (   )

_____ _____ (   ) | _____ _____ (   )

DECISION: THE WINNING TEAM IS THE_____SIDE: TEAM CODE_____

SIGNED : _____ SCHOOL_____

REASON FOR DECISION AND COMMENTS TO THE DEBATERS:

APPENDIX A

Sample Flow of Cross-Examination Policy Debate

Case flow, pg. 1 (Resolution under debate) *Resolved:* That the federal government should guarantee comprehensive national health insurance to all United States citizens.

1st Affirmative Constructive	1st Negative Constructive	2nd Affirmative Rebuttal	1st Negative Rebuttal	1st Affirmative Rebuttal	2nd Negative Rebuttal	2nd Affirmative Rebuttal
Obs. I Inherency						
SQ H.C. costs 20% GNP BW Oct 4, '93		→ extend no neg response	→ plans to bring under control Time 93	→ new argument		
Public no faith in Clinton's plan Chic Trib 9.24.93	→ plan not complete	→ no faith in poss	→ must wait and see			
Adv. I Access millions lack insur. Johnson '91	→ 1. access avail 2. many choose not to use	→ insur not avail NW 93	→ but can get care	→ not same quality care Johnson	→ evid outdated	
= 60,000 deaths annually BLK Enterprise 1992	→ 1. SQ improvements 2. not link to access	→ not enough could not afford care				

381

Case flow, pg. 2

1st Affirmative Constructive	1st Negative Constructive	2nd Affirmative Rebuttal	1st Negative Rebuttal	1st Affirmative Rebuttal	2nd Negative Rebuttal	2nd Affirmative Rebuttal
Adv 2 - Hegemony						
Rising costs of HC destroys eco Ann Arbor News '93	1. No internal link b/w H.C. & eco →	1. no ass. German plan which aff mandates			have not shown how Germany applies →	→ can work
	2. no threshold to eco decline causing war →	1. evid says must act now				
Eco strength nec for Heg. Huntington '92	3. New World order stops threat of wars For. Pol. '93 →	1. evid shows NWO stops small conflicts which will escalate →	evid stops threat	small conflicts will escalate Huntington		
Hegemony key to assure world stab For. Pol. '94	4. Other powers check world conflict Time '92 →	1. US key 2. aff evid post dates	holds in check			
U.S. leadership key to peace Wash Quart '93	5. Weak impact evidence →	1. no hegemony = war	→ why?	leadership needed NYT		
Hegemonic ↓ destroys democracy Wash Quart '93	6. Hegemony = decr. intern'l cooper. Warner '92	1. bad evid 2. no coop needed	↓ cooperation →			
Democracy prevents intern'l conflicts Foster '93						

Case flow, pg. 3

1st Affirmative Constructive	1st Negative Constructive	2nd Affirmative Rebuttal	1st Negative Rebuttal	1st Affirmative Rebuttal	2nd Negative Rebuttal	2nd Affirmative Rebuttal
Obs 2 - Solvency Germany best model NYT '93	1. Germany ∅ control costs Gershwin '93	1. not assume german plan 2. extend Brennan '42	germany no cost control '93 2. overuse lead ↓ to in access Newsweek	no overuse not applicable		= less admin. costs
Germany syst controls cost CSM '91	2. = overuse Newsweek '92	1. cost control solves 2. assumes current syst				
Transfer to US poss. Rully '92	3. German system not applicable to US	1. no reason why 2. assumes British	situations diff. 5 yrs. to implement	why still advantageous		
= less admin costs Brennan '92	4. Implementation takes 5years Wellin '93					

Plan flow, pg. 1

Affirmative Plan	Second Negative Constructive	1st Affirmative Rebuttal	2nd Negative Rebuttal	2nd Affirmative Rebuttal
1. all necessary powers	DA1 – Clinton DA			1. safeguards checkwar
	A. Popularity stable Wash Post '93	1. old impact evid →	1. protection= war NW '93	
2. implement the Germany plan	B. Links		2. empirically proven	
3. Financing through optimal means	1. Clinton doing manage comp. Adams '93	2. Case solves impacts-reverses eco ↓ →	1. case time frame too long - disad impact first	
4. Enforcement as needed	2. Causes perceived vascillation Wash Post '93	3. Not unique— Links assume poor growth →	1. uniqueness ev. brand new	1. has waffled before
5. aff speeches serve as legislative intent	C. Impacts ↓popularity=↑ protect. BW '92	4. Clinton pop. low now Wash Post '93	2. on brink of loss of control	2. link too tenous
	protectionism = NW II Kaplan '92	5. Link not unique Clinton vascillated on other issues →	1. pop. stable	
			2. evid. assumes economy	
			1. HC key issue	
			2. no evid of prev cases	

Plan flow, pg. 2

Affirmative Plan	Second Negative Constructive	1st Affirmative Rebuttal	2nd Negative Rebuttal	2nd Affirmative Rebuttal
	D A2 Federalism			
	A. Balance now → Dinkens '92	1. no brink →	1. Tenuous balance now	
	B. Links	2. impacts too weak →	1. Fed power = authoritarianism NEW ENG LAW '97	
	1. States control health care reform Public Policy '93		2. New key tim for St. power	
	2. Federal policy = coercion Indiana Law '87	3. Turn— Plan mandates state federal cooper. →	1. = fed control	1. States protect citizens
			2. any fed power = the impax	2. We turn scenario
			3. Cooper = hidden power	
	C. Impacts	4. no internal link	1. Fed. govt. gains control over HC	
	1. Federal power coercive Go + Fin '92			
	2. = tyranny Orenstein '92	5. No threshold to impacts →	1. On brink now →	1. brink evid. too old
			2. extend balance evid	2. one plant ≠ cause

APPENDIX B

Sample Flow of Lincoln-Douglas Debate

(Resolution under debate) *Resolved:* That political candidates' right to privacy outweighs the public's right to information.

Affirmative Constructive	Negative Constructive	1st Affirmative Rebuttal	Negative Rebuttal	2nd Affirmative Rebuttal
w/o st isolated decision-makers 1. election/voice of peo count 2. inf choice impt				
I. knowledge=prime A. know g better than ø know dec based on contrast opinion B. utility criteria	taking rts of some is still ø good → knowledge is impt but ø rt to know not limits →			
II. informed public nec to successful rep dem — peo only monitors of gov't	informed up to a pt don't need priv. info — to a pt			
— 1st priority to keep peo informed • rt to know more impt than rt to privacy	→ ø talking about rt to know as we know it	→ ø saying candidates were perfect	→ peo should vote on Pres.	→ info wld make better informed dec. better
• can only ex will over others when harm wld occur ∴ resolution is justified	→ T. Jefferson had affair but was good Pres. ø harming public bec public doesn't know everything	→ public can handle facts public wld not dec well ø facts	→ Jefferson was still good blurb	→ wld not have hurt

Negative Case	1st Affirmative Rebuttal	Negative Rebuttal	2nd Affirmative Rebuttal
Candidate priv shields only private life →	general will →	gen will →	gen will → Know what's involved
privacy def.	ok til you become cand. then they give things up →	don't justify taking away propriacy →	
I. Every ind has rt to priv life – freedom from intrusion – people shouldn't be in public eye →	not 2thr spotlite but do care about values →	contra →	– – –
	Rousseau - exchange of rts cand. gives up →	rts change ø und privacy →	cand are in public eye
II. Invasion of rt 2 priv violates indv. rts. peo have rts under law →	gen will - peo "want to know" ∴ resolution →	need to consider only relevant data →	who decides relevant?
III. Candidates have same rts as others →	"I don't think" unless it has a bearing →	priv info doesn't effect job Jefferson →	– – –
	peo must decide relevance	Gen will-everyone shld have priv →	gen will
FDR	Christian values must know for whom they are voting	Value & criteria argu gone →	– – –

GLOSSARY

The language of debate is specialized. It is filled with terms that are meaningful to persons who understand the concept and theory of debate. The same terms are necessary in the explanation of debate. The following list of terms, which have been used in this text and in many others, makes up the body of literature relating to debate. Each term is concisely defined. The definitions provided here were written with an effort to be consistent with the meanings and interpretations that are found in standard argumentation textbooks.

Ad hominem attack. An attack on the person rather than the person's arguments.

Additive advantage. An advantage developed by the affirmative for the first time in the second affirmative constructive speech. It is generally an advantage that flows from adopting the affirmative plan.

Advocate. (v.) To support a position. (n.) One who advocates; a debater.

Affirmative. The side that favors (affirms) changing the status quo to conform to the debate resolution.

Affirmative case brief. Used to support the affirmative case; may include arguments that extend the harms or advantages of the affirmative case or provide responses to anticipated negative arguments.

Affirmative extension brief. Used to set up a second or third line of argument.

Affirmative plan brief. Designed to defend the affirmative plan, anticipated responses to solvency and workability arguments, and negative disadvantages.

Agent of change. A person or persons responsible for carrying out the work of the plan. Sometimes this kind of plan plank need only indicate what agency, bureau, or level of government will be responsible for seeing to it that the plan mandates are carried out. The affirmative may also create a new board or agency.

Agent-of-change counterplan. An alternative way of addressing a problem. The negative might locate the agent of change at either a more global or a more local level, as opposed to a federal level.

Alternative causality. One in which a condition may be brought about by a force not considered in the original affirmative argument. This term also can be used in negative plan-meets-need arguments and disadvantages.

Alternative justifications case. An affirmative case that offers multiple justifications for the adoption of the resolution; offers multiple independent plans, as well as advantages.

Analogy. A comparison used to draw a general conclusion. The conclusion drawn is strong in relation to the number of likenesses between the things compared. Classical reasoning indicates that analogies are for clarification rather than proof; however, contemporary argumentation accepts generalizations based on strong analogies.

Analysis. The process of breaking down an idea or a proposition into its elements. In debate, analysis traditionally follows a fairly standard procedure of seeking pro and con positions on the stock issues.

Analytical fallacies. Basing a case on faulty interpretations or assumptions. Analytical fallacies include begging the question, faulty assumptions, non sequiturs, inconsistencies and emotional appeals, and ad hominem attacks.

Argument. Two senses of this term are important to debaters. In the first sense, an argument is a message consisting of a conclusion supported by a reason documented by evidence. The emphasis is on credible proof and logical structure. In the second sense, an argument is a confrontation between two parties in disagreement over a claim. The emphasis is on refutation. Thus, a debater can make an argument that is tested against the standards of evidence and logic; two debaters can have an argument with each other that one or the other wins on the basis of his or her refutation of an opponent.

Argument by generalization. Claim supported by a number of examples. Sometimes referred to as reasoning from example.

Argument from analogy. Involves comparing two dissimilar ideas, situations, things, persons, or policies.

Argument from authority. A claim whose validity is based on authoritative testimony.

Argument from expertise. Validity of argument is determined by the trustworthiness of a source. A trustworthy source is one who has been judged competent to make an evaluation by a consensus of experts.

Argument from precedent. Says one should follow an established way of doing things until and unless there is good reason for doing something differently.

Argumentation. The study or use of argument, consisting of the dual process of (1) discovering the probable truth of an issue through analysis and research, and (2) advocating it to an audience through appropriate logical, ethical, and persuasive techniques.

Assertion. An unsupported statement; a conclusion that lacks evidence for support.

Attitudinal inherency. A claim that the attitudes of the bureaucracy—i.e., government or industry—prevent the present system from solving the affirmative problem.

Audience. The person or persons to whom a message is directed. In academic debate, the audience consists of a judge who listens to the debaters, weighs the arguments presented by each side, and then makes a decision about which team's position is the most acceptable.

Authority. A person whose experience, training, position, or special study makes her or his testimony or opinion acceptable as evidence; an expert.

Backing. General area from which the warrant or data is drawn.

"Balance of arguments" judge. A kind of debate judge who bases his or her decision on which team established its arguments during the debate. The decision is based on the judge's determination as to which team did the better job of meeting its basic responsibilities. This kind of judge is likely to be much more content-analysis oriented than other judges.

Begging the question. Fallacy of the affirmative constructive arguments. It involves unreasonably expanding or narrowing the grounds of debate. Even though begging the question is primarily an affirmative fallacy, the negative also can be guilty of this fallacy.

Benefit. In a traditional need case, a positive effect of the plan in addition to the solution of the major need areas.

"Better job of debating" judge. A kind of debate judge who does not weigh the arguments to determine which team was more effective in the round, but bases her or his decisions solely on which team did the better job of debating. Decisions may be totally subjective or even impressionistic, but it is more likely that this kind of judge will use specific criteria (usually those listed on the ballot).

Bias. A prejudiced attitude on the part of the source of evidence quoted in a debate. If quoted sources are biased, their opinions are therefore questionable as credible proof. Bias exists in sources when it is shown they have some vested interest in the policy being debated. There can be political or economic bias by a lobby group or political party. As a rule, academic and scholarly research reports, or nonpartisan analytical "think tanks," are accepted as relatively unbiased sources in debate. Debaters should seek unbiased sources when possible.

Bibliographic Index. A bibliography of bibliographies.

Black's Law Dictionary. The standard work for legal terms and court precedents for concepts of law.

Books in Print. An annual listing of published works by subject, author, and title.

Brief. An outline of all the arguments on both sides of the debate resolution. An affirmative or negative brief consists of all the arguments on the respective sides of the resolution.

Brookings Institution Publications. A series of in-depth analyses of important issues.

Burden of proof. The burden of proof rests on the side that desires a change from the status quo. If the proposition was correctly stated, the burden of proof should rest with the affirmative. The affirmative must show that some serious fault is inherent in present conditions and that the proposed solution will remedy the fault in a way that is practical and desirable.

Affirmative

1. Either must prove that the status quo includes at least one important deficiency or harm or demonstrate that the affirmative plan would be superior to the status quo in one or more significant respects.

2. Must prove that deficiency is inherent to the status quo—i.e., that causal fac-

tors make the shortcoming inevitable and that a solution is impossible unless the cause or causes are removed or counteracted.

3. Presents the plan.

4. Shows that the proposal will solve alleged needs or result in the advantage.

Admitted matter

Weak points that do not matter. The negative can admit that the status quo is imperfect but that the imperfections are slight and minor changes would solve the imperfections. This would shift the focus of the debate from whether the point is true to how significant the point is and whether the status quo has the capabilities to solve it.

Waived matter

Issues that are granted for purposes of debate. For example, constitutionality is granted. Most plans would require a constitutional amendment; thus the need for amendment is granted so the debate can concentrate on more important issues.

Burden of proving. The obligation of debaters on either side to prove any argument they initiate.

Burden of rebuttal. The obligation of the negative in any debate to meet and clash with the affirmative.

Burden of refuting. The obligation of either side to respond to relevant constructive arguments presented by its opponent and to advance its own arguments.

Burden of rejoinder. Obligation to answer the opponent's arguments; the defense must show that the prosecution's case does not prove beyond a reasonable doubt that the defendant is guilty.

Card file. An organized collection of evidence recorded on index cards. A card should contain only one idea or bit of information, preferably verbatim from the source, together with complete labeling of the contents of the card and information about the source, such as the authority's name and qualifications and publication data, including the date of the source.

Case. A debate team's basic position on the resolution, made up of all the arguments that the team presents in support of that position.

Case-related disadvantages. Potentially bad consequences implied by the specific affirmative case. What is being argued is that to gain an advantage in one area of the topic will only make things worse overall. This is a powerful argument in most rounds. If it is won by the negative, the affirmative cannot win.

Causal argument. Deployed in debate for one of two purposes. First, to find the cause of a problem–to isolate conditions in the status quo that give rise to socially threatening or undesirable situations. Second, to find the causes of a successful policy so that they can be preserved or protected and the policy process can be strengthened.

Causal chain of reasoning. Linking of cause and effect. Cause is linked to effect, which itself becomes a cause of a further effect, and so on; means an effect has multiple, independent causes that together become sufficient to bring about an effect.

Causation. A relationship between two phenomena in which one is believed to cause the other.

Circumvention. Countermeasures will arise that circumvent the objectives of the affirmative plan. This area of analysis becomes particularly fertile when the case depends on the attitudes of interest groups or social agencies (attitudinal inherency). Unless the attitudes that perpetuate the problem are changed, the old problem will simply reappear in a new form. A circumvention argument always has two parts: the motive and the means. The motive for circumvention is generally isolatable from the inherency presented by the affirmative. The means for circumvention are various.

Claim. Conclusion of reasoning; it is the proposition that the arguer desires to be accepted. The claim is the end or object of making an argument.

Clash. The process of meeting and dealing directly with an argument of the opposition. Dealing with an argument implies denial or minimization, but not agreement with it.

Coach judge. A coach from one of the schools participating in a tournament who judges other participants. Coach judges are trained in debate and know the issues.

Comparative advantages case. A case in which the affirmative shows that, although existing programs could possibly be modified in the present system to achieve a solution to the problem area, the affirmative proposal could do a better job. The argument focuses on the comparison between the affirmative plan and the present system. The entire case is presented in the first affirmative constructive speech.

Comparative risks counterplan. Offers a system with less risk than the affirmative proposal. A comparative risks counterplan aims at making a subset of disadvantages unique. It is often deployed when the affirmative offers a plan that relieves or improves a dangerous situation by incremental action. The negative response is to eliminate the dangerous situation altogether, thereby reducing policy risk even more effectively than the affirmative.

Comparing processes. In this option, the counterplan enacts a superior process of addressing the affirmative concerns. Two examples of process counterplans are study and agent-of-change counterplans.

Computer indexes. One type of computer system contains items you would find in a card catalog (primarily books). Most are indexed by author, title, and subject. Another type of system carries periodical listings.

Conditional counterplan. A negative strategy of arguing the superiority of the present system over the affirmative plan.

But, on the condition that the judge agrees with the affirmative that the present system should be changed, the negative also suggests a counterplan it is willing to defend in preference to the affirmative plan. This strategy is risky because it potentially places the negative in a self-contradictory position of claiming no need for a change and then advocating a counterplan to change the present system.

Congressional Quarterly Weekly Report. A weekly resume of activities in Congress.

Constructive. (adj.) A constructive argument is one offered in support of, or in opposition to, the resolution. A constructive speech is a time period in which it is permissible to present constructive arguments.

Constructive speeches. First speeches in a debate. The affirmative and negative set out their initial positions and arguments.

Contention. A subdivision of an issue; the statement of a claim; an argument essential to support a position on an issue. Contentions may consist of either observations or indictments. In debate, a number of contentions make up the affirmative case.

Contradiction. Statements or arguments within a given position that are in direct opposition to each other.

Corpus juris secundum. A text that clarifies the implications of legal rulings or the current state of the law. Available at law libraries, major courthouses, and many general libraries.

Correlation. A statement of a logical relationship between two phenomena showing that the two appear together and that they also vary together, either directly or inversely. In other words, correlation would establish a relationship less strong than causality.

Cost-benefit ratio. An on-balance comparison of the advantages and disadvantages of alternative proposals for change. The emphasis is on quantified measures of both costs and benefits, with the greatest value assigned to the most favorable ratio between costs incurred and benefits received.

Counterargument. An argument designed to contradict a specific affirmative argument. The debater puts the argument in perspective by showing how the defeat of the particular argument affects the affirmative's case.

Counterexample. An instance that would bar the generalization.

Counterplan. Generally, the negative will agree that there is a problem in the status quo and will present a plan that it believes is better than that of the affirmative. First negative presents the plan and begins supporting. The negative must show that the counterplan is inconsistent with the affirmative plan. In other words, the negative should be ready to show that the counterplan and the affirmative cannot be adopted at the same time. The negative must assume the burden of proof for the counterplan. The counterplan cannot be resolutional; the plan must be adopted on a state, local, or voluntary level. If it requires federal action, then it has met the terms of the resolution.

Credibility. Refers to the judgment an audience makes about the believability of a source of information.

Criteria for evaluation. The means by which the values in the resolution are measured.

Criteria-goals case. An elaboration on the comparative advantages case, with greater emphasis on the policy goals of the present system. The affirmative incorporates the identification of the goal of the present system as an integral part of its analysis. Affirmative sets up the criteria to judge the fulfillment of those particular goals. The affirmative shows its proposed plan meets the criteria better than the present system does.

Critical listening. Listening theorists have identified four specific actions one can perform to become an active listener: (1) Anticipate what the opposition is likely to say. What will the next point be? (2) Continually review or summarize what the opposition has been saying. (3) Pay attention to the evidence being used. (4) Watch for "hidden meanings." What are the nonverbal messages?

Critical thinking. Developing reasons to back up a position. Analyzing a position by exploring reasons against it. Understanding the reasons behind an opponent's position and exploring the opponent's arguments to see if these arguments can refute their own position.

Cross-examination. The question-and-answer periods that follow each constructive speech. Each speaker is questioned by a member of the opposing team. Also referred to as *cross-x.*

Cross-examination (Oregon) debate. A form of debate in which debaters are permitted to ask direct questions of an opponent during specified time periods, usually immediately following the opponent's constructive speeches.

Data. The information that is offered in support of a claim. Types of data are testimony, examples, and statistics.

Debate. A contest of argumentation. The affirmative presents arguments in favor of a resolution, and' a negative presents arguments against it. The contest is won by the team that presents the best arguments in the opinion of the judge.

Deduction. A reasoning process that takes general statements or premises and draws a conclusion about particular or specific elements. In formal logic, deduction is contained in a chain called a syllogism. This form of reasoning is formal, and the validity of such an argument is based on the logical relationship between premises and conclusion, not necessarily on the truth content of any premise.

Example

Major Premise: All elementary schools are entitled to public tax support.

Minor Premise: Parochial schools are elementary schools.

Conclusion: Therefore, parochial schools are entitled to public tax support.

Defense of the present system. A refutation of affirmative claims that involves two arguments: first, that life under the present system will be worse in the future; and second, that the future looks promising in respect to the harm area isolated by the affirmative.

Definition. A formality of a debate wherein the affirmative team declares the meaning of the terms of the debate resolution. The definition of terms serves the useful function of limiting the areas encompassed by the resolution. While the affirmative team has the privilege of defining the terms, the negative team has the privilege of challenging any definition considered unacceptable. The most frequently used methods of defining terms are references to authorities, examples, or the dictionary.

Definition by authority. A definition of terms based on such sources as *Dictionary of Economics and Business, The Oxford English Dictionary, Black's Law Dictionary,* and *Random House College Dictionary,* to name a few. It may also include authorities in the field being debated.

Definition by example. The affirmative relies on numerous examples to show how a term has been applied to similar policies and then argues by analogy that the definition is appropriate.

Definition of terms. The affirmative identifies each important term in the proposition and discerns its various meanings from a number of sources.

Desirability. A condition or state of favorability; a value judgment attached to a particular outcome of a plan, especially a benefit or an advantage. Desirability is a state lower in degree than necessity.

Dilemma. A situation in which choice is between only two alternatives, both of which are undesirable.

Disadvantage. A harmful effect, or series of effects, brought about by the affirmative plan. Any disadvantage is composed of two parts: the links and the impacts. The link is the "why" part of the disadvantage. It is the proof that explains why the affirmative plan will cause an undesirable effect and why it is unique to the affirmative plan. A link may be either direct or indirect. The impact is the end result or outcome of the disadvantage.

Distortion. A misrepresentation of a piece of evidence.

Drop. To neglect to carry on an argument after the opponent's response.

Editorial Research Reports. Available only to newspapers and libraries, this publication presents in-depth analyses of currently important topics.

Elaborate alphabetical filing system. A note-card filing system that involves an affirmative file and a negative file. The cards are filed behind the major affirmative and negative headings.

Elimination rounds. Debate rounds in which teams with the best records are matched. Depending on tournament size, the rounds could begin with double octofinals, octofinals, quarterfinals, or even semifinals. A single loss in a tournament elimination round eliminates a team from the tournament, while the winner goes on to the next higher level of competition. Usually, there are multiple judges in each elimination round.

Empirical evidence. The results of controlled observation to obtain factual and inferential data.

Encyclopedia of Associations. A comprehensive list of U.S. associations.

Enforcement. That plank of a plan that provides for seeing that the performance or prohibition planks of the plan are carried out.

Ethical. Relating to the scholarliness, morality, and legality of someone's actions. Courteous behavior and use of good research practices.

Ethics. The practice or study of being ethical.

Evidence. Data that form the basis for conclusions.

Evidence card. Form used to record quotations for debate.

Examples. Instances used to demonstrate a claim's validity. Single objects or events used to show the possibility of generalized categories of similar groups of examples; a type of factual evidence. Negative examples are those used to disprove generalities.

Experimental data. The evidence reporting the results of a scientific experiment that has been conducted to explore some causal relationship. It is often considered the best debate evidence because it represents the best way to establish causation. In evaluating experimental data, the debater should ask three questions.

1. How well were the variables controlled?
2. Has the experiment been replicated with the same results?
3. Can the results of the experiment be generalized to more than just the cases that were used in the experiment?

Expert judge. A kind of judge who is familiar with the latest forensic theory and practices. He or she generally requires less explanation in apprehending the nature and weight of the argument and is less responsive to general persuasive rhetoric, as he or she understands and is concerned with the technical issues involved in debate.

Extend. To carry an argument another step forward in rebuttal; to answer the opponent's challenge and advance beyond it.

External criticism. Criticism directed at the source of evidence. This kind of criticism pertains to the excellence of the publication from which the evidence is drawn and the competence of the author of the evidence.

Extratopicality. Used in reference to the affirmative plan and its disadvantages. An extratopical plank of the plan is one that does not support the resolution. An advantage or solvency is extratopical when it is gained from means other than the resolution. An advantage is extratopical when it comes about because of a plank in the plan that is not resolutional. For example, if the plan causes unemployment by banning hazardous products, it cannot claim an advantage of employment by a plank in the plan for employment of these people or an advantage from the work these people might do in public works programs.

Fabrication. To make up evidence, considered unethical.

Fact. An actual, observable object or event in the real world. Useful as evidence in debate, facts usually fall into these categories: (a) examples, (b) statistics, (c) empirical studies.

Factual claim. Involves a statement that something either is or is not the case. Sometimes such claims are made through observation.

Fallacy. A mistaken inference; an erroneous conclusion based on faulty reasoning.

Fiat. An assured power to put a proposal into effect; a legal mandate binding on the parties involved, overriding their personal attitudes. Fiat power is limited to matters subject to law; it is not a "magic wand" to avoid substantive argument. For example, a health care bill could be adopted by fiat, but an adequate supply of doctors cannot be provided by fiat.

Figurative analogy. A comparison in which the objects have a striking similarity, but as a whole have more difference than commonness.

Flow (flow sheet). A diagram of the arguments in a debate and of their relationships. Arguments are charted (or flowed) in parallel columns, with the affirmative case written in the left-hand column, the negative arguments in the next column, the affirmative responses in the next column, and so forth. Thus, a "flow" of the arguments can be seen at a glance by tracing each argument and its responses across the flow sheet.

Forecasting. To make the audience aware beforehand of what is going to be said so it will be easier for them to understand it.

Forthcoming books. A bimonthly listing of all books scheduled for publication within the next five months.

Generalization. A series of examples which all point in the same direction; a conclusion drawn from evidence or data.

Generic policy disadvantage (policy disadvantage). A negative effect of the affirmative case deriving from its impact on society as a whole. The disadvantage derives from the policy in general and not from a specific action of the affirmative plan. The concept of generic disadvantages is based on the idea that there is no such thing as a discrete action or a delimited area; all policies are interrelated to some extent. When looking for possible disadvantage areas, the debater should first examine possible higher-order impacts—e.g., earth-ending threats.

Goal. A general objective; an aim. Systems of policy are thought to exist in order to achieve goals. Affirmative cases may be developed on the premise that a laudable goal can best be met through the affirmative proposal.

Goals case. Focuses on the goals or values toward which a policy should be directed. The affirmative identifies a goal or goals that any policy should try to obtain. The affirmative demonstrates how its proposal best meets the goal or goals.

GPO on Silver Platter. Computer index of more than 250,000 citations to government documents listed in the Monthly Catalog. Index includes periodicals, books, pamphlets, reports, hearings, maps, and other serials.

Harm. An undesirable impact resulting from the operation of a policy system. The impact may be stated in terms of deprivation of or injury to parties affected by the policy. Harm exists where needs are denied or suffering or loss of life is caused.

Highlighting. The use of well-written statements of major issues, so that the issues will be easy to remember. Highlighted contentions should be short, clear, and worded in an interesting way.

Index sheet filing system. A note-card filing system in which the evidence cards are lettered and numbered. A master notebook is kept for the entire filing system. All the material in each file box is noted on index sheets to which the debater can quickly refer for the code numbers that apply to specific subjects.

Indexes (guides). Alphabetical listings by author, title, and general subject of magazine articles that have appeared in a particular group of periodicals.

Indictment. An accusatory conclusion; a charge. A contention in a debate will usually state an indictment.

Inferences. Conclusions based on possible relationships between known facts.

Inherency. Presumption holds that the present system should be continued unless someone can prove otherwise.

Internal criticism. A kind of criticism that questions the truth of the evidence. What does the evidence say? How consistent is the evidence?

Issue. A question concerning which the affirmative and negative teams take opposite sides; a major point of disagreement.

Judge. The person who stands in for a larger audience and renders a decision in accordance with tournament custom and good educational practices.

Justification. A fulfillment of the standards of judgment. A justification argument is one in which it is charged that an affirmative case fails to "justify the resolution." As a negative strategy, the argument shows how the advantages of the affirmative case do not stem from the resolution itself but rather from other extratopical features of the plan.

Key words. A list of words put together by a researcher when investigating a subject area. Looking up the words in various indexes and the card catalog will provide a tremendous supply of possible sources.

Lay judge. A kind of judge who comes from the community. Although this kind of judge is interested in current affairs and may have a high level of intellectual accomplishment, she or he is not a specialist in debate theory and might not be an expert in the topic under discussion.

Lincoln-Douglas debate. A type of debate centered around a value proposition, in which one debater argues against another.

Lincoln-Douglas stock issues. The four stock issues in debating a proposition of value include (1) defining the object of evaluation; (2) identifying the key evaluative term in the debate; (3) establishing the criteria or standards for evaluation; and (4) establishing and justifying a value hierarchy.

Link. The "why" part of the disadvantage. It is the proof that explains why the affirmative plan will cause an undesirable effect and why it is unique to the affirmative plan. A link may be either direct or indirect.

Literal analogy. A comparison in which the objects under comparison seem to have more in common than not.

Logic. The system of analysis that shows the nature of relationships between statements, facts and conclusions, causes and effects, and deductions and premises. Logic is reasoning based on rules concerning the form in which an argument is put rather than on the nature and quality of the evidence.

Logical fallacies. Breakdowns in the connections between evidence and arguments can be divided into three main categories: (1) those relating to factual arguments; (2) those relating to value arguments; and (3) those relating to causal arguments.

Mandates. Option for conducting a comparison of the affirmative plan and the negative counterplan. The negative argues that the counterplan meets most of the affirmative goals, but stops short so as not to encounter significant advantages to a comprehensive mandate. The negative accepts the basic efficacy of the affirmative plan. Comparative workability arguments or circumvention arguments are not at issue. The focus of the debate rather is on the extent to which efforts must be made to resolve a problem.

"Maverick" judge. A kind of judge whose basis for decision making is unpredictable.

Means. Option for comparing advantages of the affirmative to the negative counterplan. The negative argues that the counterplan meets the affirmative goal better than the affirmative plan does because the counterplan enacts superior means. The negative focus on comparative plan-meet-advantage or plan-meet-need kinds of argumentation. The negative shows that the means adopted by the affirmative for the resolution of some problem for garnering some advantages have intrinsic defects that are not duplicated by the alternative counterplan.

Means of change. The affirmative may specify an exact means of enacting the resolution, or it can create a number of choices from which the board (agent of change) might choose. When the affirma-

tive wants to defend the specific alternatives, those alternatives should be listed in the plan.

Methodology. The procedure by which an empirical study is conducted. An empirical study's methodology may be challenged along such lines as the size of the sample, the amount of time, or the presence of a control group. To challenge the methodology is to test the validity of the conclusions drawn from such a study. Debaters who quote from empirical studies should be familiar with the methodology of the studies.

Minor repairs. Alterations that can be made in the present system not requiring federal action or the adoption of the affirmative plan or the resolution. The aim is to show how the present system can solve the problem with mechanisms that currently exist. For example, if the affirmative is arguing the harms of unemployment, the negative could "minor repair" by adding money to the current programs that are designed to take care of the unemployed. This would not change the structure of the present system but could solve the harm of unemployment.

Moral authority. Opinions backed with deeds, long-term commitments, and actions. Moral authority is used to support arguments about value that society is out to pursue.

Mutual exclusivity. Refers to the impossibility of adopting both the plan and the counterplan at the same time. There are several conditions under which this might evolve. First, if there are opposing legal mandates, then policy makers could not undertake opposing actions at the same time. Second, if there were a limited, non-expandable pool of resources, then resources such as trained personnel, rare materials, and so on could not be used for two different purposes.

Need. An evil or harmful situation inherent in the status quo, which the affirmative plan will remedy. The need is a necessary element of a traditional need case.

Need case (Traditional need case). A kind of case that develops the argument that a need for change exists. The case develops the plan and shows how the plan meets the need. The case develops the argument that the plan would be beneficial.

Negative. In a debate, the side that opposes (negates) the affirmative position and, therefore, the resolution.

Negative block. The section of a debate that consists of the second negative constructive speech and the first negative rebuttal.

Negative case brief. Involves negative arguments that are being made against affirmative contentions or advantages. Basically, these case briefs are organized around the stock issues—topicality, inherency, and significance.

Negative extension brief. Answers to the anticipated affirmative responses to negative arguments.

Negative philosophy. Position the negative will take against the affirmative case.

Negative plan brief. Directed at the specific solvency/workability of the affirmative plan or at the disadvantages that will result if the plan is adopted.

Negative position. Requires proof and consistency in establishing what is the probable truth, and it enhances the power of the negative by increasing its focus on its strongest argument. For the negative to develop a position it must (1) assume a burden of proof, and (2) make arguments that consistently reinforce one another.

Net benefits case. A kind of case based on systems analysis. The case incorporates four steps: (1) apply systems analysis to the problem area; (2) determine the components that make up the system and the rules that govern how the components are interrelated; (3) analyze and project the differences that can be predicted following

a change in policy governing the interrelationships; and (4) determine the most favorable ratio between the costs and the benefits of the proposed change in the system.

NewsBank. Computerized newspaper service of the *Chicago Tribune.*

NFL (National Forensic League). Sponsor of high school speech and debate activities. Located in Ripon, Wisconsin.

Non sequitur. A Latin phrase that means "does not follow." It is used by logicians to describe any fallacious argument in which the conclusion does not follow from the evidence.

Nontopicality. Refers to an affirmative case that fails to justify all the terms included in the resolution.

Novice division. A division for beginners who enter a tournament for the first time or are just beginning in a forensic career.

Observation. A descriptive conclusion or assumption.

Observational data. Information that reflects controlled observation of events. Types of observational data include statistics and carefully-developed examples. The main criteria for judging the quality of observational data are validity and reliability.

Offset counterplan. A counterplan that accepts the mandates of the affirmative plan and requires that other actions be taken that are antithetical to the direction of the resolution.

On-balance judgments. The affirmative and negative are asked to weigh the issue or instance and convince the judge that, on balance, the proposition should be accepted or rejected.

Open division. A tournament division that mixes beginners and advanced students.

Operational definition. The terms of the resolution are defined by way of the affirmative plan. The plan serves as an example of the resolution. When using an operational definition, the affirmative merely states this fact after stating the resolution.

Opinion evidence. A kind of evidence that is divisible into two categories: expert testimony and testimony from a lay person. Expert testimony is the only variety that can be used for proof. Testimony from lay people should be reserved for the persuasive effect of illustration.

PMN or PMA (Plan-Meet-Needs or Plan-Meet-Advantages). Does the plan meet the need or advantage of the affirmative case? While general research can be done ahead of time, specific application will generally need to be done after hearing the affirmative plan. For example, if the affirmative argues that people are unemployed because of U.S. trade policies, the negative would want to demonstrate that the number of unemployed is a fairly constant number and that to change the trade policies would not change the overall unemployment figures. At best, the plan may only shift unemployment from one sector of the work force to another.

PO (Plan Objection). An objection that is generally the responsibility of the second negative. These arguments include a combination of workability, plan-meet-need arguments, plan-meet-advantage arguments, or disadvantages.

Parallel organization. A method of organization based on contingency. The team argues that if any one of several contingencies is true, the proposition should be accepted.

Parameters of the resolution. The collegiate topic committee provides a statement of what the committee had in mind when framing the resolution. Although this statement is not binding on the debater, it does help the negative to build a framework for a topicality argument against any off-the-wall affirmative definitions.

Permutations. The rearrangement or reordering of things. A permutation as a standard of competitiveness substantially favors the affirmative. Using this standard,

the affirmative argues that any parts of the counterplan that could be done at the same time as the affirmative plan become reasonable additions in a world where the plan is affirmed.

Philosophical competitiveness. That there are two different value approaches to a case area and the values are not commensurable; that is, they do not stem from the same outlook or general set of social purposes. Perhaps the weakest means of testing competitiveness of the counterplan. The reason it is weak is that in a pluralistic society different value positions can be brought together to work for the same end.

Plan. The specific program proposed by the affirmative team to implement the debate resolution. The plan is a necessary part of every affirmative case.

Plan plank. A specific provision within the affirmative plan; a set of particulars about the plan. Individual planks might specify (1) goal or intent, (2) agency of change, (3) duties or powers, (4) enforcement, or (5) financing.

Plan spikes. A provision in the plan designed to eliminate a potential disadvantage or a plan-meets-need argument.

Policy. A means of achieving a goal; an action. In a narrow sense, a policy is a governmental program, such as the financing of public schools through property tax revenues. In debate, a policy proposition is the proposal of some new governmental program that the affirmative team claims should be adopted.

Policy claim. Involves a statement about what should or should not be done. Policy claims involve questions of action.

Policy debate. Consists of two teams (two people on each team); the debate centers around a policy proposition. There are two policy debate formats—**standard** and **cross-examination.**

Policy direction. Counterplan involving the comparison of policy direction. This form of counterplan mandates that action be taken in a direction opposite to the outcome stipulated by the resolution. A negative might argue a counterplan that basically accepts the mandates of the affirmative plan but requires that other actions be taken that are antithetical to the direction of the resolution. This strategy is sometimes called an offset counterplan.

Post hoc fallacy. A logical fallacy based on the assumption that, because one event is closely followed by another event, the first is the cause of the second. (**Post hoc** is Latin for "after this.")

Power match rounds. Matches based on the accumulated records of teams at the tournament.

Preempt. A plank in the plan to prevent the development of a negative disadvantage. For example, if a plan causes unemployment, some sort of subsidy might be provided to prevent the disadvantages of harms to unemployment.

Preliminary rounds. Debate rounds usually consisting of four, six, or eight debate matches per team, with each team alternating sides between affirmative and negative. The teams with the best record advance to the elimination rounds. Usually, there is one judge.

Premise. A general statement of a goal or value from which arguments and conclusions may be drawn.

Preparation time. In a debate, the time that elapses before the beginning of each debater's speech. After the first affirmative speech, each team has a strictly regulated amount of cumulative preparation time allocated to it for the entire debate, which the team members may utilize as they wish. The amount of time and the rules governing its use are determined by the tournament director.

Preset match. A round set by the tournament host before the tournament begins.

Presumption. Traditionally, the assumption that conditions and policies should remain as they are. The affirmative side has the burden to prove that the status quo should be changed. The present system is presumed to be adequate until the affirmative team meets its burden to prove that a change in the status quo is needed or would be advantageous. Presumption is analogous to the legal principle that the accused person is presumed to be innocent until proven guilty.

Presumptive validity. Meaning that almost everyone believes that the argument is true.

Prima facie. The Latin phrase may be translated as "at first look." In debate, a *prima facie* case must include a specific plan to implement the resolution and a justification for the plan—either an inherent need in the status quo, a comparative advantage of the plan over the status quo, or some other accepted justification. Such a case would be accepted "at first look," with a minimum of evidence required to meet the burden of proof.

Probability. (1) The relative degree of certainty with which an inference may be drawn. (2) In statistical language, the level of confidence that may be placed in a conclusion expressed as a percentage.

Problem area. The domain of issues that pertain to a topic. A problem area includes issues of longstanding social concern.

Process disadvantage. A flaw in the affirmative method of producing results. It relates neither to the particular content area of the topic nor to extrinsic considerations of policy effect. The judge is asked to reject the case because the plan is an inappropriate method of achieving any advantage.

Proof. That which reduces uncertainty and increases the probable truth of a claim. Evidence is transformed into proof through the use of reasoning, which demonstrates how and to what extent the claim is believable. Proof is a relative concept, ranging from possibility through probability to certainty. The amount of proof needed to establish a claim depends on a number of variables, such as the importance of the claim, the strength of opposing claims, and the credibility of the person making the argument.

Proposal. The specific affirmative plan.

Proposition. A debatable statement; a statement open to interpretation; a statement about which reasonable people may accept arguments on either side. Debate theory incorporates three types of propositions: fact, value, and policy.

Proposition of fact. A statement about a person, thing, or event, the truth or falsity of which is determinable by direct investigation.

Proposition of policy. A statement calling for a specific action. A proposition of policy requires that the debater (1) find the facts that afford a sound basis for making predictions, (2) reason cogently from these facts to the probable results, and (3) show that these consequences would be desirable.

Proposition of value. A statement offering a value judgement about a person, thing, or event. Two sides could agree on all the facts of a case but disagree about whether the facts constitute justice or whether the actions were prudent.

ProQuest. Computerized index of eight newspapers—*The New York Times, The Wall Street Journal,* the *Washington Post,* the *Christian Science Monitor,* the *Los Angeles Times,* the *Chicago Tribune,* the *Boston Globe,* and the *Atlanta Constitution.* A user can search by subject. The index provides citations and abstracts.

Qualifier. Term that expresses the degree of confidence that one has in the relationship between data and claim.

Qualitative significance. Affirmative tries to show that present policy violates core values.

Quantitative significance. Deals with the quantity of the harm (numbers or the body count).

Quote cards. Material (evidence) recorded on index cards for use in debate rounds.

Rationale. (1) The philosophical framework within which a case is constructed. (2) The criteria for accepting a premise or conclusion.

Readers' Guide to Periodical Literature. A reference listing titles of articles in such general circulation periodicals as *Time, Newsweek, Fortune,* and others.

Rebuttal (Toulmin model). A possible condition under which the relationship between data and claim would not hold.

Rebuttal. A short speech devoted to (1) rebuilding arguments that have been attacked, (2) refuting opposing arguments, and (3) summarizing the debate from the perspective of the speaker.

Rebuttal sheets. Sheets on which the arguments most likely to arise in a debate are listed, along with the replies and the best evidence. Rebuttal sheets also can be made without specific reference to pieces of evidence.

Redundancy. Stating what doesn't need to be repeated.

Refutation. An attack on the arguments of the opponent.

Reliability. A criterion for evidence that asks if the same results would be obtained if the observations were repeated or if they had been gathered at the same time by a different observer.

Research. To search again; to gather information and evidence and to classify it so that it is easily retrievable for use.

Reservation. An announced exception to the rule; a point at which one accounts for why the warrant does not really hold.

Residues case (Lincoln-Douglas debate). A residues case is one that eliminates all alternatives except for the one that the affirmative desires.

Risks. The dangers of accepting a belief or taking an action.

Running refutation. Indicting the affirmative evidence at each and every point.

Sandbagging. The practice of presenting an argument initially in skeletal form, with little or no evidence, so that it appears weak, and saving a bulk of evidence for second-line presentation only if the argument is attacked. The strategy is to make your strongest point look like the weakest so that the opposition will focus the debate there.

Senior (varsity) division. A division for more experienced debaters.

Serial organization. A method of organization in which each argument depends on the preceding argument for its support. If one argument can be destroyed, the whole case or series of arguments fails.

Shift. To abandon an original position and take up a different one.

Shift in presumption. Traditional presumption rests with the present system, meaning that any change in the present system must be justified. A shift in presumption would mean that presumption would now rest with change, that change should be adopted unless a reason not to change is justified.

Shotgun. (1) A strategy of presenting a profusion of unrelated, scattered attacks against an opponent's case; (2) a loud, bombastic style of delivery.

Should. A term generally defined by the affirmative as meaning "ought to but not necessarily will." The word means that the proposal of the affirmative would be the most desirable policy at the present time.

Should/would argument. Negative claims that the affirmative plan will never be adopted rather than discussion of whether or not it should be adopted. The affirmative need only demonstrate that legislators should vote for a change. The affirmative does not suggest that the policy change will be enacted, nor that it can be adopted, but that the change ought to be made.

Sign argument. Based upon a correlation of characteristics and objects; gives a sense of measurement, features, or characteristics of things or situations.

Significance. (1) The degree of importance of a conclusion. Significance may be qualitative or quantitative. Qualitative significance rests on an established value; quantitative significance rests on concrete units of measurement. (2) In statistical language, the level of confidence at which a predicted conclusion may not be rejected, usually ".05 level of significance," or "95 percent probability."

Signposting. Tells the judge where the debater is at a particular time in the speech. After developing an argument, all the debater has to do is provide the judge with a brief perspective. Signposting lets the judge see what an argument means in terms of a particular segment of the case, or what else has to be done to finish the analysis.

Simple alphabetical filing system. A note-card filing system that involves dividing the evidence cards into subject areas and filing them accordingly.

Sine qua non. A Latin phrase meaning "without which not." It signifies something that is indispensable or essential. As a test for the post hoc fallacy, the sine qua non question is "Would the second event have occurred if the first had not occurred?"

Slippery-slope argument. A radical departure from precedent creates opportunities for counterarguments. If one precedent can be overturned, then why not others?

Social Issues Research Series (SIRS). Carries full text of magazine and newspaper articles about current issues; works much the same as the *Readers' Guide* abstracts.

Solvency. Encompasses the affirmative plan's ability to solve the harm or to bring about the advantages identified in the affirmative case.

Source credibility. A social-psychological term that refers to the judgment the receiver makes of the believability of the source of a message.

Speaker awards. Recognition given to contestants who have accumulated the greatest number of quality points during the preliminary rounds. Many tournaments drop the highest and lowest points awarded each speaker. Ties for awards are often broken by comparing ranks.

Squirrel case. A case idea that the affirmative tries to work into the topic. It usually involves an unusual definition that will incorporate the case idea. To challenge a squirrel case, the negative challenges the definitions by placing them back into the resolution. Most of the time, when this is done the resolution will make no sense.

Standard debate format. Consists of two types of speeches—constructives and rebuttals. Involves two teams, each with two persons. Each team debates the affirmative and negative side of the topic.

Statistical abstract of the United States. An exhaustive summary of current statistics.

Statistical non sequitur. A claim in which the statistics are valid, but the evidence and the conclusion pertain to two different things. Therefore, the evidence does not follow from the conclusion, even if the evidence and the conclusion separately are valid.

Statistics. Information gathered by mathematical sampling techniques and scientific methods; used to demonstrate the widespread effects of a claim.

Status quo. The present system; the existing order; that which would be changed by adopting the affirmative plan.

Stock issues. Issues that must be addressed by the affirmative to present a prima facie case. These include topicality, inherency, harm, and solvency. For the negative a fifth stock issue is included—disadvantages.

Straight refutation. For every claim that the affirmative asserts is true, the negative offers a counterclaim asserting that what the affirmative says is false.

Strategic refutation. Requires spending a good deal of time to disestablish—that is, show false—an important claim. Strategic refutation proceeds by (1) casting doubt on the opponent's evidence, (2) introducing contrary evidence, and (3) stating the importance that winning the argument in question has for the other stock issues.

Strategy. Overall plan or approach to arguing or speaking, or any technique debaters use to win.

Structural inherency. The affirmative argues that the problem cannot be corrected until basic changes have been made in the structure of the present system. The problem cannot be solved simply by doing more of what is presently being done, nor can it be corrected simply by spending more money on present methods. Generally, the affirmative will identify some law(s) or set of regulations that stand in the way of the affirmative solution.

Student judge. A kind of debate judge who is a peer of the participants in a tournament.

Study counterplan. Includes all approaches that involve a delayed commitment to action. Sometimes negatives will argue that a policy should be submitted to referendum, court decisions, extended public debate, and so on. The idea is that no decision should be reached at this moment because there is sufficient uncertainty about the nature and solution of the present problem. It is important to show (1) that the situation does not require immediate attention, and (2) that taking action now will foreclose important options in the future. The more prudent action, then, is to wait and see.

Summarizing. Involves reminding the judge of what has come before. Most logical units of the debater's presentation (such as major contentions) should be capped with a very short summary of the argument. A one- or two-sentence summary at the end of a speech can help solidify the major ideas in the mind of the judge.

Sweepstakes awards. Recognition given to the schools who have had the best performance at a tournament.

System analysis. Assumes that policy develops in an environment that is constantly changing because of growth in population, economic fluctuations, and demographic trends. Also, it assumes that policies already exist in all the problem areas considered by the current policymakers.

Tabulation room. The place at the tournament in which results are tracked for purposes of power matching and selection of elimination round participants. Tabulators also keep track of the ballots and distribute the results at the end of the tournament.

Tactics. The specific techniques to be used to fulfill the plan. When and how will the arguments be presented? What will each speaker do? What evidence would be the best to use during the debate? What style of presentation would be the best to use?

Testimony. Opinion that is offered on behalf of the truth of a claim.

Threshold. A point in time when conditions are ripe for change.

Topicality. A jurisdictional question. For a case to be topical, it must come under the jurisdiction of the resolution. For it to be nontopical, it must be beyond the jurisdiction of the resolution. For example, if a judge has the power to decide whether a person is guilty or innocent of a felony and someone brings to court a question of drunk driving, the judge does not have the power to say whether the person is guilty or innocent, because drunk driving is not a felony.

Toulmin model of argument. Based on a theory that logic and argument should lead to truth, this model demonstrates how practical argumentation takes place, with all its varying degrees of certainty and probability. Elements of the model include the claim, data, warrant, backing, reservation, and qualifier.

Treaties in Force. The Department of State's annual list of all the treaties to which the United States is bound.

Trends of the present system. A defense of the status quo based on the assumption that new programs or measures have been designed to combat the problem to the extent possible, and additional efforts (by the affirmative) would be premature—perhaps even making the situation worse. The logic behind this position is that the multifaceted present system is better than the single approach suggested by the affirmative.

Turnaround. An argument that the meaning of an opponent's contention is the opposite of its apparent intent so that it counts against the opponent. For example, if the negative team makes a disadvantage argument, and the affirmative rebuttalist points out that the result of that disadvantage is more positive than negative, then the argument becomes a turnaround for the affirmative team.

Uniqueness. In comparative advantage analysis, the condition of inherency or inseparability of the proposal and the effects that are claimed to result from it, either advantages or disadvantages.

United States Government Printing Office: Congressional Information Service Index. Contains annotated listings of all publications from the legislative branch since 1970.

United States Government Printing Office: Monthly Publications Catalog. A reference catalog listing all government publications by subject headings.

Validity. A criterion for evidence that asks whether the observer actually observed what he or she claimed to be measuring.

Value assertions. A value assertion proposition is a categorical judgment stated in positive or negative terms. A positive value assertion states that some person, belief, custom, practice, event, or instrument is good. A negative value assertion states the opposite, depicting "bad" as unjust, worthless, detrimental, or harmful.

Value claim. Involves a statement about what an individual thinks is good or bad. Value claims apply to what people hold to be important, sacred, and clear.

Value comparison. A value comparison proposition is structured along the lines of the statement "x is better than y." Such values can be abstract or they can be concrete. When debating a comparative value proposition, the affirmative has to show that under most or all circumstances the proposition is true.

Value exclusivity. Value exclusivity propositions ask that a certain person, event, thing, custom, belief, practice, or class be judged above all competitors.

Value hierarchy. Provides the method for comparing the values presented in the case with other competing values. Sometimes the resolution will provide the hierarchy (setting out two values to be compared); at other times, resolutions will give the affirmative considerable leeway. Once the hierarchy has been established, the affirmative must justify that value hierarchy by discussing it in the context of the subject area of the resolution.

Value premise. The key evaluative term in the debate. It identifies the affirmative's highest value.

Vertical file index. Listing of pamphlets published each year by lobbying groups, foundations, and academic departments, established by most libraries.

Voting issues. Issues in debate that are crucial to determining whether the affirmative or negative wins.

Warrant. Certifies the relevance and importance of the relationship between data and claim; also called inference.

Who's Who in America. A standard source for substantiating the qualifications of authors.

Workability. A criterion for judging the affirmative's plan. The negative bases its attack on an "even if" analysis. Even if a need for a change exists and even if the affirmative's proposal could meet the need, even in theory, the affirmative's plan would be unworkable. The attack focuses on the mechanisms of the affirmative's proposal. As a negative issue and argues that the plan is not feasible, either because it lacks a crucial internal step in its creation, or because it depends upon resources that are not available, or requires actions that are impractical.

World Almanac. Lists more than 25,000 organizations and their addresses.

BIBLIOGRAPHY

Bailey, Patricia A. and Dukes, Marilee. "The Lay Judge: The Antithesis of Lincoln-Douglas Debate." *The Forensic Educator* (1991/92): 8–11.

Baron, Joan Boykoff and Sternberg, Robert J. *Teaching Thinking Skills: Theory and Practice.* New York: W. H. Freeman and Company, 1987.

Bartanen, Michael D. and Frank, David A. *Lincoln-Douglas Debate: Preparing for Value Argumentation.* Lincolnwood, IL: National Textbook Co., 1993.

Branham, Robert. *The Debate Flowsheet.* Kansas City, MO: National Federation of State High School Associations, 1987.

Branham, Robert J., ed. *The New Debate: Readings in Contemporary Debate Theory.* Washington, D.C. Information Research Associates, 1975.

Brock, Bernard L., et al. *Public Policy Decision Making: Systems Analysis and Comparative Advantages Debate.* New York: Harper and Row, 1973.

————. "The Comparative Advantages Case." *The Speech Teacher* 16 (March 1967): 118–23.

Brydon, Steven R. "Presumption in Non-Policy Debate: In Search of a Paradigm." *Journal of the American Forensic Association* 23 (Summer 1986): 15–22.

Burgoon, Judee and Montgomery, Charles. "Dimensions of Credibility for the Ideal Debater." *Journal of the American Forensic Association* 12 (Spring 1976): 171–77.

Cheseboro, James W. "Beyond the Orthodox: The Criteria Case." *Journal of the American Forensic Association* 7 (Winter 1971): 298–315.

Church, Russell T. and Wilbanks, Charles. *Values and Policies in Controversy: An Introduction to Argumentation and Debate.* Scottsdale, AZ: Gorsuch Scarisbrick, 1986.

Colbert, Kent R. "Standards for Resolving Value Debates." *The Forensic Educator* 3 (1988/89) 5–9.

Copeland, James M. *Cross-Examination in Debate.* Lincolnwood, IL: National Textbook Co., 1981.

Coulter, Skip. "Debate Drills for Coaches in the Fast Lane." *Rostrum* February 1992: 7–8.

Coverstone, Alan. "The Question Is . . . Rediscovering the Lost Art of Cross-Examination." *Debater's Research Guide: Effluents and Affluence: The Global Pollution.* Winston-Salem, NC: Wake Forest University, 1992.

Cox, J. Robert. "Attitudinal Inherency: Implications for Policy Debate." *Southern Speech Communication Journal* 40 (1975): 158–68.

Cross, John D. and Matlon, Ronald J. "An Analysis of Judging Philosophies in Academic Debate." *Journal of the American Forensic Association* 15 (Fall 1978): 110–23.

Dempsey, Richard H. and Hartman, David T. "Mirror State Counterplans: Illegitimate, Topical, or Magical?" *Journal of the American Forensic Association* (Winter 1985): 161–66.

Dick, Robert C. *Argumentation and Rational Debating.* Dubuque, IA: Wm. C. Brown Co., 1972.

Dowling, Ralph E. "Debate as Game, Educational Tool, and Argument: An Evaluation of Theory and Rules." *Journal of the American Forensic Association* 17 (Spring 1981): 235–36.

Dudczak, Craig A. "Direct Refutation in Propositions of Policy: A Viable Alternative." *Journal of the American Forensic Association* 16 (Spring 1980): 232–35.

Ehninger, Douglas and Brockriede, Wayne. *Decision by Debate.* 2nd ed. New York: Harper and Row, 1978.

Eman, Virginia and Lukehart, Jeffery. "Information Use in Academic Debate: An Information Theory Perspective." *Journal of the American Forensic Association* 12 (Spring 1976); 178–83.

Fisher, Daryl. "Should a Coach Research and Develop Arguments for Debaters?" *The Forensic Educator* 1 (1986/87): 15–16.

Flanigam, Carl D. "Value-Centered Argument and the Development of Decision Rules." *Journal of the American Forensic Association* 19 (Fall 1982): 107–14.

Fogelin, Robert J. *Understanding Arguments: An Introduction to Informal Logic.* 3rd ed. New York: Harcourt Brace Jovanovich, 1987.

Freeley, Austin J. *Argumentation and Debate: Reasoned Decision Making.* 6th ed. Belmont, CA: Wadsworth Publishing Company, Inc., 1986.

Fryar, Maridell, Thomas, David A. and Goodnight, Lynn. *Basic Debate.* 3rd ed. Lincolnwood, IL: National Textbook Co., 1988.

Goodnight, G. Thomas and Zarefsky, David. *Forensic Tournaments: Planning and Administration.* Lincolnwood, IL: National Textbook Co., 1980.

Goodnight, Lynn. *Getting Started in Debate.* 2nd ed. Lincolnwood, IL: National Textbook Co., 1993.

Hansen, R. Terry. "Summer Clinics—What Value?" *Rostrum* April 1993: 45–46.

Hanson, Jim. *Dictionary of Debate.* Lincolnwood, IL: National Textbook Co., 1990.

Hensley, Dana and Carlin, Diana. *Mastering Competitive Debate.* 4th ed. Topeka, KS: Clark Publishing, 1994.

Herbeck, Dale A. "A Permutation Standard of Competitiveness." *Journal of the American Forensic Association* 22 (Summer 1985): 12–19.

Herbeck, Dale and Dyer, Gerald. "The 'More the Merrier': Using Lay Persons as Forensic Coaches." *The Forensic Educator* (1986/87): 17–19.

Herbeck, D. A. and Katsulas, J. P. "The Affirmative Topicality Burden: Any Reasonable Example of the Resolution." *Journal of the American Forensic Association* 21 (1985): 133–149.

Herbeck, Dale and Katsulas, John. *Paradigms of Debate.* Kansas City, MO: National Federation of State High School Associations, 1988.

Herbeck, Dale A. and Katsulas, John P. *Writing the Affirmative Case.* Kansas City, MO: National Federation of State High School Associations, 1987.

Herbeck, Dale A. and Leeper, Karla K. "Policy Debate As a Laboratory for Teaching Argumentation Skills." *The Forensic Educator* 6 (1991/92): 23–28.

Hoaglund, John. *Critical Thinking.* Newport News, VA: Vale Press, 1984.

Hollihan, T. A. "Conditional Arguments and the Hypothesis Testing Paradigm: A Negative View." *Journal of the American Forensic Association* 19 (1983): 171–178.

Hunsaker, Richard A. *Lincoln-Douglas Debate: Defining and Judging Value Debate.* Kansas City, MO: National Federation of State High School Associations, 1988.

Hunsaker, Richard. "Lincoln-Douglas Debate: What Is It and How Should It Be Judged?" *The Forensic Educator* 1 (1986/87): 10–14.

Hutson, David. "What Should Be the Goals of Academic Debate? An Examination of Prioritization." *The Forensic Educator* 1 (1986/87): 8–9.

Hynes, Thomas J., Jr. "Risk, Vulnerability, and Policy Analysis: Implications for Public Argument." *Argument and Critical Practices*. Proceedings of the Fifth SCA/AFA Conference on Argumentation.: 113–117 Annandale, VA: SCA, 1987.

Kahane, Howard. *Logic and Contemporary Rhetoric: The Use of Reason in Everyday Life*. 4th ed. Belmont, CA: Wadsworth Publishing Co., 1984.

Kalmon, Stevan. "Recommendations Regarding Summer Debate Institutes." *The Forensic Educator* 1 (1986/87): 20–21.

Kaplow, Louis. "Rethinking Counterplans: A Reconciliation with Debate Theory." *Journal of the American Forensic Association* 17 (Spring 1981): 215–26.

Katsulas, John P. "A Skeptical View of Debate Handbooks: A Reply to Walker." *The Forensic Educator* 7 (1992/93): 11–14.

Kay, Jack. "A Plea for Using Non-Expert Judges in Lincoln-Douglas Debate." *The Forensic Educator* 6 (1991/92): 5–7.

Kemp, Robert L. *Assignment: Directing the School's Forensic Program*. Clayton, MO: Alan Company, 1985.

Klopf, Donald W. *Coaching and Directing Forensics*. Lincolnwood, IL: National Textbook Co., 1982.

Laird, Madison. "Comparing Elementary Theory." *Rostrum* May 1993: 29.

————. "Paterno's 'Bad Advocacy.' " *Rostrum* April 1992: 12–13.

Lichtman, Allan J. and Rohrer, Daniel M. "The Logic of Policy Dispute." *Journal of the American Forensic Association* 16 (Spring 1980): 236–47.

Madsen, Arnie. "Pairing Debate Rounds." *The Forensic Educator* 7 (1992/93): 26–30.

Madsen, A. and Louden, A. D. "Jurisdiction and the Evaluation of Topicality." *Journal of the American Forensic Association* 16 (1981): 73–83.

Mayer, Michael. "Epistemological Considerations of the Studies Counterplan." *Journal of the American Forensic Association* 19 (Spring 1983): 261–66.

Mayer, M. "Extending Counter-Warrants: The Counter-Resolutional Counterplan" *Journal of the American Forensic Association* 19 (1981): 122–127.

Meyers, Chet. *Teaching Students to Think Critically*. San Francisco: Jossey-Bass Publishers, 1986.

Mezzera, David and Giertz, John. *Student Congress & Lincoln-Douglas Debate*. 2nd ed. Lincolnwood, IL: National Textbook Co., 1989.

Mitchell, Gordon. "New Tools for the Negative: International Fiat and Plan-Inclusive Counterplans." *Debater's Research Guide: Effluents and Affluents*. Winston-Salem, NC: Wake Forest University, 1992.

Paterno, Jim. "Bad Advocacy." *Rostrum* February 1992: 15–16.

Patterson, J. W. and Zarefsky, David. *Contemporary Debate*. Boston: Houghton Mifflin Company, 1983.

Penetta, Edward M. and Dolley, Steven. "The Topical Counterplan: A Competitive Policy Alternative." *Journal of the American Forensic Association* 25 (Winter 1989): 165–177.

Perella, Jack. *The Debate Method of Critical Thinking: An Introduction to Argumentation*. Dubuque, IA: Kendall/Hunt, 1986.

Perkins, Dallas. "Counterplans and Paradigms." *Journal of the American Forensic Association* 25 (Winter 1989): 140–149.

Pfau, Michael W., Thomas, David A. and Ulrich, Walter. *Debate and Argument: A Systems Approach to Advocacy:* Glenview, IL: Scott, Foresman and Company, 1987.

Prentice, Diana and Kay, Jack. *The Role of Values in Policy Debate*. Kansas City, MO: National Federation of State High School Associations, 1986.

Richards, Jeffrey A. *Moving From Policy to Value Debate.* Lincolnwood, IL: National Textbook Co., 1992.

Rowland, Robert C. "The Debate Judge as Debate Judge: A Functional Paradigm." *Journal of the American Forensic Association* 20 (Summer 1984): 183–93.

Rowland, R. C. "The Relationship Between Realism and Debatability in Policy Advocacy." *Journal of the American Forensic Association* 22 (1986): 125–134.

Rowland, Robert C. "Tabula Rasa: The Relevance of Debate to Argumentation Theory." *Journal of the American Forensic Association* 21 (Fall 1984): 76–88.

Sanders, Gerald H. *Introduction to Contemporary Academic Debate.* 2nd ed. Prospect Heights, IL: Waveland Press, Inc., 1983.

Sayer, J. E. *Argumentation and Debate.* Sherman Oaks, CA: Alfred Publishing, 1980.

Shelton, Michael W. "In Defense of the Studies Counterplan." *Journal of the American Forensic Association* (Winter 1985): 150–55.

Shelton, Michael W. "Political Correctness in Academic Debate." *Rostrum* November 1992: 4–5.

Solt, Roger. "Counterplan Competition: Permutations and Beyond." *Debater's Research Guide: Clarifying Water Policy.* Winston–Salem, NC: Wake Forest University, 1985.

————. "Negative Fiat: Resolving the Ambiguities of 'Should.' " *Journal of the American Forensic Association* 25 (Winter 1989): 121–139.

Strickland, Glen. "Topicality or Topic Justification? The Response is Misapplied." *Rostrum* April 1990: 11–12.

Thomas, David A. and Hart, Jack. *Advanced Debate: Readings in Theory, Practice and Teaching.* 4th ed. Lincolnwood, IL: National Textbook Co. 1992.

Ulrich , Walter. *Common Debate Fallacies.* Kansas City, MO: National Federation of State High School Associations, 1993.

————. "Debate as Dialectic: A Defense of the Tabula Rasa Approach to Judging." *Journal of the American Forensic Association* 21 (Fall 1984): 89–93.

————. *Guidelines for the Debate Judge.* Kansas City, MO: National Federation of State High School Associations, 1986.

————. *An Introduction to Debate.* Kansas City, MO: National Federation of State High School Associations, 1986.

————. *Judging Academic Debate.* Lincolnwood, IL: National Textbook Co., 1986.

————. "Judging at High School Tournaments: Some Advice to Former Debaters." *The Forensic Educator.* 6 (1991/92): 29–30.

————. "The Strategic Limitations of the Spread." *Debate Issues* (January 1984): 3–11.

————. *Understanding the Counterplan.* Kansas City, MO: National Federation of State High School Associations, 1986.

Walker, Gregg B. "Debate Handbooks Have Merit: Walker Responds." *The Forensic Educator* 7 (1992/93): 15–16.

————. "Teaching Research: Some Instructional Ideas." *The Forensic Educator* 3 (1988/89): 17–20.

————. "The Utility of Research Handbooks." *The Forensic Educator* 7 (1992/93): 5–10.

Warnick, Barbara. "Arguing Value Propositions," *Journal of the American Forensic Association* 18 (Fall 1981); 109–19.

INDEX

Credits

Photographs and original illustrations:

Bettmann, pages 255, 357; Jeff Ellis, pages 9, 28, 46, 59, 147, 173, 213, 240, 287, 292; Lincoln High School, Lincoln, Nebraska, courtesy of Steve Foral, Debate Coach, pages 320, 321, 355, Appendix B; Glenbrook South High School, Glenview, Illinois, courtesy of Matt Whipple, Head Debate Coach, page 176; Bijan Marashi, page 366; National Forensic League, Ripon, Wisconsin, pages 7, 188, 215, 274, 377, 380; National High School Institute, Northwestern University, Evanston, Illinois, pages 2, 83, 86, 99, 142, 165, 184, 245, 251, 324, 330, 336, 343, 348, 357; Oak Park and River Forest High School, Oak Park, Illinois, courtesy of James Hunter, Debate Director, pages 226, 268, and 374; University of Oregon, courtesy of Dave Frank, Forensics Director, page 303; Jeff Roberson-Pool/Getty Images, page 6; Rick Wilking/CORBIS, page 20; Rick Wilking/Reuters/CORBIS, page 314.

Excerpts:

The quotations from an interview with Malcolm X and speech by President John F. Kennedy (Chapter 1, page 4) are from the *Forensic Educator 1993-1994,* page 20, published by the National Federation of State High School Associations, Kansas City, Missouri. The quotation from a speech by President Lyndon Baines Johnson (Chapter 1, page 7) is from the *Rostrum,* January 1991, page 6, published by the National Forensic League, Ripon, Wisconsin.